T5-CCV-267

SELF-GUIDED
France

SELF-GUIDED
France

*With 54 illustrations and photographs;
55 maps in color and black and white*

LANGENSCHEIDT PUBLISHERS, NEW YORK

Publisher:	Langenscheidt Publishers, Inc.
Managing Editor:	Lisa Checchi Ross
U.S. Editorial Adaptation:	Stephen Brewer, Gertrude Buckman, Mary E. Johnson, Lenore Malen, Lisbeth Mark, Jacolyn A. Mott, Donald S. Olson, Dana Schwartz, Larry White
Cartography:	Veronika Hummel and Karl Rothballer. Adaptation by Polyglott-Redaktion
Illustrations:	Margit Rein and Katharine Zsivkovics
Cover Design:	Diane Wagner
Cover photograph:	Marvin Newman, Image Bank, New York
Text Design:	Irving Perkins Associates
Production:	Ripinsky & Company
Photographs:	No. 1, No. 4, No. 5, No. 9, No. 10, No. 11, Bavaria, Munich, W. Germany; No. 2, No. 3, No. 6, No. 7, No. 8, French Tourist Office; No. 12, Eugen-Egon Hüsler
Translation:	Translation Company of America
Original German Text:	Paul Gnuva (author); Angélique Blanche (food essay); Polyglott-Redaktion (editorial)
Letters:	We welcome your comments and suggestions. Our address: Langenscheidt Publishers, Inc. 46–35 54th Road Maspeth, New York 11378

© 1989 by Langenscheidt Publishers, Inc.
All rights reserved under international and Pan-American copyright
conventions.
Manufactured in the United States of America.
ISBN: 0-88729-202-X

Contents

Foreword

In this land where art has contributed so much to life, life itself is perhaps the highest art form. To tour France is to treat yourself to what Hemingway so aptly described, though referring to Paris alone, as "a moveable feast." From sophisticated Paris to Breton fishing villages, and rugged Alpine ski resorts to ultrachic Mediterranean beaches, all France is a celebration of the senses—where wine, food, fashion, and *amour* are taken as seriously as painting, cinema, architecture, and the written word—written *en français,* of course.

Langenscheidt's *Self-Guided France* is written especially for seasoned travellers by writers who specialize in the areas they cover. This unique guide offers extensive tours of Paris, France's other great cities and the spectacular countryside. Travellers will find all the information they need to explore France at their own pace and follow their own interests.

Self-Guided Tours

The heart of this book is its self-guided tours. Walking tours of each major city describe all important sites and put them in historical perspective. Travel routes connect major cities and areas of interest, crisscrossing the country and each other to give travellers the opportunity to change direction and create their own itinerary. Detailed maps outline every route.

Because most travellers begin in Paris, our tours start with a selective guide to the "City of Light" and its nearby attractions. Following Paris are tours through some of France's other important cities—Marseille, Lyon, Bordeaux, Strasbourg, and Dijon. Then, 25 Travel Routes cover the most scenic and interesting areas of the country. A tour of the Mediterranean island of Corsica is also included.

Using This Guide

This travel guide helps you plan, organize, and enjoy your holiday in France. In "Getting Your Bearings," a brief rundown of the pleasures to be found in France's different regions will help you choose the areas in which you'd like to spend the most time. It also offers insights into French culture. An historical chronology and an essay on the arts provide helpful background and perspective on the sights you'll be seeing. We've included a special chapter on the cuisine of France to describe the fabulous regional fare you'll want to sample along the way.

Langenscheidt's writers also offer a subjective guide to the most appealing sights. Our unique three-star system appears throughout the guide:

*** Worth a special trip—don't miss it!
  ** The most important sights on the tour
   * Highlights

Other sights along the way are also worth seeing, but are not necessarily as important as the starred sights.

Total mileage is provided in kilometers and miles from the departure point of each tour. Major towns and sights appear in boldface for easy reference, while other notable places appear in italics. Numbers in parentheses correspond to locations on the maps.

The guide concludes with a Practical Information chapter divided into two parts. The first is General Trip Planning, to help you gather information you'll need before you depart for France. The second part is specific information—such as local tourist information offices, transportation, and hotels—listed town by town.

Notes and Observations

Travel information, like fruit, is perishable. We've made every effort to double check information in this guide. But hotels do close and museums do shut down for renovation, so check ahead whenever possible.

We welcome your comments and updates of our information. Please write us at:

Langenscheidt Publishers, Inc.
46–35 54th Road
Maspeth, New York 11378

Getting Your Bearings

Regions of France

France is subdivided into 22 political regions, which are not always identical with the older and better-known provincial and regional names.

Among the sights well worth seeing in the major industrial region of *Alsace and Lorraine* are the cathedral in Strasbourg; Matthias Grünewald's Isenheimer altarpiece in Colmar; the ancient, partially walled village of Riquewihr; the Alsace Wine Route and the Crest Route through the Vosges; Verdun; Domremy (birthplace of Joan of Arc); Colombey-les-Deux-Églises (tomb of Charles de Gaulle); Alsace, one of the best-preserved Medieval towns; and the elegant city of Nancy.

The large territory of *Aquitaine* in the southwest corner of France on either side of the Garonne River is full of natural contrasts. It encompasses the forested hill country of the Dordogne with the prehistoric paintings in the Lascaux caves, the truffle country of the Périgord, and the southern regions of Gascony and Béarn. Closer to the coast lies the area where Bordeaux wines are cultivated and the ancient port city of Bordeaux, which is now a major industrial center, as well as the Arcachon Basin, and the extensive moors and forests of the Landes (one of the largest forested areas in Europe). Beaches of the picturesque Côte Basque surround the great seaside resort of Biarritz. Slightly to the west, in the Pyrenees, is the enchanting Basque country. The unique dialect of this region is still spoken today.

Outstanding features of the spectacularly beautiful area of the *Auvergne* in the Massif Central are the craters of the long-extinct volcanoes, such as the Puy de Dôme and the Puy de Sancy (puy is the French term for these formations); many lakes; health spas, of which Vichy is the most famous; and the cities of Clermont-Ferrand, which is a modern town with a well-preserved Medieval center, and Le Puy, situated between two huge pinnacles of lava rock. The rugged tablelands called the "Causses" lie to the south. Sancy, a chain of 60 volcanic peaks that are a relatively young 10,000 years old, is also in the Auvergne.

Normandy (*Basse-Normandie and Haute-Normandie*), a land of livestock and apple trees, of sparkling cider and Calvados (apple brandy), extends to either side of the lower course of the Seine. Rouen on the Seine is France's largest river port. Along the coast are rocky promontories like those at Étretat, and the beach sites of the Allied invasion of Europe in 1944, such as Omaha Beach and Utah Beach.

There are big ports, including Le Havre and Cherbourg, and famous seaside resorts like Le Tréport, Honfleur, Dieppe, Trouville, and Deauville. In the 19th century many French and English artists were attracted to these resorts.

Among Normandy's major sights are the unique citadel church of

Mont-Saint-Michel; the cathedrals at Caen, Lisieux, and Rouen; the famous Medieval tapestry of Bayeaux; and the bridge over the Seine at Tancarville.

There are many relics of Celtic civilization in *Brittany (Bretagne)*, a stretch of land lying in the farthest reaches of northwestern France. The menhirs, which are upright stones, and dolmens, which have upright stone walls and a single stone slab for a roof and may have served as tombs, are important cultural monuments from prehistoric times. Thousands of menhirs can be found in Carnac. Pointe du Raz, a spur of rock projecting into the ocean, is the most westerly point in Brittany. Also worth seeing are the Medieval fortified city of Vitré; the cliffs at Cancale; Saint-Malo, the city of corsairs; the resort town Dinard, often called the "Pearl of the Emerald Coast"; and Pont-Avon, the 19th-century artists colony.

The mighty duchy of *Burgundy (Bourgogne)* was a center of European civilization in the late Middle Ages. Artistic monuments of the first rank are the old capital city of Dijon; the Hôtel-Dieu, a Medieval hospital in Beaune; the Romanesque cathedrals at Auxerre, Vézelay, and Autun; and the church in the suburb of Brou, near Bourg-en-Bresse.

The magnificent vineyards of Burgundy were first planted during the Roman settlement of Gaul and were improved upon by the early Cistercian monks. The Burgundy Wine Route is a spectacular drive through the Côte d'Or, a stretch of low-lying hills between Dijon and Santenay.

The *Centre* region encompasses the valley of the Loire River, the areas around Orléans and Touraine, the province of Berry, and the region around Chartres. Chartres cathedral is one of the great Medieval monuments. The Renaissance châteaux at Blois, Chenonceau, Chambord, and Beauregard are well worth seeing.

Champagne (and the Ardennes) is the northeastern region that contains the forested area of the Ardennes (an extension of the Belgian Ardennes), the chalk plains of Champagne, and many lakes. The large lake in the Fôret d'Orient is a waterfowl preserve.

The region is also famous for its vineyards and the art treasures of such cities as Troyes, Provins, and Reims with its spectacular cathedral.

The fourth-largest island in the Mediterranean, *Corsica (Corse)* lies approximately 175 km. (105 miles) south of the French mainland. Almost entirely mountainous, Corsica has 1,033 km. (620 miles) of magnificent coastline, such picturesque cities as Ajaccio, Bastia, Calvi, and Bonifacio, and inland wilderness along with mountain trails and caves.

Franche-Compté (Upper Burgundy), located on the Swiss border between the Rhine and the Rhône rivers, is upland country with green meadows cut by mountain streams. The former citadel of Belfort and the pilgrimage church of Ronchamp, built by Le Corbusier, are in Franche-Compté, which means "free country."

The southernmost province of *Languedoc–Roussillon* stretches along the Mediterranean from the western edge of the Rhône delta to the eastern segment of the Pyrenees. Its long sandy beaches constitute a second Riviera. The region's most popular vacation resort is La Grande-Motte, near Montpellier, and its most famous site is the Medieval fortress of Carcassonne, restored in the 19th century.

Limousin is a farming region situated to the east of the Charente. Its major cities are Limoges, known for its porcelain, and Aubusson, famous for its tapestries.

The province known as *Midi-Pyrénées* stretches from the southwestern part of the Massif Central through the Garonne basin to the highest peak in the Pyrenees, Pic du Midi-de-Bigorre. The region's major attractions include the Cirque de Gavarnie, a natural amphitheater, and Lourdes, city of pilgrims. Other places worth visiting are Toulouse, chief city of the Midi; Albi, with its fortified church; the health spa of Luchon and the nearby winter sports resort of Superbagnères; the tiny independent state of Andorra; and in the northeastern corner of the region, Roquefort, famous for its cheese. The wild ravines of the Gorges of the Tarne are also noteworthy.

The lively capital of the agricultural province of *Nord–Pas-de-Calais* is Lille. The "Opal Coast" stretches for 130 km. (80 miles) and is famous for its dunes, steep cliffs, and such resorts as Le Touquet-Paris-Plage. The major fishing port is Boulogne-sur-Mer. Passenger ships set out for England from Calais, which until 1558 was England's last stronghold on the Continent. In Calais stands the famous monument by Rodin, *The Burgers of Calais,* a reminder of this 200-year domination.

Pays-de-la-Loire, which borders the Atlantic, encompasses departments that lie to the north and south of the Loire. The chief city in this province is Nantes, which has a large commercial port.

The flat country of *Picardy* (*Picardie*), bounded on the west by the English Channel, is one of the major industrial areas of France. The great plains of the region, however, continue to be cultivated, primarily with wheat and sugar beets. Sights of major interest are the Medieval cathedrals at Amiens, Soissons, and Laon.

The reputation of the western province of *Poitou–Charente* rests on its oysters, its butter, and its cognac, made in the town of Cognac. Other attractions include the Romanesque churches in Poitiers and Saintes, the picturesque old Huguenot port of La Rochelle, the seaside resort of Royan, and the wide beaches on the island of Oléron. The marshes of the Poitou country are negotiated on flatboats called *plates.*

Provence–Côte d'Azur lies to either side of the lower reaches of the Rhône. To the east it encompasses the old capital city of Aix-en-Provence and the port of Marseille, the second-largest city in France. Provence offers a wealth of major tourist attractions and boasts some of the best-preserved Roman ruins in Europe: the theater in Orange; the cemetery Les Alycamps in Arles; the arenas in Nîmes and Arles; and the best-preserved aqueduct, the Pont du Gard. Medieval sights include the castle at Tarascon, the ruined city of Les Baux, the marshlands of the Camargue with the maritime fortress of Aigues-Mortes, and the Palace of the Popes in Avignon. Also of interest is Matisse's exquisite Chapelle du Rosaire in Vence. The Mediterranean resorts of Cannes, Saint-Tropez, and Nice—the Riviera—are located in the southeastern corner of the province.

Paris, one of the great metropolitan areas of the world, is located in the *Île-de-France.* Ten million people live in the *Région Parisienne* surrounding Paris, a broad belt of countryside, crossed by numerous streams and rivers. Also located in the Île-de-France are the celebrated palaces at Versailles and Fontainebleau.

The province of *Rhône–Alps* encompasses the Rhône Valley and the ancient regions of Savoy and Dauphiné, including the French Alps. The varied landscape of the western portion of the region extends from the Jura uplands, with its ridges and lakes, to the Cévennes mountains, part of the Massif Central, to the hilly vineyards of Beaujolais. Lyon, the region's capital, is a big commercial city, but it is also noted for its fine food and extraordinary museums. Southeast of Lyon is Grenoble, a major industrial town surrounded by snow-capped mountains, which lies near Europe's highest mountaineering and winter sports area, and popular resort villages such as Briancon-Sainte-Catherine. Major attractions in the Alps are Chamonix, with its glaciers and funicular railway (it goes up to the Aiguille du Midi and over the Vallée Blanche, with Mont Blanc in the background); the lake of Annecy; and the church at Assy. The Route des Grandes-Alpes goes over the highest passes. The Route Napoleon from Grenoble to Nice is of great historical importance.

Location and Size

Situated at the edge of the European continent, France is a land of extraordinary physical variety that covers an area of 547,026 sq. km. (186,456 sq. miles) including Corsica, about twice that of the combined area of New York State and New England. Its mainland territory, with a population of 54.7 million, is bordered on the north by the English Channel, Luxembourg, and Belgium; on the west by the Atlantic Ocean and the Bay of Biscay; on the south by Spain and the Mediterranean Sea; and on the east by West Germany, Switzerland, and Italy. The French island of Corsica is located in the Mediterranean, south of Genoa, and has an area of 8,722 sq. km. (5,233 sq. miles) with some 1,000 km. (600 miles) of coastline. France's seacoasts extend for 3,120 km. (1,939 miles).

Topography

France's proximity to both the Atlantic Ocean and the Mediterranean Sea subjects it to several climatic influences: Continental, oceanic, and Mediterranean. It shares with other European countries both ancient and relatively new mountain ranges. The three youngest ranges are the Alps, the Pyrenees, and the Jura. The lofty Alps, part of a chain that extends through Europe, are the natural barrier between France and Italy; the majestic Pyrenees in the south create a natural border with Spain. The Jura mountains in the northeast near Switzerland have parallel ridges that extend from north to south.

Remnants of the more ancient and lower ranges include the Ardennes and the Vosges in the east. Farther to the west is the ancient mountainous plateau of the Massif Central, which covers one-sixth of France. The hilly ridges of Brittany and Normandy are part of the ancient Massif Armorican.

The extensive lowland areas of France consist of northern plains, which extend from the Ardennes to the Artois near Belgium; the Paris, or Seine, Basin in north-central France; the much smaller Aquitaine, or Garonne, Basin in the southwest; the narrow valley of the Rhône, which

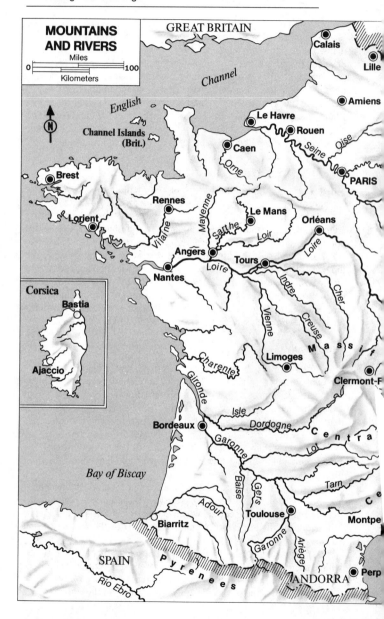

MOUNTAINS AND RIVERS

Miles
0 — 100
Kilometers

N

GREAT BRITAIN

Calais

Lille

Channel

English

Amiens

Channel Islands (Brit.)

Le Havre

Rouen

Oise

Seine

Caen

Orne

PARIS

Brest

Rennes

Le Mans

Orléans

Vilaine

Mayenne

Sarthe

Loir

Loire

Angers

Tours

Nantes

Loire

Indre

Cher

Lorient

Vienne

Creuse

M a s s i f

Corsica

Bastia

Limoges

Clermont-F

Ajaccio

Charente

Gironde

C e n t r a l

Isle

Dordogne

Bordeaux

Lot

Garonne

Baïse

Bay of Biscay

Gers

Tarn

C e

Adour

Toulouse

Montpe

Biarritz

Garonne

Ariège

SPAIN

P y r e n e e s

ANDORRA

Perp

Rio Ebro

Golfe du Lion

spreads out to meet the coastal plain of Languedoc in the south; and the Loire plains, which follow the Loire Valley.

The coastline of France is as varied as the countryside. Parts of the French coastline are etched with bays and high headlands, while other coastal areas are alluvial plains with extensive lagoons. Near the North Sea the coastline is characterized by great sandy dunes, eastern Normandy is known for its beautiful white chalk cliffs, while Brittany has a variegated coast cut by capes and reefs. Of the four major river systems, the Seine, the main river of the Paris Basin, drains into the English Channel; the Loire, the longest river, and the Garonne, in the southwest, both drain into the Atlantic; the Rhône, which originates in Lake Geneva, drains into the Mediterranean.

Constitution and Representation

France has been a democratic republic (Republique Française) with a centralized parliamentary government since 1871. The present Fifth Republic, based on the constitution of 1958, gives considerable powers to the Président, who is the country's primary political force. Elected by popular vote for a seven-year term, the Président appoints the Prime Minister, who is constitutionally subordinate to him. Upon the recommendations of the Prime Minister, the President also appoints the other

ministers who comprise the Council of Ministers (Cabinet), over which
he presides. Commander in chief of the Armed Forces, and with considerable personal powers in the case of national emergency, the President is
constitutionally empowered to dissolve the National Assembly, but cannot himself be relieved of his position by the Assembly.

The French Parliament has a legislative body, the Assemblée Nationale, whose 577 members are directly elected for a five-year term, and an
advisory body, the Sénat, with 322 members elected by regional assem-
blies for a nine-year term. Both divisions pass laws, but in disputed cases
it is the Assemblée Nationale that makes the final decision. It also has the
power to bring down the government by a vote of no confidence. All
citizens over 18 have the right to vote.

The country, highly centralized, is divided into 96 départements,
which are grouped in 22 administrative regions. In 1985 a form of pro-
portional representation was introduced, in which votes cast were dis-
tributed on a departmental basis, thus abolishing majority rule. France's
overseas departments include Martinique, Guadeloupe, Réunion, and
Guyana, all of which send representatives to the French Parliament.

A founding member of the European Community (EEC), of which it is
the largest country, France is also the seat of the European Parliament,
which meets in Strasbourg. France left the North Atlantic Treaty Organization (NATO) in 1966.

Customs and Manners

France, a country of great and long-established traditions, is also, in
many ways, the most advanced nation in Europe. It is a country with
consistently high standards of achievement in fields as diverse as medical
research and fashion design. Chic, sophisticated, passionate, charming,
difficult, haughty, chauvinistic—the list of adjectives applied to the
French is seemingly endless, generally biased, and often at least a little
bit true. They are, to be sure, a complicated people, with a long, dramatic
history of extraordinary individuals and momentous events. And they
are a proud people—aware of their cultural significance in all the arts,
and sometimes viewing themselves as the last standard-bearers of civilization. But if you stop to think of it, what country has contributed more,
or been so much in the forefront of modern intellectual and artistic movements, from Impressionism to avant-garde literature and textual anal-
ysis? Over the centuries, hundreds of artists and free-thinkers have
migrated to France, and found a spiritual home there because of the
peculiar French attitude of *savoir faire*—a willingness to accept and
value all aspects of life, even when they contradict one's personal values.
The French reputation for "naughtiness" stems from the French accep-
tance of pleasure as part of life's rich bounty. It is true that the French take

themselves very seriously, whether they are upholding a time-honored tradition or destroying it. Their humor, as might be expected, is less broad than it is sharp, caustic and cerebral.

In a manner less paradoxical than deftly well-assimilated, the French are able to combine physical *joie de vivre* with a respect for things of the mind. In this sense, they have refined many aspects of daily life, such as cooking and conversation, to a very fine art. A certain conservative emphasis is consequently placed on proper form—the correct (i.e., French) way of doing things—and this can reach, to the outsider's more casual eye, intimidating heights. It's often in matters of food that the French tendency towards chauvinism is expressed. In polite French society, for example, never attempt to cut the nose off the cheese. This *faux pas* will be met with incredulous stares, even gasps of horrified astonishment, for in France the ripe end-section of the cheese is always sampled by each guest. Friendship and entertaining, too, can take a certain distinct form in France. New acquaintances are more likely to be entertained in a café or restaurant than in a French home, for domestic and social life tend to be kept separate.

This is not to say that the French are invariably stiff, pompous and impenetrable, for such is not the case, especially outside of Paris. They are a people of great personal charm and friendliness, and visitors who can speak even a little of their language will be rewarded for the effort. Influenced by television and other media, certain aspects of traditional French culture and manners are undergoing what many observers call an "Americanization," with greater emphasis placed on informality, convenience, and openness.

For all of their homegrown sophistication, and perhaps because of it, the French have tended towards a certain insularity. Until fairly recently, for instance, most French vacationed within their country. This is changing, and more and more French are now travelling to other countries— but in smaller numbers than their European neighbors. Since France has everything a vacationer could possibly want—from mountains to Mediterranean beach resorts—this self-imposed isolationism is certainly understandable. Their colonial past (and present) has put the French in touch with many exotic cultures, which have been assimilated into the country's culture and cuisine.

After politics, sports are a Frenchman's passion—especially soccer and rugby. The famous long-distance cycle race, the Tour de France, is a major highlight of the French sporting year, and is avidly followed throughout the country.

There's actually a great deal of truth in the time-worn cliché that France is a land of artists and lovers. French artistry is for life itself, which they love, exalt, revere, and put into those forms that are so uniquely, so persistently French.

Chronology

390 B.C.: The Gauls sack Rome.

58–51 B.C.: Caesar conquers Gaul, bringing its language and culture under the influence of Classical Rome.

A.D. 486: Franks become unified in Gaul under Merovingian King Clovis I and adopt Christianity. Clovis I baptized a Catholic in Reims.

508: Clovis makes Paris his capital.

732: Charles Martel defeats the Moors at Poitiers.

751: Founding of Carolingian dynasty.

768–814: Carolingian King Charlemagne rules France, Germany, and Italy as Holy Roman Emperor.

910: Founding of Benedictine abbey at Cluny.

987: Hugh Capet, first of the Capetian kings, unifies France, making Paris its center.

1066: William, Duke of Normandy, invades and conquers England at the Battle of Hastings.

1096: Crusades begin.

1150–1300: Rapid growth of cities and towns; building of Gothic cathedrals.

1152: Eleanor of Aquitaine, divorced from Louis VII of France, marries Henry Plantagenet, who becomes King Henry II of England in 1154. Their union brings much of France under English control.

1257: The Sorbonne, one of the world's first universities, is founded in Paris.

1309–1378: Popes reside in Avignon.

1337–1453: Hundred Years War, ending with British defeat at Calais.

1431: Joan of Arc, who defeated the British in the Battle of Orléans in 1429, is burned at the stake.

1481–1482: King Louis XI adds Anjou, Maine, Provence, Burgundy, and Picardy to the royal domain.

1532: Brittany annexed to France.

1572: Protestants throughout France are murdered in the Saint Bartholomew's Day Massacre.

1580–1587: Montaigne publishes his essays.

1598: Edict of Nantes grants freedom of worship.

1628: Cardinal Richelieu seizes absolute power; captures Huguenot stronghold La Rochelle.

1643: Académie Française is founded.

1685: Edict of Nantes is revoked, forcing Huguenots to emigrate.

1643–1715: Louis XIV, the Sun King, establishes absolute monarchy, launches costly wars, moves court to Versailles, selects ministers from haute bourgeoisie; Paris becomes cultural center of Europe, and home of writers and playwrights such as Boileau, La Fontaine, Molière, Racine, and Corneille.

1715–1774: Louis XV reigns for 59 years, a time of enlightenment, as evidenced in works of Voltaire, Diderot, Rousseau, Montesquieu, et al.; economic instability continues.

1756–1763: Seven Years War; France loses colonies in North America, India, and West Indies.

1789: With the States-General, France attempts to establish a constitution. On July 14 of that year, the citizens of Paris storm the Bastille. The French Revolution begins.

1791: King Louis XVI and his wife, Marie Antoinette, attempt to flee France but are apprehended.

1792: Crowds storm the Tuileries, where the King and Queen are confined.

1793–1794: Louis and Marie Antoinette are beheaded. Thousands of Frenchmen die during the Reign of Terror, the dictatorship of Robespierre and his followers.

1796–1797: Napoleon Bonaparte, a young Corsican general, wins the attention of all Europe with his brilliant military campaign in Italy.

1799–1804: Napoleon takes over the leadership of France as First Consul, securing Belgium and much of Italy, and, at home, putting revolutionary gains on a secure footing.

1804–1814: Napoleon rules as emperor, conquering an empire that stretches from Rome to Hamburg and from Brest to the Bay of Kotor, but meets defeat in Russia in the winter of 1812.

1814: Napoleon abdicates, is exiled to the island of Elba.

1815: Napoleon returns to France for 100 days, but succumbs to forces massed against him at Waterloo.

1821: Napoleon dies on island of Saint Helena.

1830: The July Revolution puts an end to the repressive antidemocratic measures of restored Bourbon Kings Louis XVIII and Charles X.

1848: King Louis-Philippe is overthrown when he refuses to institute universal suffrage.

1848: Louis Napoleon, nephew of Napoleon I, is elected president.

1852–1870: Louis Napoleon rules as emperor.

1854–1856: In the Crimean War, France defeats Austria in northern Italy, winning back Savoy and Nice.

1871: France is defeated in Franco-Prussian War, which ends in the siege of Paris.

1879–1894: France colonizes extensive portions of Central Africa, Tunis, Indochina, Madagascar, and Morocco.

1894–1906: The Dreyfus affair, in which anti-Semitic forces wrongly accuse a Jewish officer of treason, creates a political crisis.

1914–1918: Much of World War I is fought on French soil, as evidenced by huge military graveyards in the north of the country; 1.3 million Frenchmen die in the fighting.

1939–1945: World War II. France and England declare war on Germany September 3, 1939; Germans enter France in the spring of 1940; France surrenders to Germany and Marshal Pétain establishes his Nazi-backed government in Vichy; Allied troops land in Normandy in the summer of 1944; by October, much of the country is liberated by the Allies. Unconditional surrender of Germany is signed at Reims May 7, 1945.

1958–1969: As President, Charles de Gaulle lays the groundwork for modern industrial France.

1968: The "Events of May," student uprisings in Paris, rock the country and threaten the government.

1981: President François Mitterrand ushers in France's first Socialist government.

1986: Jacques Chirac elected Prime Minister, begins dismantling institutions and programs instituted under Mitterrand.

1988: Mitterrand reelected.

The Arts of France

Prehistory and the Ancient World

The whole of Western culture is mirrored in the arts of France. The very earliest surviving artworks in the world, dated from about 15,000–10,000 B.C., are located deep in the caves of the Dordogne in southwestern France. Twenty-five of the 1,200 ancient caves in the region contain paintings and drawings of animals that were rendered with astonishing naturalism. The best-known cave, Lascaux, is located at Montignac; the other caves are slightly south, near Les Eyzies.

About 1500 B.C., a new culture arose in northwestern France in what is now Brittany. What remains of this civilization are thousands of huge, rough-hewn stones called megaliths, some standing 21 meters (70 feet) high that were fashioned into menhirs or dolmens. Menhirs are single stones set on end and arranged in parallel lines, which sometimes extend for miles; dolmens consist of several large stones standing on end covered by a large slab.

Although the ancient Greeks settled in the area around Marseille about 600 B.C., it was Roman colonization of the Rhône Valley in the first and second centuries B.C. that is responsible for the great number of Classical monuments that can still be seen in southern France. Western Provence was the center of the Roman province of Gaul. Some of the monuments erected by the Romans are the best preserved in Europe outside of Italy: the theater and the triumphal arch in Orange; the arenas in Nîmes and Arles; the aqueduct Pont du Gard, which serves as a crossing over the river Gard; the Roman temple, Maison Carrée, at Nîmes; La Trophée des Alpes at la Turbie; and thousands of sarcophagi, baths, bridges, mosaics, and Roman statues.

In the early Middle Ages, Roman Gaul was overrun by the Germanic migration of Franks and Visigoths, and it was not until around A.D. 1000 that the culture we think of as characteristically French began to emerge.

Romanesque Art

The year A.D. 1000 was a turning point in Europe. The great migrations had ceased; political and cultural consolidation of various provinces was under way; and pilgrims began visiting the relics of the saints. Saint James, perhaps the most venerated saint of that era, was buried at Santiago de Compostela in northern Spain. Dozens of cathedrals were constructed along the routes to Spain to accommodate the pilgrims—among them Nôtre-Dame in Le Puy; Saint-Sernin in Toulouse; Sainte-Foy in Conques; Saint-Martin at Tours; La-Madeleine at Vézelay; Saint-Lazare at Autun; Saint-Pierre at Moissac; Saint-Trophime in Arles.

These cathedrals were the first stone edifices constructed since antiquity. They shared certain characteristics: semicircular barrel-vaulted
ceilings, heavy stone walls, radiating chapels off the apse that housed
relics, and Roman arches; hence the name of the style—Romanesque.

Inspired by surviving Roman sculpture, Romanesque craftsmen
began sculpting reliefs on the portals of the cathedrals and on the capitals
of the interior columns (historiated capitals). The reliefs, which illustrated scenes from the Old and New Testaments, including the Last Judgment, became a vivid, sometimes terrifying reminder of the moral
obligations of a Christian life. Some of the best of these reliefs can be
seen at Saint-Trophime at Arles, Saint-Pierre at Moissac, Saint-Lazare at
Autun, and La Madeleine at Vézelay.

The most progressive of the Romanesque-style churches is
Saint-Étienne in Caen, begun by William the Conqueror. Its soaring
piers and ribbed vaults that permitted light from the clerestory to enter
the central aisle ushered in the Gothic style.

William the Conqueror's invasion of England in 1066 was illustrated
on the famous 70-meter- (230-foot-) long embroidered frieze, *the
Bayeux Tapestry,* which hangs in Bayeux's Centre Culturelle.

Gothic Art

The Gothic period, which dates from approximately 1150, started as a
local development in the Île-de-France and gradually extended to all of
Europe. Abbot Suger of Saint Denis, an adviser to Louis VI, is credited
with the first purely Gothic design. Gothic architecture is characterized
by designs that evoke a sense of graceful, soaring weightlessness in contrast to the massive solidity of the Romanesque. Arches are pointed
rather than rounded and flying buttresses deflect the weight of the interior walls to the outside of the building. Huge clerestories and rose windows permit colored light from stained glass to flood the interior. The
very construction of these churches was based on a philosophy of numer-
ical harmonies and on a belief that light was endowed with symbolic
qualities. One of the first great Gothic cathedrals was Nôtre-Dame in
Paris, followed by the cathedral in Chartres. The style saw its height in
the soaring verticality of the cathedrals at Amiens and at Reims. The
cathedral of Saint-Urbain at Troyes and the Sainte-Chapelle in Paris are
later refinements; Saint-Maclou in Rouen was built even later in what is
called the Flamboyant Gothic style.

French Gothic is no less impressive in secular structures: in the grandiose, marvelously preserved fortified cities of Aigues-Mortes and Carcassonne; the Papal Palace in Avignon; the fortress of Villeneuve; the
fortified castle of King René in Tarascon; the castle of Chinon; Jacques
Coeur's urban mansion in Bourges; the hospital in Beaune; and in court-

houses, town halls, and bridges, such as the three-towered bridge in Cahors.

The walls of public buildings and even the ambulatories of churches were hung with tapestries, of which two famous examples are the *Tapestries of the Apocalypse* in Angers and the *Lady and the Unicorn Tapestry* in Paris.

During the Gothic period sculpture became freestanding for the first time since antiquity. Individual statues, like the *Virgin of Paris* in Nôtre-Dame, are noted for their grace and refinement. Some of the most remarkable small-scale reliefs are found in quatrefoil frames on the façade of the cathedral at Amiens.

The art of manuscript illumination, which survived throughout the early Middle Ages in isolated monastic outposts, reached its peak with the beautifully illustrated *Très Riches Heures de Duc de Berry,* which contains popularized scriptures and an illustrated calendar. The calendar depicts in charming naturalistic detail the everyday life of both aristocrats and peasants.

The waning of the Middle Ages and the beginning of the Renaissance is often associated with the kingdom of Burgundy, which, in its heyday, nearly rivaled Florence for power and influence. Burgundy had close political ties with Flanders, and some of the greatest Flemish artists of the period worked for the Burgundian dukes. The Flemish sculptor Claus Sluter produced four of his finest works for the portals and interior of the Chartreuse de Champmol in Dijon; the Flemish painter Rogier van der Weyden's *Last Judgment* still adorns the walls of the Hôtel-Dieu in Beaune, for which it was commissioned in about 1443.

The best French painters of this period—Jean Fouquet, the court artist, and Enguerrand Quarton, associated with the school at Avignon—were strongly influenced by both Italian and Flemish art.

The Renaissance

The term Renaissance comes from the French word "rebirth," but this period came to France much later than to Italy. The Renaissance in the north began about 1500. Even as late as 1528, however, Saint-Pierre at Caen, built by Hector Sohier, was designed with a French Gothic choir.

It was François I (1494–1547), best remembered by the regal and icy portrait of him painted by Jean Clouet, who defined the Renaissance in France. His court was a magnet for artists from all over Europe and he made Mannerism, a late-Renaissance style, into the dominant style in 16th-century France.

François I was the first modern monarch to be obsessed with a passion for architecture. He built several of the early châteaux on the Loire, including the Château de Chambord. When he moved to the Paris region in 1528 he commissioned the master mason Gilles le Breton to build the Château de Fontainbleau. Nearly 20 years later he demolished the Medieval château on the site of the Louvre and began a reconstruction based on a Classical Italian Renaissance style. It was not completed until the 17th century.

Beginning around 1550, France's artists took a new direction. They modeled their work on the style of the late period of Classical antiquity, revived in Italy by Palladio, and created buildings of a noble and aloof detachment in the Classical style. From it developed the French Baroque, which combined dignity and pomp with measure and clarity. The square court of the Louvre, begun in 1546 by Pierre Lescot, is a synthesis of traditional Medieval château style with Italian Renaissance palazzo. However, the rich sculptural decoration by Jean Goujon that covers much of the wall surface is typically French. The tall narrow windows, high-pitched roof, and numerous vertical accents are also characteristic of French design.

The Baroque and Rococo

Under the "Sun King" Louis XIV (1638–1715), France became the cultural center of Europe. In literature the severe regularity of form in the plays of Corneille and Racine set French taste apart from the histrionic style of the rest of Europe. In painting, Classicism, influenced by French humanism, was the official court style. The two most famous French artists of the period were Nicolas Poussin (1594–1665), whose Classical themes and austere, intellectually rigorous style had lasting impact, and the more lyrical landscapist Claude Le Lorraine (1600–1682). Lorraine is remembered for his idealized mythological views of the Roman countryside.

After Poussin and Lorraine, perhaps the two greatest artists of the 17th century were the provincial painters Georges de la Tour (1593–1652), influenced by the dark, dramatic naturalism of the Italian school of Caravaggio, and Louis Le Nain (1593–1648), who worked in a more earthy Realist style derived from the Flemish-Dutch tradition. Both artists were all but forgotten after their deaths. Some other important artists of this period were Hyacinthe Rigaud, Nicolas de Largillière, Philippe de Champaigne, Simon Vouet, and Eustache Le Sueur.

The foundations of Baroque architecture were established early in the 17th century by François Mansart (1598–1666), who designed the Orléans wing of the château at Blois. Colbert, Louis XIV's influential minister, was responsible for organizing the completion of the Louvre, which was finally undertaken by Claude Perrault (1613–1688), Louis Le Vau (1612–1670), and Charles Le Brun (1619–1690). The plan for the Louvre, a symbol for centralized authority of the state, masterfully integrated French Classical and Italian elements into a building with stately proportions. Meanwhile Louis XIV, with the help of Charles Le Brun, began transforming the royal hunting lodge at Versailles into a gigantic palace. The outstanding feature, the garden façade, was begun by Louis Le Vau and continued by Jules Hardouin-Mansart (1646–1708). Conceived in a typically grandiose Baroque style, the whole center block of the palace contains a single room, the Hall of Mirrors. An enormous park, designed by André Le Nôtre (1613–1700), consists of formal gardens designed as if they were outdoor rooms for fêtes and spectacles. Another Baroque masterpiece by Jules Hardouin-Mansart is the church of the Invalides in Paris.

The production of Baroque sculpture was also closely tied to the royal patronage system organized by Le Brun. Three of the best-known Baroque sculptors were François Girardon, Antoine Coysevox, and Pierre Puget.

By the mid-17th century the Academy had replaced the time-honored apprentice system as the method for training artists. Founded in 1648 and directed by Poussin and Le Brun, the Royal Academy of Painting and Sculpture had a rigid curriculum and an absolute standard of taste. Yet by the time Antoine Watteau (1684–1721), the famous Rococo painter, entered the Academy in 1717 taste had changed. Upon the death of Louis XIV the rigid Classicism of the French Baroque period gave way to a style of refinement and elegance. Rococo paintings are intimate in feeling, often small in scale, and many of them are playfully erotic. After Watteau, the best-known Rococo artists were Jean Honoré Fragonard (1772–1806), François Boucher (1703–1770), and Jean-Baptiste-Siméon Chardin (1699–1779).

In architecture the Rococo style was expressed largely in the interior decoration of the many newly constructed Hôtels, urban dwellings for the aristocrats. Rococo is typefied by sinuous curves, irregular shapes, a profusion of mirrors and porcelain, and motifs drawn from Turkish and Chinese objects. Place Stanislas in Nancy and the Salon de la Princesse in the Hôtel de Soubise by Germain Boffrand in Paris epitomize the Rococo decorative style.

Neoclassicism and Romanticism

Revolutionary sentiments were in the air for decades before the French Revolution occurred, manifesting themselves in a revolt against the frivolity of Rococo and in a revival of Classicism. The Neoclassicism that emerged was inspired by archaeological discoveries at Pompeii and Herculaneum and was associated with the republican virtues of ancient Greece and Rome rather than with the absolute monarchy of Louis XIV. Anti-Rococo sentiment can be seen in the moral tales of peasant life painted by Jean-Baptiste Greuze (1725–1805). The Classical allegories of Jacques-Louis David (1748–1825) also typified the moral currents of the time.

The period after the Revolution is distinguished by wide swings in artistic taste, prompted by a romantic nostalgia for the past. Until the mid-18th century, Classical, Gothic, Renaissance, and Baroque styles were alternately revived. David's successor was the Neoclassicist Jean-Auguste-Dominique Ingres (1780–1867), but David's pupil Antoine Jean Gros (1771–1835) became a Neo-Baroque Romantic. Théodore Géricault (1791–1824) and Eugène Delacroix (1798–1863) also fell under the spell of Romanticism. The paintings of Delacroix, the quintessential Romantic, are characterized by a poetic and imaginative detachment from contemporary life and by a penchant for the exotic.

Late 18th- and 19th-century architecture is also distinguished by the Romantic adaptation of various historical styles. The ultimate phase of Romantic architecture can be seen in the heavily ornamented, Neo-Baroque Paris Opéra designed by Charles Garnier (1825–1898). The 19th century saw the gradual introduction of new building techniques and new materials such as iron; the materials were often partially disguised to conform to a revival style. An early example of this trend can be seen in the Bibliotèque Sainte-Geneviève in Paris by Henri Labrouste (1801–1875), where exposed iron columns are designed in a Renaissance revival manner.

Realism and Impressionism

The harsh political realities of mid-19th-century France ushered in a new interest in Realism. This style was exemplified by Honoré Daumier (1808–1879), who contributed more than 4,000 lithographic caricatures of middle-class city dwellers to various political journals. At the same time in the forests of Fontainebleau, 58 kilometers (40 miles) southeast of Paris, Jean-Baptiste-Camille Corot (1796–1875), Charles-François Daubigny (1817–1878), Théodore Rousseau (1812–1867), V.N. Diaz de la Peña (1807–1876), and Jean-François Millet (1814–1875) founded a school of landscape art, whose poignant realism had affinities with the Dutch Realist landscape art of the 17th century. The leading Realist painter in Europe was Gustave Courbet (1819–1877), who believed that the purpose of art was to present life "just as it is" and thus brilliantly depicted the social order of mid-19th-century France. His successor, Edouard Manet (1832–1888), considered the first modern painter, maintained that art should embrace the essence of contemporary life. Manet was a forerunner of the Impressionists: Claude Monet (1840–1926), Camille Pissarro (1830–1903), Auguste Renoir (1841–1919), and Edgar Dégas (1834–1917). What united these artists was their interest in painting the leisure activities of the middle class and in recording scenes that the eye could behold in a moment of time. Monet was especially obsessed with the nature of color and light, and in his later paintings the solidity of objects was all but dissolved in order to present purely optical sensations.

Sculpture made far less of an impact than painting in the 19th century. In the first half of the century it displayed the same range of stylistic influences as did painting. Jean-Antoine Houdon (1741–1828) was a Neoclassical portraitist and François Rude (1784–1855) worked in a style that was theatrically Baroque. Antoine-Louis Bayre (1795–1855) was a Romantic sculptor whose animal groups were reminiscent of Delacroix's paintings. Jean-Baptiste Carpeaux (1827–1875) created a famous Neo-Baroque sculptural group, *The Dance,* for the façade of the Paris Opéra. The greatest sculptor of the era was Auguste Rodin (1840– 1917), who ushered in the 20th century by broadening the repertory of sculptural themes and by interpreting the human figure in a style that was part romantic, part naturalistic, and part psychological.

Post-Impressionism

Several artists were associated with Post-Impressionism. Paul Cézanne (1839–1906) believed in the prolonged observation of nature rather than in the depiction of an instant in time. His firmly structured still lifes, landscapes, and portraits reveal the subjectivity of the artist's gaze. Georges Seurat (1859–1891) created an appearance of frozen calm, superimposed on a casual everyday experience. Paul Gauguin (1848– 1903) used primitive art and flat unnaturalistic color to evoke emotional states. The subjects of Vincent Van Gogh's (1853–1890) paintings were his alternately rapturous or tormented inner states. Henri-Marie-Raymond de Toulouse-Lautrec (1864–1901) was a chronicler of the demi-monde. Other artists of note from this period were Odilion Redon, Pierre Bonnard, and Edouard Vuillard. The Symbolist movement that developed during the late 19th century challenged artists to abandon literal representations of subject matter for an art that depended on abstract harmonies or on imaginative symbols and poetic feelings. This artistic philosophy paved the way for abstraction.

The 20th Century

Paris continued to be the unrivaled center of the art world until World War II. Numerous movements developed in Paris in quick succession. Fauvism, which stressed violent distortion of form and outrageous unnaturalistic color, was launched in 1905 by André Derain (1870– 1954), Henri Matisse (1869–1954), Albert Marquet (1875–1947), and Maurice de Vlaminck (1876–1958). Matisse had a passion for color, which he daringly used to alter proportions and spatial relations, creating an art of glowing serenity. The iridescent surfaces of Expressionist Georges Roualt's paintings, on the other hand, poignantly drew attention to the suffering of humanity.

Cubism, created in Paris by Georges Braque (1882–1963) and Pablo Picasso (1881–1973) in 1909, quickly attracted a number of artists, including Juan Gris (1887–1927), Fernand Léger (1881–1955), Albert Gleizes (1881–1953), and Jean Metzinger (1883–1956). All of these artists were searching for the essence of form by analyzing objects in space. Deeply influenced by Cubism, Robert Delaunay (1885–1941) and Sonia Delaunay (1885–1979) used color as a means of creating forms in space, producing some of the first purely abstract paintings.

The turn of the century saw a renewal of interest in sculpture. One of the more conservative 20th-century sculptors was the Classicist Aristide Maillol (1861–1944). Many painters, including Matisse and Picasso, produced sculpture. Cubism was the formative influence on the Russian-born, French-naturalized sculptor Jacques Lipchitz (1891–1973). Henri Laurens (1885–1954) was exclusively a Cubist sculptor.

Dada, an artistic movement of the absurd, and Surrealism, a movement whose subject matter was fantasy and the subconscious, were founded in the years surrounding World War I. Marcel Duchamp (1887–1968), the most interesting practitioner of Dada, was French. Surrealism, founded as a literary movement by André Breton and Philippe Soupault, attracted many artists including the Belgian René-François-Ghislain Magritte (1898–1967), French-born American Yves Tanguy (1900–1955), and the French Jean Arp (1887–1966).

Certainly the greatest architectural movement of the 20th century was the International style, so named for its widespread use in a geographical sense. The style is distinguished by having building exteriors designed according to distribution of interior space and by having interior spaces opened onto one another. According to this style, a house was conceived as a "machine for living," and "form followed function." Reinforced concrete was used as a basic material. Concrete had been employed with great success early in the century by the French architect Auguste Perret (1874–1954) and later by Le Corbusier (1887–1965), the Swiss-born architect working in France, who designed the famous International style Villa Savoye at Poissy, near Paris, between 1929 and 1931.

After World War II, the avant-garde shifted to the United States, but many gifted artists remained in France, and one can see the up-to-date artworks in the contemporary art galleries in Paris. Three of the most famous postwar French artists are the Expressionist Jean Dubuffet, the Dadaist sculptor Jean Tinguely, and the Pop artist Yves Klein.

The Cuisine of France

French cuisine has long been the standard by which all other Western cuisines are judged. The French attitude toward food was perhaps best characterized by the writer and critic Brillat-Savarin (1755–1826), who defined French gastronomy as "the intelligent knowledge of whatever concerns man's nourishment." French cooking is one of the few codified cuisines in the world. Foods are typed according to their method of preparation and their sauce. Soups, for example, are subdivided into *consommés* (clear soups), *veloutés* (made with a white sauce), *crèmes* (cream soups), and *potages* (thick soups).

French cuisine is typified by its delicate sauces prepared from long-simmering stocks. Hundreds of sauces have been created to enhance the flavor and texture of foods. French cooking is also distinguished by its practice of using fine wines as an accompaniment to food. The French have cultivated more than 400 varieties of wine and hundreds of types of cow- and goat's-milk cheese.

The history of French *haute cuisine* dates to the arrival of Catherine de Médicis at the French court and her marriage to Henri II in the 16th century. Catherine's cousin, Marie de Médicis, who married Henri IV, further advanced the culinary arts. Before the 16th century, French food was characterized by its crudity and its extravagance. At each meal huge quantities of beef, mutton, pork, or game were roasted on spits or stewed in cauldrons. Spices such as ginger, cinnamon, cloves, and nutmeg were used to obscure the taste of spoiled foods.

The Médicis and their Florentine cooks introduced foods that we now consider typically French, including truffles, artichokes, aspics, sweetbreads, and quenelles of poultry. Louis XIV was deeply interested in French cuisine. At Versailles he established the custom of serving dishes in a specific order rather than serving all of them at the beginning of the meal. It was during his reign that the fork became widely used and fine porcelain was made into dinnerware. After the Revolution, advances in French cuisine took place in restaurants, rather than in the châteaux of the aristocrats.

Some of the greatest French chefs and culinary authorities were François-Pierre de LaVarenne (1618–1678), who presided over Marie de Médicis's table; Antoine Carême (1784–1833), called the aristocrat of French cuisine, employed by Tallyrand; Prosper Montagné (1864–1938), who wrote the *Larousse Gastronomique* (1938); and Georges-Auguste Escoffier (1836–1935), a zealot for culinary simplification. In recent years French cuisine has been greatly simplified. *Cuisine Minceur,* created by Michel Guèrard, calls for the elimination of fats and sugars; *Nouvelle Cuisine,* created by Fernand Point and his disciple Paul Bocuse and other chefs, also specifies that sauces be made from the reduction of puréed vegetables rather than from stock, butter, and flour.

Just as rich and considerably more varied than the haute cuisine of France is the cuisine of the French provinces. This cooking, which depends almost entirely on the use of local ingredients, has its roots in an earlier time when the provinces of France were all politically independent entities with their own languages and unique cultures.

Central France

Paris and Île-de-France. Historically, the farmland of the Île-de-France was the breadbasket of Paris. Today, anything harvested in the distant provinces of France arrives in Paris daily, and in huge quantities. Some well-known dishes that originated near Paris are *cerises Montmorency* (cherries from Montmorency) and *Crème Chantilly,* from Chantilly. Traditionally, the haute cuisine of France has been centered in Paris. At the same time one can find a wide range of simpler dishes in the capital, including *crêpes Suzette* (thin egg pancakes flambéed with orange liqueur), *matelote* (fish soup), *soupe à l' oignon gratinée* (onion soup with grated cheese), *boeuf de Mironton* (beef stew), *veau sauté Marengo* (braised veal stew), *gibelotte* (wild rabbit in wine), and *gigot d' agneau* (leg of lamb).

Paris is known throughout the world for its desserts. Some favorites are *choux à la crème* (puff shells filled with custard), *mille-feuilles* (puff pastry leaves filled with cream), and *petits fours* (tiny iced cakes).

A few local cheeses are *Coulommiers* (a disk of soft cow's-milk cheese resembling Brie), *Fougeru* (an aged Coulommiers), and *Fontainebleau* (a cow's-milk dessert cheese).

Wines. All of the wines of France are available in Paris. Beer is also popular.

Loire River and Valley and the Sologne. This region is located between Brittany and Burgundy. The Loire River flows from east to west amid forested valleys and Renaissance châteaux. Lakes and rivers are filled with tiny fish called *éperlans, goujons,* and *gardons,* which are traditionally served fried. Game and wild mushrooms (*cèpes* and *coprins chevelus*) are plentiful in the deciduous forests.

Specialties from Orléans and Blois are the *Pâté de Pâques* (Easter veal and pork pie), *andouilettes* (tripe), *saucisses* (sausages), and *civet de lièvre de Sologne* (rabbit stew). From Tours and Angers come *rillettes de Tours* (minced pork or goose cooked in earthenware), *côques* (black pudding), *boudin blanc* (white sausage), *brochet au beurre blanc* (perch or pike with white butter sauce), and *truite au Vouvrey* (trout with a wine sauce).

Chèvre (goat's-milk cheese) is the predominant cheese of the region. Try the *chabichou, selles-sur-Cher, Pouligny-Saint-Pierre,* or *Sainte-Maure.*

For local desserts try the prunes stuffed with marzipan and preserved in Vouvray wine, the *tarte à la citrouille* (pumpkin pie) or *tarte Tatin* (apple tart), the *pralines* (caramelized almonds) from Montargis, or honey from Gatinais.

Wines. The best of the Loire wines are whites, both sweet and dry. The region is known for its sparkling whites from Saumur. The internationally known liqueur *Cointreau* is produced in Angers. The nine major wine districts of the Loire are Anjou, Coteaux du Loir, Jasnières, Muscadet, Pouilly-sur-Loire, Quincy, Reuilly, Sancerre, and Touraine.

Burgundy. The cuisine of Burgundy strongly reflects its ancient heritage: Pork was prepared in ancient Gaul; snails, honey, mustard, olives, and grapes were delicacies in Roman settlements in Gaul; garlic and parsley came from Egypt; sugar, cinnamon, pepper, ginger, saffron, and shallots were brought to Burgundy during the Crusades.

Each city is known for a specialty: Beaune for *oeufs en meurette* (eggs poached in red wine); Mâcon for *coq au Chambertin* (chicken in red wine) and *escargots* (snails) with garlic; Morvan for wild boar and chestnut stew; Charolles for beef with marrow; and Auxerre for pike and trout mousse.

Burgundian hors d'oeuvres include *cerneaux* (fresh walnuts with a vinegar taste), *cèpes* (marinated mushrooms), pork sausages and pâtés, and warm pies, the best known of which is *la gougère* (a seasoned cheese pastry). Burgundy also specializes in ham dishes, including *jambon persillé* (parsleyed ham in aspic), and *saupiquet* (ham and vegetables).

Most fish in Burgundy is cooked in wine and herbs, enriched with cream and occasionally with mustard. In Burgundy a fish stew prepared with white wine is called *la pauchouse* and with red wine *à meurette.*

The Romans used honey, spices, and pepper in their pastry, and so do the Burgundians. The famous *pain d' épice* is a Burgundian gingerbread from an original Medieval recipe. Also popular are *beignets* (fritters), *clafoutis* (cherry custard pie), and *nonnettes* (honey and almond cakes).

In Burgundy *chèvre* (goat's-milk cheese) is eaten everywhere. Cow's-milk cheese is served fresh in desserts or is whipped with herbs. The best-known soft fresh cheeses are *Sainte-Marie-des-Laumes* and *Sainte-Reine-d'Alise.* Some other popular cheeses are *Charolais, Langres,* and *Epoisses,* the latter known for its orange crust.

Wines. Crème de Cassis, a black currant liqueur, is a product of Burgundy, as is *kir,* an apéritif made from white wine and cassis. The greatest wines of this region come from the Côte d'Or, a low range of hills along the western edge of Burgundy beginning north in Dijon and ending in the south just above Lyon. Wines of the north—the Côte de Nuits—include *Nuits-Saint-Georges, Chambertin, Romanée,* and *Musigny.* Wines from the south—the Côte de Beaune—include the red *Pommard* and whites such as *Meursault* and *Montrachet*. Other wines of the region are *Givry, Mercurey, Montagny, Beaujolais, Morgon,* and *Brouilly*.

The Auvergne. The Auvergne is a rugged mountainous area in central France that specializes in hearty meats and cheeses. A sampling of local dishes includes *aligot* (puree of potatoes and garlic), and *tonne* (curded cheese), *pounti* (pork, swiss chard, and prune loaf), *lentilles du Puy* (tiny green lentils served with sausages and ham), *saucisson sec* (dried salami), and *petit salé aux lentilles* (salt pork with lentils).

Some desserts of the region are the *gâteau de la châtaigneraie* (chestnut cake), chocolates from Royat, *dragées* (sugared almonds) from Aigueperse.

Among the approximately fifteen varieties of cheese produced in the Auvergne are *Cantal-Laguiole, Bleu d'Auvergne, Saint-Nectaire, Gaperon,* and *Saint Marcellin*.

Wines. Although the wines of Auvergne are not considered to be of the highest quality, the *Châteaugay, Corent, Saint Pourçain,* and *Chanturgues* vintages are worth trying.

Champagne and Ardennes. Champagne and Ardennes are located in an area of rolling hills and wheat fields a few hours east of Paris. The region is not known for its fine cuisine, but for its simple specialities, including *pieds de porc à la Sainte-Menehould* (pigs feet), *pâté de pigeon en croûte* (pigeon pâté), *brochet* (freshwater pike), and *truite* (trout) from Montmirail.

This region is world famous for its *Brie de Meaux,* a soft cow's-milk cheese and *Brie de Melun,* similar in taste but available in smaller sizes than *Brie de Mieux*. Other cheeses of note are the *Maroilles, Rollot,* and *Boulette d'Avesnes,* all made from cow's milk.

Wines. Some of the most ancient vineyards in Europe are located in Champagne. Sparkling wines, however, were only developed in the 17th century. The champagne producers are in Reims, Châlons-sur-Marne, Bar-sur-Aube, Château Thierry, and Épernay. A few of the great champagnes are *Tattinger, Moët et Chandon, Krug,* and *Bollinger*.

Northern and Northwestern France

Normandy. Normandy is a region of pastoral farmland abutting the sea. It is best known for its *Camembert* (a soft cow's-milk cheese), butter, cream, pear and apple cider, and its *Calvados*—an apple brandy named for a department in Normandy. The region abounds in seafood. One can find oysters from Saint-Vaast-la-Hougue, fresh *crevettes grises* (tiny shrimp) from Deauville and Trouville, mussels from Villerville. Some traditional dishes of Normandy are *poulet vallée d'Auge,* (chicken in cider and cream sauce), *pain brié,* (a rectangular loaf of dense white bread), *tripes à la mode de Caen,* (beef tripe cooked in cider and Calvados).

Along with Camembert, Normandy is known for its *Pont-l'Evêque* and tangy *Livarot* cheese, and *Neufchâtel* and *gervais* cream cheese.

Brittany. Bordering on the Atlantic Ocean, the sea has heavily influenced Brittany's cuisine. The province is known for its sea salt, its *praires* (tiny clams), its scallops from the Saint-Brieuc bay, and tiny bay scallops called *olivettes*. *Langoustine* (spiny lobster) and *homard* (lobster) are served grilled or roasted. A particularly flavorful dish is *homard grillé à la crème*. Two varieties of Breton oysters are the flats or *plates*, of which the best known are the tiny Belon oysters and the *Creuse*, which have crinkled shells. Of the latter, try the *papillon* (butterfly) variety from the Claires oyster beds near Marennes or the *spéciales* from the beds near La Rochelle and Marennes-Oléron.

Brittany is also highly regarded for its cakes, among them the famous *Breton crêpes* (thin wheat pancakes) and *galettes* (thin buckwheat pancakes). Also from Brittany are the *far breton* (a cake or flan made of sweetened wheat and filled with prunes or raisins), *craquelin* (a flat peasant dough cake), *kouignamann*, (a buttery yeast cake), and *gâteau breton* (Brittany butter cake). One of the best known cheeses of Brittany is *Port du Salut*.

Wines. Cider is a traditional drink. Wines from the Muscadet vineyards near Nantes are the only ones in Brittany to be classified. They are the perfect accompaniment to seafood. Varieties include *Muscadet, Muscadet de Sèvre-et-Maine, Gros Plant,* and *Muscadet des Coteaux de la Loire.*

Picardy. This northern province is known for its fine assortment of fish and shellfish, including North Sea herring, *huîtres* (oysters), *coques* (cockles), and *crevettes* (shrimps). A few popular local dishes are Flanders *hochepot* (thick stew, usually of oxtail), *pâté de bécasse* (woodcock pâté), *carbonade* (beef braised in onions and beer), *bouillabaisse de la Manche* (fish soup), *cassolette d'escargots à l'anis* (snail and anise stew), and duck pies, a specialty of Amiens. The best known cheeses are the *Gris de Lille, Dauphin, Rollet, Vieux Lille, Marvilles, Mont des Cat,* and *Goyère.*

Wines. This region produces no wine, but it makes beer, cider, and *Genièvre,* a juniper-flavored spirit.

Eastern and Northeastern France

Alsace and Lorraine. Throughout history Alsace and its northern neighbor Lorraine have shared a border with Germany and have been occupied alternately by the French and Germans. The hearty peasant cuisine of this region borrows from both French and German cooking.

Specialties from Alsace are *choucroute garnie à l'alsacienne* (sauerkraut, sausage, bacon, pork, and potatoes), *tarte à l'oignon* (onion tart), *flammekueche* (cheese and onion tart), *potée alsacienne* (pork and vegetable soup), *Beckenoffe* (beef, lamb, pork, potatoes, and onions cooked in wine), *quenelles de foie* (liver dumplings), or *coq au Riesling* (braised chicken with white wine). For dessert sample the *birwecka* (fruit and brandy bread). The most popular Alsatian cheese is *Munster.*

The cuisine of Lorraine is similar to that of Alsace. Popular dishes are sausages from Metz, roast goose with apples, *pâté Lorraine* (meat and vegetable stew), *perdrix aux choux à la Lorraine* (partridge with cabbage).

Desserts in Lorraine range from *dragées* (sugared almonds) from Verdun to *macaroons* from Nancy to jam from Bar-le-Duc.

Wines. There are more than 130 varieties of wine in Alsace. *Riesling* and *Gewürztraminer* are the finest wines of the region. Some other varieties are *Sylvaner, Traminer, Muscat d'Alsace, Tokay d'Alsace, Pinot Gris,* and *Chasselas.* Beer is also popular.

The Alsatian vineyards extend in a north-south band along the eastern edge of the Vosges mountains. The most noteworthy wine areas are between Riquewihr and Ribeauvillé and the clusters of vineyards around Barr and Guebwiller. Tourists often drive along the Route de Vin, setting out from Strasbourg and travelling south to Colmar.

Clear fruit brandies such as *Framboise* (raspberry), *Poire* (pear), *Kirsch* (cherry), and *Quetsche* (plum) are produced in Alsace. Sample the *ratafia* (mixture of sweet wine and brandy) at the Distillerie Massenez.

Franche-Comté, Savoie-Dauphiné, and the Vallée du Rhône.

This region, which extends eastward from the Rhône valley to the Jura mountains and Switzerland, includes the towns of Savoie and Bresse and the city of Lyon. Lyon is considered second only to Paris in its gastronomic sophistication.

For hundreds of years Bresse has been known for its *poulet de Bresse,* a succulent bird raised on a special diet. The production of this bird is controlled by the French government. Other specialties of the region are the smoky *Morteau* sausage and the *galette bresanne* (sugar and cream tart).

Some of the cheeses of eastern France are *Beaufort, Emmentaler, Reblochon, Tamie,* and *Tomes de Savoie.*

Wines. Vineyards abound on the banks of the Rhône, yet only wines from the central section bear the name *Côtes du Rhône. Tavel, Châteauneuf-du-Pape* and *Hermitage* are the best-known Rhône wines. *Kirsch,* a cherry flavored brandy, is also made in this region.

Southern and Southwestern France

Pays Basque and Aquitaine. Its long Atlantic coastline and proximity to the Pyrenees are responsible for the very diverse cuisine of this region. A few specialties of the Pays Basque are *piperade* (eggs, tomatoes, peppers, and ham), *aubergine farcies* (stuffed eggplant), *poulet basquaise* (chicken with tomatoes and peppers), and *tripoxca* (calf's or sheep's blood sausage with peppers). For desserts in the Pays Basque try the *gâteau basque* (black cherry cake), *tourtière landaise* (apple, prune, and Armagnac strudel). The best-known cheese of the region is *Brebis,* made from sheep's milk. *Eaux-de-vie de poire* (pear brandy) and *eaux-de-vie de prune* (plum brandy) are savored in this province.

North of the Pays Basque is the region surrounding the port city of Bordeaux, where simple local ingredients are favored. Sample the *éclade de moules* (grilled mussels), *mouclade* (mussel stew), *pibales* (tiny eels), *lumas* and *cagouilles* (land snails). *Mojette* (fresh or dry white beans) prepared with ham are a specialty of the area.

Wines. Bordeaux may be the most important wine district in France. About one quarter of the finest and most expensive wines of the world are produced here. Not all wines grown in the district are labeled Bordeaux; to be worthy of the appellation wines must adhere to certain standards and requirements. Red wines are made to the north of the city and whites to the south. The following are but a few of the fine reds of Bordeaux: *Haut-Médoc, Margaux, Pauillac, Pomerol, Saint-Émilion, Saint-Estèphe,* and *Saint-Julien.* Bordeaux whites include *Sauternes, Barsac, Entre-Deux-Mers, Graves Supérieures,* and *Premières Côtes de Bordeaux. Côtes de Bourg, Graves, Blayais,* and *Premières Côtes de Blaye* are among the Bordeaux wines that may be white or red.

The Dordogne. An agricultural province whose ancient name was Périgord, the Dordogne region is known for its *foie gras* (goose or duck liver), truffles, *confit* (preserved duck or goose), goat cheese called *cabecou,* and *eaux-de-vie de prune* (plum brandy). The term *périgourdine* refers to a rich sauce made with truffles and *foie gras.* The Dordogne has been for many years France's primary source of strawberries.

Wines. Good local wines to sample with the *foie gras* are *Côtes de Duras* and *Côtes de Buzet.*

Gascony and Toulouse. Southwestern France was occupied by the Arabs for 800 years and their influence can still be seen in the cuisine of the region. *Tourtière* is a dessert that resembles the Arabic baklava and *cassoulet* may be a French version of an Arabic fava beans-and-mutton stew. *Confit* (preserved goose or duck), *foie gras* (goose or duck liver), and wild mushrooms are popular in this region.

Around Toulouse, ducks, geese, turkeys, and pigs are bred in great quantities, and local restaurants specialize in foods that use these animals as a base. Try the famous *Saucisse de Toulouse,* made from coarse cut saddle of pork. *Les violettes des Toulouse* (candied violets) are a traditional dessert. Local cheeses made of ewe's milk are generally excellent. The best-known cheeses are *Gris de Lille, Dauphin, Rollet, Vieux Lille, Marvilles, Mont des Cat,* and *Goyère.*

Wines. This region produces no wine, but it makes beer, cider, *Genièvre,* a juniper-flavored spirit, and the famous *Armagnac* brandy, which is full-bodied and pungent.

Limousin. A cattle-breeding region, Limousin produces not only beef but *gigot* (leg of lamb) from Montmorillon and *jambon* (ham) from Saint-Mathieu. Specialties include *Bréjaude* (bacon and cabbage soup, eaten with rye bread), truffled meat pâtés, and *lièvre en chabessa* (rabbit).

Clafoutis (cherry custard pie) is popular for dessert as are *noisettes aubussonaises* (hazelnut cake) and *flaugnarde* with apples. Few cheeses apart from the *Brach,* which is like Roquefort, are produced.

Languedoc. This region is situated on a vast plain just west of Provence. The cooking, whose staple ingredients are olive oil and garlic, is extremely varied and includes such specialties as *cassoulet* (white bean, goose, and mutton stew) and *rouille de seiche* (cuttlefish in garlic sauce). In Roussillon, Catalan cuisine is emphasized. Sample the *moules* (mussels) from the Bassin de Thau, *civet de langouste* (lobster stew), *ovillade* (bean and cabbage soup), and *perdreau à la Catalane* (young partridge with bitter oranges). In the Camargue, near Provence, try the *gardiane* (stew of bull meat, wine, and black olives). In Bouzigues, try the *moules de Bouzigues.* This town produces one-third of the mussel crop of France.

For desserts try *crème Catalane,* an anise-flavored custard. The plain of Roussillon accounts for the entire French apricot production, and this fruit appears in pastries and in many other desserts.

Roquefort, one of the best-known cheeses in the world, is produced from aged sheep's milk in the town of *Roquefort-sur-Soulzon.* Also of interest are *cabécou,* a sheep's-milk farm cheese, *Pelardon des Cévennes,* a goat's milk cheese, and the widely-known *bleu des Causses,* made from cow's milk.

Wines. Languedoc produces some of the least expensive table wines of France. Even so, many of them are respectable. The better wines are the white *Clairette du Languedoc,* the red *Minervois,* and the sturdy varieties of *Corbières.*

Corsica. The cuisine of the island of Corsica has been influenced by France, Italy, Spain, and North Africa. Corsican sausages are delicious, as are many dishes made from organ meats such as *rifreda* (liver and lung of lamb or kid) and *tripettes* (tripe). Other exotic island specialties are *azimu,* a Corsican fish soup, *pâté de merle* (blackbird pâté), and *tianu di cignale* (roasted boar).

The best cheeses are those from the villages of Fastelicaccia, Niolo, Coscione, and Venaco. *Broccin,* a cheese made from whey and whole milk, is widely used in Corsican cooking.

Wines. The finest Corsican wine is *Patrimonio Rosé,* grown near Bastia. The other good wines of the region are the whites from Cape Corse, *Rogliano* and *Centuri,* and the reds of Sartène and Figari.

Provence and Côte d'Azur. Provence is a land of exquisite beauty with silver-tinged olive trees and lavender fields. The Greeks and Romans brought olive oil and wine to the region. Today Provence is known for its love of garlic, anchovies, and a special blend of spices called *aromates* (dried and fresh herbs and zest of citrus fruit).

There are at least 400 dishes that are original to Provence. Perhaps the best known is *aïoli,* which was extolled by the 19th-century Provençal poet Frédéric Mistral (1830–1914): "Aïoli gently intoxicates, charges the body with warmth, bathes the soul in rapture." Essentially *aïoli* is a creamy garlic mayonnaise served with cold fish and vegetables. Other Provençal specialties include the famed *bouillabaisse* (fish and saffron stew), *la bagna caudo* (raw vegetables and anchovies dipped in hot olive oil), *tapenado* (black olives, anchovies, and capers), *soupe au Pistou* (basil, garlic, and cheese soup), *aïgo boulido* (garlic soup), *pissaladièra* (bread baked with purée of onions, anchovies, and olive oil), *brandade de morue* (salt, cod, olive oil, and milk), *ratatouille Niçoise* (mélange of green peppers, tomatoes, eggplant, onion, and garlic), and *salade Niçoise* (tuna and vegetable salad).

For dessert in Provence try the fresh figs, the *Bugnes Arlésiennes* (fried cakes), *tarte de blettes* (raisin, pine nut, and chard cake), and the special *carnissouns* (or *calissouns*), lozenge-shaped sweets made from ground almonds, melon preserve, and fruit syrup.

Sheep- and goat's-milk cheeses, especially those from Picodon and Banon, are the specialty of the region.

Wines. Most wines of Provence are little known outside their own region. The Rhône extends into Provence and some of the best wines fall under the heading of *Côtes-du-Rhône,* among them the famous *Châteauneuf-du-Pape,* whose vineyards are located several miles south of Orange. Other wines worth trying are those of *Lirac* and the *Tavels,* whose bouquet is similar to the fragrance of young strawberries. East of the Rhône are the vineyards under the name *Côtes du Ventoux.* From Aix to the Var valley are the *Côtes de Provence.* The wines of Bandol, Cassis, and Palette are also of interest.

***Paris

Like other great cities of the world, Paris is highly individual—in appearance, in atmosphere, in tempo, and in tone. Like the others, it appeals to many different kinds of visitors, whatever their backgrounds, expectations, and tastes. It has grandeur as well as intimacy, cool elegance as well as warm-hearted charm. For generations the very name of this city has conjured up the ideas of romance and excitement and a quality expressed by the phrase *je ne sais quoi*—that inexpressible something that lends it a special mystery and grace, however often one may encounter it. It comes as no surprise that Paris is called The City of Light, for it is that on many levels. It may not be all things to all people, but it comes pretty close.

Its glamour and capacity to stimulate and please have not diminished over the centuries, despite the inevitable incursions of the uglier aspects of contemporary life, and the unrelenting armies of visitors it welcomes annually. It is one of the places in the world that every traveller should visit once, if not many times. (There is nothing stern, only seductive, about this imperative.) It is not "See Naples and die," but "See Paris and live!"

History

In 52 B.C., one of Julius Caesar's lieutenants seized the river fort of the Gallic Parisii tribe on the ancient site of what is now the Île de la Cité— the delightful island in the Seine River that separates the left bank from the right. The settlement, which the Romans called Lutetia, later became a thriving commercial center, and several Roman emperors stayed there. In the year 360, Lutetia was named Paris, and after the departure of the Romans it was saved, according to legend, from an invasion by Attila's Huns in 451 by the prayers of Sainte-Geneviève, who became the city's patron saint.

In the first decade of the sixth century, Clovis, King of the Franks, made Paris his capital, and the city remained in Merovingian hands for nearly 250 years until Pepin the Short, father of Charlemagne, ousted the last successor of the Merovingian dynasty. There followed a period of frequent Norman raids on the city. The great siege of Paris in 885–886 ended in the defeat of the Normans by Count Eudes, who was made King of France in 887. The principle of monarchy in France became established with the Capetians, who ruled from 987–1328; it was during the reign of Philippe I that the building of one of Paris' greatest monuments—Nôtre-Dame cathedral—was begun. The fortress of the Louvre was erected under Philippe Auguste (1180–1223), who also constructed a defensive wall around the city and laid the foundation of the University of Paris, one of Europe's greatest Medieval centers of learning. The Sorbonne was established by Louis IX (1223–1285), who was later canonized; another Paris landmark—Sainte Chapelle—was built during his reign, and the basilica of St. Denis, prototype of the new Gothic style, was worked on.

Under the Valois kings, France entered a chaotic period in which war with England was a constant factor. There was a popular uprising among the people of Paris in 1358, under the leadership of the mayor of the city. The Bastille was erected under Charles V the Wise; during the reign of his successor, the weak Charles VI, Paris was captured by the English king, Henry V. The city remained in English hands from 1420–1453.

Paris prospered under Louis XI (1461–1483)—a school of medicine was established and the first printing press was set up. François I (1515–1547), a great patron of the arts, helped to introduce the Italian Renaissance to France, and began the reconstruction of the Louvre. From 1559–1589, the city was the scene of murderous conflicts between Catholics and Protestants, culminating in the St. Bartholomew's Day Massacre in 1572, when 3,000 Huguenots were murdered in Paris.

The Louvre and the Tuileries palace, first begun under Catherine de Médicis, were extended under the Bourbon king, Henry IV, who also created the beautiful Place des Vosges and completed the Pont-Neuf. The size, influence, and architectural magnificence of Paris grew steadily during the 17th century, known as "Le Grand Siècle." Marie de Médicis built the Luxembourg palace, while Cardinal Richelieu founded the Académie Française and built the Palais-Royal. Paris became a bishopric in 1622.

By the mid-17th century, Paris was an important and sophisticated city of half a million inhabitants. The educational journey to Paris—the so-called "Gentleman's Tour"—became indispensable for every European of rank or social pretension. The splendor of the court of Louis XIV, the "Sun King" who built Versailles, Les Invalides, the Louvre colonnade, and the Comédie Française, turned the eyes of the world to Paris. Louis XIV, however, abolished the office of mayor and the municipal institutions of Paris, and tightened the grip of the centralized power of the monarchy by placing Paris under the rule of the state, a situation that was to remain in effect until the Revolution. Despite the ensuing crisis and growing popular discontent with the monarchy, Paris continued to be ennobled by the building of the Panthéon, the Palais-Bourbon, and the Place de la Concorde.

Paris was the scene of one of the great turning points in French and world history when, on July 14, 1789, a mob stormed the Bastille and set in motion the events leading up to the French Revolution. During the Reign of Terror, 2,800 people were executed in Paris alone, many of them on guillotines set up on the Place de la Concorde. It was also a time when countless works of art were marred or destroyed because they either had or were thought to have royalist themes.

With the advent of Napoleon, who in 1799 appointed himself First Consul of France, Paris entered into a new period of material expansion and prosperity; the city was terrorized, however, by the excesses of Napoleon's secret police. In 1804, Napoleon had himself crowned emperor in Nôtre-Dame cathedral. France became the ruler of Europe until 1814, when Paris, which had become the center of Europe, was captured by the invading allied armies. The Bourbon monarchy was restored, but the short-lived July Revolution in Paris (1830) ousted the Bourbon Charles X in favor of Louis-Philippe of the Orléans line. Modernization began in Paris with the opening of the first French railway line and gas lighting.

The "Citizen King," Louis Philippe, spent a fortune upgrading the city, and beginning in 1853, the architect Baron Haussmann (1809–1891) transformed Paris from a large Medieval town to the most modern city in the world by creating the Grand Boulevards and 20 great squares. The famous and extravagant Paris Opéra was built in this period.

The city suffered great damage in 1871 when the Commune, a revolutionary government, briefly took power, but had recovered sufficiently by 1889 to host the World Exhibition, whose symbol was the cast-iron tower by Gustave Eiffel.

The first Métro line opened in 1900. Relatively little physical damage was done to the city in the two World Wars.

Postwar Paris has seen the addition of several controversial buildings and urban renovation projects, including the skyscrapers of La Défense, the Tour Montparnasse, the Pompidou Center, and the Forum des Halles, which replaced the old Halles market. The most recent architectural controversy revolves around the new glass pyramid, which is being built in the courtyard of the Louvre.

You can wander endlessly in Paris, with ample reward. You can make preliminary surveys by taking buses. You can examine a bird's-eye map of the city and strike out on impulse, but since Paris is so large, we advise some planned tours, such as the series of walks given here, that provide a circular tour of the City of Light (see map on pages 34–35).

WALK 1: ***Louvre–*Tuileries Gardens–**Place de la Concorde

See color map.

(*Métro stations: Louvre; Palais-Royal; Tuileries; Concorde*)

The Louvre, first stop on this walking tour, is among the world's greatest museums, filled with countless masterpieces. Its collection is so vast that you may want to spend at least one day exploring it. From the Louvre you can stroll through the delightful Tuileries Gardens, an example of urban landscape art at its best, to the imposing and historically important Place de la Concorde.

***The Louvre** (1) began as a Medieval fortress that was part of the city walls and became over three centuries and 17 reigns a royal residence—a residence like no other for sheer size and for the number of architects involved in its extended construction. Once royal patronage provided house and studio room for artists here, now it's art's supreme showplace. From its magnificent courtyard you can see—through the triumphal *Arc du Carousel*—right down the Tuileries and the Champs-Elysées to the Arc de Triomphe, a vista made possible through the city's splendidly organized plan.

The extensive and varied Louvre collections—of Oriental and Egyptian antiquities, Greek and Roman antiquities, sculpture, paintings and drawings, furniture, and objets d'art—make it one of the richest museums in the world. It is so rich, in fact, that it can be bewildering, even to dedicated museumgoers. One visit will hardly suffice to acquaint you with any but the most celebrated masterpieces. Chief among these are the *Winged Victory,* mounted like a presiding angel on the first landing of the grand staircase on the left, Leonardo da Vinci's *Mona Lisa,* and the *Venus de Milo*. There is a gem of quite another order in the 137-carat "Regent" diamond in the French crown jewels in the *Galerie d'Apollon*. There is a world to choose from in the Louvre. Guided tours are available, and advisable, but there are also maps of the museum and indicators of suggested routes to get you through the endless huge salons to the works that interest you most.

West of the Louvre are the ***Tuileries Gardens** (2) by the 17th-century master of the formal-garden landscape André Le Nôtre, as part of the Palace of the Tuileries, which was destroyed by the Commune in 1871. The gardens, flowerless though they are, provide a very pleasant area of dappled light to stroll and sit in, a lovely retreat from the streets or for the gallery-weary, where you can take refreshment at a café table under the trees and people-watch at leisure. At the far end of the gardens, on either side of the gate leading to the Place de la Concorde, are two pavilions. The one on your left, nearest the river, is the *Orangerie,* once the palace greenhouse; the other, the *Jeu de Paume,* once the tennis court (which is what the name means), was until recently (1985) the home of the famous collection of French Impressionist paintings that have been transferred to the **Musée d'Orsay* (see Walk 4) across the Seine. Both pavilions now serve as galleries for changing exhibitions.

The beautiful and spacious late-17-century **Place de la Concorde** (3) once held the guillotine by which, during the Reign of Terror, royals, aristocrats, and revolutionaries alike met their deaths. The writer André Maurois deemed it the most beautiful architectural ensemble on the planet. But even allowing for French chauvinism, it is certainly impressive, with its mansions, fountains, sculpture, pavilions, the deluxe Hôtel Crillon, and the rosy-hued central *obelisk from Luxor* (more than 3,000 years old). Of course there is also, given modern Paris, a nonstop flow of traffic, which can pose some difficulties for appreciating the wonderful vistas in all directions: to the north

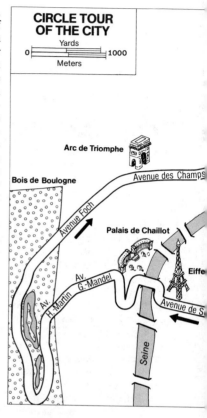

CIRCLE TOUR OF THE CITY

Yards
0 |⊢⊢⊢⊢⊢⊢⊢| 1000
Meters

Arc de Triomphe

Bois de Boulogne

Avenue des Champs

Av. Foch

Palais de Chaillot

Eiffe

Av. H.-Martin   Av. G.-Mandel

Avenue de S

Seine

through the Rue Royale to the church of the Madeleine; to the east through the Tuileries to the Louvre; to the south over the bridge to the Classical Palais-Bourbon; to the west up the Champs-Élysées, its entrance marked by the Marly statues of wild horses from Louis XIV's château, to the Arc de Triomphe.

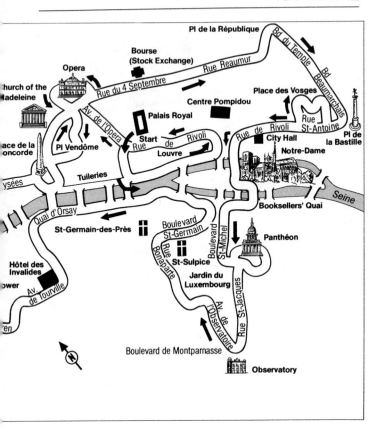

WALK 2: *Champs-Élysées–**Arc de Triomphe

See color map.

(Métro stations: Franklin D. Roosevelt; Étoile)

Walk 2, a continuation of Walk 1, takes you down the Champs-Élysées, a grand thoroughfare that begins at the Place de la Concorde and ends at the equally famous Arc de Triomphe.

*Avenue des Champs-Élysées, a long boulevard whose name is known throughout the

world, is the main avenue leading to the monumental ****Arc de Triomphe** of Napoleonic inspiration, under which lies the *Tomb of the Unknown Soldier.* The avenue is one of twelve boulevards that lead, like the petals of a daisy, to the arch, and the whole complex is known as the ***Place de l'Étoile** (4).

These avenues end in the *Place Charles de Gaulle,* a daunting traffic circle which you can cross through an underground passage. In earlier times the Çhamps was a favorite and fashionable promenade for carriages and riders, as it is these days for tourists and organized political demonstrations. The first section of the avenue from the Place de la Concorde to the *Rond-Point* (an intersection for several roads) is still parkland of a sort, and the traffic circle is charming, with its fountains and greenery. Several celebrated restaurants are situated here, as well as the two important exhibition halls of the *Grand* and *Petit Palais.* Beyond the circle, the Champs—although lined with trees—has become highly commercialized, with shops, cinemas, cafés, hotels, restaurants, office buildings, and showrooms. The city's

Arc de Triomphe

Tourist Information Office is also located here. All in all, however, the avenue retains its fabled attraction.

When you have reached the *Arc de Triomphe,* examine the wealth of its sculpture, especially the lively relief on the left, known as *"La Marseillaise,"* the name it shares with the French national anthem. By all means take the elevator to the top for an enthralling view of the entire geometric layout of the Étoile and of more distant Paris.

WALK 3: **Musée d'Art Moderne de la Ville de Paris– *Palais de Chaillot–***Eiffel Tower–*UNESCO

See color map.

(*Métro stations: Trocadero; Champ-de-Mars; La Motte-Picquet*)

Starting at the Musée d'Art Moderne de Paris, with its collection of contemporary art, Walk 3 takes you to yet another quintessential Parisian landmark, the Eiffel Tower. After passing the École Militaire, the walk ends at the modern Maison d'UNESCO, a venue for cultural events.

From the Arc de Triomphe follow Avenue d'Iéna to the intersecting Avenue du Président Wilson, where you'll find the **Musee d'Art Moderne de la Ville de Paris** (5), housed in the *Palais de Tokyo,* which was built for the World Exposition of 1937. Most of its major holdings of modern paintings have been transferred to the Pompidou Center (see Walk 5) and to the Musée d'Orsay (see Walk 4), but there are many fine works from its permanent collection still shown here—Cubist paintings by Picasso and Braque, and works by Matisse and Modigliani among others—along with temporary exhibitions.

In the *Place du Trocadero* along the Avenue du Président Wilson, you come to the **Palais de Chaillot** (6), built in 1937 for the Paris Exhibition, and consisting of architecturally fairly ordinary Classical-style wings. But from its fountained terrace you get an absolutely spectacular vista across the river of both old and new Paris. Inside the Chaillot Palace is a cultural center, with a cinema and film library, the *Théâtre Nationale de Paris,* the *Musée de la Marine,* and the *Musée National des Monuments Français,* which offers an art-history survey of great works of every description, age, and category from all over the country. The important anthropological museum, *Musée de l'Homme,* is also housed here, and many kinds of theatrical productions—ballet, opera, plays, and concerts—are regularly presented.

Continue down the avenue to the *Pont d'Iéna* and cross the river to the *Champ-de-Mars,* the huge field which for centuries was used for parades and military exercises, later as a race course, and now as the park fronting the ***Eiffel Tower** (7) one of the city's most potent symbols, though it was built in 1889 by the engineer Gustave Eiffel as a temporary structure, with a projected life span of only 20 years. It has served as a tourist draw ever since. This ingenious, brilliantly conceived, daringly tall structure has been attacked and praised with great passion by distinguished artists and writers. Apart from its unusual character, it has proved of practical use as a radio and television tower, and on a clear day, or at sunset, it provides a glorious, vast view—although you may prefer the more interesting views from its lower levels. All the platforms are accessible by elevator, and the tower offers a range of amenities, including restaurants, a nightclub, a post office, and a bank. You can decide for yourself whether this once merely decorative tower is an abomination, or the "Queen of Paris," as Jean Cocteau called it.

Walk away from the tower and river through the Champ-de-Mars to the *École Militaire** (8), a handsome 18th-century military academy. The columns, porticos, and pediment, as well as the courtyard, are traditionally Classical, but the building was enlarged in the 19th century. The young Napoleon Bonaparte was a cadet here at the age of 15, and his report unequivocally promised success for the young man.

*Maison d'UNESCO (9) had three modern architects, two of whose names—Pier Luigi Nervi and Marcel Breuer—are well known. As a structure primarily intended for the work of the United Nations Educational, Scientific, and Cultural Organization, it contains many conference rooms, but it is also a venue for cultural events, films, and lectures, and something of a museum for works by renowned artists such as Picasso, Miró, Le Corbusier, Lurçat, Giacometti, Henry Moore, and Alexander Calder.

WALK 4: **Hôtel des Invalides–**Musée d'Orsay– *Palais Bourbon

See color map.

(*Métro stations: Invalides; Chambre des Députés*)

A continuation of the previous walk, Walk 4 takes you first to the Hôtel des Invalides and its 17th-century church where Napoleon's tomb is located. Personal mementoes of the emperor are on display at the Musée de l'Armée. The genius of the sculptor Rodin is to be seen in the excellent Musée de Rodin, while across the river is Paris' great Impressionist collection, formerly in the Jeu de Paume, now housed in the city's newest museum, the Musée d'Orsay.

From the UNESCO building, walk northeast on the Avenue de Lowendal to the Avenue de Trouville, where you will see the beautiful architectural complex ****Hôtel des Invalides** (10). The ***church of the Invalides,* a masterpiece of 17th-century architecture, is a Baroque church with Classical elements—pediment, Doric columns, a columned drum crowned by a magnificent dome, meant always to be covered in gold leaf. It was commissioned by Louis XIV from the architect Hardouin-Mansart, and contains many works by artists of the period. *Napoleon's tomb* is in the center, under the dome. He was buried in a series of six coffins of different materials, including wood, stone, lead, and metal, one inside the other. The tomb is surrounded by art work celebrating his victories and achievements. His remains were brought here from Saint Helena 40 years after his death, apparently in a fine state of preservation. Side chapels hold the tombs of his brothers and his son, as well as French military figures.

Across the *Cour d'Honneur,* an arcaded formal court with cobbled

Napoleon's tomb

pavement, where military ceremonies take place, and where
Captain Dreyfus was publically
disgraced, is the *Musée de
l'Armée*. It contains a great deal of
what one would expect to find in
any historical military museum—
arms, the elaborate uniforms of
the times, plans, portraits, ban-
ners, paintings. The Napoleonic
items have a special interest; here
is his personal equipment and furniture; his white horse (stuffed);
his death mask, recently acquired;
and miniature suits of armor, the
maker's samples.

From the Boulevard des
Invalides on the east side of the
museum, the Rue de Varennes
branches off to the east. At
Number 77 on this street is the
Musée de Rodin (11), housed
in the spacious 18th-century Classical *Hôtel Biron*. This building
was at one time an arts center
where Isadora Duncan, the German poet Rainer Maria Rilke, and
Auguste Rodin himself (from
1907 until his death in 1917)

lived. Many of Rodin's greatest
sculptures are in this museum,
both in the house and in the garden, along with interesting items
from his personal art collection.

Cross the *Esplanades des
Invalides* to the river, where you'll
come to the *Pont Alexandre III*
(12), the most elaborately decorated bridge over the Seine, built
in 1900 and named after a czar. Its
lavish style is typical of its period,
with an abundance of sculptured
creatures, garlands and objects,
and with imposing lamps along its
length. Without crossing the
bridge, turn right on the Quai
d'Orsay to what had been the Gare
d'Orsay, a railway station, now
transformed into Paris' newest
museum, the **Musée d'Orsay,**
which opened in 1986 to house the
superb Impressionist collection
from the Jeu de Paume. Here you
will find brilliant works by Degas,
Manet's *Déjeuner sur l'Herbe,*
considered to be the first Impressionist painting, and his *Olympia,*
and the celebrated *Cathédrals de
Rouen* paintings by Monet.
Renoir, Cézanne, and Van Gogh
are all represented on the top of the
museum's three floors. You will
also find sections devoted to
French decorative arts and furnishings, and special areas
devoted to the Paris Opéra and
Baron Haussmann, the architect
of 19th-century Paris.

West of the museum, fronting
on the Seine across from the Pont
de la Concorde, is an 18th-century
building that was designed to look
like a Greek temple. This is the

**Palais-Bourbon (13), built in 1722, seat of the Chambre des Députés, or French parliament. From here you can look across the river and the Place de la Concorde to the church of the Madeleine, whose Classical façade echoes the one of the Palais, providing a fine view of the urban landscape.

WALK 5: **Grands Boulevards–**Place Vendôme– *Palais Royal–**Centre Georges Pompidou

See color map.

(Métro stations: Madeleine; Opéra; Palais Royal)

Several centuries and styles are spanned on Walk 5, which begins at the church of La Madeleine, begun under Napoleon. The several Grands Boulevards are the result of Baron Haussmann's massive urban planning scheme of the 19th century and the taste of that era is nowhere better reflected than in the Paris Opéra. The ultra-chic Place Vendôme, on the other hand, belongs to the 17th century; in its vicinity are most of the exclusive shops that have made Paris synonymous with fashion. Modern Paris is represented here by the Centre Georges Pompidou and the surrounding area known as the Beaubourg.

From the Place de la Concorde, the Rue Royale leads directly to **La Madeleine** (14), the church whose construction was begun by Napoleon in 1806 to commemorate the glory of the Grande Armée. It was not consecrated as a church until 1842, when it was at last completed, and only after several other possible uses had been suggested for it. It is prominently situated in its own square of flower markets, and is impressively grand, with a stepped entrance and 52 Corinthian columns.

The ****Grands Boulevards,** which radiate from this point, were created in the second half of the 19th century by Baron George-Eugène Haussmann; his grand design adapted itself well to the development of modern transport and street lighting thus bringing Paris from the Middle Ages into the modern era. The streets were deliberately made wide to prevent barricading in the event of future street fighting or revolutions, and to accommodate marching troops. These broad thoroughfares became fashionable promenades, and they still have elegance and vivacity despite the onslaught of commercial enterprises of every sort and heavy motor traffic.

The first two sections of the Grands Boulevards (actually one long avenue), the **Boulevard de la Madeleine* and the *Boulevard des Capucines,* are the most attractive, lined as they are with fine restaurants, hotels, cafés, and luxury shops. They feed directly into the very lively junction of the *Place de l'Opéra* (15), dominated by the great **Opéra** itself. The flamboyant structure, designed by Charles Garnier and built between 1862 and 1875, is a collage of architectural styles in the grand and heavily opulent manner of the Second Empire, with gilded sculptural decoration inside and out. In addition to performances of opera and dance, the Opéra also serves as a gala society ballroom and showplace, its grand staircase providing a wonderful background for display of ballgowns and evening dress. An underground lake discovered during construction inspired the story of *The Phantom of the Opera*. More recently, Marc Chagall painted the famous frescoes on the auditorium ceiling. A new opera house now under construction on the Place Bastille will provide additional performance space.

Head down from the front entrance onto the *Avenue de l'Opéra*. Branching off to the right is the *Rue de la Paix,* whose lustre as a luxury fashion street is now somewhat tarnished. It leads, however, to the exquisitely proportioned and arcaded **Place Vendôme** (16), designed by Jules Hardouin-Mansart in honor of the Sun King, Louis XIV. Completed in the last year of the 17th century, it is a time-honored setting for exclusive fashion and jewelry shops, art dealers, banks, and one of the most famous hotels in the

Place Vendôme

world, the *Ritz.* The statue of Louis XIV that once stood in the center was destroyed during the Revolution, and the replacement figure atop the column (itself a replacement of one knocked down by the Commune in 1871) shows Napoleon costumed as a Roman emperor.

The street crossing the river side of the Place Vendôme is the *Rue Saint-Honoré,* for centuries a shopper's paradise, filled with boutiques, galleries, jewelers, perfumers, and designers' studios. Here you will find internationally known haute couturiers such as St. Laurent, Cardin, Lanvin, Gucci, Hermès, Dior, as well as many antiques shops. Around the corner, on the *Rue Royale* in front of the Madeleine, is that restaurant of song and story, *Maxim's,* and a shop that sells Lalique glass.

Head back toward the bottom end of the Avenue de l'Opéra to *Place André Malraux,* with its attractive fountains, and the home of the prestigious *Comédie Fran-çaise,* where the classical tradition of French drama is maintained in performances of Molière, Corneille and Racine. Modern plays are also performed here. Almost adjacent is the ***Palais Royal** (17), built for Cardinal Richelieu in the early 17th century, and bequeathed by him to Louis XIII. The name refers to both the palace and the adjoining gardens with their apartments, galleries, and shops. The delightful complex was once the scene of political and artistic activity—and gambling, revelry, and debauchery as well. In our times it has been home to such celebrities as Colette and Jean Cocteau.

Continuing east on the Rue Saint-Honoré you'll find the ***Forum des Halles,** the former site of the great food market dating from the 12th century (the market has been moved to the suburb of Rungis). The alterations to this area have turned the square into a fashionable and lively shopping center, filled with boutiques, restaurants, shops, and garden areas. It is now also a setting for theatrical productions and cinemas, and there are many cafés and restaurants on the side streets. Whatever the nostalgia for the old Les Halles, the leveling of the market has opened up interesting views of, for one, the *Bourse* (Stock Exchange) in its outwardly serene guise of a classical temple, and for another, the soaring **church of Saint-Eustache,* built on a Gothic plan with Renaissance and Classical additions. It is known especially for its organ concerts, the organ here being one of the largest in Paris. It also has some remarkable stained-glass windows and associations with many notables in the country's history: Cardinal Richelieu, Madame de Pompadour, and Molière were baptized in it, and Louis XIV celebrated his first communion here.

Take the Rue Rambuteau east, past Forum des Halles, and you will reach the enormous cultural center, ****Centre Georges Pompidou,** known as *Beaubourg,* after the surrounding area, or simply *Centre Pompidou.* Its unconventional design at first shocked those who were accustomed to the grace of the city's past architecture, but the controversy has long since died down. Its naked structure, that of a building turned inside out, and its exterior escalator rising to the gallery levels, signaled a new age in public architecture. Inside there are art galleries, the **National Museum of Modern Art,* theaters for dance, drama, and film, a laboratory for contemporary music, a design center, a bookshop, and a restaurant. The views from the restaurant make this complex well worth seeking out. Entertainments of every sort take place in front, and the entire area between the center and the Forum des Halles is now very trendy and heavily thronged with visitors and residents alike. In the middle of this area is a popular square dominated by a beautiful Renaissance fountain—the *Fontaine des Innocents.*

WALK 6: *Les Quais–Pont Neuf–**Île de la Cité–***Nôtre-Dame

See color map.

(*Métro: Pont Neuf; Cité*)

Perhaps the most romantic walk in Paris is this one, which starts along the riverside quay and takes you to the Île de la Cité. On this ancient island in the Seine you can visit the 13th-century Saint-Chapelle, with its extraordinary stained-glass windows, and the beautiful cathedral of Nôtre-Dame.

The walk along the quais of the Seine on either side of the river across from the Île de la Cité are particularly engaging. On the Left Bank are the wooden stalls of the *bouquinistes* (second-hand booksellers), and on the Right Bank are vendors of birds and small pet animals. In good weather fishermen line the banks of this picturesque river, which is crossed by many bridges.

Quai du Louvre begins at the Louvre, where an iron footbridge spanning the Seine, the *Pont des Arts* (18), offers an outstanding view and leads to the gold-domed *Institut de France,* home of two important cultural institutions: the *Bibliothèque Mazarin,* a public library established by Cardinal Mazarin, whose tomb is here, and the *Académie Française,* founded by Richelieu. Membership in the Académie is limited to 40 individuals from many cultural disciplines, although it is mostly literary. Its official dictionary is dedicated to the guardianship of the French language. Académie members, nicknamed "The Immortals" (though many brilliant immortals never became members) did not allow a woman into their proud ranks until the election of Margaret Yourcenar in 1980.

Continue along the Quai de Conti to the *Pont Neuf,* which despite its name ("New Bridge") is the oldest—and longest—in Paris. Here you can cross to the **Île de la Cité,** the island that is the most ancient part of Paris. In the *Place Dauphine,* on your right, is an equestrian statue of Henri IV, popular ruler, liberal idealist, and irrepressible womanizer. Behind the Place Dauphine stands the massive complex of the **Palais de Justice** (19), an ancient palace that was for centuries the center of the city's government. The two most interesting parts of the complex are the *Conciergerie and the unique ***Sainte-Chapelle.** The Conciergerie, once the palace dungeon, has an entrance flanked by two round Medieval towers. It was a notorious prison, especially during the Revolution, when it held some of the city's most notable citizens. Despite its grim associations, the building also contains remarkably beautiful chambers, especially the Gothic *Salle des Gens d'Armes* (where the palace guards lived) and their connecting kitchens with enormous ovens.

The main gate of the Conciergerie leads directly to a mid-13th-century masterpiece, the incomparable *Sainte-Chapelle*, which you enter on the lower level. Climb the winding stair from what was the chapel of the palace staff to the upper chapel, intended for the king and his personal retinue. Here you enter a world that seems to be made entirely of stained glass. When light pours through the windows, the colors glow with unequalled splendor. The window tracery framing the glass is delicately beautiful. This is not abstract art, however; the windows tell the old familiar Biblical stories.

The gargoyles of Nôtre-Dame

It's a short walk past the *Préfecture de Police,* home of Interpol, to the Place du Parvis Nôtre-Dame, on which stands the Gothic cathedral of *****Nôtre-Dame** (20). It rests on ancient sacred foundations, and is so important historically that its western entrance is the starting point for calculating distances in France. Its 13th-century purity has been many times altered; the particularly lovely north *rose window,* however, is intact. Many portions of the cathedral were stripped of their decorations during the French Revolution. Some of them, along with pieces of the Roman temple from the cathedral site, may be seen at the *Musée de Cluny* (see Walk 7).

The three *portals* contain Medieval sculptures of exceptional quality, depicting scenes such as the Resurrection and the Weighing of Souls, and the Last Judgment; figures of Christ in Majesty, the Virgin, and Saint John are on the tympanum. There are also legendary and mythical figures, and natural elements such as flowers and fruit.

The cathedral is especially noted for its flying butresses on the marvelous **apse,* the Gothic Revival gargoyles (by the 19th-century architect Viollet-le-Duc), the very tall spire, and the largest organ in all of France. Perhaps the most satisfying view of Nôtre-Dame is from the opposite bank of the river.

Behind the cathedral the little *Pont Saint-Louis* crosses to the *Île Saint-Louis,* a charming villagelike community with elegant—and expensive—residences. There are small shops and cafés, delightful quays and views, and a peaceful ambience.

WALK 7: *Latin Quarter

See color map.

(Métro stations: Saint-Michel; Cardinal Lemoine)

This walk provides a good introduction to the Latin Quarter on the Rive Gauche (Left Bank), which is the students' quarter of Paris. Several fine old churches can be visited as well as the splendid Musée de Cluny, home of the Lady and the Unicorn tapestry and countless treasures of Medieval art. From the Sorbonne, the walk continues on to the Panthéon, where some of France's greatest men are buried.

The *Boulevard Saint-Michel* on the Left Bank is the heart of the students' quarter. It is known as the Latin Quarter because Latin was the language used at the Sorbonne, the city's major university, until 1798. If you enter the Latin Quarter from the Pont Saint-Michel, you will find, on your left, the *Rue de la Harpe,* lined with Middle Eastern pastry shops and small restaurants. That street leads to the Rue Saint-Séverin and the very fine late-Gothic **church of Saint-Séverin** (21), the university church, built between 1414 and 1520, and enlarged in 1670. Its double *ambulatory,* with an amazing Flamboyant Gothic column and its *stained-glass windows,* are of special interest. Organ and choral concerts are frequently given here.

From Saint-Séverin head down the Rue Saint-Jacques, which runs parallel to the Boulevard Saint-Michel. At the Boulevard Saint-Germain, turn right, and you'll find the ***Hôtel de Cluny** (22), which houses the *Musée de Cluny,* a magnificent collection of Medieval art. The ***Lady and the Uni-* *corn* tapestry of the early 16th century is an especially prized item. Constructed by the Burgundian abbots of Cluny as a city residence, the building is the oldest Gothic residential structure in Paris; its battlements and towers are merely decorative. Roman baths were excavated on its grounds, and the city's oldest Roman relic, the so-called *Boatman's Pillar* from the time of Tiberius (first century A.D.) is kept in what was once the frigidarium of the baths, the *Salle Romaine.*

Continue on the Rue Saint-Jacques and you will come to the ***Sorbonne** (23), founded as a theological college in the mid-13th century. It was rebuilt in the early 17th century, but the present barrackslike building dates from 1885–1900. The *chapel,* dating from 1635, is the only original part left and contains the tomb of Cardinal Richelieu, who paid for the rebuilding of both structures. Every December 4, the anniversary of his death is commemorated. The Sorbonne, with its long, distinguished, and turbulent history, became a part of the

University of Paris after the student riots of 1968.

Continue down Rue Saint-Jacques to the Rue Soufflot, turn left, and you will reach the ***Panthéon** (24), originally the church of Sainte-Geneviève. In 1791, it was converted into a temple to honor and serve as the burial site for the great men of France. It is an imposing building, with a great dome resting on columns atop a pedimented portico with enormously tall Corinthian columns. Its interior contains paintings, some by Puvis de Chavannes, and monuments.

Rousseau, Voltaire, Victor Hugo, and Émile Zola are among the notables interred in the crypt.

To the right of the Panthéon steps is a very attractive late-Gothic church with a triple pediment, ***Saint-Étienne-du-Mont** (25). A 16th-century marble ***rood screen,* and the curving marble stairs are its most notable features, but you might care to look at the *shrine of Sainte-Geneviève,* and the *tombs* of Racine and Pascal. The Rue de Clovis leads you the short distance to the métro station Cardinal Lemoine.

WALK 8: *Saint-Germain-des-Prés–*Luxembourg Gardens and Palace–*Montparnasse

See color map.

(Métro stations: Saint-Germain-des-Prés; Vavin)

Paris is a city of distinctive quarters, and Walk 8 takes you from the literary center of Paris—the café-filled area of Saint-Germain-des-Prés—to Montparnasse, the old Bohemian quarter. In between there is a stop at the beautiful Luxembourg Palace and Gardens.

The Boulevard Saint-Germain owes its fame to the presence and activities in the area of the Existentialists (followers of the philosophy of Jean-Paul Sartre), and the artists and intellectuals who made its cafés and jazz clubs their headquarters during the 1950s. Although many of the avant-garde now flock to the Forum des Halles/Centre Pompidou area (see Walk 5) on the Right Bank, and most of the jazz clubs have been replaced by discothèques, the Left Bank is still a literary center of Paris, full of publishing houses and bookshops, and close to the Académie Française.

Opposite the métro station Saint-Germain-des-Prés is the ***church of Saint-Germain-des-Prés** (26). Once a sixth-century Benedictine abbey, it is the oldest church in Paris, with considerable Romanesque remains. Destroyed by the Normans and rebuilt in the 11th century, it became a center for literary and religious studies, drawing many scholars. The building itself has undergone many changes and restorations over the centuries: The presbytery was built in the 18th century, and the deteriorating steeple was replaced in the 19th century.

Across from the church, on the same side of the boulevard, are two famous cafés, the *Deux-Magots* and the *Café de Flore.* In the 1950s, these were crowded with artists, writers, and philosophers; the celebrity of these former patrons continues to lure tourists, even though most of them have fled to other scenes or died. Nevertheless, the two cafés retain a literary ambience because of the nearby publishers and bookshops, and they are still pleasant places in which to sit (if you can find free seats) and watch the fascinating Parisian parade. Across the boulevard is the renowned *Brasserie Lipp,* with its hearty Alsatian food and unchanged, turn-of-the-century decor; it, too, is perpetually crowded, well attended by the celebrated and the influential and those not daunted by the current high prices.

Across the boulevard, opposite the church, go down Rue Bonaparte to the *Place Saint-Sulpice,* with its 19th-century *Fountain of the Four Bishops* and shady chestnut trees. The square is a reconstitution of the one dug up for the sake of an underground car park. The ***church of Saint-Sulpice** (27), a heavy Classical structure of the 17th and 18th centuries, is noted for its organ concerts. In its interior are a ceiling and two frescoes painted by Delacroix.

Take Rue de Sulpice (on the left of the church) to Rue de Touron, turn right, and you'll come to the idyllic and popular ***Palais du Luxembourg** (28) and gardens. The Palais du Luxembourg, built in Florentine style, was commissioned by Marie de Médicis, Henri IV's second wife, who lived there for a few years after 1625. After her exile and death, the palace had a checkered history: It was a monastery, a prison, a German military headquarters, and simply an abandoned palace. Now it houses the French Senate. In the 19th century, the interior was almost completely altered. The library contains imaginary portraits of Dante, Virgil, and Alexander the Great painted by Delacroix. (The Rubens paintings of Marie de Médicis are now in the Louvre.)

The **gardens* are particularly delightful and civilized, with statues of French writers and artists, a lively Baroque fountain, old trees, and exotic plants, with the *Orangerie* serving as a greenhouse. There is also a museum with changing exhibitions.

The broad Avenue de l'Observatoire, an extension of the gardens, contains an exuberant fountain representing the four quarters of the globe, and leads you along a chestnut-lined path to the Boulevard Montparnasse, marked by a **statue of Marshal Ney.* Turn right to the *Boulevard Raspail* (29); the junction, marked by Rodin's *statue of Balzac,* was once the heart of the Bohemian quarter. Its cafés and artistic life flourished in the 1930s, and the large cafés, *La Coupole* and *La Rotonde,* are now patronized by visitors and would-be artists. The associations with famous writers, artists, and personalities of the past, however, are still vivid in these streets and in the nearby Montparnasse cemetery, where so many of them are buried.

WALK 9: *Tour Saint-Jacques–*Place de la Bastille–**The Marais Quarter

See color map.

(*Métro stations: Châtelet; Bastille; Saint-Paul; Pont-Marie; Chemin-Vert; Rambuteau*)

Walk 9 covers a fascinating historical area north of the Île de la Cité. Starting with the 19th-century theaters at Place du Châtelet, and the 16th-century tower of Saint-Jacques church, the walk goes on to the Place de la Bastille, where the French Revolution was set into motion. From the Hôtel de Ville, the city hall, the walk leads you into the 17th-century urban landscape known as the Marais, full of wonderful restored hotels and museums.

To the north of the Île de la Cité, on the right bank of the Seine, lies the **Place du Châtelet,** an open square with two theaters—the large *Théâtre Musical de Paris,* where operettas, ballets, and operas are performed, and the *Théâtre de la Ville,* once Sarah Bernhardt's theater, which still preserves the dressing room of the great tragic actress, and where popular entertainments are now given. In a small park in the northeast corner stands the *Tour Saint-Jacques* (30), a notable Gothic remnant of a 16th-century church from which pilgrims used to set out on their long journey to Santiago de Compostela in Spain. The tower, which figured prominently in the work of the Surrealists, currently serves as a meteorological station.

Walk east along the Rue de Rivoli to the *Hôtel de Ville (31), which stands on the site of two earlier city halls—the first in 1357, the second in 1789. The latter became the headquarters of the Revolutionary Committee after the storming of the Bastille, and the large square became a public execution ground. Burned down by the Commune in 1871, it was replaced by the present Renaissance-style structure, whose interior is noted for its fin-de-siècle extravagance. When the office of mayor of the city of Paris was re-established in 1977, the Hôtel de

Ville became his headquarters. Visitors can view sessions of the city's 109 councils from a public gallery.

The historic **Marais District**, or simply "The Marais" (so-called because it was once a marsh) fully rewards exploration of its winding streets, beautiful houses, and its noble *Place des Vosges.*

You can walk along the Rue Antoine (the eastern extension of the Rue de Rivoli) to the *Place de la Bastille (35), which, in the 14th century, was a fortress that was part of the city fortifications. It became a prison under Richelieu. The Bastille was stormed several times, but it is the July 14, 1789 siege that is so enthusiastically celebrated in France as a victory over oppression. The Bastille itself was demolished within a year of that date, and a line of cobblestones on the west side of the square demarcates the former building. The *Colonne de Juillet* (July column) that now stands in the Place de la Bastille honors the dead of the 1830 revolution, and is crowned by a statue of the Spirit of Liberty. The new Paris Opéra is being constructed on this site; when completed, its concert halls will triple the capacity of the current Opéra, and there will be a new media center as well.

**Marais District

You can start on the east side of the Hôtel de Ville, walking along Rue François Miron to the early 17th-century **church of Saint-Gervais-Saint-Protais,** with its impressive triple-order façade, its Flamboyant Gothic nave, and its many art treasures. The historic quarter itself, covering some 300 protected acres, is rapidly being restored to its original 17th-century architectural distinction and residential desirability.

From Saint-Gervais, continue on Rue François Miron past several fine buildings to Number 68, the *Hôtel de Beauvais,* no longer intact, but with an interesting courtyard, circular entry hall, and elegant staircase. It was here that Mozart gave his first Paris concert at the age of seven, and where Queen Christina of Sweden lived for a time. At the intersection of Rue de Jouy you have a choice of continuing along the Rue de Rivoli or turning south. If you choose the second option you will come into Rue des Nonains d'Hyères and the *Hôtel d'Aumont,* an austere mid-17th-century mansion, complete with a formal garden, now a government building. Turn left here to Rue du Figuier and the beautifully restored **Hôtel de Sens,** an oddity in Paris as it was once a Gothic residence, like the Cluny Museum. Now housing the Forney Library, it was once a stagecoach terminal. You may wish to walk upriver along the Quai des Celestins to see some of the remnants of the 12th-century Bastille ramparts on the Rue des Jardins-Saint-Paul, and the house where Rabelais died. The mansion at Number 3 at the end of the quay is the seat of the splendid 17th-century *Library of the Arsenal,* with its rich and historically colorful holdings, its collection of dramatic works, illuminated manuscripts, and its fascinating decor, including rooms unchanged since the time of Louis XIII.

If you turn off any street along the quay you will find yourself in places of interest. For example, head north on Rue Saint-Paul, turn left (west) on Rue Charlemagne, make a right turn (north) past the *Lycée Charlemagne* to the Rue Saint-Antoine. On the other side of the Rue de Rivoli on the left is the old Jewish quarter, a picturesque area of synagogues, shops, and restaurants, many with signs in Hebrew. The traditionally Eastern European atmosphere has now given way to a more exotic ambience dominated by Algerian Jews. The area around Rue des Ecouffes is a particularly lively shopping section.

If you then head east on Rue Saint-Antoine, you'll come to the elaborately decorated 17th-century Jesuit *church of Saint-Paul-Saint-Louis.* On the north side of Rue Saint-Antoine, at number 62, is **Hôtel Bethune-Sully,** a restored mansion where information about guided tours of historical monuments, and good books on the subject, may be obtained. Turn left from here onto the Rue de Birague, which will take you to the ***Place des Vosges** (34), a distinguished square of mansions with steep roofs and arcaded fronts. In the center of what was once a jousting field is an equestrian statue of Louis XIII, a gift to him by Cardinal Richelieu. Some of the mansions here are magnificent, and have housed many illustrious and influential Parisians. The first floor of *Victor Hugo's house* at Number 6 is now a museum, with many of his strange watercolors, drawings, and eccentrically designed pieces of furniture.

On the north side of Place des Vosges, turn left (west) on the Rue des Francs-Bourgeois, so named for the peasants who, as feudal vassals, were exempt from city taxes. On the corner of Rue Sévigné is the ***Hôtel Carnavelet** (33), once the house of Madame de Sévigné, whose letters give such a vivid portrait of 17th-century life. Some of her furnishings and possessions are still on view in this enjoyable municipal museum, with its graphic reconstructions of a vanished way of life full of the civilized amenities the revolutionaries sought to sweep away as symbols of decadence.

Just across the street, at the corner of Rue Pavée, is the *Hôtel de Lamoignan* (16th–17th centuries), now the *Bibliothèque de la Ville de Paris,* which has a store of historical information complementary to the contents of the Carnavalet Museum. The writer Alphonse Daudet came to live here after his marriage in 1867.

Walking north on the Rue de Sévigné, a charming street in itself, then west on Rue Parc Royal, you'll pass many restored mansions. The *Hôtel Libéral-Bruant* on Rue de la Perle contains an engaging and unusual collection of historical locks, door handles, keys, and the like in its *Musée Bricard* (the name of the first collector), usually referred to as the more descriptive *Musée de la Serrure* (Museum of the Lock).

The *Hôtel Salé* at nearby 5 *Rue de Thorigny* has been restored to its 17th-century beauty, and houses the new ****Picasso Museum,** with a generous display of his work as well as many pieces by famous contemporaries from his personal collection. From the Picasso Museum walk south on the Rue Vieille-du-Temple; at Number 87 is the 18th-century *Hôtel de Rohan,* with fine Rococo interiors and an impressive grand salon. This mansion is one of a pair with the adjacent *Hôtel de Soubise,* which, like its twin, contains the **National Archives** (32) whose holdings include important documents such as the Edict of Nantes and its Revocation, the wills of Louis XIV and Napoleon, the Declaration of the Rights of Man, and letters of Joan of Arc and Voltaire. The sumptuous Rococo interior decoration of the private apartments, which you can visit, conveys an idea of the social occasions that must have been celebrated here when the building was the private mansion of the Prince and Princess de Soubise. Around the corner in the exquisite 17th-century *Hôtel Guenegaud,* at 60 Rue des Archives is the *Musée de la Chasse et de la Nature,* a rather specialized hunting museum.

WALK 10: **Montmartre

See color map.

(Métro stations: Pigalle; Blanche)

Montmartre, the old Bohemian artist quarter, remains one of the most picturesque sections of Paris. Besides its narrow streets and steep stairs climbing the hillside, the landmark basilica of Sacré-Coeur, and the raucous areas of Place Pigalle are covered on this walk.

Montmartre means martyrs' hill, and probably refers to the legend of the beheading in A.D. 272 of Saint-Denis and his companions. Located in the northern part of the city, the celebrated Montmartre quarter climbs a hill, *La Butte,* which is dominated by the enormous white ***basilica of Sacré-Coeur** (38), built between 1876 and 1914 in a bastard Roman-esque-Byzantine style. What this landmark of Paris lacks in architectural distinction it makes up for in the view from its terraces and domes. The simplicity of the *church of Saint-Pierre,* just beside Sacré-Coeur, contrasts starkly with the basilica; the third-oldest church in Paris, it is a former abbey, incorporating some ancient stones and arches.

Sacré-Coeur

Montmartre is best known for having been a center for artists and writers who were able to live and work there in inexpensive, sympathetic, and picturesque surroundings. The streets of Montmartre are narrow and the stairs are steep, but it is possible to avoid the climb by taking the funicular from the Place Saint-Pierre below Sacré-Coeur. ***Place   Pigalle** (36) has become a rather sordid tourist trap, filled with restaurants, cafés, cinemas, and bad art, but the streets around it are still worth exploring. The *Rue des Martyrs, Boulevard de Clichy,* and *Rue des Abbesses* are especially picturesque, and still hold some of the piquant charm and originality that once characterized the entire area. Another photogenic corner of old Montmartre is the **crossroads* (37) where Rue Norvins, Rue Saint-Rustique, and Rue des Saules meet. The central square of Montmartre, **Place du Tertre,* is always teeming with tourists, with

artists hawking their work, with caricaturists sketching on the spot, with restaurants and café tables, and with a general air of fizzy excitement that seems about as authentic as a musical comedy. Yet, serious artistic pursuits are still followed here, and a good place to renew one's sense of genuine artistic tradition is the **Musée de Montmartre,** 17 Rue St.-Vincent, where many artists of the past once lived; to the right of the museum's terraced garden is the last surviving vineyard within the boundaries of Paris, where the grapes are harvested in a festive atmosphere on October 1 of every year. At the intersection of Rue St.-Vincent and Rue des Saules stands the old Bohemian cabaret **Lapin Agile.* Take Rue St.-Vincent to Rue Girardon and turn right. The *Moulin de la Galette,* one of the two old windmills of the area, stands in the Rue Cailaincourt. Just below it lies the **Montmartre Cemetery* (39), where such French notables as the writer Stendhal and the composers Berlioz and Offenbach are buried. The cemetery is a poignant reminder of the quality of the artists—in every field—who once made Montmartre radiant with their genius and vitality.

THE ENVIRONS OF PARIS

****Fontainebleau**

By train: regular service from the Gare de Lyon to Fontainebleau station, with connecting bus service to the palace. *By car:* 60 km. (37 miles) from Paris via A6, the Autoroute du Sud.

Fontainebleau palace, a royal residence from the 12th century onwards, has a rich history and an intriguing charm. Most of the French sovereigns lived here for a time. The inimitable François I (1494–1547) is primarily responsible for the great **château,** with its royal apartments and splendid formal gardens. In 1528 he had most of the Medieval structure demolished, and erected a new château, which was built according to the latest Renaissance principles from Italy. Look for François I's symbol—the fire-breathing salamander: It's carved in stone and wood throughout the building. The palace was added to by Henri II, Catherine de Médicis, and Henri IV, which accounts for its accumulation of buildings from different periods built around five courtyards.

If you have sufficient time, approach the palace through the *formal gardens* designed by Le

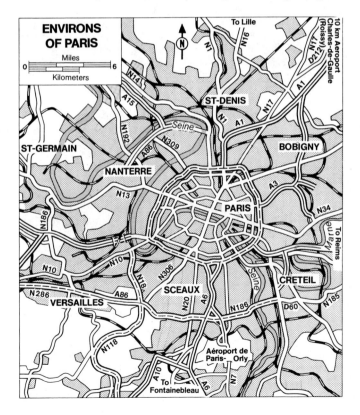

Nôtre in 1664. Here you'll see all the elements of 17th-century garden design: parterres, curious statues, and a carp pond. The fountain from which the palace derives its name—*fontaine belle eau* (place of beautiful water)—lies to the southwest of the pond. On the north side of the palace is the lovely *Garden of Diana*. From here you can pass into the *Cour du Cheval Blanc*, also known as the *Cour des Adieux* (Courtyard of Farewells) because it was here that Napoleon took final leave of his guard. The courtyard has an unusual double horseshoe staircase which leads to the public entrance of the palace. Before entering, you may wish to look at the *Fountain Courtyard*, located to the right of the stairway; the famous *gilded door* of the palace may be seen through another archway.

Inside there are rooms of particular period interest, the most notable being the *François I Gallery*, which was decorated by Italian artists and craftsmen between 1534 and 1537. The enormous *ballroom* was added during the reign of Henry II, while the *apartments of the King and Queen* reveal the heavy, grandiose taste of King Louis-Philippe. The series of *Napoleonic rooms* includes the Emperor's Throne Room, bedroom, and council chamber; a bee—Napoleon's symbol for industry and discipline—figures prominently in the ornate decoration.

Exploring the vast **forest of Fontainebleau*, which surrounds the palace and town of Fontainebleau, could easily take a day. The forest, with its time-worn boulders and rock formations, is crisscrossed with drives originally laid out by Henri IV to make hunting easier. Today, this *Route Ronde* (circle route) crosses the loveliest parts of the forest. In its northeastern section is the village of *Barbizon*, where the intimate landscape painters of the Barbizon school—Corot, Millet, Daubigny, and others—established themselves.

The town of *Fontainebleau*—with its leafy avenues and large houses—has a quiet, prosperous charm of its own.

**Saint-Denis

By métro: Saint-Denis Basilique. *By train:* all lines from the Gare du Nord, except Crépy-en-Valois. *By bus:* Nos. 153, 155, 156, 170, 177. *By car:* Routes A1 or N 14 north from Paris.

The major sight and the main reason to come to this industrial suburb 11 km. (7 miles) north of Paris is the **Basilique de Saint-Denis**, the burial place of French kings from Clovis I, who died in A.D. 511 to Louis XVIII, who died in 1824. A Benedictine abbey was founded in the seventh century on the grave and chapel of Saint-Denis. The saint was said to have walked, head in hand, to this site after being decapitated in Montmartre. Abbot Suger, a friend of Louis VII, decided to replace the abbey church with a new basilica. Begun in 1137 and substantially completed by the end of the 13th century, Saint-Denis was the first monumental structure in France to use the Gothic pointed arch and rose window, and it thus prefigures the flowering of Gothic art and architecture in the ensuing centuries. The basilica became a royal mausoleum under Louis IX (Saint-Louis), who erected the first *royal tombs* in the choir, having symbolic effigies created for his ancestors back to the seventh century. Dating from the death of Philippe the Bold in 1285, however, tomb effigies were modeled on real portraits. Joan of Arc dedicated her armor in Saint-Denis. During the French Revolution, the 800 royal bodies were unceremoniously pitched into a communal grave under the north transept; the tombs, which had been removed for safety, were saved from destruction. Attempts at restoration of the much-damaged basilica were largely incompetent and insensitive until Viollet-le-Duc took over the work in the mid-19th century.

A short walk will take you from the basilica to the *Musée d'Art et d'Histoire,* which helps to fill out the historical picture of Saint-Denis.

*Malmaison and **Saint-Germain-en-Laye

These two châteaux, both to the west of Paris, can easily be combined in a day trip.

Malmaison: *By métro:* Rueil-Malmaison. *By train:* RER (Réseau Express Régional) to Rueil-Malmaison. *By car:* N 13 west from Paris via La Défense.

**Château Malmaison,* 15 km. (10 miles) west of Paris, was built in the early 17th century and became the home of Napoleon's wife, Josephine (who had been the widow Beauharnais) after their marriage. She was happy here as the mistress of a literary salon, and after her divorce from Napoleon she retired here and cultivated her garden. The château later went through several royal hands, and the Empress's possessions were dispersed. It was ultimately bought and refurbished by a private citizen, who then presented it to the state. As a museum, it has since made further authentic and historically important acquisitions. Josephine's tomb is in the nearby church of Rueil. Another museum very close to Malmaison, the *Musée du Château de Bois-Preau,* is in a building Josephine bought, and which contains portraits and memorabilia of the time and of persons connected with her.

Saint-Germain-en-Laye: *By métro:* St. Germain-en-Laye. *By train:* RER to St. Germain-en-Laye. *By car:* N 13 west from Paris via La Défense.

**Saint-Germain-en-Laye* is an elegant suburb 21 km. (12 miles) west of Paris, with very attractive streets, interesting shops, and a château located in the forest, high above the Seine. The château was rebuilt by François I in the 16th century. Only the 12th-century keep remains intact. A number of French kings were born here— Henri II, Charles II, Louis XIV— and Henri XIII died here. Before Versailles was finished, it was an important royal seat. The château contains the *Musée des Antiquités Nationales.* The Gothic *chapel, where royal baptisms were celebrated, is of great interest despite some unwise alterations. It was the work of Pierre de Montreuil, the architect of Sainte-Chapelle. There is a view down the Seine to Paris from the beautiful *terrace.*

***Versailles

By train: from Gare des Invalides, Gare Montparnasse. *By car:* N 10 or Autoroute A 13 to N 321, where you turn south.

Versailles is 21 km. (12 miles) from Paris; it is one of the major tourist attractions of France for its palace and gardens. It is one of the largest and most splendid palaces ever built, and some may consider it to be one of the most pretentious monuments that a man ever erected for his own glorification. Louis XIV drained the treasury to accommodate his fantasy, and the statistics are fantastic—more than 30,000 workmen were used to build the palace, which had room for 2,500 horses and 2,000 carriages; thousands of servants and courtiers were, of course, required

for its daily operation. The façade of the palace has no less than 375 windows.

It is as brilliantly impressive, both in the public salons and the private apartments, as one would expect. Le Vau and then Jules Hardouin-Mansart were the architects (starting in 1661, work continued for over half a century), while Le Brun was responsible for the interior decoration. The stables are to the left and right of the vast *Place d'Armes* in front of the palace. From here you enter the enormous *courtyard,* with its equestrian statue of Louis XIV. The entrance is to the right of the courtyard. From the *chapel,* a sumptuous creation in gold and white, you can pass into the *state apartments.* Everyone wants to see the great *Galerie des Glaces* (Hall of Mirrors) and the *Chambre du Roi* (King's bedchamber) at dead center of the palace, where Louis XIV's ceremonial bed was the setting for the ritual called the Lever et Coucher du Roi (the Rising and Retiring of the King); this was an occasion for rivalry among the nobles, all of whom sought the privilege of attending to the monarch in these intimate moments. On September 1, 1715, the Sun King died on this bed. At the opposite end of the Hall of Mirrors are the *Queen's apartments,* including *Marie Antoinette's bedroom,* from which she fled before the enraged mob. You can also see the huge painted *Hall of Battles* as part of a guided tour, and the Royal Opera.

The gardens are vast and formal, the work of the landscape architect Le Nôtre who designed the Tuileries in Paris, and you reach them by marble stairs from the broad terrace. The major showpieces are the *Bassin de Neptune,* the *Bassin de Latone,* and the *Grand Canal,* all of which mirror the sky.

Two pleasure palaces lie in the northwest corner of the park—the *Grand Trianon,* built of rose and white marble for Madame de Maintenon, and the *Petit Trianon,* built by Louis XV for Madame de Pompadour, who died before its completion (she was replaced as the King's mistress by Madame du Barry). Marie Antoinette adored it, and Napoleon's sister, Pauline Borghese, lived in it for a time.

For visitors who find the self-conscious grandeur of the palace daunting, there is an engaging contrast in Marie Antoinette's miniature farm *l'Hameau.* It is strangely appealing in its toylike architecture, scale, working equipment, and setting. Here the Queen tried her hand at butter churning, and other rustic conceits, but of course, servants worked the little farm.

You can return to Paris via the Avenue de Paris, with a stop at the *Sèvres* porcelain factory and the *National Museum of Ceramics* or on Route N 186 to *Sceaux,* where there is a castle park designed by Le Nôtre in 1677. The Château d'Ecouen houses the *Musée de l'Île-de-France* with artistic and historical exhibitions and a "Grand Siècle" park, with pavilions dating from the 17th and 18th centuries. It is about 11 km. (7 miles) from Sceaux to Paris.

Marseille

Marseille, with a population of about 900,000, is the oldest city in France, and is situated on a series of limestone hills overlooking a broad bay in the Gulf of Lyon. Crowning the hills is the Neo-Byzantine church of Nôtre-Dame-de-la-Garde, the first landmark to come into view when approaching the city by sea.

Marseille is a gritty, noisy, industrial town, but with an unmistakably Mediterranean flavor. It has a history of political independence and the Marseillais are an earthy, hard working people, traditionally known for playing a unique form of bowling called *petanque* and for having created a glorious saffron fish stew, bouillabaisse. At the *Vieux Port* (old port), visitors can still watch fishermen sing the virtues of their daily catch.

Today Marseille is a major force in the economic life of France. The second largest city and the largest commercial seaport in the country, Marseille conducts a lucrative trade with North Africa and Asia. The Marseille-Rhône canal connects the thriving port with the interior of France.

History

Phoenician merchants settled in Marseille as early as the eighth century B.C. Around 600 B.C. Greeks from Phocaea founded a city on the site, naming it Massalia. Commanding the natural trade route on the Rhône, the city prospered, establishing commerce throughout the European continent, and as far as the west coast of Africa. Marseille first allied itself with Rome, becoming one of the principal rivals of Carthage. Its university was praised as a seat of learning by Cicero and Tacitus, and eventually became the last center of Greek learning in the West. Later, however, it struck an alliance with Julius Caesar's political adversary Pompey, and upon Pompey's defeat, Caesar besieged the city and partially demolished its fortifications. In the second century A.D. Marseille fell to the Visigoths. Later it was overrun by the Franks and it was eventually ruled by the Burgundian kingdom of Arelat. In the Middle Ages the city prospered greatly as a starting point for the Crusades. By the beginning of the 13th century it had formed a republic around what is today the Vieux Port. The discovery of the Americas, and the consequent shifting of trade to the Atlantic coast ports of Bordeaux and La Rochelle, was a major economic setback for Marseille. During the 17th century the city prospered again, but was devastated by the plague of 1720, which killed half of the city's 80,000 inhabitants. Sixty years later the remaining population participated vigorously in the French Revolution. After the French conquests in North Africa and the opening of the Suez canal in

1869, Marseille became the "port of the empire." Its harbors were later extended to accommodate the huge ocean liners entering the Mediterranean. The city and harbor suffered extensive damage during World War II. Since the war Marseille has once again become a powerful center of industry and an increasingly modern city.

Attractions

See map below.

The vibrant heart of the city is the intersection of the famous boulevards (called "cours" in Provence), **La Canebière** (1) with the Cours Belsunce and the Cours Saint-Louis. A street of elegant shops and cafés, La Canebière forms the dividing line between the rich and the poor parts of Marseille. Follow La Canebière west to the center of the old port city, known as the ***Vieux Port** (2) which ends at the lively *Quai des Belges*. Recently renovated, the area has been transformed into a pedestrian zone filled with book-

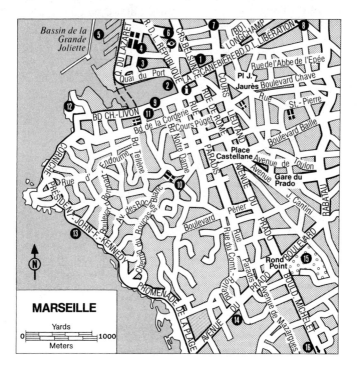

stores, boutiques, charming cafés, and restaurants. Marseille's only harbor until 1844, the Vieux Port forms a long rectangle, at the end of which is a narrow outlet to the sea guarded by two 17th-century forts—Saint-Nicolas on the south side and Saint-Jean on the north. The forts were used by the Vichy government (1940–1944) to imprison Allied airmen forced down over France.

From the northeast corner of the Vieux Port, the Quai du Port—its waterfront avenue—runs west leading to the **Hôtel de Ville** (3), a Baroque edifice built between 1663 and 1683. This was one of the few buildings spared when the Germans demolished much of the picturesque—and disreputable—old port quarter of the city in 1943. Also saved was the *church of Saint-Laurent,* located where the Quai du Port turns into the Quai de la Tourette at the Fort Saint-Jean. These two historic buildings are now incongruously situated in a bland high-rise apartment district which has replaced the more characteristic Marseille tenements.

At the junction of the Quai de la Tourette and its continuation, the Quai de la Joliette, is the **Cathédrale Sainte-Marie Majeur** (4), also known as the New Cathedral, built between 1852 and 1893 in a ponderous 19th-century style, with alternating layers of white and dark green limestone. Next to the New Cathedral stand the remains of the so-called *Old Cathedral,* a Provençal-Romanesque structure built in the 12th century. In 1481 the *Chapelle Saint-Lazare* was installed in the left transept of the church, and it contains a striking Romanesque altar and a white ceramic bas-relief by Luca della Robbia. From the west terrace you can look out over the New Port and the bustling port train station, **Gare Maritime de la Jolliette** (5), completed in 1953. From the north end of the Gare Maritime the Boulevard des Dames leads east to the **Arc de Triomphe** (6) of 1832, adorned with sculpture depicting scenes of France's struggles under the First Republic and the First Empire. Passing the **Gare Saint-Charles** (7), Marseille's principal railway station, you reach the Boulevard de la Libération, the continuation of La Canebière. By going 2 km. (1.2 miles) north and turning left on the Boulevard Philpon, you come to the *Palais Longchamp,* the north wing of which houses the **Musée des Beaux-Arts** (8). Be sure to see the museum's excellent *Daumier Room on the top floor, which has numerous portraits and lithographs by the famous caricaturist, Honoré Daumier, who was born in Marseille in 1808. On the ground floor there are rooms devoted to the works of the Marseillais sculptor Pierre Puget (1622–1694); the central hall displays work of Renaissance and Baroque masters and local Provençal painters. The south wing of the building contains a natural history museum and there is a zoological garden in the back.

Back in the Vieux Port, go

south on the Quai des Belges, around the port basin to a point almost at the end of the Quai de Rive Neuve (9), where you will find steps and a road south to the **Basilique Nôtre-Dame-de-la-Garde** (10), the church that dominates the city and the bay. (The ascent to the church must be made by car or on foot since the funicular no longer runs.) Its bell tower is crowned with a gilded statue of the Virgin Mary. The church, designed in a Neo-Byzantine style, was erected between 1853 and 1864, replacing a 13th-century pilgrim's chapel. The church's terrace offers a fabulous view of Marseille's port and docks, with Cap Croisette to the south and the Estaque Peninsula to the northwest.

If you continue on the Quai de Rive Neuve rather than ascending to the basilica, shortly before the Fort Saint-Nicolas (and the entrance to the traffic tunnel under the Old Port) you will come to the **basilica of Saint-Victor** (11), named after the third-century Roman officer who died a martyr in Marseille. The church, the oldest in the city, was built in the 11th century on the site of an earlier church constructed in the fifth century by Saint Cassian. The remains of the older church can be seen in the crypt and catacombs. The vaulting of the nave of the basilica displays both late-Romanesque and early-Gothic elements.

If you pass *Fort Saint-Nicolas,* you come to the **Parc du Pharo** (12), where you can get a beautiful view of the city and port. The *monument* here commemorates the "Heroes of the Sea." In the park there is a *château* that once belonged to the Empress Eugénie, and that now houses a medical and pharmaceutical center. France's outstanding Institute for Tropical Diseases occupies the adjacent building. Southeast of this small park begins the ***Promenade de Corniche** (13), also known as Corniche President J.F. Kennedy. The road follows the coast for 9 km. (5.6 miles) as far as *Cap Croisette,* and offers constantly changing vistas of the sea and islands. After approximately 5 km. (3 miles) the Promenade passes the *Place du Prado,* which has swimming facilities, cafés, and restaurants. Here the wide **Avenue du Prado** (14) leads away from the sea to the northeast, passing the *Parc Borély.* The *Musée d'Archéologie Borély* is located here in an 18th century château. The museum's Mediterranean collection includes some of the finest Egyptian antiquities in Europe, as well as Etruscan, Greek, and Roman finds. Archaeological pieces from Provence are on view in the *Musée Lapidaire.*

Following the Avenue du Prado, the **Parc Amable Chanot** (15), begins just on the other side of the Rond Point. Two interesting museums are located here: the *Musée du Vieux-Marseille,* with a fascinating folk art collection that reflects the city's 2,500 year history, and the *Musée de la Marine et de la France d'Outre Mer,* devoted to France's maritime and colonial history. From the Rond Point it is another 1.5 km. (just over a mile) to **La Cité Radieuse** (16), a 17-story residential complex built on concrete piles by the great French architect Le Corbusier (1887–1965). The buildings, erected between 1947 and 1952, created an international sensation when they opened, and the complex is now considered a landmark in the history of modern French architecture.

Museums

Many of the museums of Marseille are in the process of being modernized. Aside from those already mentioned, there are several others that are well worth a visit:

The **Musée des Docks Romains** (at 28, Place Vivaux) stands on the site of the Greek and Roman harbor docks and houses the ruins of the docks and a warehouse dating from Roman times. They were discovered in the 1940s after the Germans demolished this part of the city. Also on display are objects found in the area of the Roman city and in ancient shipwrecks discovered along the coast.

Located in the Palais de Bourse, on La Canebière, the **Musée de la Marine** specializes in the history of the port of Marseille from the 17th century to the present. Numerous ship models depict the development of sailing vessels in this important Mediterranean port. Close by, in the Rue Barbuss, north of the museum, remains of

the walls and docks of ancient Massalia have been uncovered.

Musée Grobet-Labadié, at 140 Boulevard Longchamp, was founded by the painter and musician Louis Grobet, who was an avid collector of paintings, weapons, musical instruments, tapestries, sculpture, furniture, and ceramics.

Environs

In addition to a tour of the Vieux Port, you should not miss the motorboat excursion (crossing time 30 minutes) to the tiny island fortress of ***Château d'If,** which owes its reputation to the popular French novelist Alexandre Dumas. The fort was the setting of his 12-volume novel, *The Count of Monte Cristo*. Built by François I in 1524 to protect Marseille from the Spaniards, it was later converted to a prison dreaded for its dungeons. Some of the walls still display carvings made by the Huguenot (Protestant) prisoners incarcerated here before being sent to Toulon to become galley slaves, and there is a memorial to the 3,500 Huguenots condemned to the galleys between 1545 and 1750.

Nearby are the islands of *Raton-neau* and *Pomegues*, which are linked by a jetty that protects the *Port du Frioul*, the quarantine station that sequestered returning sailors.

Other places to visit on the dramatic coastline near Marseille are **Les Calanques,** the fjordlike coves in the rocky shore of the Massif de Puget southeast of Marseille. The best way to see them is to make a half-day excursion by boat. *Cap Morgiou,* which juts out into the Mediterranean between the Calanque de Sormiou and the Calanque de Morgiou, is especially impressive. Other calanques (Port-Minou, Port-Pin, En-Vau) lie southwest of Cassis (see Travel Route 19).

To the west of the city is **L'Estaque,** the mountain often painted by Cézanne. A tunnel cut into the peninsula for 6.5 km. (4 miles) allows ships access to the Rhône River. A 27-km. (16-mile) drive on the southern shore of the **Estaque Peninsula** first passes extensive port facilities, then climbs 200 meters (650 feet) to *Le Rove* and follows the L'Estaque Ridge before descending through a wild valley to the seaside towns of *Rouet-Plage* and *Carry-le-Rouet.* If you put off your return until the late afternoon you may get a splendid view of Marseille bathed in the golden light of the setting sun.

*Lyon

A city of about 420,000 people, with perhaps a million more in the surrounding suburban area, Lyon is the center of the French textile industry. The heart of the city is located on a narrow peninsula between two mighty rivers, the Rhône to the east and the Saône to the west. In the 15th century, the Lyonnais learned from the Italians how to manufacture silk products, and the city was soon famous throughout Europe for its silk. Joseph Marie Jacquard's 1802 invention of the mechanical loom moved production from the cottage to the factory, and made Lyon a busy textile center. Today, synthetic fibers are the mainstay of the Lyon textile industry, and the town presents its goods every spring at the Lyon sample fair.

This city is also second only to Paris for its gastronomic excellence. There is a seemingly endless choice of fine restaurants, bistros, and cafés, offering everything from *haute cuisine* to simple but excellent local specialties.

History

Lyon has been an important city since ancient times, and celebrated its 2,000th anniversary in 1958. Known to the Romans as Lugdunum, it was the capital of the province of Gallia Lugdunensis, which included most of the area between the Seine, the Loire, and the present-day eastern border of France. A favorite city of several Roman emperors—including Nero, Trajan, and Hadrian—the city boasted many temples, theaters, and baths. In the second century, the city became the center of Christianity in Gaul. By virtue of the Treaty of Verdun in 843 (which divided the Carolingian Empire among the three sons of Louis I), Lyon became part of Burgundy, and was thus joined for a time to the Holy Roman Empire. Conquered in 1312 by Philippe le Bel (Philip the Fair), Lyon came fully into French possession in 1552 and developed into a mighty industrial and commercial city. The first stock exchange in France was established here in 1506. During the French Revolution, Lyon refused to follow the leaders of the Terror, who sent an army against it. After a two-month-long siege, the city was taken; 6,000 inhabitants were slaughtered, and part of the city was reduced to rubble. Only the death of Robespierre saved Lyon from further destruction. Napoleon rebuilt Lyon in the early years of the 19th century. In World War I, the city was again nearly destroyed; it has since been rebuilt.

Attractions

See map on page 66.

The main center of the city is the wide **Place Bellecour** (1), laid out in 1617 and ornamented with an equestrian statue of Louis XIV; at the southeast corner of the plaza, next to the main post office, stands a *bell tower* built in 1665. Running north from the northwest corner of the square are the two main commercial streets, the **Rue de la République** (a pedestrian street) and the **Rue du Président-Herriot** (2), named for the longtime mayor of the city and two-time premier of the Third Republic. If you continue north on this street for about 750 meters (half a mile) you will come to the **Église Saint-Nizier** (3) on the left. Most of this late-Gothic church dates from the 15th century; it has a 16th-century Renaissance portal that stands on the site of the city's first Christian house of worship. An oratory was built here by Saint Pothin in the second century, and a crypt beneath the choir dates from the sixth century. A little farther ahead the street ends in the **Place des Terreaux,** which gets its name from the loads of earth used to fill in the Roman canal that once connected the Rhône and the Saône. On this site in 1642, the Marquis de Cinq-Mars and François de Thou were beheaded for conspiring against Cardinal Richelieu, the uncompromising chief minister under Louis XIII. The figures on the fountain here symbolize the rivers

hurrying to the sea. At this point you are at the slope known as the *Croix Rousse,* on which the weavers' quarter, *Les Traboules,* is located. The name comes from the passages (*traboules*) that lead from street to street through houses and courtyards. These passages acted as avenues of escape during a 19th-century weavers' uprising—and served their purpose again for the Resistance movement during World War II. Before the Industrial Revolution as many as 60,000 handweavers lived and worked on Croix Rousse. Today, in the few workshops that remain, you can watch weavers creating fabrics from traditional patterns.

On the south side of the Place des Terreaux stands the **Musée des Beaux-Arts** (4) with a beautiful sculpture collection that includes antique work and pieces by Auguste Rodin, Aristide Maillol, and Antoine Bourdelle. The museum also houses a rich collection of late 19th- and early 20th-century paintings by such artists as Van Gogh, Renoir, Manet, Corot, and Gauguin. On the east side of the square stands the ***Hôtel de Ville** (5), one of the handsomest city halls in France. The structure, dating from the mid-17th century, encompasses two courtyards and is surmounted by a belfry (originally a watchtower) with a lovely set of chimes. A gable in the main façade is decorated with a representation of King Henri IV on horseback. Heading south on the Rue de la République,

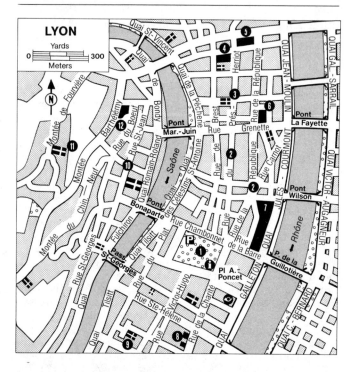

you soon come to the imposing **Palais du Commerce et de la Bourse** (Chamber of Commerce and Stock Exchange) (6). Built between 1855 and 1860, the massive edifice reflects the importance of trade to Lyon. French President Marie François Sadi Carnot was assassinated in front of its portal in 1894. To the south of the stock exchange stands the **church of Saint-Bonaventure,** which dates from the late-14th and early-15th centuries. It is named for the Tuscan Bonaventura, who brought about the renewal of the Franciscan

Order; born in 1221, he died in Lyon in 1274. Mostly Gothic, the church boasts 17th-century Aubusson tapestries. From here it is just a few steps to the quais of the Rhône, which is crossed by a dozen bridges. Upstream is the magnificent *Parc de la Tête d'Or,* with its attractive lake, zoo, botanical gardens, and a pavilion where fairs are held. Turning south along the river you will soon encounter the magnificent **Hôtel-Dieu** (7), a historic hospital. Begun in 1741, the **façade*—designed by Soufflot, builder of the Pantheon in Paris—took 100 years to construct. A *court of honor* dating from the 17th century and a charming *chapel* built in 1645 are also notable features.

From the southwest corner of the Hôtel-Dieu you can see the Place Bellecour, lined with cafés and restaurants. From the southeast corner, the Rue de la Charité leads south to two neighboring museums (8). The **Musée des Arts Décoratifs** houses Lyonnais furniture, mostly from the 18th century, as well as tapestries from the Lyon Gobelin factory, and Aubusson and Beauvais tapestries. There is also an important collection of Lyon china and Italian faïence, and an unusual collection of wallpaper. Next door is the unique ****Musée Historique des Tissus,** which has an incomparable collection of textiles of all kinds, from silks, velvets, and brocades to embroideries and tapestries. There are also examples of ancient textiles from Greece, Rome, and more exotic places of the ancient world.

Farther along the Rue de la Charité you come to the *Place Ampère,* with its monument to the great physicist André Marie Ampère (1775–1836), a Lyon native. Walk west on the Rue des Remp d'Ainay to the ***church of Saint-Martin-d'Ainay** (9). This Romanesque structure, the oldest church in Lyon, was erected on the site of a Roman temple and consecrated in 1107. The six plain columns of the nave may be of Roman origin; the four columns at the crossing are probably from the altar of Roma and Augustus, which once stood on the hill of Croix-Rousse. From the church, follow the Quai Tilsitt upstream along the Saône, cross the river by way of the *Pont Bonaparte* and walk north.

The **Cathédrale Saint-Jean** (10) stands behind a cluster of houses. The church was built over the course of 400 years, beginning in the 12th century. The transept with its astronomical clock from 1598 is Romanesque; the apse is Burgundian Romanesque with a Gothic vault; the main nave, richly decorated with Medieval stained glass, is early-Gothic; and the façade, with a rose window dating from 1393, is late-Gothic. From the Pont Bonaparte you can see west beyond the flat-topped towers of Saint-Jean to the **Basilique Nôtre-Dame-de-Fourvière** (11). This church, which has been the destination of many pilgrims, is located above the city and is reached by funicular from the Cathédrale Saint-Jean. The building is richly gilded and decorated with paintings and mosaics. From the northeast tower, which also serves as an astronomical observatory, there is a lovely view over the city and its surroundings. Just to the north of the basilica rises the lofty *Tour Métallique,* a metal tower that was erected in 1893 and is now a television tower. To the south of the church are the remains of two *Roman theaters,* where outdoor performances now take place during the summer. Visit the nearby *Musée de la Civilisation*

Gallo-Romaine, which opened in 1975 and is devoted to the history of Lyon from prehistoric times to the coming of Christianity. The old city, known as *Vieux Lyon,* is located just west of the Cathedrale Saint-Jean, and has houses dating from the 15th through the 17th century. The *Quartier Saint-Jean* (12), whose center is the Rue Saint-Jean, is especially interesting. Museums in the quarter include the *Musée Historique de Lyon* and the *Musée de la Marionette,* which has exhibits on puppet theater.

Environs

Charbonnières-les-Bains, 10 km. (6 miles) to the west of Lyon on Route 7 is a lovely thermal spa with a casino, park, and race track. In March it is the scene of a popular motor rally.

Île-Barbe, 6 km. (3.7 miles) to the north, is an island in the Saône River. The belltower of the 12th-century abbey of Nôtre-Dame is located here.

Rochetaillée, about 12 km. (7.5 miles) to the north, is a restored château that now houses an automobile museum.

Pérouges, a village 36 km. (22 miles) in the direction of Geneva, west of Autoroute A 42, is a throwback to the 16th century, with many churches and well-preserved houses. You may want to sample the Medieval food and drink offered at the local restaurants. Not far from Pérouges is the industrial town of *Villefranche-sur-Saône,* known as the center of the Beaujolais wine area.

The **Plateau de Dombes,** called the "land of a thousand lakes," is 26 km. (16 miles) northeast of Lyon on Route 83. Those interested in natural history will be enchanted by the *Dombes Ornithological Reserve,* which boasts over 400 species of birds.

*Bordeaux

Bordeaux (population 650,000) is an important port city. It is some 100 km. (62 miles) from the sea, but is linked to it by the Garonne River and the long, narrow, funnel-shaped estuary of the Gironde. It is the regional stem, so to speak, holding together an encircling cluster of famous vineyard districts—Graves, Pomerol, Médoc, and Saint Émilion. Approximately five million bottles of its famous wines are shipped yearly from docks here to appreciative oenophiles throughout the world. The wine trade goes back some 2,000 years to when the Romans wisely noted the suitability of soil and climate and planted the first vines. Although it basically is not a tourist city, visitors will nonetheless find a great deal to appreciate in and along its grand boulevards and squares. A preponderance of Neoclassical buildings from the 18th century, which was a period of prosperity and town planning, gives parts of the old city an elegant and impressive air.

History

Bordeaux was founded by the Romans and under the name of Burdigala was the capital of the province of Aquitaine. In 412 it fell to the Visigoths; in 507 to the Franks. With the marriage of Henry Plantagenet (who became Henry II of England) and Eleanor of Aquitaine, the city came under English rule and remained so from 1152 to 1453. The Black Prince held his court here, and his son, eventually to become Richard II, was born in Bordeaux. At the end of the Hundred Years' War France won it back. King Charles VII, to retain French control, built two fortresses (Château du Hâ and Château Trompette), but the populace revolted against centralized authority many times over the next several centuries, and it was not until the 18th century that Bordeaux again prospered economically. Large sums were spent at this time to embellish the city. From 1870 to 1871 and again in 1914, the seat of French government was transferred from Paris to Bordeaux. Likewise, after the fall of France in 1940, the government moved here, but it was supplanted two weeks later by the Vichy government. Bombed by the Germans and the Allies, it was liberated on August 28, 1944.

The two big cultural events of the city both take place in May. The International Festival of Music and Dance schedules events in the cathedral, the public gardens, and famous châteaux, while the International Fair uses newer buildings in the Quartier du Lac.

Attractions

See map on page 71.

The heart of Bordeaux is the *Place de la Comédie*. Among the buildings facing it is the ****Grand-Théâtre** (1). A stunning Neoclassical building considered by many to be the most beautiful in the world and, justifiably, the pride of the city, it was built between 1773 and 1780 by the architect Victor Louis on the site of a Roman temple. Its main façade is fronted and flanked by a magnificent colonnade of 12 Corinthian columns; statues of 12 muses and goddesses line the balustrade. You can go into the lobby, but to see the dazzling interior you have to buy a ticket for a performance. The architect Charles Garnier was so impressed by the Grand-Théâtre that he borrowed details from it for the Paris Opéra. Not far to the north is one of Europe's largest squares, the **Place des Quinconces** (2). From the east terrace of the tree-lined square, laid out between 1818 and 1828 on the site of Charles VII's demolished Château Trompette, you have a lovely view over the wide, smooth-flowing Garonne and the port facilities. *Monument des Girondins,* erected in 1895, completed in 1902, dismantled in 1943, and reinstalled in 1982, is on the semicircular west end of the square; on the longer north and south sides are statues of two of the great sons of Bordeaux: the essayist Montaigne (1533–1592), who was mayor for five years, and the philosopher Montesquieu (1689–1755). A few blocks to the northwest is the **Jardin Public** (3), with a lake and botanical gardens laid out between 1818 and 1828 as a promenade and altered in 1858. A botanical library and the *Natural History Museum* are located in an 18th-century building on the grounds. Walk northwest to the nearby **Palais Gallien** (4), the remains of a Roman amphitheater dating from the third century A.D. Though the structure was neglected and severely damaged during the Revolution, one entrance, with a lofty, walled arch, has been preserved.

If you walk inland from the Garonne for a few blocks you come to the ***church of Saint-Seurin** (5), whose vestibule dates from the 11th century (unfortunately, it is hidden by a 19th-century fake Romanesque façade). Portions of the choir are from the 12th century, and the elaborate south portal with its sculptured figures dates from the 13th century. The two Romanesque bell towers were given upper stories in the 16th and 18th centuries. Marble sarcophagi in the crypt date from the sixth century. Walking southeast, farther into the old city, you reach the **Place Gambetta** (6), the liveliest square in Bordeaux, surrounded by houses in quintessential Louis XV style. During the Terror, a well-honed guillotine was kept busy in the center: 300 heads rolled in what is now the garden. From here, in the same south-

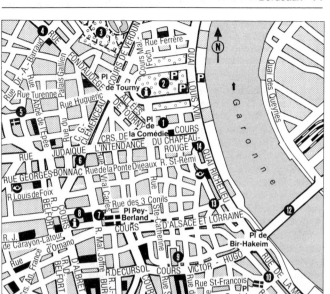

east direction, you can see the 81-meter- (266-foot-) tall, unusually slender spires of the city's principal church, the **Cathédrale Saint-André** (7). The main 12th-century west façade is fairly uninteresting; it is the *Porte Royale* on the north side, with its sculpted tympanum of the Last Supper and 13th-century statues, that is noteworthy. A freestanding 15th-century bell tower, the *Tour Pey-Berland,* rises next to the choir and is crowned with an unattractive gilt statue of the Virgin Mary, added in 1863. Within, the huge 15th-century choir presents a striking contrast to the aisleless 12th-century nave.

Across from the cathedral to the west is the *city hall,* formerly the archbishop's palace (1772–1781), and behind it is the colorful *Jardin de la Mairie* (city hall garden), flanked by two galleries. If you go south, you come to the *Musée d'Aquitaine,* reopened in 1986. The completed upper floor is devoted to local history and ethnography; the ground floor, when completed, will encompass aspects of Aquitaine from prehistory to 1715. To the north is the gallery housing the ***Musée des**

Beaux-Arts (8), with a surprisingly good collection of paintings. Here you will find works by Veronese, Titian, Perugino, Rubens, Brueghel, Van Dyke, Delacroix (whose *Lion Hunt* is a showpiece of the collection), Renoir, and Matisse. The museum also has an extensive collection of *paintings by Albert Marquet (1875–1947), who was born in Bordeaux. One block to the north is the ***Musée des Arts-Déco-ratifs,** which displays work of artists and artisans from Bordeaux and is beautifully furnished as it might have been two centuries ago.

Head farther southeast, and near the *Grand-Marché* you can't miss the immense ***Tor Grosse-Cloche** (Big Bell Gate) (9). It is 41 meters (135 feet) high and has a 15th-century belfry above one of the two gateways. Continue in the direction of the Garonne and you will come to the **Église Saint-Michel** (10), a triple-naved Gothic church from the 14th to 16th centuries (recently closed because of its unsafe condition). The magnificent pulpit dates from 1753 and the modern stained glass by Max Ingrand was installed after the original glass was shattered in 1940. In front of it is a free-standing bell tower, at 110 meters (330 feet) the highest structure in southern France, the ***Tour Saint-Michel,** whose remarkable and beautifully restored 12-sided spire was built from 1376 to 1492. Underneath the tower, but not for the faint-hearted, is the *Caveau des Momies,* the crypt of mummies, where a guide will shine his light to show you what you may not want to see and, if he's feeling playful, pull a corpse's beard or caress a dusty breast.

Go a little farther to the southeast to reach the Romanesque **Église Sainte-Croix** (11), once the church of the richest abbey in Bordeaux. Its remarkable façade, "restored" by Abadie, is framed by two flat-topped towers. Inside there is not much to see, save Romanesque capitals and a tiled floor in the north transept. The bank of the Garonne is just ahead, and from here you can see, across the river, the suburb of *La Bastide,* with its modern residential development, the *Cité de la Benauge.* Here also is the famous stone bridge ***Pont de Pierre** (12), with 17 arches, built between 1810 and 1821. North of the bridge, near the Quai de la Douane you encounter the ****Porte de Cailhau** (13), handsomest of the city's old gateways. The structure, dating from 1495, is 34 meters (112 feet) high, with four irregular, conical turret caps.

Go a little farther north along the bank of the Garonne, where you will find the loveliest square in the city, the ****Place de la Bourse** (14). Designed between 1733 and 1751 by Gabriel, it is framed by 18th-century buildings, including the *Customs House* and the *Stock Exchange,* which opened in 1749 and gave the square its name. The central building houses the *Musée de la

Marine, with ship models from the 17th to the 19th centuries, figureheads, old admiralty maps, engravings, and seascapes. Finally, you may wish to stop in at the *Centre National Jean-Moulin,* the city's World War II Resistance museum, located on Place Pey-Berland.

Environs

Most excursions from Bordeaux lead to seaside resorts or wineries with world-famous vintages. The *Maison du Vin,* just north of Place de la Comédie, is a marvelously helpful wine information center. Free literature and information about some of the 7,000 wine châteaux are available, and you can conveniently make arrangements (as well as appointments if they are necessary) for visits to various châteaux in the region.

While most wines are named after the general region in which they are cultivated, such as Champagne or Burgundy, the wines of the *Bordelais* region bear the name of the central city, Bordeaux. To become acquainted with the surrounding area, there are two trips to consider. The first goes out Route D 2 to the ***Haut-Médoc,** 50 km. (31 miles) to the north. This area, one of the most favored in France for wine growing because of its soil and temperate climate, has some 130,000 hectares (321,000 acres) planted in vines. The wine-growing region of the *Médoc* extends for 80 km. (50 miles) along the west bank of

the Gironde, reaching inland 10 to 20 km. (6 to 12 miles); Haut-Médoc is its southern portion, the part closest to Bordeaux. The first stop along the way, at just under 31 km. (19 miles), is *Margaux,* famous for its wineries that produce the "Roi du Médoc." Another 18 km. (11 miles) brings you to *Saint-Julien,* where "Château Beychevelle" is grown. Then comes *Pauillac,* with vineyards whose very names intoxicate wine connoisseurs: *Château Latour, Château Lafite-Rothschild,* with a palatial new *chai* (*cave* or cellar) designed by the Spanish architect Ricardo Bofil, and **Château Mouton-Rothschild,* usually open weekday mornings only and closed in August. Here there is a museum thematically dedicated to the glories of the grape and of the Rothschilds growing it. Finally, with the wide Gironde still in view, comes *Saint-Estèphe,* with its strong wines, where the Haut-Médoc territory ends. Smaller châteaux will post signs on the road if they sell their vintages to the public.

The second trip on Route N 89 takes you in just a little less than 40 km. (25 miles) through *Libourne,* where you pick up D 670, to ***Saint-Émilion,** a renowned wine town high in the hills and one of the loveliest small cities in France. A large portion of its 13th-century walls have been preserved. The restored *Église Collégiale* has an impressive late-13th-century Gothic cloister. A free-standing bell tower rises over the

Place des Créneaux. The major attraction is a remarkable underground church, the **Église Monolithe.* The Benedictine successors of Saint Émilion, who lived in the adjacent hermitage in the eighth century, began hacking this Romanesque chapel out of the rock in the ninth century. The irreplaceable stained-glass windows of Chartres cathedral were stored here during World War II. An underground passage originally connected to the church now leads to partially excavated catacombs of great antiquity; there are guided tours. The little *Musée Arché-ologique* is of no great interest, but you may want to sit at a table in the 14th-century *Cordeliers' cloister* and sample a bottle of sparkling wine.

From Saint-Émilion, the route goes 65 km. (40 miles) south through the wine-growing area of *Entre-Deux-Mers* to ***Cadillac,** with the imposing but long derelict château built by the dukes of Epernon between 1598 and 1620, now under restoration. The 35-km. (22-mile) return trip to Bordeaux follows the right bank of the Garonne.

**Strasbourg

Strasbourg (population approximately 260,000) is the ancient capital of the much disputed province of Alsace. It is a fascinating city; an Episcopal see, a university town, an international communications center, and the seat of the Council of Europe. Alsace is wholly French, but with historical roots in both Germany and France. The oldest Strasbourgeois were educated in German and speak that language as fluently as French. One of the main prizes of the three modern wars between France and Germany (1870, 1914, 1940), Strasbourg has been claimed by both sides not as conquered territory, but as an integral part of the country. It is not uncommon for a citizen of this city to have a grandfather who fought for Germany in 1914, and a father who fought for France in 1940.

Strasbourg is at the crossroads of western Europe. The center of the city is less than a day's drive from Austria, Switzerland, Belgium, Luxembourg, and the Netherlands, and only a few miles from the West German border. Once the focus of national enmities, Strasbourg has auspiciously become a symbol of European cooperation as the home of the Council of Europe, the political arm of the Common Market.

History

Almost surrounded by the Ill River, near the Rhine and the Vosges mountains, the site of Strasbourg was an obvious choice for human habitation from the earliest times. Originally a Celtic fishing village, it was located on the main route between Germany and Gaul and became a garrison town under the Romans in 15 B.C. The Romans called it Argentoratum. When it was conquered by the Franks in the fifth century, it took the name Strateburgum, meaning city at the crossroads. During the Merovingian dynasty the city became the seat of a bishop. Charlemagne's heirs ended their fraternal strife here in 842 with oaths of alliance, the "Strasbourg oaths." Charles II the Bald, King of West Franks, and Louis I, the German King of East Franks, took an oath called the *Serment de Strasbourg*, a text of which is the earliest document in old French.

Although Strasbourg was nominally a part of the Holy Roman Empire (which was aptly described as neither holy, nor Roman, nor an empire) until the 17th century, it had long been virtually self-governing. As early as the 13th century, the city's citizens destroyed the power of the ruling bishop and Strasbourg officially became a free city of the empire governed democratically by a guild of citizens. Several leaders of the Reformation settled here, including John Calvin from 1538 to 1592, and Martin Bucer from 1523 to 1549. The city's university was founded in 1566. Among Strasbourg's most famous residents were Johannes Gutenberg, who worked here between 1434 and 1444 to perfect the printing press, and the poet and dramatist Goethe, who was a student at the university from 1770 to 1771. Louis XIV seized the city in 1681 and its annexation to France was legitimized by the Treaty of Ryswyck in 1697. Strasbourg surrendered to the Prussians in 1870 after a 50-day siege and bombardment. The following year it was joined to the newly formed German Empire, along with the rest of Alsace-Lorraine. On November 22, 1918, the city once again became part of France. In 1940 Nazi Germany annexed Alsace-Lorraine and expelled 100,000 people who were deemed irretrievably French. The city was liberated on November 23, 1944.

Attractions

See map on page 78.

The main square of old Strasbourg, **Place Kléber** (1), is named after Jean Baptiste Kléber, a Strasbourgeois and general of the French Revolution whose monument and tomb are located in the square. Kléber was assassinated in Cairo in 1800. On the southeast corner of the square begins an old street of shops, the **Rue des Grandes Arcades** (2). Follow the street south to its end at the *Place Gutenberg,* with its statue of the famous printer in the center. On the west side of the square is the *Chamber of Commerce,* housed in the former Hôtel de Ville. Built in 1585, the building was the site of pre-Revolutionary violence, looted by a mob on July 21, 1789, while royal troops watched—unable, or unwilling to quench the mob's fury.

Start at the southwest corner of the Place Gutenberg and walk south down a narrow street called Rue Mercière. Through a cleft in the old gabled houses there suddenly looms—astonishing and overpowering—the lofty façade of the ***Cathédrale Nôtre-Dame.*** (3), which traces its history to 496, when Clovis built a church on the site. This edifice was rebuilt by Charlemagne, but sacked in 1002 and struck by lightning five years later. A Romanesque church was begun, but in the 13th century its nave was rebuilt and the construction of the present French Gothic cathedral began. The west façade was built between 1277 and 1339; the octagonal tower, with its spire, was completed in 1439.

The *west façade,* built by Erwin von Steinbach and his son Jacob between 1277 and 1339, is noted for its tracery and elaborate statuary. Unlike traditional Gothic façades, it was conceived as a separate piece of decoration, rather than as an intrinsic part of the building's design. Unfortunately, the portals were mutilated at the time of the French Revolution and some of the statues are replicas.

The north tower of the cathedral is the work of Ulrich von Ensingen, the architect of Ulm cathedral. The original plan called for twin towers of equal height to rise from a second story; instead, the two unfinished towers were

Strasbourg's Cathedral

joined by a platform on the third story, above which a daring tower, decorated with statuary, rises to a height of 142 meters (455 feet). Johann Hultz of Cologne built the pierced spire atop the tower between 1420 and 1439. You can climb to the top and, on a clear day, have a splendid view of the city, Alsace, and the Black Forest.

In the enormous interior of the cathedral, the effect of the harmonious proportions is further enhanced by the beauty of the 13th- and 14th-century window tracery and the stained glass. The carved stone *pulpit* was made by Johann Hammerer in 1486. The vaulting in the south transept is supported by the *Angels' Pillar,* with its statues of angels blowing trumpets for the Last Judgment, built in 1230. Worthy of note is the famous *astronomical clock,* which was originally constructed by Conrad Dasipodius in 1571. Reconstructed in 1842, it still

keeps time, setting a multitude of figures in motion daily at precisely 12:30 P.M.

Directly on *Place de la Cathé-drale* is the *Pharmacie du Cerf,* a half-timbered house with a stone ground floor, built during the 15th and 16th centuries. To the left of the cathedral is the wonderful **Kammerzell House* with an elaborately carved façade and interior murals. Now a popular restaurant, its ground floor was built in 1467, and the overhanging upper stories date from the 16th century. On the south side of the cathedral is the 18th-century **Place du Château** (4) named after the Château des Rohan. The château was the home

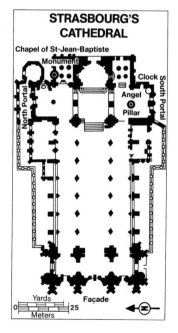

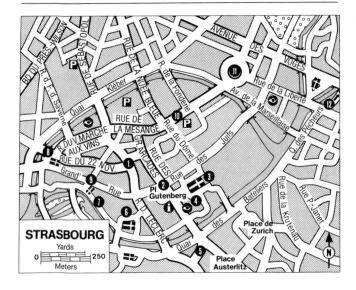

of four bishops who were members of the Rohan family, and briefly housed the university in the 1870s. It was restored after being damaged during World War II, and its Rococo rooms now contain the *Musée des Beaux Arts.* Art of the Upper Rhine, Renaissance, and Baroque masterpieces, memorabilia of the Rohan family, and an archaeological collection are on display. On the southwest corner of the square stands the **Maison de l'Oeuvre Nôtre-Dame,** which has a crenelated gable over its Gothic wing dating from 1347, and a richly decorated gable surmounted by an armed figure over the wing that was built by Thomann Uhlberger in the German Renaissance style in the 16th century. In 1349 the building became the headquarters for the

architects of the cathedral. The edifice has been restored since 1944 and now contains the important *Musée de l'Oeuvre Nôtre-Dame,* whose 40-odd rooms contain Medieval and Renaissance art, including original statues from the cathedral. Here you will find the original of *The Synagogue and the Church,* which has been removed from the façade of the cathedral to protect it from air pollution.

Behind the Maison is a romantic old square, the *Place du Marché-aux-Cochons-de-Lait,* and a little farther to the southwest is the former *Grande Boucherie* (1586–1588). This building now houses the *Musée Historique,* whose collection is devoted to the history of Strasbourg. Immediately to the west is a replica of the *Ancienne Douane* (customs house), built in 1356 but destroyed in 1944. The *Musée d'Art moderne,* with works by Renoir, Dégas, Vuillard, Gauguin, and others, is located within.

Crossing over the Ill River by the nearby *Pont du Corbeau* you come to the *Place du Corbeau* (5). To the left is the old *Cour du Corbeau,* an inn that housed many famous guests, including the Prussian King Frederick the Great in 1740. To the right is a 17th-century merchant's house that is now the *Musée Alsacien,* containing folk art, furniture, domestic objects, and costumes.

Recrossing the Ill and going west you soon come to **Saint-Thomas** (6), a Protestant church with Romanesque and Gothic towers that contains the sculptor Jean-Baptiste Pigalle's **tomb* (1756) of a French Marshal, Maurice of Saxony (1696–1750). On the Silberman organ here Albert Schweitzer began a tradition of concerts in 1908 to commemorate the death of Johann Sebastian Bach on July 28, 1750. By following the Rue de la Monnaie north, and then turning west on Rue des Dentelles, to the north and west, you will come to the **Rue du Bain-aux-Plantes** (7), a street that runs through the old **tanners' quarter* and is lined with many picturesque half-timbered houses. The "petite France" cluster of houses is especially noteworthy. Also in this district are two towers which are restored remains of Medieval fortifications. From the *Quai de la Petite-France* three bridges cross the Ill; although they lost their roofs in 1784, they are still called the *Ponts Couverts.* You can get an excellent view of the Medieval towers from the *Ponts Barrage Vauban,* which spans the Ill just to the west. From here, continue north to the Rue du Maire Kuss, and turn on the *Pont Kuss.* From here you can see the rather austere façade of the church called **Saint-Pierre-le-Vieux** (8), which was divided in 1681 into a Catholic church and a Protestant church. The Catholic section was rebuilt in 1867. The **Grand' Rue** (9), with many well-preserved old houses, runs in front of the church and ends, to the east, in the Place Gutenberg. By going east from Place Gutenberg on the Rue des Hallebardes and turning left on the Rue du Dome, you reach the **Place Broglie** (10), which is surrounded by 18th-century administration buildings, including the *Hôtel de Ville.* Behind the Place Broglie, the *Theater Bridge* leads over the *canal* to the broad **Place de la République** (11), with many fine public buildings, including the *Palais du Rhin,* built from 1883 to 1889 in Neo-Renaissance style for the German Kaiser. To the east, the Rue de la Liberté leads across two branches of the Ill to the *Place de l'Université,* behind which stand the buildings of the *University.* From here the **Allée de la Robertsau** (12) branches off to the northeast, leading past the city park called the **Orangerie* (1806) to the **Palais de l'Europe,* the seat of the Council of Europe.

**Dijon

Dijon, with a current population of 150,000, was once the capital of the Medieval duchy of Burgundy, a vast territory that stretched as far as the North Sea. Although the duchy has long been incorporated into France, its historic capital retains much of its former grandeur as a center of gastronomy, wine, and fine art. With its many restored Medieval houses and well-preserved old buildings, Dijon is indeed a city of remarkable landmarks; and happily for the traveller, most of these are concentrated in one relatively small area.

History

Called Divio, or Castrum Divionense, the city was first fortified by the Romans in A.D. 273. At about the same time, the settlement was converted to Christianity by Saint Benignus. In early Medieval times Dijon became the capital of the Burgundian kingdom and the seat of a powerful Valois duchy. Destroyed by fire in 1137, the city was rebuilt and fortified by Duc Hugues II. Following its restoration, Dijon flowered for several hundred years as the site of the dazzling Burgundian court, whose dukes were among the most splendid figures of Medieval France.

The Duchy of Burgundy was bestowed on Philippe le Hardi (Philip the Bold) in 1364 by his father, King John II. Philippe became the most powerful prince in Christendom when he put down a rebellion of Flemish rebels and, in 1384, inherited Flanders. His son, Jean sans Peur (John the Fearless), carried on his father's struggle against the French king, taking advantage of King Charles VI's defeat by the English (under Henry VI) to seize the throne. He was assassinated in 1419 at a meeting with the Dauphin (later Charles VII).

Philippe le Bon (Philip the Good) avenged his father's death by allying Burgundy with England, which had great territorial ambitions in France. It was then that the duchy reached its greatest territorial extent, stretching from the heartland between the Loire River east to the Jura mountains and north to large portions of the Low Countries. A great patron of the arts, Philippe maintained his court in a lavish style that astounded all of Europe.

In 1476, Charles the Bold—Philippe's son—died at the Battle of Nancy, leaving no male heir. The French king, Louis XI, invoked a law prohibiting female inheritance and seized the province, which has been part of France ever since.

Attractions

See map below.

The busiest square in Dijon is the **Place Darcy** (1), between the train station and the Old City. At one end is the Porte Guillaume, dating from 1788, behind which begins the Rue de la Liberté, the main traffic artery of the city. This street leads to the **Place de la Libération** (2), a splendid, broad, semicircular plaza. Built in 1682 by Jules Hardouin-Mansart, one of the architects of Versailles, the plaza graces the area in front of the **Palais des Ducs de Bourgogne** (3). This great building was once the center of Burgundian rule, then the residence of the king of France; it serves now as the Hôtel de Ville and houses a fine museum. Parts of the building are Medieval, but the buildings around the *Cour d'Honneur* were erected between 1686 and 1701, and those around the *Cour de Flore* were built between 1783 and

1787. Many parts of the Medieval castle were never completed, but they are nonetheless fabulous to see. The *Tour de Bar,* a 14th-century tower in the courtyard (*Cour de Bar*), is flanked by a handsome staircase called the Escalier de Bellegarde (1614); the *Tour de Philippe le Bon* lies behind the center segment of the Cour d'Honneur. The vaulted *Salle des Gardes* is today part of the ****Musée des Beaux-Arts** (4). Established in 1799, the museum is one of the richest in France. The entrance is on the east side of the palace complex in the *Place de la Sainte-Chapelle* (the chapel itself was destroyed in 1803). Beneath its Medieval vaulting, the ground floor of the museum houses a *sculpture collection* by such artists as Claus Sluter, who died in Dijon (Room B); François Rude, a native of Dijon (Room A), whose masterpiece, the sculptural group known as the *Marseillaise,* graces the Arc de Triomphe in Paris; and

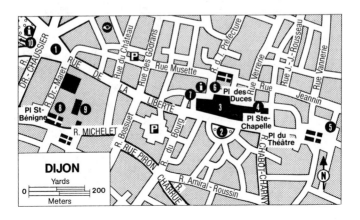

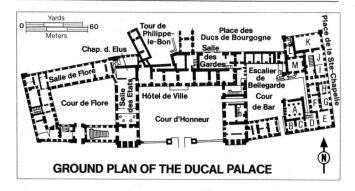

GROUND PLAN OF THE DUCAL PALACE

the Burgundian animal sculptor François Pompon (Room K). Room C, the former kitchen of the ducal palace, dates from about 1435; it has six huge hearths whose flues all come together in a single chimney.

Upstairs is a 22-room *picture gallery* with works by Italian, French, Flemish, and German masters. All that remains of the ducal apartments, the Salle des Gardes, is between rooms 13 and 14. Here are the world famous **tombs,* which were once kept just outside the gates of Dijon in the Chartreuse de Champmol (see below). A likeness of Philippe le Hardi, watched over by two angels, is carved in stone. Around the sarcophagus are 41 *pleurants* (mourners)—maidens of the town, court ladies, monks, and knights forming a funeral procession in stone. Nearby are the *tombs of Jean sans Peur* and *Marguerite de Bavière,* his consort. The Salle des Gardes also houses two noteworthy altarpieces by Jacques de Baerze (1390–1399).

Just east of the museum stands the **church of Saint-Michel** (5) built between 1499 and 1529. Its naves and choir are late-Gothic; its *façade,* one of the finest in France, is Renaissance. The sculptures on the façade show Christian motifs side by side with scenes from pagan mythology.

To the north, behind the Palais des Ducs, stands the remarkable **church of Nôtre-Dame** (6). Built in the early 13th century, it is

The tomb monuments of Dijon

considered the most complete example of the Burgundian Gothic style. Along its marvelous ****façade** are two long rows of arches with delicate columns over the entries to the vestibule, and three wide friezes bearing false waterspouts. Two slim towers elegantly unite the ensemble. The right-hand tower houses a **clock* that Philippe le Hardi brought back as booty from the Flemish town of Courtrai in 1382. The church's light and harmonious interior is a pleasing place to visit. Worthy of special attention are the stained-glass windows from the 13th century, a 12th-century Madonna, and a modern tapestry depicting the two liberations of Dijon—in 1513 and 1944.

Only a few steps south of Nôtre-Dame is the **Rue des Forges** (7), which is lined by many private houses dating from the 13th through the 16th centuries. Among the most interesting are the *Hôtel Chambellan* (1490) at Number 34, housing the local tourist office; the *Hôtel Milsand* (or *Maillard*) (1561) at Number 38; the 13th-century *Hôtel Aubriot* at Number 40; the *Hôtel Morel-Sauvegrain* (15th century) at Number 52–56; and the *Hôtel Rochefort* (15th–16th centuries) in the courtyard of Number 56. The Rue des Forges ends at a plaza named for the sculptor François Rude (1784–1855), who was born nearby. Walk down the Rue de la Liberté and turn left on Rue du Dr.-Maret to reach the Burgundian Gothic **Cathédrale Saint-Bénigne** (8). The crypt of the holy martyr Benignus, who died in the third century, is believed to be here. Although Medieval church authorities doubted the authenticity of the tomb, it became an object of pilgrimage and the chief reason for the construction of a succession of ever-larger churches. The present cathedral is a vast Gothic structure begun in 1280 and it incorporates the apse of the former Romanesque basilica. Northeast of the church in the former abbey is the **Musée Archéologique** (9), which contains Gallo-Roman findings, remains from the old basilica of Saint-Bénigne, and a **bust of Christ* by the Dutch sculptor Claus Sluter, which was once part of Moses' Well (see below).

Outside the Old City, 1 km. (about half a mile) west of Place Darcy, stands the **Chartreuse de Champmol** (10), the monastery where the Valois dukes are buried. Originally built between 1384 and 1394 and destroyed in 1793, it has been a psychiatric hospital since 1843. The preserved **portal,* decorated with figures executed by Claus Sluter, depicts a courtly scene of Philippe le Hardi being presented to Mary, Queen of Heaven, by Saint John; his consort, Marguerite, is presented by Saint Catharine. Under a protective roof in the courtyard is the most important sight here, the ****Moses' Well** (1395–1404), by Claus Sluter. The fresco was originally the base of a calvary scene rendered in brilliant polychrome.

The fragment that remains shows six naturalistic figures of prophets, including Moses. Some art scholars consider this work to be even finer than the Moses of Michelangelo.

Environs

The most charming excursion from Dijon is to the south through the vineyards of the *Côte d'Or* to *Cîteaux Abbey,* the motherhouse of the Cistercians. The entire trip is about 92 km. (57 miles). Route D 122, the first half of the **Route des Grands Crus** (the wine route) runs parallel to Route N 74, the second half of the wine route; both roads pass or run through many towns famed for the wines—past and present—they have produced. The Côte d'Or is called the heart of Burgundy. In *Chenôve* there are two wine presses dating from the 13th century, and on display in *Clos du Rois* in *Fixin* is a monument by François Rude, *Napoleon Awakening to Immortality,* which was erected by Noisot, the former Commander of the Imperial Guard, at his estate as a token of his unbroken loyalty to the emperor. Napoleon's favorite wine came from the vineyard *Champ de Bertin* in *Gevrey-Chambertin*. Probably the most famous vineyard in the region, however, is the *Clos de Vougeot*. The château, built in the 12th century and renovated during the Renaissance, is now the headquarters of the Chevaliers de Tastevin, the order of winetasters.

Near *Vougeot,* the Route des Grands Crus intersects Route N 74 and follows it for 3 km. (2 miles) to the village of *Nuits-Saint-Georges*. From here you have the choice of driving toward *Beaune,* with its Medieval home for the aged, the Hôtel-Dieu, or of going 13 km. (8 miles) east to the *Abbaye de Cîteaux,* now consisting of modern buildings but on an important site in cultural history: The Cistercian Order, founded here in 1098, eventually grew to encompass some 1600 monasteries by the late Middle Ages.

25 Travel Routes through France

Modern autoroutes (superhighways) cover all of France, making it possible to reach any major point in the country without leaving the highways. Although we have mentioned the shortest and fastest ways on the autoroutes between locations in the following 25 Travel Routes through France, we have placed greater emphasis on the scenic routes—those smaller highways and roads that reveal far more intimately the country's rich cultural heritage. By following these suggested routes, you can experience the incomparable beauty of the French landscape, and become better acquainted with France's historic and artistic treasures. Whether you take a main highway or a road less travelled, the most important and remarkable sights are described along with information that allows you to stop off at noteworthy cities and places of scenic, cultural, historical—or even culinary—interest along the way.

The first Travel Routes describe scenic drives from Paris east through the Vosges, followed by two routes to the city from the Channel coast, and the north. The next 12 tours fan out from Paris in every direction, linking the city to the Atlantic coast, the Mediterranean, and the mountainous regions to the southeast. The remaining travel routes are devoted to other important areas of France, such as a circular tour of Provence and a trip along the spectacular Côte d'Azur. Travel Route 20 is devoted to the Mediterranean island of Corsica. Before choosing and travelling on any one of our self-guided travel routes, you may wish to read the chapter called *Getting Your Bearings,* which briefly describes the characteristic landscapes, and cities in each region of France. Also, many of the travel routes intersect each other, offering the flexibility to change direction to suit your interests.

TRAVEL ROUTE 1: Through the Vosges

See color map and map on pages 92–93.

From Paris there are three routes that lead to the Vosges. All of them pass through the ancient provinces of Lorraine and Alsace, via either Nancy or Épinal.

The Vosges mountains are covered by woods that form the western extension of the Black Forest. Along the mountains' eastern edge extends the plain of the Upper Rhine, with many old cities and towns such as Strasbourg, Colmar, Obernai, and Riquewihr. There are fortresses such as Haut-Koenigsbourg; monasteries and convents such as Sainte-Odile. Travellers can pick up sections of the Route du Vin d'Alsace (Alsation Wine Route) from north to south along the foothills of the Vosges between Strasbourg and Colmar and then follow the Route des Crêtes (Crest Route) that passes between Colmar and Belfort (see Travel Route 1 D).

TRAVEL ROUTE 1 A: ***Paris–Nancy–**Strasbourg (460 km.; 286 miles)

See color map and map on pages 92–93.

Travel Route 1 A takes you on a quick but interesting trip west of Paris to Strasbourg along Route N 4. Along the way you'll pass industrial cities and forested tracts before touring the city of Nancy, a masterpiece of 18th-century urban planning; you can also visit the crystal town of Baccarat. The final stretch of the trip takes you over the Vosges to Saverne, an important town during the Middle Ages, before continuing toward Strasbourg.

From Paris take N 4 east for 52 km. (32 miles) to *Rozay-en-Brie* where about 2 km. (1 mile) south of the village you can see the *Château de la Grange-Bleneau.* The Marquis de Lafayette, friend of George Washington and hero of the American Revolution, lived here from 1802 to 1834.

Continuing east on N 4 you pass through Sézanne, Vitry-le-François, which was laid out by King Francois I, and the bustling industrial city of *Saint-Dizier.*

If you wish, you can make a short (24 km.; 14 mile) detour via N 35 to **Bar-le-Duc** (population 22,000). This was once the capital city of the old Duchy of Bar, which was incorporated into France in two stages, in 1301 and 1766. In 1916, one French regiment after another marched through this town into the "Hell of Verdun." The town is known for another grim reminder of death, the famous—and macabre—**Skeleton,* a statue by sculptor Ligier Richier (1500–1567) in the *church of Saint-Pierre.* This work grew out of a strange request by the Prince of Orange to be depicted on his tomb in the way his body would look after being in the grave for three years. Out of gray stone the sculptor created a work that is striking in its realism.

Rejoin N 4 at *Ligny-en-Barrois* where you can pick up Travel Route 1 C or continue eastward to the former bishop's city and citadel of **Toul** (population 20,000). *Saint-Étienne,* the former cathedral, was built between 1204 and 1490. It has a splendid 15th-century façade in the Flamboyant style (named for the typical decorative motif of an elongated flame). The *cloister of Saint-Gengoult* was built in the same style.

The road continues in a long

The Eiffel Tower, the most recognizable symbol of Paris, was constructed for the International Exhibition of 1889.

PARIS
(DOWNTOWN)

Yards
0 ⊢⊢⊢⊢⊢⊢⊣ 1000
Meters

WAGRAM

DE CLICHY

TERNES

BD DES BATIGNOLLES

Pl de la Pt des Ternes

Porte Maillot

AV DES TERNES

AV PEREIRE

DE VILLIERS

DE COURCELLES

Parc Monceau

MALESHERBES

Gare St-Lazare

Gare St-Lazare

RUE ST-LAZ

Amsterdam

Rue de Clichy

AV DE LA GRANDE ARMÉE

Pl des Ternes

BOULEVARD

Rue

du

DE FRIEDLAND

BD

Vignon

Rue

Opéra

Av. Foch

AVE DE

Av. VICTOR-HUGO

AVENUE KLEBER

AVENUE D'IENA

AVENUE DES CHAMPS-ELYSÉES

Faubourg

ST

Honoré

Pl de la Madeleine

AVENUE MARCEAU

Grand Palais

LA REINE

Pl de la Concorde

RUE

QUAI DES TUILERIES

Pl du Trocadéro

AV. DU PRÉS.-WILSON

C. ALBERT 1er

C. LA

Seine

Q. A.-FRANCE

Q. VOLTAIRE

RUE DE RIVOLI

NEW YORK

Pt de l'Alma

Pl des Invalides

D'ORSAY

Gare des Invalides

Gare d'Orsay

Pont d'Iéna

QUAI

BRANLY

AVENUE

Rue

Saint-

INVALIDES

ST-

Dominique

BOULEVARD

Pont de Bir-Hakeim

Parc du Champ

de

Rue

Rue

GERMAIN-

de

Grenelle

SAINT-

Av. DE LA BOURDONNAIS

Av. DE SUFFREN

Av. BOSQUET

PICQUET

de Mars

AV. DE LA MOTTE

Rue

DUQUESNE

DE

DES

Rue

de Varenne

Vaneau

RUE DU FOUR

RENNES

DE SÉGUR

BRETEUIL

DES-

SÈVRES

GRENELLE

BD GARIBALD

SUFFREN

PRES-

Rue

RASPAIL

AV. ÉMILE-ZOLA

RUE DU COMMERCE

Rue Cambronne

Pl de Breteuil

DE

Rue

BD PASTEUR

GRENELLE

RUE LECOURBE

BD DE Vaugirard

BOULEVARD DU MONTPARNASSE

MONTPARNASSE

Gare Montparnasse

The remarkable Galerie des Glaces (Hall of Mirrors) is among the stunning sights at Versailles.

Strasbourg's Gothic Cathedral of Nôtre Dame boasts an exquisite red sandstone façade and awesome Rose Window.

ROUTE 1
Vosges to Paris

Miles
0   30
Kilometers

To Luxembourg

WEST GERMANY

Dillingen
Saarlouis
Saarbrücken
Zweibrücken
Kaiserslautern
Pirmasens
Landau
Wörth

To Paris

Metz
St-Avold
Morhange
Bitche
Haguenau

Pont-à-Mousson

Sarrebourg
Phalsbourg
Saverne
Marmoutier

To Karlsruhe

Nancy
Toul
Lunéville
N4
Blâmont
Marlenheim
Rosheim
Strasbourg
(Straßburg)
Kehl

To Paris
St-Nicolas-de-Port
N59
Obernai
WEST GERMANY

Domrémy-la-Pucelle
Baccarat
Ste-Odile
Andlau

Mirecourt
St-Dié
Koenigsbourg
Le Bonhomme
Sélestat

Neufchâteau
Vittel
D166
Épinal
N415
Kaysersberg
Munster
Ribeauvillé
Colmar
Breisach
Freiburg

Contrexéville
Gérardmer
Remiremont
C. de la Schlucht
1139
Neuf-Brisach

Plombières-les-Bains
Bussang
Grand Ballon
424
N66
Cernay

St-Maurice
Giromagny
Thann
Mulhouse

Ronchamp
N93
Belfort

Vesoul
Basel

To Dijon
Besançon
Pont-de-Roide
Delémont
Olten

To Zurich

Biel
Langenthal

Neuchâtel
Lac de Neuchâtel
SWITZERLAND
Langnau

To Lausanne
BERN
To Lucerne

Sarre
Moselle
Saône
Saône
Ognon
Doubs
Doubs
RHEIN

From the Middle Ages through World War II, the cliffs of Falaise d'Aval in Normandy have been the scene of many turbulent battles.

Mysterious menhirs, such as these standing in the heath at Carnac in Brittany, date back to the Stone Age.

Chenonceaux, built over the Cher River, was a gift from Henri II to his mistress, Diane de Poitiers, and was once a showplace for magnificent Renaissance festivals.

The Renaissance hunting castle of Chambord, with its turreted roofs, sits in an enclosed national wildlife preserve.

straight stretch through forest toward *Nancy*. If you don't have time to visit this city, you can continue directly on the bypass road, which joins Route N 4 after 10km. (6 miles) west of Lunéville.

Nancy

See map below.

Founded in the 11th century, Nancy (population 100,000, much more including suburbs) was the seat of the dukes of Lorraine, who followed one another in unbroken succession from 1049 to 1735. Surrounded by enemies, these rulers were forced to defend their territory from all sides. The powerful Burgundians, in particular, were bent on conquering Lorraine, because the duchy lay between their heartland and their northern possessions (see Dijon, page 80). In 1735, Louis XV set his father-in-law, the 58-year-old deposed King of Poland, Stanislas, on the ducal throne of Nancy, with the understanding that after his death Lorraine was to revert to the French Crown. But Stanislas lived another 31 years, and spent his time in Nancy building with vigor, enthusiasm, and taste. Thanks to Stanislas, Nancy is one of the marvels of city planning in Europe.

**Place Stanislas (1). The plaza was laid out from 1752–1760 by the architect Emmanuel Héré. It is surrounded by six buildings, including the palace of King Stanislas. The plaza is enclosed by magnificent gilded wrought-iron gates made by the master metal craftsman Jean Lamour. North of the plaza is the *Triumphal Arch* (2) in honor of Louis XV. Through this arch one enters the *Place de la Carrière* (3), once used as a jousting field. The *Palais du Gouvernement,* fronted by an oval colonnade, is at the end of the plaza.

Contrasting with this Rococo ensemble is the Medieval quarter of Nancy with its **Palais Ducal** (4), dating from the early 16th century. It houses the *Musée Historique Lorrain,* one of the more interesting provincial collections of its kind in France, with engravings by Jacques Callot and paintings by Georges de la Tour. There is a Judaica section on the second floor.

To the left of the ducal palace stands the **Église des Cor-**

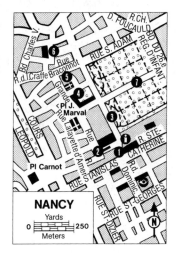

NANCY

Yards

0 ⊢━━━━━┤ 250

Meters

deliers (5), the church in which the dukes of Lorraine are buried. Of particular interest is the *tomb* of the Duchess Philippa de Gueldre, built by Ligier Richier around 1550. Grande Rue, the main street of the old city of Nancy, ends at the *Porte de la Craffe* (6), the sole but powerful remains of the city fortifications of the 15th century. The gate is ornamented with thistle, symbolizing Lorraine, and two crossbars—the *cross of Lorraine*—which became the symbol of the Free French under General De Gaulle during World War II.

In the center of Nancy is the *Parc de la Pépinière* (7) a beautifully laid out park containing a monument by Rodin in memory of the Lorraine painter Claude Lorrain (1600–1682).

Following N 4 eastward for 12 km. (7.5 miles) you come to the town of *Saint-Nicholas-de-Port*. The pilgrimage *church of Saint-Nicholas-de-Port* is one of the great sights of France. It was built in the late 15th and early 16th centuries. Its façade is late-Gothic, but the two towers were built in the 17th century. Joan of Arc is known to have prayed here. The next important town is **Lunéville** (population 24,500), historically important for the "Peace of Lunéville," the treaty concluded here in 1801 between France and Austria that ended the French Revolutionary wars. The treaty awarded France the left bank of the Rhine. The city retains its 18th-century appearance. Sights of interest include the *palace* and its *park* with the *Promenade des Bosquets*; the *Église Saint-Jacques*, the only Baroque church in Lorraine; and the *city museum*, which has a fine collection of Lunéville faïence.

From Lunéville, you can make a 25-km. (14.5-mile) detour on Route N 59 to **Baccarat** (population 5,600), on the western edge of the Vosges. Famous for the manufacture of tableware, decanters, bottles, vases, and goblets, all of leaded crystal, the town displays its products in the *Crystal Museum*. From here, you may continue on Travel Route 1 B.

From Baccarat travel north via D 935 to return to Route N 4. Turning eastward you will soon come to the small fortress of *Blâmont* with the five towers of a ruined castle, and then to the town of *Sarrebourg*. Beyond is the town of **Phalsbourg,** which became French in 1661 and was fortified in 1680. The fortress held the Prussians at bay for four months in 1870.

The road ascends slightly across the rolling Lorraine plateau and then begins its climb over the Vosges to the *Col de Saverne* (Saverne Pass). Just before the highest point (410 meters; 1,345 feet), there is a fountain that marks the boundary between Lorraine and Alsace. The road then descends through the plain of the Upper Rhine to wooded countryside with lovely views, and the small city of **Saverne.** The name is derived from the Roman *Tres*

Tabernae (three taverns). This was the principal town of the Wasgau region in the Middle Ages. Louis René de Rohan, Bishop of Strasbourg, built a **palace* here in the 1780s. Its majestic main façade faces a lovely park. Saverne lies at the entrance of the Saverne valley, through which the Zorn River flows, dividing the Middle Vosges from the Northern Vosges. The river, the Rhine–Marne Canal, the railroad, and the highway run side by side through the valley beneath red limestone cliffs.

Continuing on N 4 in a southerly direction, the next town is *Marmoutier,* with its old *church of Saint-Maurus,* that has a Romanesque façade dating from the 12th century. Continue on N 4 to ***Strasbourg* (see page 75), the principal city of Alsace, with its stunning cathedral.

TRAVEL ROUTE 1 B: ***Paris–Nancy–Colmar (443 km.; 275 miles)

See color map and map on pages 92–93.

This route highlights the sights between Lunéville and the beautiful Alsatian towns of Kaysersberg and Colmar, both notable as stops along the Route du Vin d'Alsace.

Leave Paris on Route N 4 and follow the tour described in Travel Route 1 A through Nancy as far as Lunéville. From Lunéville proceed southeast on N 59 through the crystal-producing town of *Baccarat* (see page 88), down the valley of the Meurthe River through *Raon-l'Étape* to **Saint-Dié** (population 28,000), a city surrounded by wooded heights. In World War II, it was deliberately destroyed by the Germans in their 1944 retreat, but it has been rebuilt. The main street, **Rue Thiers,* has been restored just as it was laid out by Emmanuel Héré, the great architect of Nancy, in 1757. The cathedral, the Romanesque chapel of *Nôtre-Dame-de-Galilée* (12th century) and its Gothic cloister (14th century) are worth a visit.

Proceed on Route 415 southeast as it ascends in large loops through pastureland and fir woods up to the **Col du Bonhomme,** the pass that cuts off the crest through the *Diedolshauser Gap.* To the right the magnificent ***Route des Crêtes* branches off (see page 97).

The road then descends to the birthplace of the great theologian, physician, musician, and Nobel Peace Prize winner Albert Schweitzer (1875–1965), the small but popular wine town of **Kaysersberg** (population 3,000). The house where he was born is now a museum. The town's fortified bridge dates from 1511; its Renaissance *Hôtel de Ville* was built in 1521. The *church* houses a *carved altarpiece* (1584) by Johann Bongartz of Colmar.

Continue on N 415 a few miles farther to **Colmar** (population 65,000), situated along the eastern edge of the Vosges mountains. Colmar was a Carolingian royal possession in the ninth century and by 1226, when it became a free city associated with the Holy Roman Empire, it was already the most important commercial center in Upper Alsace. With the exception of the years 1870 to 1918 when it was under German control, the city has been French since the 17th century.

Colmar was the birthplace of the painter Martin Schongauer (1420–1491) and of Auguste Bartholdi (1834–1904), sculptor of the Statue of Liberty in New York Harbor. However, it is more famous for the painter Matthias Grünewald's masterpiece, the **Isenheim Altarpiece** (1510–1515), on exhibit in the *Musée d'Unterlinden*, which is just north of the center of the old part of the city. The museum is housed in buildings that surround the cloister of a former Dominican convent founded in the 13th century. The freestanding altarpiece, considered by many scholars to be the greatest work of German painting of the late-Gothic period, consists of several panels, the most notable

Colmar: Pfister House

of which is the **Crucifixion of Christ**. Grünewald painted the altarpiece for the former Isenheim monastery near Guebwiller, 25 km. (15.5 miles) south of Colmar.

Upon leaving the museum, turn right along the Rue des Têtes, then left along the Rue des Boulangers to reach the Dominican church that currently houses the superb *Madonna in the Rose Hedge* by Martin Schongauer.

Colmar still has many old houses. The *Pfister House* at the corner of the Rue des Marchands and Rue Mercière dates from 1537 and the *Maison des Têtes* in the Rue des Têtes, a Renaissance building dating from 1607, are the most handsome.

For excursions from Colmar, particularly to the picturesque villages on the Route du Vin d'Alsace, see Travel Route 1 D.

TRAVEL ROUTE 1 C: ***Paris–Épinal–Mulhouse (477 km.; 296 miles)

See color map and map on pages 92–93.

This approach to the Vosges region provides a richly historical and picturesque route west. Among the highlights are Domrémy, the birthplace of Joan of Arc, the spas of Vittel and Plombières-les-Bains, the high mountain passes, the wine market town of Thann and the fabric-producing city of Mulhouse.

Follow Route N 4 from Paris to Ligny-en-Barrois as described in Travel Route 1 A. From Ligny-en-Barrois, take Route D 966 through *Gondrecourt-le-Chateau* through the valley of the Meuse River to the village of **Domrémy-la-Pucelle** (population 350). This town is the birthplace of Jeanne d'Arc (Joan of Arc), the Maid ("la pucelle") of Orléans. The cottage in which she was born sometime between 1410 and 1412, which has been restored many times, is near the church, with an adjacent museum. About 1.5 km. (1 mile) past the village, on the left is the *Basilica of Bois-Chenu,* built in 1881 on the spot where Joan was said to have heard the voices telling her to drive the English from France.

About 10 km. (6 miles) to the south is the town of **Neufchâteau** (population 10,000). During the Middle Ages the old city, situated on a hill above the Meuse, was a constant object of dispute among the dukes of Lorraine and the counts of Champagne. When Neufchâteau participated in the rebellion known as the "Jacquerie," Riche-lieu had the castle and the city walls torn down.

You now have the option of taking Route D66/166 directly to *Mirecourt* and *Épinal* or making a worthwhile detour of 20 km. (12.5 miles) through Vittel on Route D 164. The road goes through a changing panorama of rolling hills to *Contrexéville* (population 5,000), a spa. About 5 km. (3 miles) to the east is ****Vittel** (population 7,000). This is a beautifully situated health spa famous for its mineral water. From a visitors' gallery in the bottling plant you can watch bottles being filled and labelled at a rate of about 200,000 per hour. The **spa park* covers 62 acres; a casino, golf course, and racetrack contribute to Vittel's reputation for being the most elegant spa in the Vosges.

From Vittel, you can continue east on Route D 3 then north on D 4 to **Mirecourt** (population 10,000). Italian craftsmen brought the art of making stringed instruments here in the 17th century, and the town is still a center of their manufacture. A national school of stringed instruments ("de lutherie") was established

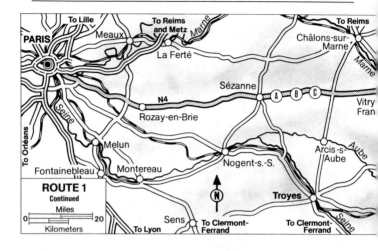

here in 1970. The stone halls of the market date from 1617.

Route D 166 now proceeds into the High Vosges to **Épinal** (population 42,000). The city is beautifully situated in the middle of a thickly forested area. It grew up around a convent for noblewomen founded in the 13th century. Today the city's main industry is processing cotton, but it is famous for the manufacture of popular colored prints, the *images d'Épinal*. These 18th-century works may be seen at the **Musée Departmental des Vosges et Musée Internationale de l'Imagerie*.

Continue south on N 57 to **Remiremont** (population 12,000). The old city, with its arcade-lined *Grand' Rue,* now the Rue Charles de Gaulle, is historically significant as the site, on the nearby Saint-Mont, of a famous 11th-century convent for noble ladies whose abbess enjoyed princely rank in the Holy Roman Empire.

Detour west on N 57 for 14 km. (8.7 miles) for a short side trip to **Plombières-les-Bains** (population 4,000). This is a health resort that was popular with the Romans and was much visited by princes and kings in the late Middle Ages. The indoor swimming pool dates from the 18th century (it was modernized in 1935); the spa park merges into magnificent woods.

Return to Remiremont and join N 66 for the journey directly to Mulhouse (see page 94), or take the alternate travel route along D 417 via Gérardmer and Colmar described below.

This extremely scenic route through the Vosges begins at Remiremont and joins Travel Routes 1 B and 1 D at Colmar.

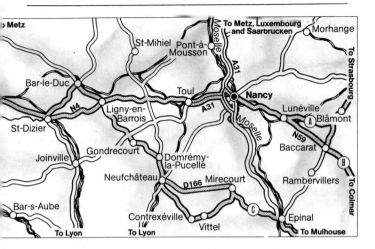

From Remiremont drive east on D 417 about 30 km. (18 miles), passing by the foot of the *Saint-Mont,* through the Moselle Valley, and going through *Le Tholy* then past the *Lac de Gérardmer* to **Gérardmer** (population 11,000), the most popular winter resort in the Vosges and an important summer resort as well. It was destroyed by the Germans in 1944 and rebuilt with little regard for its former character.

Continuing on D 417 through the forest, you pass the *Lac de Longemer* and the smaller *Lac de Retournemer.* The *Roche du Diable* looms in the background. Next, you will come to the ***Col de la Schlucht** (1,139 meters; 3,737 feet). This pass sat on the border between France and Germany before the Treaty of Versailles restored the whole area to France in 1871. Just south of the pass stands the third highest peak of the Vosges, the *Hohneck.* From the summit, at 1,361 meters (4,465 feet)—reached by chair lift—you have a spectacular *view in all directions.

Descending into the Munster Valley, you will soon come to the

Col de la Schlucht

town of **Munster** (population 16,000), whose name is derived from the *Gregorian Minster,* a monastery that was torn down in 1790. Munster cheese gets its name from this town and this is also the starting point for the so-called Route du Fromage (Cheese Route) into the Vosges.

The road now climbs toward the health resort of *Hohrodberg* and passes beneath a peak known as the "Great Hohnack." From here you have a wonderful *view across the Rhine plain all the way to the Black Forest in West Germany. Next you will reach *Les Trois Épis,* a place of pilgrimage with a 17th-century church. The road then winds down to *Turckheim,* a picturesque old wine town. *Colmar* is only a few miles farther east (see page 90).

If you opt to go directly from Remiremont to Mulhouse, continue southeast on N 66. The road ascends the valley of the Moselle, which becomes ever narrower as you climb. You will pass through the town of *Le Thillot,* famous for its weaving, and *Saint-Maurice-sur-Moselle,* which originally was a station on the ancient Roman road between Basle and Metz. The road continues its ascent. Near the summit of a mountain called the Ballon d'Alsace there is a magnificent view of the whole range of the Vosges, the Jura, and the Black Forest. When the weather is especially clear (rarely in the summer) you can see the Alps from here. Continue through the resort town

of *Bussang* and the *Col de Bussang.* N 66 descends through a beautiful ravine of rocks and trees in a series of switchbacks to the valley of the Thur River. You will soon arrive at the town of **Thann** (population 9,000), which is situated at the entrance of the Thur Valley. The most important Gothic church in Alsace after the Strasbourg cathedral is located here. It is the *Collégiale Saint-Thiébaut,* built from 1332–1498. The tower—76 meters (250 feet) high—was completed in 1519. Especially noteworthy are the *main portal* and the north *side portal* and, inside, the **choir stalls** and the *windows.* Thann also marks the beginning of the Route du Vin d'Alsace which winds its way north toward Strasbourg (see Travel Route 1 D).

Route N 66 continues through the plain of the Upper Rhine to the end of this Travel Route, **Mulhouse** (population 114,000, nearly 250,000 including the suburbs), an important industrial city that specializes in the manufacture of woolen and cotton cloth, printed linens, and muslin. The city has been a part of France since 1798.

Sights worth seeing include the *Place de la Réunion,* surrounded by the modern city, and the lovely rebuilt *church of Saint-Étienne,* with beautiful stained-glass windows dating from the 14th century. Across from the church is the *Hôtel de Ville* which was built in 1552 and is the most notable relic of old Mulhouse. Its walls are covered with murals painted in 1698 and restored many times (the last restoration took place in 1968). This building houses the *Musée Historique,* which displays a charming and varied collection of items from the area.

The *Musée des Beaux-Arts,* housed in an old merchant's town-house at 4 Place des Bonnes-Gens, contains paintings by Peter Brueghel the Younger, along with works of Alsatian artists. The *Musée de l'Impression sur Étoffes* on the Rue des Bonnes-Gens has displays of the whole process and history of printing on cloth, as well as many examples of the rich and colorful late 18th-century materials that were manufactured here.

If you love cars, don't miss the remarkable collection of over 450 automobiles in the *Musée National de l'Automobile* at 192 Avenue de Colmar, northwest of the center of the city. The *Musée Français du Chemin de Fer,* with an impressive collection of locomotives (some dating back to 1844), dining cars, and coaches, is located west of the city in the suburb of Dornach.

TRAVEL ROUTE 1 D: **The Vosges Route (244/311 km.; 152/193 miles)

See color map.

This route rambles leisurely through picturesque Alsace from Strasbourg to Belfort, including detours to some of the loveliest spots in the southern Vosges. It generally follows the eastern edge of the mountains as far as Colmar, touching several wine towns along the Route du Vin d'Alsace, and then runs south along the Route des Crêtes to Belfort.

As you leave Strasbourg (see page 75) Route D 392 takes you across the plain of the Upper Rhine for 21 km. (13 miles) to the outskirts of *Dorlisheim.* There you turn left onto a secondary road and follow it for 4 km. (2.5 miles) to the wine-making village of ***Rosheim** (population 3,500). The Roman-esque **church of Saint-Peter-et-Saint-Paul* (12th century) has an eight-sided tower dating from the 14th century. The 12th-century *Maison de Païen* (pagan house), located on the west end of the Grande Rue, is thought to be the oldest stone house in Alsace. Continue on the secondary road to ***Obernai** (population 9,500), a quintessential Alsatian town that was once the residence of the dukes of Alsace. The town's most famous native is Sainte-Odile, a duke's daughter who was born blind in the seventh century.

In the ****market square,* un-changed since the 16th century is the **Six Bucket-Well* (1579). Sur-rounding the square are the **Hôtel de Ville* (1523); the Gothic *chapel* *tower*; and the *corn market build-ing* (1554), which houses a museum of local history.

From Obernai you drive directly on Route N 422 through the foothills of the Vosges by way of the wine market town of Barr to *Sélestat* (23 km.; 14 miles)—or take a delightful detour west on secondary roads for 50 km. (31 miles) through the village of Klingenthal, known for the production of swords and rapiers, to ****Mont Sainte-Odile.** The convent located here at this wooded ridge was founded in the seventh century by Sainte-Odile, the patron saint of Alsace, who was said to have miraculously received sight at her baptism. The convent burned to the ground in 1546 but was subsequently rebuilt.

The ridge, at an elevation of 750 meters (2,460 feet), provides a great **view of the plain of the Upper Rhine and the Black Forest. Mont Sainte-Odile has been a fortress of refuge since prehistoric times. The remains of the "pagan wall," a Celtic work that is more than 10 km. (6 miles) long, surrounds the ridge.

Leaving Mont Sainte-Odile the road passes through a magnificent forest for 10 km. (6 miles) to the summer resort of *Le Hohwald.* From there it is another 8 km. (5 miles) through a wooded ravine to **Andlau** (population 2,000), where there is a restored Romanesque church dating from the 9th–11th centuries. The road returns to the plain for 17 km. (11 miles) to the town of **Sélestat**

(population 18,000). Of significance in the old quarter are the Romanesque **Église Sainte-Foy* (12th century) with its 43-meter- (141-foot-) high tower; the Gothic *Église Saint Georges* (13th–15th century), with a rose window (14th century) and a Renaissance pulpit dating from 1552; and the *chapter house* of the abbey of Ebersmunster, with a Renaissance portal from the 16th century. Near Sainte-Foy is the *Biblioteque Humaniste,* which includes the library of Beatus Rhenanus, Humanist scholar and friend of Erasmus. The collection includes more than 2,000 manuscripts and incunabula.

From Sélestat drive west 12.5 km. (8 miles) to ****Haut-Koenigsbourg,** the largest fortress in Alsace. Originally built in the 12th century, it was destroyed and rebuilt many times. In 1900, when Alsace was part of Germany (1870–1918), the fortress was restored by Kaiser Wilhelm II to look like a late-Medieval building. From the ramparts—750 meters (2,460 feet) high—there is a fine **view to the Kaiserstuhl mountains.

The next town on the Vosges Route is **Ribeauvillé** (population 5,000), which is famous for its wine. Looming over the town are the ruins of three citadels that date from the 11th–14th centuries. Among its many interesting old houses, the most notable are the 16th-century **Ave Maria House* (also known as the *Pfifferhüs*) in the Grande Rue. Ribeauvillé's wine market takes place in July and Pfeiffertag (Musician's Day), the first Sunday in September, ushers in a week-long folklife festival.

Just 5 km. (3 miles) farther south is the popular and picturesque wine-making town of **Riquewihr** (population 1,400), which has changed little since the 16th century. Its attractions include the charming half-timbered houses of the local gentry; the old city walls; the *Dolder* (1291), one of the finest tower gates of the Middle Ages, which now houses a museum; the *Thieves Tower,* with its torture chamber; and the castle of the dukes of Württemberg (now a postal museum). Riquewihr hosts a Reisling festival in August, followed by a two-weekend wine festival in September.

From Riquewihr it is only 11 km. (6.5 miles) to the lovely and interesting city of *Colmar* (see page 90). You can also proceed

Ribeauvillé: "Pfifferhus"

directly to *Kaysersberg* (see page 89), another town on the Route du Vin d'Alsace, where you may join Travel Route 1 B. Another worthwhile journey will take you from Kaysersberg to the Col du Bonhomme, the beginning of the **Route des Crêtes where the road runs on the west side of the ridge. At the *Col du Louchbach,* 5 km. (3 miles) south of the Col du Bonhomme, a side road goes off to the left for 5 km. (3 miles) to the lovely *Lac Blanc and *Lac Noir.

The Route des Crêtes intersects the road from Colmar to *Gérardmer* at the *Col de la Schlucht,* described as an alternative route to Travel Route 1 C on page 93. The **section of the Route des Crêtes from the Col de la Schlucht to the Grand Ballon mountain is particularly beautiful. For 30 km. (18.5 miles) the road curves in wide arcs through upland pastures, past the peak of Hohneck to *Le Markstein,* a summer and winter resort 1,200 meters (3,937 feet) high. Here the Route des Crêtes, still following the contour of the ridge, turns almost due east and after 7 km. (4.5 miles) comes to Grand Ballon, at 1,424 meters (4,671 feet), the highest peak in the Vosges. From the road there is a path leading to the summit (the climb takes about a 15 minutes).

The road descends 6 km. (3.5 miles) to *Col Amie* at an elevation of 825 meters (2,707 feet) where it divides. Both roads lead to Belfort: one by way of Vieil-Armand and Cernay, the other through Bussang and Ballon d'Alsace.

The Route des Crêtes is the eastern fork at Col Amie, where it continues straight and begins to climb again. After 5 km. (3 miles) you will see on the left the national monument at *Vieil Armand* (or Hartmannsweilerkopf), the most disputed and fought-over piece of land in Alsace during World War I. Of the 60,000 men who fell here some 12,000 could not be identified. Their remains lie in the crypt of the war memorial, which is surrounded by a military cemetery. If you climb to the top of the rise above the cemetery you can still distinguish trenches and shell holes.

From here, the Route des Crêtes drops down to *Cernay,* an industrial city heavily damaged in both world wars, and ends at route N 83. Follow this road south 35 km. (21 miles) to the fortress town of Belfort.

If you opt to take the other road at Col Amie, it branches to the right and leads into the Thur Valley to Route N 66. Follow N 66 to *Saint-Maurice-sur-Moselle* and make a sharp left turn onto Route D 465. This road runs through the forest, then over pasture land for about 10 km. (6 miles) to the mountain known as the Ballon d'Alsace. The pass is a watershed; one side drains to the North Sea, the other to the Mediterranean. From the pass it is a 30-minute climb to the summit (elevation 1,250 meters; 4,100 feet) where you are rewarded with a superb *view in all directions. At the top of the pass is the *Monument à la

Mémoire des Démineurs (memorial to the bomb disposal troops).

Route D 465 descends the mountain in switchbacks with wonderful views to the south. It then proceeds on a flatter course to *Giromagny* (population 3,200). A road to the right leads to *Ronchamp,* famous for Nôtre-Dame-du-Haut, a chapel designed by Le Corbusier in 1955. From Giromagny it is another 12 km. (7.5 miles) to **Belfort** (population 58,000), the birthplace of more generals than any other city in France.

Since ancient times there has been a fortress in Belfort to bar the Burgundian Gate, the swath of lowlands that divides the Vosges in the north from the Jura mountains in the south. The Trouée de Belfort (Belfort Gap), has been a route for migrating peoples and marching armies through the ages. It was closed for two centuries after the great military engineer Vauban (1633–1707) built a fortification in Belfort after the city was conquered by France in 1648. So well did he do his work that when in 1870 the *citadel* was bombarded by 200 pieces of heavy artillery, the city held out for 103 days and capitulated only after the armistice was concluded. This gallant resistance achieved two things for Belfort: Bismarck's decision not to annex the city and the ensuing flood of Alsatians that streamed into this "free zone" and laid the groundwork for its industrial growth.

In 1878, Auguste Barholdi created the red-sandstone *Lion of Belfort,* a grim-looking lion 22 meters (72 feet) long and 11 meters (36 feet) high. From the platform at the lion's feet there is a marvelous view of the city and the Vosges mountains.

TRAVEL ROUTE 2: Mons–Compiègne–***Paris (245 km.; 152 miles)

See map on page 100.

This Travel Route begins at Mons, just over the Belgian border, and takes you south to Paris. Along the way you can visit historic cities such as Saint-Quentin and Noyan, as well as Compiègne and its great château.

The city of Mons in Belgium lies only 12 km. (7.5 miles) north of the French border. Cross the border and take Route N 2 to the industrial city of *Maubeuge* (population 40,000) on the Sambre River. The town, heavily damaged during World War II, was rebuilt in an exemplary modern style, but its best feature is still the *Ports de Mons,* the handsome 17th-century city gate.

Route N 2 continues south through *Avesnes-sur-Helpe,* site of a former fortress, to *La Capelle.* Here you can pick up Route N 29 through *Guise,* an ancient town on the Oise River with a brick citadel from the 16th century to ***Saint-Quentin** (population 75,000). Named after the martyr Quintinus, who was beheaded here in the third century, Saint-Quentin was a renowned weaving city in the Middle Ages. Philip II built the monastic castle of *El Escorial* in Madrid in commemoration of his victory in a battle here in 1557,

and the town was later part of the dowry of Mary, Queen of Scots. The town was badly damaged when German divisions broke through the British front on March 21, 1918, during the Second Battle of the Somme.

The *Hôtel de Ville* has a magnificent Flamboyant **façade* (1509) and a tower with 37 bells that can be heard in carillon. The bones of Quintinus lie in an 11th-century crypt in the spacious *collegiate church of Saint-Quentin* (13th–15th century), with rose windows and a transept that is divided by a double ambulatory. A fine collection of 87 pastel portraits by Maurice-Quentin de la Tour (1704–1788), a native of the town, as well as other 18th-century French paintings are on display in the *Musée Lucuyer,* while the *Musée d'Entomologie* houses one of the biggest butterfly collections in Europe.

From Saint-Quentin follow route D 930 for 20 km. (12.5

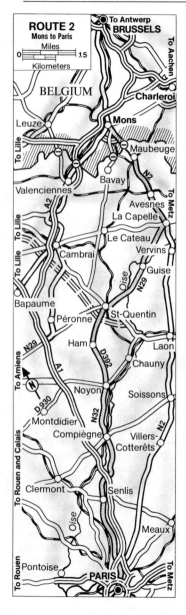

ROUTE 2
Mons to Paris

miles) to **Ham** (population 4,300), where, in a ruined 15th-century castle, Napoleon III was held captive from 1840 to 1846. He escaped by disguising himself as a workman. The *church of Nôtre-Dame* dates from the 12th and 13th centuries. From Ham, Route D 932 proceeds to ***Noyon** (population 15,000). This historic city, birthplace of the reformer John Calvin (1509–1564), is graced by a particularly beautiful example of Transitional architecture, the ****cathedral of Nôtre Dame** (12th–13th century), which combines the sober earthbound strength of Romanesque style with the lighter and more daring grace of the Gothic style. Except for some later additions, construction of the cathedral was completed in 70 years. Worth noting are the rounded-off *transept, the wide vestibule formed by incorporating the bases of the towers, the adjoining *chapter hall, the Gothic *cloister, and a 16th-century *library.

Like so many other towns in this battle-scarred region of the Somme, Noyon lay in ruins after aerial bombardments at the end of World War I. In 1940, during World War II, it was the scene of violent fighting in its streets, and it was bombarded again before finally being liberated by American troops in 1944.

From Noyon, Route N 32 follows the north bank of the Oise for 24 km. (15 miles) to ***Compiègne** (population 45,000), on the northwestern edge of the majestic 14,500-hectare (35,800-acre) oak and beech forest, *Font de Compiègne*. Compiègne gets it name from the Gallo-Roman fortified camp of *Compendium* that once guarded the crossing of the Oise. Since the fifth century it was a favorite spot of French monarchs who would visit Compiègne after being crowned at Reims. Charles VII came to Compiègne in the company of Joan of Arc, who was captured and imprisoned here a year later.

Louis XV, eager to escape the pompous and stultifying court life of Versailles, commissioned architect Ange Gabriel to replace the old palace of Charles V. Although curiously static, the Neoclassical **château* he built from 1751 to 1788 is, after Versailles and Fountainbleau, one of the great palaces of the French monarchs. The scene of dazzling court feasts up to the time of Napoleon III, the château also served as a backdrop for the first meetings between Louis XVI and Marie Antoinette (1770) as well as those of Napoleon I and Marie-Louise (1810), who were married in the large ballroom. Eugénie and Napoleon III found it congenial for their extravagant weekend parties. Many of the apartments are open to the public. The intriguing ***Musée de la Voiture et du Tourisme* adjoining the château offers a large collection of vintage vehicles you won't see on any modern highways, including many carriages and coaches, early bicycles and cars, a 1900 Renault and a 1907 de Dion limousine.

Inhabited since the Stone Age and still bearing traces of Druid sacrifices, this area has borne witness to more than its share of momentous events. Among the most important of these was the signing of the armistice of November 11, 1918, which brought an end to World War I. The document was signed in the railway saloon car of Marshal Foch in a forest clearing 5 km. (3 miles) outside of Compiègne. In 1940 Hitler gleefully humiliated the French by having them sign terms of surrender in the same carriage, then destroyed the railway car. A reproduction of the historic car stands in place of the original and you must pay a fee to enter.

A detour (14 km.; 8.7 miles) from Compiègne takes you to the enormous bulk of the **Château de Pierrefonds* (1407), long considered an outstanding example of Medieval military architecture, although some recent critics have deplored Viollet-le-Duc's scholarly "restorations" of the mid-19th century. After another 17 km. (10.5 miles) you come to the little Romanesque *church of Morienval*, built on ancient Roman foundations. The detour past *Champlieu*, an important site for Roman and Gallic excavations that include a 4,000 seat coliseum, leads back to Route D 932.

From Champlieu continue 32 km. (20 miles) on D 932 A to ***Senlis** (population 15,000), surrounded by splendid beech forest.

Starting as a Gallo-Roman settlement, the town developed into an important religious center as early as the third century. The *cathedral of Nôtre-Dame* was built in 1155–1191. In 1240 a magnificent **spire was added to the tower on the right. Of special interest is the main **portal whose 13th-century scenes from the life of the Virgin Mary signaled a trend that earned for the period the label "Century of the Virgin." A triforium gallery, some splendid vaulting, and a chapter house with 14th-century glass, are also notable. In the old town surrounding the cathedral there are many fine old houses, particularly in the *Rue du Châtel* and the *Rue de la Treille,* and fragments of the ancient Gallo-Roman walls that once enclosed them. Remains of an enormous 10,000 seat Roman arena, located west of the town, provide a good indication of the area's prominence in ancient times.

From Senlis it is 44 km. (27 miles) to *Paris* on either Route N 17 or the Autoroute A 1 (enter by the Porte de la Villette or the Porte de la Chapelle). Left of the autoroute in *Roissy-en-France* is the big Parisian airport, *Charles-de-Gaulle,* known locally as "Roissy."

TRAVEL ROUTE 3: Dunkerque–***Paris (274 km.; 170 miles)

See map on page 105.

If you are travelling from Great Britain to France, you may take a ferry to Dunkerque on the northwest coast. The trip southeast to Paris will take you through Flanders and the northern regions to the cathedral city of Amiens, as well as to Chantilly, with its fabulous château.

Dunkerque and Paris both lie at 0 degree longitude on the Greenwich Meridian, and a traveller between the two cities heads either due south or due north. You have a choice of two routes. You can either take the Dunkerque-Lille expressway (A 25) and connect with the Autoroute du Nord (A 1) in Lille or follow the national highways through Amiens to Paris.

Dunkerque (48,000 population), in 1940 the scene of the extraordinary and valiant rescue of 350,000 British and French soldiers from the advancing German army, was almost completely destroyed in World War II. This historic event is re-created with models and audio-visual installations in the *Musée des Beaux-Arts,* which also contains a large collection of ship models and some good paintings. The town has another museum, the *Musée d'Art Contemporain,* and there is also an *aquarium.* France's northernmost town, its third port, and the terminus for cross-Channel ferries,

Dunkerque takes its name (Dune Church) from the church in the dunes, *Nôtre-Dame-des-Dunes* (16th century), which stands to the northeast on the road to the seaside resort of *Malo-les-Bains.* Malo's esplanade, the *Dique de Mer,* runs for 2 km. (1 mile) along a sandy beach. The French maritime hero Jean Bart (1651–1702) was born in Dunkerque.

From Dunkerque, Route D 916 takes you 9 km. (5.6 miles) to **Bergues** (population 5,000), which has fortified towers, moats, and monumental city gates that still make it look like the strongly fortified, Medieval Flemish city it once was. Two towers of the *abbey of Saint-Winoc* (11th century) have been preserved and the city *museum* has several noteworthy paintings by Flemish and French painters.

From Bergues, it is another 18 km. (11.2 miles) on Route D 916 to **Cassel** (population 2,900), situated on a hill 175 meters (575 feet) above the great plain of Picardy. The splendid view from the castle esplanade extends all the way to Dunkerque and Ghent. The brick-built *church of Nôtre-Dame* dates from 1298.

Route D 916 continues through *Hazebrouck* to **Lillers** (population 9,500), with a much-restored Romanesque church that houses a famous *wooden crucifix* (12th century). The 12th-century Artesian well in the courtyard of the old Dominican monastery is said to have been the first such well in France. Route D 916 then continues through the old market town of *Saint-Pol-sur-Ternoise* and on to *Doullens,* where the Allies gave Marshall Foch the supreme command of the Western Front in March 1918. The former town hall, dating from the 15th to the 17th centuries, has a graceful belfry, and an ancient convent is now the *Musée Lombart,* housing local antiquities and paintings. The road goes on to *Talmas.* About 3 km. (2 miles) west of the town, near *Naours,* there is a "city of refuge" 35 meters (115 feet) underground that was laid out in the ninth century as a hiding place from marauding Normans. An area of 2 km. (1.5 miles) of subterranean streets, storerooms, and chapels has been excavated.

At this point, you are only 16 km. (10 miles) from ***Amiens** (population 128,000), the capital of Picardy. Its ****cathedral of** *Nôtre-Dame,* the largest church in France, is considered a Gothic masterpiece. The dimensions of the cathedral, built from 1220–1270, are overwhelming: The length of the nave is 145 meters (476 feet); the vault is 42 meters (138 feet) high; the rose window measures 13.5 meters (44 feet) in diameter; the tower extends to a height of 113 meters (371 feet). The entire structure was restored by Viollet-le-Duc in the mid-19th century. During World War I the exterior was protected by sandbags and escaped serious damage even though it was struck by nine shells.

The finest section of the **west façade has three **portals with rich statuary, including the

**Beau Dieu, a Christ figure on the central pillar of the main portal. A colossal statue of Saint Christopher blesses travellers from the south façade.

The interior of the cathedral is dazzling for the graceful and light-saturated simplicity of its enormous space. Windows occupy almost half the total height. An old saying has it that "the choir of Beauvais, the nave of Amiens, the portal of Reims, and the towers of Chartres would together form the finest church in the world." Be sure to examine the **choir stalls dating from the early 16th century and reputed to be the most beautiful in France. The wrought-iron grill screen from the 18th century, and the **Vierge Dorée, the often copied Golden Madonna surrounded by angels on the central pillar of the south portal of the transept, are also noteworthy. Three rose windows glow with a rich display of glass; the groined vaulting of 1270 in the transepts is the earliest in France.

Amiens also has a fine collection of paintings in the *Musée de Picardie, ranging from Frans Hals to Salvador Dali, with almost everyone in-between represented. The collection includes 15 pictures (15th to 16th century) from the Puy Notre Dame d'Amiens, a pious fraternity that established competitions among poets and painters. The palatial Maison de la Culture is a legacy of the 1960s, when de Gaulle's culture minister, André Malraux, had a chain of such arts centers built throughout the country. You can also explore the curious Hortillonnages in the eastern suburbs, a low-lying area of market-gardens and orchards on a series of canals. Pierre Choderlos de Laclos (1741–1803), author of the notorious Les Liaisons Dangereuses was a native of Amiens, and Jules Verne (1828–1905) spent most of his life here.

From Amiens Route D 916 continues to Beauvais, with its large, unfinished **cathedral of Saint-Pierre (see page 107). A museum immediately west of the cathedral has a collection of objects saved from its previous site, which was destroyed in 1940. The church of Saint-Étienne is built in two distinct styles, and reveals a striking contrast between the restored Romanesque nave and the late-Gothic choir (1506). Also worth seeing is the Galerie de la Tapisserie, where finely woven tapestries of wool and silk were produced well into the 19th century. From Beauvais you can proceed directly to Paris on Route N 1 or make a loop through Clermont on the Breche River and Creil on the Oise River on Route N 31 to ***Chantilly** (population 12,500), a lovely small city well known for its horseraces, which have been held here since 1836, and for the fabulous ***Château de Chantilly,** which came into the possession of the Montmorency family in 1484. The Petit Château of 1560 and the Grand Château rebuilt in 1876–1882, stand on two islands in the middle of a lake stocked with carp, are connected and surrounded by a beautifully parterred

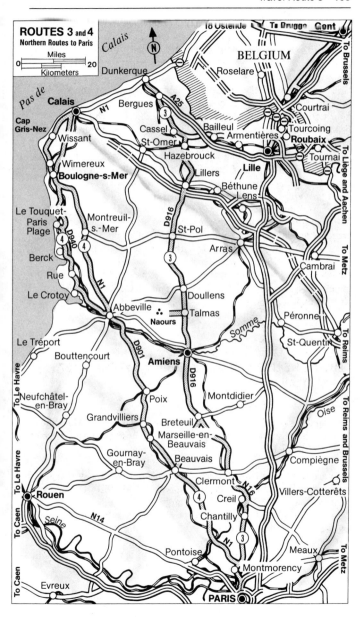

ROUTES 3 and 4
Northern Routes to Paris

Miles
0 ————————— 20
Kilometers

To Ostende   To Brugge   Gent

Calais

BELGIUM

Dunkerque

Roselare

Pas de Calais

Calais   N1   Bergues   Cassel

Cap Gris-Nez

Wissant

Wimereux

Boulogne-s.-Mer

Courtrai

Tourcoing

Bailleul   Armentières   **Roubaix**

St-Omer

Hazebrouck

Tournai

Lillers

Lille

Béthune

Lens

Le Touquet-
Paris
Plage

Montreuil-
s.-Mer

St-Pol

Berck

Arras

Cambrai

Rue

Le Crotoy

Abbeville

Doullens

Talmas

Naours

Péronne

Somme

St-Quentin

Le Tréport

Bouttencourt

Amiens

Neufchâtel-
en-Bray

Poix

Montdidier

Oise

Grandvilliers

Breteuil

Marseille-en-
Beauvais

Compiègne

Gournay-
en-Bray

Beauvais

Clermont

Villers-Cotterêts

Rouen

Creil

Chantilly

Meaux

Seine   N14

Pontoise

Montmorency

Evreux

PARIS

To Brussels

To Liège and Aachen

To Metz

To Reims

To Reims and Brussels

To Metz

To Le Havre

To Le Havre

To Caen

To Caen

park designed by Le Nôtre. In the Grand Château Molière's *Les Précieuses Ridicules* was given for the first time in 1659. Excess has always been the order of the day here. A maître d'hôtel committed suicide in 1671 because he thought the fish would be late for a Friday night dinner to be attended by Louis XIV. The world-famous *Musée Condée* is housed in the apartments of the Petit Château and is magnificently decorated with **paintings* by Raphael and Filippino Lippi (around 1457–1504) and 40 ***miniatures* by the great French painter Jean Fouquet (1420–1480), done for the *Book of Hours* of the Dukes of Berry. On display in the Jewel Room is the huge pink diamond known as Le Grand Conde.

Don't miss the *Musée Vivant du Cheval*, or "living-horse museum," built under orders from Louis Henri, Prince de Condé, in 1912. The hall, which has stable room for 240 horses and 420 dogs for stag and boar hunts in the nearby forest, is 186 meters (200 feet) long. There are dressage performances daily in the rotunda and an exciting cross-country competition is held every fall in the nearby Parc de Sylvie.

The splendid Renaissance **château of Ecouen* (1530–1551), which serves as home to the Legion of Honor, lies almost on the edge of Paris on Route N 16.

On its approach to Paris, N 16 passes through *Saint-Denis,* with its famous Gothic ***basilica* (see page 54).

TRAVEL ROUTE 4: ***Paris–Boulogne–Calais (275 km.; 171 miles)

See map on page 105.

This route crosses the Picardy region through Beauvais and Abbeville to the seaside resorts and port towns dotting the northernmost stretch of France's Channel coast.

Leaving Paris through the Porte de la Chapelle and Avenue Président Wilson, you will come after 11 km. (6.8 miles) to the suburb of **Saint-Denis** (population 110,000). The **Basilica of Saint-Denis* (see page 54) is well worth a visit. It provides a concentrated lesson in French history. This Gothic cathedral stands on the site of a church and abbey that were founded in the fifth century and built over the saint's grave. The structure was rebuilt in the eighth century, looted during the Revolution, and finally restored in the mid-19th century. It houses many of the *gisants* (tombs with reclining statues) of the kings and queens of France including Louis

XVI, Marie Antoinette and Catherine de Médicis. Saint-Denis is easily accessible by the Paris Métro (the Saint-Denis Basilique stop) and is a pleasant day trip from the city.

You can bypass Saint-Denis to the east on Route N 1. As you cross the Oise River, the countryside might seem familiar. The area around the tiny village of *Auvers,* although a favorite subject of artists such as Cézanne, Corot, Daumier, and Pissarro, is most closely associated with Vincent Van Gogh, who died and is buried in the town.

The 17th-century *Château de Nointel* lies between Saint-Denis and Beauvais. The gardens, painted by Jean Honoré Fragonard, have been restored and the castle is open to visitors. Route N 1 crosses the Oise River near *Beaumont-sur-Oise* through *Île-de-France* and continues for some 66 km. (41 miles) to ***Beauvais** (population 55,000). This town was virtually leveled in World War II bombing attacks, but has been largely rebuilt. While the nearby houses exploded into rubble, the magnificent *******cathedral of Saint-Pierre* somehow survived. It was planned as the largest church in 13th century France and, indeed, the vaulted roof soars as high as 43 meters (141 feet)—higher than that of Nôtre-Dame in Paris. However, the ambitiously conceived façades proved too delicate, and in 1284, a portion of the choir collapsed—at 48 meters (157 feet) it had been the tallest choir ever

built. A 153 meter- (502 foot-) high tower was built in 1569, but it toppled in 1573. Nevertheless, construction continued for the next two centuries and the results are breathtaking.

Note the Renaissance doors of carved oak, the work of Jean le Pot, and the jewellike beauty of the rose windows. Tapestries from the Gobelin factory, founded in Beauvais in 1664, are on display. At the north portal you will see the famous astronomical clock made in 1866 which is a duplicate of the one in Strasbourg. The work of local craftsmen, it has 52 dials and 90,000 parts. Figures appear on the hour with a representation of the Last Judgment visible at noon. The Basse-Oeuvre, a portion of the original cathedral dating from the tenth century, is incorporated into the transept.

East of the cathedral is the *Galérie Nationale de la Tapisserie* featuring exhibits of the intricate needlework. West of the cathedral are two towers that mark the entrance to a *museum* housed in the former Palais de Justice. It displays a variety of tapestries, Medieval sculptures, ceramics, local archaeological finds, and paintings (including works by Delacroix and Sisley).

The Gothic and Romanesque *church of Saint-Étienne* has a rose window of the Wheel of Fortune in the north transept.

Route D 901 proceeds from *Beauvais* through *Marseille-en-Beauvais* and *Grandvilliers* for 44 km. (27 miles) to the town of *Poix.*

Continue another 42 km. (26 miles) across the plateau of Picardy (keep an eye out for windmills) and over the Somme River to the port town of **Abbeville** (population 25,000). Although the town was leveled by bombs in World War II and has been rebuilt, several buildings remained intact, including the late-Gothic *church of Saint-Vulfran.* Beyond the Renaissance door panels, you can walk in the steps of Mary Tudor and Louis XII who were married in the church in 1514. The 18th-century *Château de la Bagatelle,* decorated in the period style, is open to visitors.

Two routes lead north to Calais from Abbeville. The faster inland highway N 1 passes through the citadel town of *Montreuil-sur-Mer.* The ramparts of the citadel are still intact and provide a grand view of the area. N 1 continues for 80 km. (50 miles) through rolling countryside to *Boulogne-sur-Mer* and from there 34 km. (21 miles) more to Calais (see page 109).

Coastal route D 940 is a more languorous journey. It runs along the Soame River to the *Baie de Somme* and to the small seaside resort of **Le Crotoy.** The writer Jules Verne lived here from 1865 to 1870 at number 9 on the street named in his honor. The road cuts back inland to the little town of **Rue** (population 3,000). It has the lovely late-Gothic *Chapelle du Saint-Esprit,* built in the 15th–16th centuries. Because the town is situated on a marsh, bird-watching is particularly good.

About 19 km. (12 miles) farther along, the road comes to the first of the large seaside resorts on the Pas de Calais (known across the Channel as the Straits of Dover): **Berck-Plage** (population 20,000), where the large **Hôpital Maritime* of the city of Paris is located.

Continue north 18 km. (11 miles) to ***Le Touquet-Paris-Plage** (population 5,000; 60,000 in the summer), a fashionable summer resort since the 19th century. Lighthouses guard the bay formed by the mouth of the Canche River. Hotels, health spas, shops, and restaurants line the waterfront, and spectacular villas sit back among the birch and pine trees. An airport provides a 20-minute air shuttle to England. The route continues for 39 km. (24 miles) through the fishing port of *Étaples,* past the resort town of *Hardelot-Plage,* to **Boulogne-sur-Mer** (population 55,000). Both Julius Caesar (in 55 B.C.) and Napoleon (in 1803) studied the far coastline from this vantage point while they contemplated adding England to their empires. Boulogne is principally a fishing port and fish-processing center. The modern *port* was rebuilt after having been the target of repeated bombing raids during World War II. The *"upper town"* is surrounded by the **ramparts* of a Medieval castle. The *Nôtre-Dame Basilica,* remarkable for its enormous domed roof, houses an 11th-century crypt and the ruins of a third-century Roman temple. The

Musée des Beaux-Arts has a fine collection of *Greek vases*. The "*lower town*" has a pleasant shopping district.

As you leave Boulogne on the **coast road (Route D 940) toward Calais, you will pass on your right the 53-meter- (174-foot-) high *Colonne de la Grande Armée*, a memorial to the camp Napoleon set up here from which he launched his ill-fated attempt to take England. The scenic road climbs to the top of the cliffs and continues through the small resort towns of *Wimereux* (where you may enjoy a fabulous view of Boulogne), *Ambleteuse*, with an old fort designed by military architect Vauban, and *Audresselles*.

About 2 km. (1.3 miles) past Audresselles, a side road branches off for 3.5 km. (2 miles) to *Cap Gris-Nez* where the English Channel joins the North Sea. On a clear day, you can look beyond the 24-meter (79-foot) lighthouse and get a marvelous **view of the famous white chalk cliffs of Dover.

The road now descends toward *Wissant* and its sandy beach. This was the site of the ancient port of Itius where, in 55 B.C., Julius Caesar and his legions set sail to conquer England.

**Cap Blanc-Nez* lies 6 km. (3.7 miles) beyond Wissant. Its chalk cliffs offer the highest vantage point for a beautiful view of the English coast. The road then winds down toward *Sangatte* as the craggy cliffs level into the Flemish plain. En route, you pass

the monument to Blériot who made the first Channel crossing in an airplane in 1909. The road continues 10 km. (6 miles) to **Calais** (population 80,000), a terminus of cross-Channel ferries and the aeroglisseurs (hovercraft) to ports in England. The city is divided into Calais-Nord, the older maritime section lying between the harbor and the Citadel, and Calais-Sud (Saint-Pierre), the textile manufacturing district. Auguste Rodin's monument to **the Burghers of Calais* (1894) stands opposite the Parc Saint-Pierre, in front of the Hôtel de Ville. It depicts a group of prominent citizens leaving the city as hostages of King Edward III during his seige of Calais in 1347. The English maintained control until 1558. The city was a British base during World War I and endured repeated bombing raids during both World Wars. The port has been rebuilt since 1944. The *Tour de Guet,* a watch-tower, was

Rodin's "The Burghers of Calais"

built in 1224, then used as a light-house until the mid-19th century. The *Musée des Beaux Arts et de la Dentelle* in the Parc Richelieu has a collection of watercolors and lace (lace and other textiles are produced in Calais).

From Calais, it is 36 km. (22 miles) along Route N 1 to *Dunkerque* (see page 102).

TRAVEL ROUTE 5: ***Paris–*Rouen–Le Havre–Le Treport (230/312 km.; 143/194 miles)

See map on page 112.

Although decidedly agricultural, Normandy is also a region that bustles with industry and bears the marks of a rich history. All facets of Normandy can be sampled along this travel route as you pass through some of its most charming towns and fishing villages, handsome châteaux and majestic cathedrals, as well as the important cities of Rouen and Le Havre.

This Travel Route offers three different routes that connect Paris and Rouen: an expressway, the *Autoroute de Normandie* (A 13); the national highway (N 14); and the departmental roads that follow the course of the Seine.

Paris to Rouen on the Autoroute

Follow the route marked "1" on the map.

You can leave Paris either through the Porte Maillot or through the Porte de Saint-Cloud. The two routes intersect in Saint-Cloud, after you cross the Seine and get on the *Autoroute de Normandie* (A 13). Soon thereafter the expressway enters a long tunnel. It crosses the *Marly forest* and links up with Route N 15 in *Louviers,* situated on the bank of the Eure River. N 15 crosses the Seine on the *Pont-de-l'Arche,* a 410-meter- (quarter-mile-) long bridge, and follows the river for 10 km. (6 miles) to Rouen (138 km.; 86 miles from Paris).

Paris to Rouen via Route N 14

Follow the route marked "2" on the map.

Route N 14 leaves Paris through the Porte de Clignancourt and proceeds in a northeasterly direction towards **Pontoise,** a charming ancient city on the banks of the Oise River. Despite serious damage during World War II, Pontoise retains its historical appeal. Amid the red-roofed houses sits the *church of Saint-Maclou* with its early-Gothic choir and exquisite 16th-century stained-glass windows. The *Tavet-Delacour Museum* is within the walls of a turreted mansion and features sculptures ranging from the late Gothic period through the 18th century. The *Pissarro Museum* features paintings by the artist who once lived here. The road then heads directly northeast passing through *Magny-en-Vexin, Ecouis, Fleury-sur-Andelle,* and *Boos* before reaching Rouen (123 km.; 76 miles from Paris).

Paris to Rouen through the Seine Valley

Follow the route marked "3" on the map.

At the beginning of this route, which passes through the most scenic areas of the Seine Valley, leave Paris and enter the Autoroute de Normandie (described above) and take it as far as **Mantes-la-Jolie** (population 44,000). The *church of Nôtre-Dame* (12th–13th centuries) is the "little twin" of the cathedral of Nôtre-Dame in Paris. The statuary embellishing the portals and the Navarre Chapel (14th century) is particularly noteworthy. The *Porte aux Prêtres* and the *Tour*

Saint-Maclou are the remains of the ancient fortifications that once defended the riverside city.

From Mantes, Route D 913 continues west along the left bank of the Seine. After 6 km. (3.7 miles) the road passes through *Rosny-sur-Seine,* the birthplace (1559) of the Duc de Sully, the finance minister of King Henri IV, who built his château here. The road then continues through *Bonnières.* Here you leave Route D 913 and take Route N 15 along the left bank of the Seine as far as the old city of **Vernon** (population 23,500). The city's architectural landmarks include the **church of Nôtre-Dame* (11th-14th centuries); the remains of a city fortress, the *Tour des Archives,* dating from the 12th century; the **ruins* of a Medieval bridge still span part of the Seine. Nearby is the **Tour des Tourelles* surrounded by some wood and stone houses dating from the 15th century. The Poulain Municipal Museum has exhibits of local history and artifacts as well as paintings by Monet.

Route D 313 continues along the right bank of the Seine through enchanting wooded areas offering a superb view of the Seine Valley. The ruins of a fortress, the **Château Gaillard,* are visible from the road. This castle was built in 1197 by King Richard the Lion-Hearted to guard the valley. The route continues through the Seine Valley to **Les Andelys,* birthplace of the painter Nicolas Poussin (1594–1665), crosses the river, and inter-

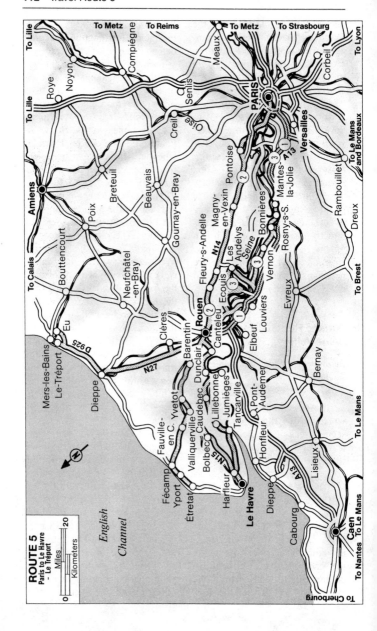

ROUTE 5
Paris to Le Havre
– Le Tréport

sects with Route N 14, the final leg to the ancient capital of the Duchy of Normandy, Rouen.

*Rouen

See map on page 114.

Including its suburbs, Rouen has a population of 400,000. This thriving port is the fourth-largest in France. It is 130 km. (81 miles) upriver from the mouth of the Seine at the Channel and 220 km. (137 miles) from Paris by the twisting path of the river. The old sections of the city have been very well restored and pedestrian malls have been added. The city is also a busy industrial center (particularly for textiles), and a cultural hub. The best way to become oriented is to drive 5 km. (3 miles) up the **Côte Sainte-Cathérine* on the southeastern side of the city to the *Corniche de Rouen*. From here, you get a splendid *view* of the neat grid of the city plan.

Originally a Roman settlement, Rouen was overrun by the Normans in 876. Their leader established the Duchy of Normandy here in 911. When the Norman William the Conqueror became king of England in 1066, Rouen suddenly belonged to England. It was held by England until 1204, and again from 1419 to 1449 during the Hundred Years War. Joan of Arc, the Maid of Orléans, was burned at the stake in the *Place du Vieux Marché* on May 30, 1431. By the 16th century, the brightly colored cotton fabric textiles pro-

duced here (called "Rouenneries") were being exported around the world. More than half of its Huguenot (Protestant) citizens left Rouen after the revocation of the Edict of Nantes in 1686. The city eventually revived its textile and faïence-ceramic industries in the 18th century and they continue to flourish. During World War II, Rouen was badly scarred in June 1940 by a citywide fire and, again, in 1944 by bombs. The port was rebuilt by 1949. Famous native sons include playwright Pierre Corneille (1606–1684), the painter Théoodore Géricault (1791–1824), and novelist Gustave Flaubert (1821–1880), creator of *Madame Bovary*.

Begin your tour of Rouen in the *Place du Vieux Marché* (1), site of the reconstructed market square. A cross 27 meters (88.5 feet) high marks the exact spot where Joan of Arc was burned alive. Archaeologists uncovered the site of the funeral pyre during the construction of the modern *church of Sainte-Jeanne d'Arc*. The church, built in 1979–1980, is in the shape of a capsized boat. The *Musée Jeanne d'Arc* is also on the square. A few steps to the south stands the **Hôtel de Bourgtheroulde** (2) with an *inner courtyard* (1501–1537) that is an attractive blend of late-Gothic and Renaissance architectural elements and details. Just to the east of the old market is the **Palais de Justice** (3), a Gothic masterpiece (1508–1509). Although damaged during World War II, the *façade* is magnifi-

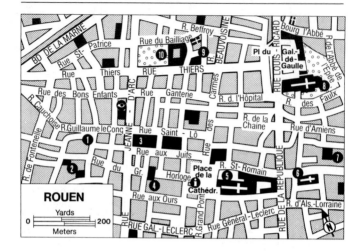

cent. Enigmatic Jewish relics found during excavations in 1976 date to the 12th century. One of the grand rooms within is nicknamed the Room of Lost Steps, because lawyers pace here waiting for their cases to be called. The Rue Thouret leads from the Palais de Justice to the bustling Rue du Gros-Horloge with its Renaissance pavilion. To the right stands the **Tour du Gros-Horloge** (4) consisting of a belfry (1389), a Renaissance arch (1525) that spans the street, and a large *clock* (1447). To the left of the clock tower is the ****Cathédrale Nôtre-Dame** (5), one of the great Gothic churches of France. Constructed between 1201 and 1530, the church reflects early-Gothic to late-Gothic styles. It might appear familiar for it was the subject of Monet's famous series of paintings depicting the variations of light on

the main *façade*. This splendid façade is representative of the late Flamboyant Gothic style. It is flanked by two towers of unequal height. The tower on the left is 82 meters (269 feet) high and dates from the 13th century. Here hangs the nine-and-a-half ton *Jeanne d'Arc Bell*. The *tower on the right is 77 meters (253 feet) high and was added between 1485 and 1507. It contains the 58-bell *carillon*. The cathedral's spire soars 151 meters (495 feet) high, the tallest church tower in France. The *Portail des Libraires,* the north portal, is the most richly designed of the transept portals, and features 150 "medaillons" depicting scenes from the Bible and from Medieval fables. Also of interest are the 51-meter (167-foot) *lantern* over the enormous transept and the chapel with the *tombs of the cardinals of Amboise.*

Behind the cathedral stands the **church of Saint-Maclou** (6) (1437–1581), a fine example of late-Gothic architecture. However, its lofty crossing tower was not added until 1688. The treasure inside is a rare Renaissance organ. Behind the church, to the northeast, is a half-timbered building known as the **Aître de Saint-Maclou** (7), which houses a crypt where citizens who died from the plague were buried throughout the Middle Ages. Note the morbid carvings in the wood beams. To the north is another Gothic masterpiece, the **church of Saint-Ouen** (8) (14th–15th centuries), with a crossing tower that is 82 meters (269 feet) high. Because of its crenelated top, it is called the "Crown of Normandy." From Saint-Ouen, proceed diagonally across the *Place-de-Gaulle* to the Rue Thiers. Here are two important museums, the *Musée le Secq des Tournelles* (9), with its intriguing collection of wrought-iron objects, and the **Musée des Beaux-Arts** (10), one of the best art museums in France. It houses a large collection of paintings from the 15th through the 20th centuries including works by Clouet, Poussin, Rubens, Velásquez, Fragonard, Ingres, Delacroix, Monet, Sisley, Renoir, and Dufy. In the *Musée de la Céramique* (1 Rue Faucon), you will find a fabulous collection of Rouen-crafted faïence. There are also smaller *museums* devoted to Corneille and Flaubert and the *Musée des Antiquités* within the walls of an old monastery, featuring relics from Roman times.

There are a number of possible routes to take from Rouen to Le Havre and other points on the west coast.

Rouen to Le Havre via Route N 15

Route N 15 leaves Rouen to the northwest and climbs to the top of a plateau, where it comes to the valley of Sainte-Austreberthe and to the industrial town of **Barentin** (population 12,200), which is situated along a 550-meter (1,650-foot) brick railroad viaduct. The town is also noted for works by the sculptor Bourdelle (1861–1929) and the *Walking Man* by Rodin. After another 18 km. (11 miles), N 15 comes to **Yvetot** (population 10,000) which was largely destroyed in World War II and rebuilt. The unusual round *church of Saint-Pierre* (1955) has enormous windows designed by Max Ingrand. Just 2 km. (1.2 miles) to the southwest is **Valliquerville** where a 1,000-year-old oak tree with two small chapels carved into its trunk still stands at the Allouville church. The next village is **Bolbec** (population 13,000). From here, a road bears to the northwest for 25 km. (15.5 miles) to the seaside town *Étretat* (see page 117). Route N 15 then comes to **Harfleur,** a port founded by the Romans. The *church of Saint-Martin* is crowned with an elegant Gothic spire. The town is a suburb of **Le Havre** (population 200,000; 88 km.; 55 miles from Rouen), France's second-largest port after Marseille. The city was founded in 1517 by François I. It endured centuries of tug-of-war fighting between France, England, and Holland. Four-fifths of the city was reduced to rubble during World War II, so the town center, largely the work of architect Auguste Perret (1874–1954), gives a distinctly 20th century impression. The maze of docks is at the south end of town. Le Havre accommodates many of the transatlantic cargo ships as well as several cross-Channel ferries.

The *Place de l'Hôtel de Ville*, the work of Perret, is one of the largest city squares in Europe. Perret also laid out the broad *Avenue Foch* leading to the sea, and built the lofty reinforced-concrete *church of Saint-Joséph*. The *Nouveau Musée des Beaux-Arts*, built entirely of metal and glass, houses an extensive collection of important works by famous Impressionists, including 250 paintings by Eugène Boudin (1824–1898), one of whose students was Monet, and 65 by Raoul Dufy (1877–1953).

Rouen to Le Havre via Route D 982

As D 982 leaves Rouen to the west it follows the Seine, then leaves the river and climbs to the village of *Canteleu*. The views are superb and the 11th-century *church of*

Saint-Martin de Boscherville is well worth a visit. The road rejoins the river just before Duclair. From Rouen to the sea, the river is navigable for ocean-going ships and flows between majestic white cliffs. From Duclair, a side road leads 3 km. (2 miles) south to the 11th-century ruins of the **abbey of Jumièges*. Route D 982 now hugs the right bank of the Seine to **Caudebec-en-Caux** (population 2,900). The town's *church of Nôtre-Dame* (1425–1539) is a late-Gothic gem. Henri IV described it as "the most beautiful chapel in my kingdom." The Medieval *Maison des Templiers* provides a charming setting for its museum. The next town on D 982 is **Lillebonne** (population 9,700) which in Caesar's time was a lively port city of 25,000 inhabitants and was known as Juliobona. The remains of a small *amphitheater* stand as a reminder of the Roman occupation. In 1066, William the Conqueror assembled his forces for the invasion of England in the town's citadel. A *tower*, which was added in the 13th century, survives. The road descends slightly to **Tancarville,** with its castle, the *Château de Tancarville* (14th–18th century). Inside the castle is an art gallery, a museum and model workshops from the 11th–15th centuries. The impressive **Bridge of Tancarville,* completed in 1959, spans the Seine.

From Tancarville, the road follows the *Canal de Tancarville* past enormous oil refineries to Le

Havre (92 km.; 57 miles from Rouen; see above).

On the opposite side of the ever-widening Seine estuary lies the picturesque port town of **Honfleur** (population 9,600). This town, the birthplace of Eugène Boudin (1824–1898), was an artists' colony. The *church of Sainte-Cathérine* and its bell tower, built by local shipbuilders at the end of the 15th century, is made entirely of wood. Also of interest is the *Museum of Norman Folk Art*. There is a magnificent view over the town with its old houses of wood and slate from the **Côte de Grace*, a hill that rises 90 meters (295 feet) above the estuary. The nearby farm of *Saint-Simeon* was once a rendezvous point for Impressionist painters.

Rouen to Fécamp and Étretat

This route through the lovely farm country of the Pay-de-Caux region follows the Rouen–Le Havre trip on the N 15 described on see page 115 as far as *Valliquerville*, where the road turns off to the right from N 15 and proceeds 33 km. (20 miles) through *Fauville-en-Caux* to the most scenic part of the chalky Normandy coast. The main town here is **Fécamp** (population 24,000), a fishing port situated between two steep white cliffs. The town's pilgrimage *church of Sainte-Trinité* (1175–1220) is an early-Gothic structure of the Norman school with Renaissance decorations. Note the clock (1667) in the north transept. Rue A. Legros is lined with folk-art museums and shops.

Part of the *Musée de la Bénédictine* is an old distillery. Here, in 1510, a Benedictine monk brewed aromatic herbs he found growing on the cliffs. It was intended for medicinal purposes. That concoction was the liqueur that has become known throughout the world as Benedictine. Fécamp is the birthplace of writer Guy de Maupassant.

A winding, scenic coast road runs 20 km. (12.4 miles) through the small resort town of *Yport* to the seaside resort of **Étretat** (population 1,600; 86 km.; 53 miles from Rouen). The town lies nestled along a pebble beach between high sea-carved white cliffs known as **falaises*. To the north is the *Falaise d'Amont*, a chalk cliff atop which stands a monument to the aviators Charles Nungesser and François Coli who disappeared in 1927 during an attempt to make the first east-west Atlantic crossing. Other rock formations rising from the sea include the **Falaise d'Aval*, the **Manneporte*, and the *Aiguille d'Étretat* (the Étretat Needle). The composer Offenbach often worked here, drawing his inspiration from the seascapes.

Rouen to Dieppe and Le Tréport

From Rouen, Route N 27 continues over a plateau then descends the steep coastline to

Dieppe (population 45,000). Situated on a shallow bay, the city is an important fishing port and terminus for ferries to and from England. In the 16th century, Dieppe was the home port of the dreaded privateer Jean Fango and his fleet. At the edge of the cliffs on the western side of town stands the imposing *château* (14th–17th century), which houses a *museum*. The exhibits include a collection of Dieppe ivory carvings and the first piano owned by composer Camille Saint-Saëns whose father was a farmer in the area. The views from the castle are stunning. From Dieppe, Route D 925 proceeds northeast to the old fishing port of **Le Tréport** (population 7,000; 88 km.; 55 miles from Rouen) and its popular seaside resort, *Mers-les-Bains.* Because Le Tréport is the closest resort to Paris and the sea, it is a favorite holiday spot for Parisians. The 100-meter- (328-foot-) high hill *Calvaire des Terrasses* provides a glorious view of the coastline. Just 3 km. (2 miles) beyond Le Tréport lies the old city of **Eu** (population 9,000) where the *collegiate church of Saint-Laurent* (1186–1280) is located. The tombs of the Counts of Eu of the House of Artois (14th and 15th centuries) are in the crypt.

TRAVEL ROUTE 6: ***Paris–*Caen–Cherbourg (341 km.; 212 miles)

See map on pages 120–121.

Normandy, one of France's richest provinces, abounds in natural beauties. In the spring, apple blossoms make it look like one vast, snowy orchard; but its farms produce more than apples (although they've gained special notice through a famous applejack called *Calvados*). There is an abundance of other fruits, vegetables, and dairy products, not to mention the fruits of the sea—for the Normans ply the North Atlantic as adventurously as did their Viking ancestors, though more peacefully. In addition to its superb food, Normandy is known for picturesque scenery, turbulent history, and architecture that influenced English building from cathedrals to cottages.

This Travel Route takes you from Paris to some of the region's ancient cities and Medieval structures which sharply contrast with the elegant resorts along the Atlantic coast. A somber reminder of Normandy's more recent role in historic events are the monuments honoring Allied forces that landed on the coast on D-Day during World War II.

The Autoroute de Normandie, A 13, heads west from Paris past the ornate splendor of Versailles, then turns northwest. Follow it nearly to *Vernon;* then exit the expressway and continue west on Route N 13. About 100 km. (62 miles) from Paris, you come upon the first of several towns with notable examples of Norman architecture.

*Evreux (population 50,000) is a center for marketing local produce and the most important town of the department of Eure. It began as a Roman settlement and was already established by the reign of the Emperor Augustus. Unfortunately, Evreux was attacked repeatedly from the ninth century to World War II and suffered severe damage each time. First among several important buildings still standing is the *cathedral of Nôtre-Dame,* a successful blend of styles from the 12th to the 17th century. The basically Romanesque structure has a splendid Renaissance main façade and a late-Gothic north façade in the Flamboyant style. Inside, the woodwork and stained-glass windows are especially fine (the 14th-century windows are outstanding examples of that period, the 15th-century windows in the Lady Chapel have well-executed and well-preserved stained glass, and the rose windows in the transepts are good 16th-century work).

The *Bishop's Palace,* south of the cathedral, is now a museum, displaying Gallo-Roman artifacts, pottery from Rouen, enamels from Limoges, English carvings in alabaster, and paintings. The heavily restored Flamboyant structure was built in 1481.

You can take a very pleasant stroll along the river from the back of the cathedral to the Flamboyant-style clock tower. On the way, you can see remnants of the moat and ramparts of the old town. If,

on the other hand, you follow the Rue de Verdun east from the cathedral, you'll come to the Norman *church of Saint-Taurin,* named after the local saint Taurinus, who was reputedly such a fierce fighter against evil that he broke off one of the Devil's horns. The building has Romanesque and Renaissance elements and an 18th-century west façade, but the overall effect is 14th century. Lovely 16th-century stained glass can be seen in the choir. The church contains a masterpiece of Medieval smithing: the gilt reliquary of Saint Taurinus, dating from the 13th century.

From Evreux, N 13 provides a direct route to Lisieux (72 km.; 43 miles). However, a short scenic detour southwest along Route D 830—18 km. (11 miles)—takes you to the lovely town of **Conches-en-Ouche** (population 3,800), whose name is thought to derive from a famous pilgrimage site, Conques, in the south of France. Soldiers returning home brought a relic of Saint Foy from Conques in about 1035. The saint, a martyr whose name means *faith,* was widely venerated during the Middle Ages, especially in France and England. The *church of Sainte-Foy* dates from the 15th and 16th centuries and has splendid Renaissance *stained-glass windows.* There are a number of half-timbered houses from the 15th and 16th centuries in the town, and the ruins of a 12th-century castle can be seen from the terrace behind the church.

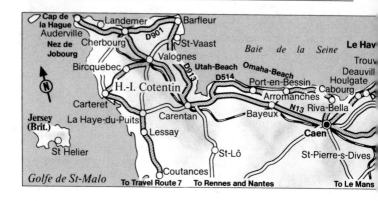

Route D 140 then heads west through *Beaumesnil,* with its elegant 17th-century château set in gardens by Le Nôtre. From there, it is 34 km. (21 miles) to **Bernay** (population 12,000). From its *Promenade des Monts* there are excellent views of the countryside. The *church of Sainte-Croix,* which dates from the 14th and 15th centuries, has a monumental 17th-century altarpiece on the high altar and Renaissance and 17th-century woodwork on the organ and pulpit. The *church of Nôtre-Dame-de-la-Couture* is a 15th-century basilica with an elaborate wooden roof, black-and-white checkered walls, and a contemporary statue of the Virgin.

An abbey was founded at Bernay in 1031 by Judith of Brittany, who was William the Conqueror's grandmother. The abbey church, built in the 11th century, altered in the 15th and 17th centuries and later abandoned, has been restored. Its south transept is quite lovely. The *Hôtel de Ville* occupies part of the 17th-century additions to the abbey, and a museum has been installed in the former *Abbot's Lodge.* Made of checkered brick and stone, it houses a collection of Gallo-Roman silver, pottery from Rouen, and Norman furniture.

Continue northwest on Route D 138 to return to Route N 13, which leads west to **Lisieux** (population 28,000). It is the gateway to the department of Calvados in Lower Normandy. Lisieux is also the major town of the Pays d'Auge, a distinctive region of impressive manor houses, scenic river valleys carved in a chalk plateau, and dairy farms that make Camembert cheese.

Unfortunately, Lisieux's quaint old town was devastated during World War II. Among the surviving buildings is the oldest Gothic church in Normandy, the *cathedral of Saint-Pierre.* Mainly built around 1170, the cathedral was changed and enlarged until the 15th century, when the imposing

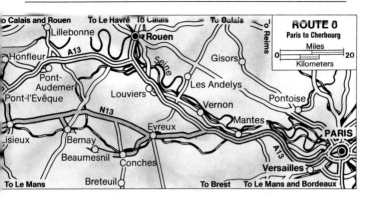

o Calais and Rouen   To Le Havré   To Calais   Tu Oalais   ROUTE 0
Lillebonne   Rouen   Reims   Paris to Cherbourg
Honfleur   A13   Gisors   Miles
Pont-   Seine   0   20
Audemer   Louviers   Les Andelys   Kilometers
Pont-l'Evêque   Vernon   Pontoise
                      N13   Mantes
               Evreux   PARIS
isieux   Bernay   A13
       Beaumesnil   Conches   Versailles
To Le Mans   Breteuil   To Brest   To Le Mans and Bordeaux

Lady Chapel was added. The tall, dignified nave and the south portal exemplify early-Gothic architecture.

The façade of the nearby *Bishop's Palace,* now the Palais de Justice, is in the style of Louis XIII. A few old houses remain in the vicinity. But Lisieux's present-day fame rests on its association with Saint Theresa of the Infant Jesus. Born Thérèse Martin (1873–1897), she was canonized in 1925. Many places in Lisieux have associations with the saint, including the Carmelite convent where she spent the last eight years of her life. The most prominent, however, is the huge domed *basilica of Sainte-Thérèse,* built in 1937. After Lourdes, it is the most famous pilgrimage church in France and attracts huge crowds each year on August 15 and in late September.

From Lisieux, Route N 13 goes west 46 km. (29 miles) to *Caen.* Route D 579 is 23 km. (14 miles) longer and swings north through the charming **valley of the Touques* for 17 km. (10.5 miles) to *Pont-l'Evêque,* a town that is famous among gourmets for its cheese.

From Pont-l'Evêque, Route N 177 follows the river valley for another 11 km. (6.6 miles) to ****Deauville-Trouville** (population 6,661 and 5,743, respectively), which together form the most elegant seaside resort in Normandy. During its short season, mid-July to the end of August, Deauville attracts the rich and famous from around the world for sailing, swimming, horse racing, gambling, and golf—or simply strolling alongside its beautiful beach on the **promenade des planches* (boardwalk), which is bordered by a profusion of colorful flowerbeds. Trouville, the oldest seaside resort in France, attracted writers like Alexandre Dumas and Gustave Flaubert, as well as painters like Gustave Courbet, Claude Monet, and James Whistler. Trouville is both a fishing port and a resort. It has long sandy beaches, an impressive casino, a yacht club, and its *promenade des planches* was once known as "the summer boulevard of Paris."

Route D 513 will take you west from Deauville to Cabourg. Along the way, it passes through the coastal towns of *Blonville, Bénerville,* and *Villers-sur-Mer.* It then curves behind the long, dark *cliffs of the Vaches Noires* (Black Cows) and comes back to the sandy shore at *Houlgate.* This drive—past summer homes with exotic plants, past orchards, and meadows full of wildflowers—will give you some idea why this part of Normandy is called the *Côte Fleurie* (flowery coast). *Dives-sur-Mer,* now an industrial town, was once an important seaport. From its harbor, long since choked with sand, William the Conqueror set out to invade England in the summer of 1066.

Cabourg (population 3,000) has a rather distinctive layout—its streets fan out from the casino. This very popular resort has a long, sandy beach and a fine promenade along the shore. It was particularly loved by Marcel Proust, a frequent visitor, who made Cabourg the model for Balbec in the novel *Remembrance of Things Past.* From Cabourg, it is 24 km. (15 miles), still on Route D 513, to ***Caen** (population 120,000), the leading town of the department of Calvados and an important port. Its chief glory, however, is the magnificent architecture inherited

from the past. The survival of such a rich heritage is remarkable because Caen has been a prize in many wars since its founding in the 11th century. It had to be largely rebuilt after World War II.

At opposite sides of the town are two of its three principal monuments: the **Église Saint-Etienne* to the west and the **Église de la Trinité* to the east. They were part, respectively, of the *Abbaye aux Hommes,* built by William the Conqueror, and the *Abbaye aux Dames,* built by his wife, Mathilda. The king and queen were cousins who had married without the special permission that was needed from the pope. They founded the abbeys as penance and to lift the threat of excommunication.

Saint-Étienne is a powerful Romanesque structure, one of the finest in France. It measures 115 meters (377 feet) long and 24 meters (79 feet) high. The bold but severe style of the church—the huge buttresses that divide the west façade, the tall square towers (capped, however, by Gothic spires added in the 13th century), and the lack of decoration—seems to symbolize the man of action who commissioned it. His wife's La Trinité, on the other hand, seems softer and more approachable in its size, its comfortable proportions, and the carved decoration. The interior of La Trinité has the groined vaults that are typical of early-Romanesque ceilings; the ribbed vaults that developed from them can be seen in Saint-Étienne. Lighter and easier to build and stabilize, ribbed vaults evolved into the Gothic style. The airy grace of Saint-Étienne's interior is also characteristic of the transition from Romansque to early-Gothic, leading logically to the Gothic choir, which was added in the 13th century. La Trinité, too, has a notable Gothic addition: a lovely, delicate 13th-century chapel in the south transept.

Nearly midway between the two abbeys is the *castle* built by William the Conqueror. It occupies high ground on the north side of Caen, and its 12th-century ramparts provide a fine view of the town. The fortress itself is in ruins, but the grounds are laid out as an attractive garden, and there are other buildings of interest within its precincts. The *Musée des Beaux-Arts,* for example, contains paintings by Perugino, Tintoretto, Titian, Veronese, Van Ruisdael, and Van der Weyden, as well as an impressive collection of prints.

The descent from the castle leads directly to one of Caen's most prominent landmarks, the magnificent *bell tower of Saint-Pierre* (built in 1308, restored after World War II). Construction of the church was begun in the 13th century in Gothic style and continued into the 16th century, when the ornate Renaissance apse was built.

Route N 13 goes directly from Caen to Bayeux, a distance of 27 km. (17 miles). Route D 514 offers a longer drive (55 km., 33 miloo) along the coast where English and American forces invaded Normandy in World War II. The beaches became famous overnight: Sword, Juno, Gold, Omaha, Utah. These landing sites stretch northwest from *Riva-Bella,* which is situated only 14 km. (8 miles) from Caen. Throughout this area, now so placid, are poignant and evocative reminders of the liberation—bunkers, huge cemeteries, and war memorials.

At *Courseulles-sur-Mer,* a side road leads to the *chateau of Fontaine-Henry,* a graceful blend of the Medieval and the Renaissance. It contains fine furniture and paintings.

Returning to the coast road, Route D 514, and continuing west, you will come to **Arromanches-les-Bains,** which was the site of the man-made "Mulberry Harbor," built to assist in the Normandy invasion. It was created by sinking caissons filled with cement. Dubbed "Port Winston," it handled up to 9,000 tons of military equipment every day. Models can be seen in the Arromanches museum that commemorates the landings. It is the best of its kind in Normandy. Only 10 km. (6 miles) southwest of Arromanches via Route D 516 lies **Bayeux** (population 15,000), the first town to be liberated during the Normandy invasion in World War II. It has picturesque old buildings, and the magnificent *cathedral of Nôtre-Dame* is a

Bayeux: Tapestry

splendid example of Norman Gothic architecture and one of the loveliest churches in France. Yet neither liberation nor the town's architectural attributes account for the fame of Bayeux, which rests, in fact, on a piece of cloth. What is known to the world as the **Bayeux Tapestry* is called the "Tapestry of Queen Mathilda" in France. It is actually a needlepoint embroidery of varicolored wool on linen that was not made by William the Conqueror's wife, Mathilda, but was probably commissioned about 1080 by William's half brother Bishop Odo (who is a figure in the embroidery). It was meant to hang in his cathedral. The embroidery, 70 meters (230 feet) by 50 centimeters (20 inches) records the victory of William over Harold of England in 1066. It's a *long* story told in 58 scenes that are sufficiently detailed to be a source of information on costumes, weapons, ships, and military defenses of the

period. One scene shows a comet passing overhead. Fanciful beasts decorate the top and bottom bands. The embroidery is on view at the *Centre Guillaume-le-Conquérant* on the Rue de Nesmond.

From Bayeux, you can go directly to *Carentan* on Route N 13. There is a more interesting drive, however, back along Route D 516 to the coast and then west on Route D 514. After 9 km. (5.4 miles) you come to the first town of any size, the fishing port of *Port-en-Bessin* where the American and British forces met in 1944. To the west lies **Omaha Beach,** where American forces landed on June 6, 1944— D-Day—with heavy losses in 1944. The military cemetery, with 9,385 graves, overlooks the bitterly contested beach.

From a fishing village and seaside resort called *Grandcamp-les-Bains,* you can take either D 514 or D 199 south to Route N 13, which is the highway to **Cherbourg.** On the way N 13 passes through two important butter markets, *Isigny-sur-Mer* and *Carantan.* This is the southeast corner of the Cotentin peninsula, much of which is devoted to dairy farming and breeding horses.

An alternate route to Cherbourg goes along the eastern coast of the peninsula. At *Saint-Côme-du-Mont,* about 3.5 km. (2 miles) north of Carentan, you can pick up Route D 913. Follow it through the town of *Sainte-Marie-du-Mont,* and continue straight ahead 15 km. (9 miles) to the *monument of La Madeleine,* a German bunker that has been turned into a World War II memorial. This is the beginning of **Utah Beach,** where American forces landed on D-Day. The beach extends 3.5 km. (2 miles) to the *Dunes-de-Varreville,* where the Americans overcame strong German resistance. It was also the landing place of the Free French and is so marked by a pink granite monument shaped like the prow of a ship.

Passing through *Quinéville* and *Quettehou,* the coast road D 14 proceeds to **Saint-Vaast-la-Hougue** (population 2,500), a picturesque fishing port and resort. Here you can see fortifications built in the 17th century from designs by the military engineer Vauban, who also built the citadel and watchtower on the nearby island of *Tatihou.*

About 10 km. (6 miles) from Saint-Vaast along Route D 902 is the small, pleasant port of **Barfleur** (population 900) and 4 km. (2.5 miles) farther will bring you to *Gatteville,* where the *lighthouse*—one of the tallest in France— offers an extensive view of the east coast of the Calentio peninsula and the Côte du Calvados. This site, known as the *Pointe de Barfleur,* is only 27 km. (17 miles) from **Cherbourg** (population 35,000), an important

naval base and commercial port. Its strategic merits were recognized as early as the 17th century, when the engineer Vauban fortified the city and began construction of the harbor. The impressive breakwater that protects it from the fury of English Channel storms was not completed until the mid-19th century. Cherbourg served as the major supply point for the Normandy invasion in 1944. The Allies removed German mines from the harbor and laid an oil supply line called PLUTO (Pipeline under the ocean) from the Isle of Wight to Cherbourg. You can get a splendid view of the city and the harbor from the fort on the *Montagne du Roule,* a hill south of the city. It was one of the strongest German defenses in the Atlantic Wall and now houses the *Musée de la Guerre et de la Libération.*

If you wish to tour La Hague Peninsula from Cherbourg, Route D 901 heads east for 5 km. (3 miles) and intersects Route D 45, which follows the base of the steep coastline. From *Dannery,* a side road (1.5 km.; 1 mile) leads to the high granite cape called the *Nez de Jobourg,* 180 meters (590 feet) high. Here you can get a marvelous **view** over the rugged coast and the Channel Islands.

TRAVEL ROUTE 7: ***Paris–Rennes–Brest–*Quimper (803/820 km.; 482/492 miles)

See maps on pages 128–129 and 133.

Travel Route 7 presents two different routes through Normandy to get from Paris to Brittany. Each option has its temptations—you may go by way of the fabulous citadel church of Mont-Saint-Michel, or through Chartres, with its spectacular cathedral. Whichever you choose, you will find yourself in Rennes, the capital of Brittany and from there, continue to Brittany's main cities, Brest and Quimper. Brittany has some of the most rugged coastline in France and the trip provides many options for exploring it: You can tour the resorts along the Côte de'Emeraude, admire the jagged pink granite coastline of the Côte de Granit Rose, and visit the mysterious menhirs near Carnac.

There are two different routes you can follow from Paris to Rennes; one goes through Fougères, the other goes through Chartres.

Paris to Rennes through Fougeres

Follow the route marked "1" on the map on pages 128–129.

Leave Paris on the *Autoroute de Normandie* (A 13) and take the left fork at the junction with the Rocquencourt expressway. After 6 km. (3.7 miles), enter Route N 12 heading west. Passing *Houdan,* with its massive *watchtower (12th century), you go for 84 km. (52 miles) to the industrial city of **Dreux** (population 35,000). Among the town's architectural attractions are a 16th-century *watchtower and the *Chapelle Royale Saint-Louis,* with tombs of members of the House of Orléans. The stained-glass windows were designed in part by the

painter Ingres (1780–1867). You can stretch your legs along the trails in the nearby Dreux Forest before continuing west on N 12. The road bears southwest at the enchanting town of *Verneuil-sur-Avre* with its half-timbered houses and church of Nôtre-Dame.

The scenery along this stretch is delightful as the road passes through the hill country of the Haut-Perche to the north of *Mortagne.* In the middle of a fertile plain lies **Alençon** (population 34,000) nicknamed the *"Points d'Alençon"* for its many church spires. The town is known for its lacemaking and boasts a *Musée des Beaux-Arts et de la Dentelle* in a restored former Jesuit college.

Another stretch of wooded hills leads to *Mayenne,* after which N 12 runs in a long, straight stretch to **Fougères** (population 30,000), which produces one-tenth of all the shoes made in

France. This ancient town is on the border of Brittany and was meticulously described by Balzac in his novel, *Les Chouans*. Of special interest is the **château* (12th–15th century) that was once surrounded by a moat. There is a footpath along the ramparts connecting the 13 towers. From Fougères it is 47 km. (29 miles) west to Rennes (344 km.; 214 miles from Paris; see page 130) and the same distance north to Mont-Saint-Michel.

If you wish to take a side trip to Mont-Saint-Michel from Fougères, take Route D 155 northwest to *Antrain*. From there take Route N 175 to *Pontorson,* and from there take Route D 976 to ***Mont-Saint-Michel,** one of the architectural wonders of the world.

From a distance, the citadel church looks like a fantastic sand castle rising out of the sea. The church, dedicated to the Archangel Michael, is built on a granite rock rising 78 meters (256 feet) above the tidal flats. It is connected to the mainland by a causeway that is passable only by boat during high tides and the new or full moon. The beginnings of the monastic settlement on the rock go back to the eighth century. By the tenth century, there was already a chapel here called *Saint-Michel-au-Péril-de-la-Mer.* The structure has served over the centuries as a church, a basilica, an academy for monks, a temporary court for Henri II, a fortress, and a prison. The present abbey atop the summit has a spire that soars 150 meters (492 feet) above the church of Saint-Michel and dates from the 13th–16th centuries. From the bottom of the rock, the *Grande-Rue* winds through a village sprinkled with gabled houses, shops, and restaurants and climbs to the entrance of the abbey, which is guarded by a succession of three gates. The major part of the abbey, known from the time it was built (1211–1228) as *"La Merveille"* ("the Wonder"), contains the *almshouse,* which once served as a dormitory for pilgrims; the *Salle des Hôtes* a reception room for distinguished guests; the four-aisle chapter hall known as the *Salle des Chevaliers* (Knight's Hall); the *refectory;* and the *cloister.* A single flying buttress of the abbey church supports an ingenious spiral staircase, which leads to a gallery on the roof of the choir that offers a dramatic view. It is possible to hike to the rock at low tide on a sandy tract called "La Grève," but do so only with a guide. The tide rises quickly and the passage is dotted with quicksand. Be prepared to wade in some parts.

From Mont-Saint-Michel return on Route D 976 to Pontorson. From there it is 57 km. (35 miles) on Route N 175 to Rennes (see page 130). Proceed west on Route N 176 to the *Emerald Coast* for 19 km. (12 miles) to **Dol** (population 5,000), dominated by its **cathedral of Saint-Samson* (13th century). This delightful town has lovely old homes and antiques shops. The nearby town of Mont-

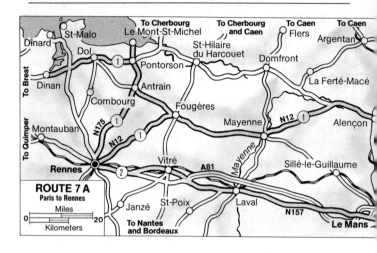

Dol is studded with windmills and provides grand views. The Pierre du Champ-Dolent, one of the most magnificent menhirs (large prehistoric monoliths) in Brittany, is 2 km. (1.2 miles) south of Dol on Route D 795. Back on Route N 176, another 25 km. (15.5 miles) takes you to **Dinan** (population 14,000). This city, sitting above the Rance River, is enclosed by Medieval walls and is crisscrossed by romantic cobblestoned streets. Craft shops may be found on the Rue du Jerzual. The city's *fortified castle* has a huge oval tower 34 meters (112 feet) high (14th century), and the *church of Saint-Sauveur* has another *tower* (1557) that rises 57 meters (187 feet) over the asymmetrically constructed nave.

In Dinan you can make connections for a side trip along the northern coast of Brittany described on page 131.

Paris to Rennes through Chartres

Follow the route marked "2" on the map above.

Leave Paris on the *Autoroute de Normandie* (A 13) and, at the junction with the Rocquencourt expressway, take the southwest extension. Near Versailles go south on Route N 10. You will pass **Rambouillet** (population 24,000), with an often-rebuilt **château* that overlooks a lovely *park* interlaced with wide canals. The present structure mostly dates from the 18th century and serves as the country residence of the President of France and as a guest house for government visitors. Occasional tours are scheduled when he is elsewhere. The château has a rich history. It was once the property of Henri IV and Cath-

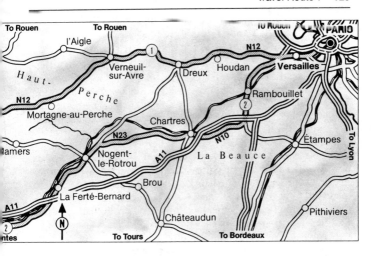

erine de Médicis. It was passed down to Louis XVI, who had a house decorated with seashells and a model dairy built on the grounds to amuse Marie Antoinette. Napoleon spent his last night of freedom here before being exiled to Saint Helena.

At *Ablis* the road makes a sharp turn to the west and cuts across the Beauce plain, the breadbasket of France. The plains are sprinkled with silos and windmills. Long before you reach ***Chartres** (population 45,000), you will see the distinctive unmatched spires, high nave, and weathered copper roof of the famous ****cathedral of Notre-Dame*. It was built on the site of four previous churches, each destroyed by fire. The austere south spire dates from the 12th century; its ornate neighbor was added in the 16th. When the building was reconstructed in the 13th

century after the last fire, religious fervor was so strong that the people of Chartres, even the men and women of the nobility, yoked themselves to carts and dragged the huge, heavy stones to the site from the quarry 8 km. (5 miles) away. Three million tourists a year visit Chartres to see the cathedral, its thousands of remarkable statues, and its magnificent stained-glass windows, which the English art critic John Ruskin called "flaming jewelry." The Gothic ambulatory contains 41 reliefs depicting scenes from the lives of Christ and Mary. The Bishop's Garden overlooks the "lower town" and the Eure Valley. The *Musée de Chartres* features exhibits tapestries, paintings, drawings, armor, and enamels.

As you cross the Eure River look back for a splendid view of Chartres. (From Chartres, you can pick up Travel Route 9.) Route N 23 continues west over the Beauce plain through the rolling countryside of *Petit-Perche* to *Nogent-le-Rotrou* (population 12,500), a lovely old market town in the Huisne Valley.

From here Route N 23 follows the Huisne River to **La Ferté-Bernard** (population 9,200), where the *church of Nôtre-Dame-des-Marais* has a Renaissance *choir* worth seeing. The town's market halls date from 1536 and there are picturesque old houses in the Rue d'Huisne and the Rue Carnot. Another 34 km. (21 miles) brings you to **Le Mans** (population 155,000). This city is world-famous for its auto races held in the racetrack 3 km. (2 miles) to the south. The big 24-hour road race is held annually in June. The track is usually open and a nearby museum boasts 150 vintage cars and motorcycles. In the old city, still surrounded by its third-century Gallo-Roman walls, is the *cathedral of Saint-Julien* (1217–1254). Of particular interest in the cathedral are the tombs of Queen Bérangère, the consort of Richard the Lion-Hearted, and that of Charles IV of Anjou. The *Maison de la Reine Bérangère* is a small museum of local crafts and history.

From Le Mans, Route N 157 heads west for 75 km. (47 miles) to *Laval* (population 55,000) on the Mayenne River. About 35 km. (22 miles) ahead lies the border of Brittany and the old citadel of **Vitré** (population 13,000). The restored *castle* (14th–15th century), with its three massive fortified towers, stands on a hill overlooking the Vilaine River. The town has several old wood-and-slate houses. About 35 km. (22 miles) farther, N 157 comes to the administrative center of Brittany, the ancient capital of the Duchy, **Rennes** (population 210,000; 361 km.; 224 miles, from Paris, including the side trip to Mont-Saint-Michel). The old city was destroyed in 1720 by a fire that raged for seven days, and Rennes now blends fanciful Medieval architecture with the sober appearance of the French Classical period. Outstanding buildings include the *city hall* (1734) by Gabriel, the architect of Louis XV, and the *courthouse* (1618–1654), whose **Grand Chambre is decorated with a painted wood ceiling (1656–1660), gilded wall paneling (1660), and tapestries that depict the history of Brittany (20th century).

The *Musée des Beaux-Arts* has a fine collection of French, Italian and Dutch paintings. West of Rennes is thought to be the site of "Broceliande"—the legendary home of King Arthur's wizard, Merlin.

Highway N 12 is the direct highway from Rennes to Brest (245 km.; 152 miles; see route marked "B" on the map on page 133). It provides access to many points along the north Breton coast. We have outlined three additional trips that intertwine with N 12 if you want to take extra time to enjoy the coast.

Rennes to Brest along the Côte d'Emeraude

Follow the route marked "1" on the map on page 133.

You can make the trip from Rennes to *Saint-Brieuc* via Saint-Malo and the Côte d'Emeraude (Emerald Coast). Take Route N 137 out of Rennes toward Saint-Malo, but after 40 km. (24.9 miles), near *La Coudraye,* turn west onto Route D 794, which takes you 11 km. (6.8 miles) to Dinan (see page 128). The road continues another 22 km. (13.7 miles) north to Dinard, then on to *Saint-Servan* with its powerful *Usine Marémotrice,* the first tidal generating station in the world, which uses tidal action to generate power.

On the peninsula stands Saint-Servan's **Fort de la Cité* (1759), incorporated into the Atlantic Wall fortification system during World War II. The esplanade called the ***Corniche d'Aleth* that circles the fort provides breathtaking views out to sea. Saint-Servan is a suburb of ***Saint-Malo** (population 62,000). This famous maritime city, which still has its old ***ramparts,* was rebuilt in the old style following devastating fires in 1944. It is now a busy Channel port, as well as a resort, and locale of the famed oyster beds which are visible at low tide. Among famous "Malouins" (as natives of Saint-Malo are called) are Jacques Cartier (who discovered the Saint Lawrence River, and explored Canada, in 1534) and the poet and statesman François-Auguste-Réné de Chateaubriand (1768–1848). A tour of the ramparts and esplanades provides the best views. Boats and planes depart Saint-Malo regularly for the Channel Islands of Jersey, Guernsey, and Sark. *Paramé,* a seaside resort, and *Cancale,* a fishing port and resort, are nearby.

Across from Saint-Malou and the Rance estuary lies the town of ***Dinard** (population 11,000). Its sandy beaches and cliff-side walks have made this resort especially popular with British vacationers since Victorian times. Next to it is *La Baule.*

Route D 786 takes you through the many resorts of the Côte d'Emeraud: *Saint-Lunaire* (where Claude Debussy is thought to have composed *La Mer*); *Saint-Briac; Saint-Cast; Saint-Aide,* where you can make a detour to *Fort La Latte,* a maritime fortress (13th–17th century) on a rocky peninsula; and ***Cap Fréhel,* where 57-meter- (187-feet-) high red cliffs provide a stunning view.

After passing through the resorts of *Sables-d'Or-les-Pins, Erquy* and *Le Val André,* D 786 leaves the coast and intersects Route N 12. Saint-Brieuc is 10 km. (6.2 miles) farther.

To Brest through the Côte de Granit Rose

Follow the route marked "2" on the map on page 133.

From Saint-Brieuc you can go directly to Morlaix on Route N 12 (86 km.; 53.4 miles)—passing *Guingamp* (population 12,000), the first town on the Paris–Brest trip where Breton is spoken. ("Brezoneg" is composed of four distinct dialects derived from several ancient languages). An alternate route is to follow the *Côte de Granit Rose* to *Morlaix* (154 km.; 96 miles) on Route 786. Heading northwest, you come first to the small port of *Binic* and the resort of *Saint-Quay-Portrieux,* then continue through scenic moorland to the fishing port of **Paimpol.** From here you can drive 6 km. (3.7 miles) to *Pointe de l'Arcouest,* where you can cross over to the **Île de Brehát** built on red granite. Its low houses turn their backs to the storms that come from the northwest and the tiny fields are protected by stone walls. From the lighthouse, the *Phare du Paon,* on the northern point, there is a sweeping view of the jagged coast of pink granite rocks and the many tiny islands and reefs just offshore. At the nearby *Cemetery of Ploubazlanec* the names of those lost at sea are inscribed on a wall.

From Paimpol, the D 786 turns west, crosses the estuary of the Trieux River and comes to **Tréguier** (population 3,600), with its *cathedral of Saint-Tugdual* (14th–15th century) and beautiful cloister. Tréguier is the birthplace of Saint-Yves (13th century) and the philosopher Ernest Renan (1823–1892).

About 18 km. (11 miles) farther west lies the old Breton city of **Lannion** (population 20,000), at the head of the Léguer Valley where many grand *châteaux* are located and which is the departing point for a trip over **Corniche Bretonne** (35 km.; 22 miles).

The corniche, a 13 km. (8 mile) panoramic highway offering marvelous views, begins at the fishing port and seaside resort of *Perros-Guirec.* Along the way the seaside resorts of *Ploumanach* and *Trégastel-Plage,* nestle between red cliffs. Many dolmens and menhirs (see page 136) line the road.

From Lannion, D 786 runs southwest for 5 km. (3 miles) to *Saint-Michel-en-Grève.* Here the road curves along a lovely bay called *Lieue de Grève,* at the end of which the scenic *Corniche de l'Armorique* branches off for 7 km. (4.3 miles) and returns to D 786 at *Lanmeur.* About 13 km. (8 miles) farther, the road reaches **Morlaix** (population 20,500). The city lies in a narrow valley above a dazzling inlet that resembles a Finnish fjord. A 285-meter- (935-foot-) long railway viaduct (1861) spans the valley at the dizzying height of 58 meters (190 feet). There are many charming old houses in the Grand'Rue and the Rue du Mûr.

Route N 12, direct from Morlaix to Brest (60 km.; 37 miles),

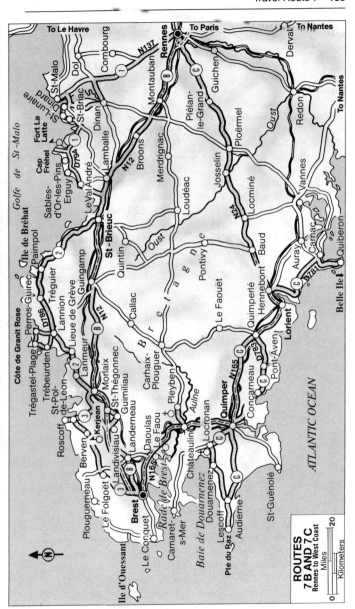

**ROUTES
7 B AND 7 C**
Rennes to West Coast

Miles
0   20

Kilometers

cuts across the northwest tip of Brittany. First, it takes you to **Saint-Thégonnec** (population 2,200). The town's ****Enclos Paroissial** (enclosed churchyard) should not be missed for it is the finest in Brittany. Enter through the massive Renaissance triumphal gate (1587) to get to the church, which has a dome-covered tower vestibule (1610) and a richly carved chancel (1685); a bell tower (1563); an *Ossuary* (1677), with a carved, sacred burial group in the crypt; and a *Calvary* (1610), a depiction of the Crucifixion that is unusually rich in sculptured figures.

While you can follow Route N 12 directly to *Landivisiau,* you may find it worthwhile to drive 5 km. (3 miles) south through *Guimiliau* to see another ****Enclos Paroissial** that is only slightly less renowned than the one in Saint-Thégonnec. Its ****Calvary** group has 200 figures, which peasants

Saint-Thégonnec: "Enclos paroissial"

carved out of granite between 1581 and 1588.

Landivisiau (9,000 population) is known for its cattle and horse market. From here, N 12 descends through the beautiful Elorn Valley to *Landerneau.* It is only 20 km. (12.5 miles) farther to **Brest** (population 175,000), France's second largest military port after Toulon. Its natural harbor covers a broad area but can be entered only through a bottleneck 1,800-meters- (1 mile-) wide called the "Goulet de Brest." During World War II the harbor was one of three bases for the German submarine fleet on the west coast of Brittany. Between the damage caused by the 165 Allied air raids, and the explosions set off by the Germans when they withdrew in September, 1944, the city was almost devastated. It has been rebuilt as a modern metropolis. The *Pont Mobile de Recourvrance,* the largest drawbridge in Europe, crosses an estuary of the Penfeld River in Brest. The *Promenade Cours Dajot,* an esplanade laid out on the ramparts atop walls designed by the military architect Vauban in the 17th century, provides fine views of the harbor. A museum of local and military history is housed in the *La Motte-Tanguy Tower* (16th century).

If you have a day to spend, you can go by boat to the small lobster-fishing port of *Le Conquet,* at the western tip of Brittany, and to the *Ile d'Ouessant,* with its rugged **cliffs. Its lighthouse, the

Phare du Créac'h, together with the English lighthouse at Land's End, signals the entrance to the English Channel for some 30,000 ships a year.

From Brest you can drive directly to *Quimper* (see page 137) on Route N 165.

To Brest through Saint-Pol-de-Léon

Follow the route marked "3" on the map on page 133.

Instead of taking Route N 12 from Morlaix to Brest, you may cross the northwestern tip of Brittany on Route D 769 heading north. About 23 km. (14 miles) from Morlaix, you will reach the major market center for the fertile Léon region, **Saint-Pol-de-Léon** (population 9,000), where there is a lovely *cathedral* and the *Chapelle du Kreisker* with a magnificent 77-meter- (253-foot-) high Gothic **tower** (15th century). Continue north to **Roscoff** (population 4,800), a crabbing port, resort, and health spa. The Brittany ferries leave regularly from here for the 8-hour trip to Plymouth, England.

You can continue the trip on Route D 788, which heads inland to **Berven.** The town has a charming *belfry* (1537).

Nearby is the *Château de Kerjean,* considered the most beautiful Renaissance castle in Brittany (1560–1590). It is still surrounded by moats and sturdy walls and is decorated with exquisite old Breton furnishings. The road continues to one of the most popular places of pilgrimage in Brittany. **Le Folgoët** (population 2,400). The town is famous for its annual pilgrimage on September 8 to the grave of a poor innocent, Salaun. The *church* (1419) has a fine belfry and an intricately sculpted late-Gothic *choir screen. A spring called the "Fontaine de Salaun" wells up under the high altar.

From here, D 788 takes you 26 km. (16 miles) to Brest (see page 134).

Rennes to Quimper

Follow the route marked "C" on the map on page 133.

Leaving Rennes on Route N 24 in a west-southwesterly direction, you will soon pass the southern edge of the great *Forest of Paimpont,* which was Merlin's magic forest in the legend of King Arthur. After 60 km. (37 miles) you come to the crossroads town of **Ploërmel** (population 7,200), location of the *church of Saint-Armel,* which contains the tombs of the dukes of Rohan. To the west, on the Brest-Nantes Canal, is **Josselin** (population 3,000), where the heavily-turreted **ancestral castle** of the Rohans, one of the country's most renowned families, is located.

Route N 24 takes you through *Locminé, Baud,* and *Hennebont* to **Lorient** (population 65,000). This port city thrived as a result of the threat the English fleet once posed to the Channel port of Le Havre. Situated on the estuaries of the Scorff and Blavet rivers, Lorient provided a safe port for merchant ships returning heavily laden with goods from the East Indies. Largely destroyed in World War II, Lorient has been rebuilt, and its *Port de Kéroman* is now the most modern fishing port in France. The *Base Sousmarine* is here: It is the home port of France's atomic submarine fleet, built in three huge bunkers left over from a German World War II base.

Carnac: Menhirs

From Lorient you can make a fascinating side trip to **Carnac** and **Belle-Ile** (104 km.; 65 miles round trip).

Leaving Lorient via the Pont de Bonhomme, a bridge over the Blavet River, take Route D 781 and drive 34 km. (21 miles) to **Carnac** (population 4,100). As you approach this small seaside resort, you will see a curious arrangement of huge upright boulders in parallel lines—the so-called *alignments*. There are 2,935 monoliths in the area, each measuring up to 20 meters (66 feet) in height.

These monumental stones, called "menhirs" (meaning "long stones") are arranged in rows of 11, 10, and 13. They may date from as far back as 3000 B.C., although their origin and significance is hotly debated among archaeologists. There are also dolmens here (meaning "stone table"). These prehistoric monuments, consisting of a horizontal stone slab atop two upright stones, apparently served as tombs. Archaeologists have identified a massive mound of heaped stones—called the *Tumulus of Saint-Michel*—as a mounded grave with a burial chamber. Materials relating to these ancient stone groupings can be seen in Carnac's *Prehistoric Museum*.

The nearby *abbeys* of Saint-Michel and Sainte-Anne offer services in Gregorian "plainsong" or chants.

From Carnac it is 18 km. (11 miles) across a narrow spit of land to the sardine-fishing port and resort town of **Quiberon** (population 4,900), where the coastline to the west is ragged, hollowed and scoured by the action of the surf.

From Quiberon, you may take an hour-long boat trip across the sea separating the west coast of Brittany from the small island of

**Belle-Île (population 3,500). *Le Palais,* the island's picturesque port town, is dominated by a citadel (1572). The main attraction on the island, however, is the steep, rugged coastline known as the ***Côte Sauvage* (Wild Coast) on the western side. Coves and rocky outcroppings known as the *Aiguilles de Port-Croton* punctuate the coastline.

From Lorient, Route N 165 leads directly to Quimper (68 km.; 42 miles). A slightly longer but more scenic route is D 783; a detour through *Pont-Aven* and *Concarneau.* Enter the road on the outskirts of Lorient near the airfield and follow it for 29 km. (18 miles) to the estuary of the Bélon, with its famous **oyster beds. About 9 km. (5.6 miles) farther is **Pont-Aven** (population 3,800), a scenic spot frequented by painters, including Paul Gauguin (1848–1903), who lived and worked here. The town lends its name to a school of Post-impressionists.

Farther along the road is **Concarneau** (population 19,500), France's largest tuna-fishing port. The **Ville-Close,* the picturesque old walled city with its narrow streets, is situated on an island in the middle of the harbor. The city was fortified with granite walls in the 15th century and the walls were reinforced by Vauban, the military architect, in the 17th century.

From Concarneau it is another 23 km. (14 miles) to the riverside city of *'**Quimper** (population 62,000; 214 km.; 133 miles from Rennes), the old capital of Cornouaille, known for its world famous faïence and lace. The two 76-meter- (250-foot-) high **towers* of the Gothic *cathedral* dominate the city. Its *Musée Départemental Bréton* houses a splendid collection of Breton folk art. The *Musée des Beaux-Arts* in the Hôtel de Ville has a rich collection of 17th-century paintings as well as works from the Pont-Aven school.

From Quimper, you can make a 114 km. (71 mile) circle tour to *Pointe du Raz.* Leaving Quimper, take Route D 765 west to the beautifully situated resort village and fishing port of *Audierne.* Lobsters and sardines are the main catches off the sandy beaches.

Continue to to the westernmost tip of Brittany, ****Pointe du Raz,** a rocky cape that affords stunning views. Another 3 km. (2 miles)

Pointe du Raz

around the *Baie des Tréspassés* brings you to another lookout point, the **Pointe du Van. Return to *Audierne* and go on through *Pont-Croix,* which has a high bell tower. Another 22 km. (14 miles) brings you to **Douarnenez** (population 20,500), the largest fishing port in France and site of a flourishing canning business. The real attraction is the sandy beach by the Treboul quarter which attracts many vacationers.

Continue to *Locronan (population 800), with its marketplace surrounded by lovely Renaissance houses, and 15th-century church; then return to Quimper. From Quimper, you can drive directly to *Brest* (see page 134) on Route N 165.

TRAVEL ROUTE 8: Paris–Orléans–Castles on the Loire (115 km.; 71 miles)

See map on pages 142–143.

The Loire Valley has something for everyone. The castles, for which the region is justly famous, range from gray Medieval residences and watch-towers to Renaissance, Baroque, and Classical palaces. In their court-yards and corridors you can't escape the feeling of stepping back into history. And the feeling grows as you visit places where Joan of Arc, Madame de Pompadour, and Catherine de Médicis played out their desti-nies. In addition to sightseeing, there are beaches for swimming and waterways for cruising and canoeing. Fishing is an especially popular sport here. The Loire Valley is also the "Garden of France" — a cheerful, green landscape of vineyards and kitchen gardens. The food is excellent: fresh vegetables and fruit, fish from the local rivers, and venison and wild boar from the forests.

This Travel Route of the eastern château district, the area around Orléans, can be combined with Travel Route 9 of the western part, the area around Tours.

Orléans marks the northernmost point in the course of the Loire River. The quickest way to get there from Paris is by Autoroute A 10. A more leisurely drive on Route N 20 goes through Month-léry, where the auto races are held, and *Arpajon,* with its 17th-cen-tury *indoor market buildings.

The road continues to *Etampes,* site of the *church of Nôtre-Dame-du-Fort* (12th–13th cen-tury), which has a lovely *south portal (similar to the one at Char-tres) and a Romanesque *bell tower 62 meters (203 feet) tall. The town clusters around an old watchtower, called the *Tour Guin-*

eiie. It was constructed in 1110 on a foundation shaped like a four-leaf clover.

Route N 20 crosses the Beauce plain to *Artenay* and continues 20 km. (12 miles) to **Orléans** (population 105,600), the major city of the department of Loiret, the site of a university since 1309, and a place inextricably linked to the memory of Joan of Arc. On May 8, 1429, the Maid of Orléans, as Joan was called, ended a year-long siege by the English. There is an equestrian statue of her in the *Place du Martroi* in the heart of the old town. Nearby is the dominant landmark, the *cathedral of Sainte-Croix*. It is nearly as large as Nôtre-Dame in Paris and was built in the 13th century on the site of a number of earlier churches; most of what exists today dates from the 17th to the 19th centuries, other parts having been destroyed by Calvinists in the 16th century. The church is a fascinating anachronism because it has maintained its Gothic style (although Marcel Proust condemned it as the ugliest church in France). The *Musée des Beaux-Arts* owns some outstanding works dating from the 15th to the 20th century—especially notable are some 18th-century oil and pastel portraits and an extensive collection of prints and drawings. The small *Musée Historique et Archéologique* also deserves a visit for its collection of local arts and crafts.

Orléans is at the center of this Travel Route which forms two loops—one to the southeast (80–88 km.; 50–54 miles, round trip) and the other to the southwest (about 158 km.; 98 miles, round trip).

To tour the castles southeast of Orléans, drive east on Route N 60 about 25 km. (15 miles) to the town of **Châteauneuf-sur-Loire** (population 6,000). Castles were built, then destroyed, on this site from the 10th to the 18th centuries; little remains of the last château, a miniature Versailles. The grounds, however, are lovely: a charming formal garden and, below it, a splendid park that is famous for its rhododendrons; it also has tulip trees, magnolias, and weeping willows beside gentle, curving streams. The *Musée de la Marine* in the park has a large exhibit on the Loire when it was the prime waterway for transportation in the region.

Only 5 km. (3 miles) farther to the southeast lies **Germigny-des-Prés** (population 400). It is famous for a Carolingian *church,* built in 806, said to be the oldest in France. Byzantine mosaics were brought from Ravenna to decorate it. Thought to have been destroyed, one mosaic was discovered in 1848 under a coat of plaster. It is the magnificent scene in the east apse, showing the Ark of the Covenant with angels.

Another 5 km. (3 miles) to the southeast is the small village of ***Saint-Benoit,** where the ancient Benedictine *abbey of Fleury* was built in the mid-seventh century. Soon after, the abbey became the shrine for the bones of Saint Benedict, the order's founder, when the original burial place in the Italian monastery of Monte Cassino was sacked by the Lombards. The abbey church is a great 11th-century *basilica*. It is considered one of the most beautiful Romanesque buildings in France. Especially noteworthy are the ornate capitals of the tower incorporated into its porch.

*Sully (population 6,000) is the farthest point on the loop of this tour. Its 14th-century *château,* surrounded by a moat, is actually a massive Medieval fortress with corner towers flanking a rectangular keep. On the third floor you can see the heavy beams of the immense chestnut roof, shaped like an upturned ship. The duke of Sully, a minister of Henri IV, acquired the fortress in the early 17th century, enlarged it, and designed the park beyond the moat. Voltaire stayed there in 1716 and 1719 while he was exiled from Paris; he also had some of his plays performed here.

You can return to *Orléans* either by reversing this route or by following the left bank of the Loire through Tigy.

The loop tour southwest of Orléans captures four great storybook castles: the châteaux of *Blois, Chaumont, Cheverny,* and *Chambord.*

Drive west from Orléans on Route N 152 along the right bank of the Loire to *Beaugency* (population 7,000), with its centuries-old bridge, a massive 11th-century **watchtower,* the 15th-century *Château Dunois,* and a Renaissance *Hôtel de Ville. Ava-ray,* 8 km. (5 miles) farther west, has a moated château with charming gardens above the river. Next, you'll arrive in *Suèvres,* with a tenth-century **bell tower.* Route N 152 continues through the park of *Menars* to the 18th-century *château of Madame de Pompadour,* mistress of Louis XV. It has a very fine interior and some equally fine structures in the terraced park that leads down to the river.

Follow the road to a fork and then bear right for access to a château that stands in the heart of one of the most attractive large cities on the Loire.

*Blois (population 50,000) has steep, twisting streets, quaint old buildings, and a lovely 18th-century bridge. But it is the *******château* that dominates the city. Built on high ground, it reflects more than four centuries of French architecture. The powerful counts of Blois built the Gothic Salle des États in the north corner. The late-Gothic northeast wing, where the main entrance is located, was built by Louis XII from 1498 to 1503. François I built the splendid Renaissance northwest wing (1515–1524). This is the most famous part of the château, and its most prominent feature is the often photographed *******spiral staircase* in the open tower on the inner court. The southwest wing, in Classical style, was begun by Mansart for Gaston d'Orléans, the brother of Louis XIII, but it was never finished. On the south side

Blois: Stair Tower

of the château are the late-Gothic *Chapelle Saint-Calais* and the Medieval *Tour du Foix,* which offers a sweeping view of the town and the surrounding countryside. The entire château is redolent of history, but the *François I wing* seems to have seen more than its share. Catherine de Médicis had an apartment there, including a study with carved wall paneling that concealed 237 compartments for hiding state documents, jewelry—and poisons. Her son Henri III had the too-powerful Duc de Guise murdered in the château in 1588. Marie de Médicis escaped her two years of exile here by her son, Louis XIII, when she climbed down from a window in 1619. The three heraldic symbols that appear repeatedly in the château are the porcupine of Louis XII, the ermine of Anne of Brittany, and the salamander of François I.

From Blois, continue on Route N 152 along the right bank of the Loire for 16 km. (10 miles) and cross the bridge to the château at **Chaumont-sur-Loire** (population 800). Situated on a cliff above the river, the *château* is a ten-minute walk from the village through a *park* shaded by majestic cedar trees. Sturdy Gothic *towers* and a drawbridge attest to the château's original purpose as a fortress, but its grimness is softened by gingerbread motifs added during the Renaissance. The building in its present form dates from the mid-15th century, except for a fourth wing to the north, which was razed in about 1740 to create a *terrace* and to open up a view over the river.

When Catherine de Médicis acquired the château, she had a secret staircase built to connect her apartment to the tower suite occupied by the Florentine astrologer Ruggieri, with whom she discussed the future. After her husband, Henri II, died in 1559, Catherine forced his mistress Diane de Poitiers to exchange her beautiful and beloved Chenonceau (see page 147) for the austere Chaumont. Diane stayed only a short while and then retired to the château that Henry II had built for her at Anet on the Eure River. When the writer Madame de Staël was exiled in 1810 for criticizing Napoleon, she was given refuge at Chaumont where she completed her book *De l'Allemagne.*

Of special interest are the luxurious 19th-century *stables* and the lovely *dovecote* in the court-

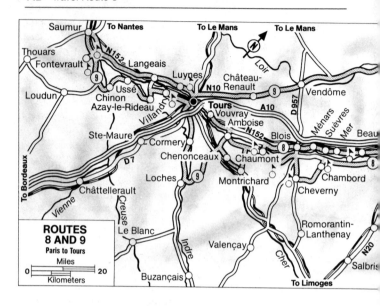

**ROUTES
8 AND 9**
Paris to Tours
Miles
0   20
Kilometers

yard. The latter was used at one time as a riding school and, for a while in the 18th century, as a factory that made terra-cotta portraits. Benjamin Franklin posed for one during a visit to the château.

From Chaumont-sur-Loire you can pick up Travel Route 9 by following Route D 751 west along the left bank of the Loire for 17 km. (10 miles) to *Amboise.* An alternative is to drive south from Chaumont 18 km. (11 miles) to Montrichard and proceed west 28 km. (17 miles) to *Chenonceaux.* However, you should consider the other treasures along this Travel Route: the châteaux of *Cheverny* and *Chambord.* Traveling east from Chaumont along a country road for 25 km. (15 miles), you

will come to **Cour-Cheverny** (population 720). The elegant, Classical ****château of Cheverny** was built in 1634. Descendants of the original owners still live here and its magnificent 17th-century **interior* is intact. There is a small hunting museum and, next door, kennels for 70 hunting dogs.

Hunting was the raison d'être for the next—and the last—château on this route. In fact, because it was a hunting lodge for kings, it became the grandest and most spectacular château in the entire Loire valley. Drive northeast on Route D 102 about 9.5 km. (6 miles) to *Bracieux* and then north 8 km. (5 miles) on D 112 to the **château of Chambord.** In majestic isolation amid sprawling private forest, the château is a ver-

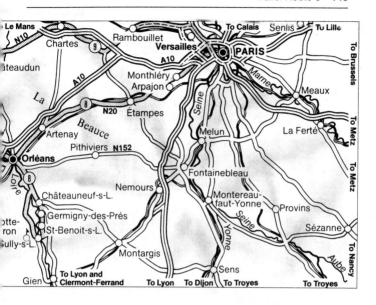

itable forest of turrets, pinnacles, gables, and chimneys. Following the taste of the Renaissance for rooftop promenades, there is a *roof terrace* offering an excellent view over the park. It seems more like a village street than a roof because of all the fanciful architecture that rises above it. The château has 440 rooms; its façade alone is 126 meters (420 feet) long. The famous *main staircase* goes from the ground floor to the roof, where it is crowned by a magnificent *lantern*. The design of this double staircase is a tour de force, often attributed to Leonardo da Vinci. It is composed of two spirals that start at different levels so that, although they cross and recross, they never meet. Thus, large groups of people could go up

and down at the same time. There are 14 other major staircases and 70 lesser ones.

Chambord was begun around 1519 by François I. It is said that 1,800 workmen labored there for 15 years, and work continued under other kings. After so much effort, ironically, the château was often empty. Louis XIV visited it only nine times during his long reign. Today, a sound-and-light show—music, recitative, and colored lights—is particularly impressive here, as the château's towers are reflected in the Cosson River.

To return to *Orléans,* take Route D 112 north for 10 km. (6 miles) to Route D 951; then travel east another 34 km. (21 miles) along the left bank of the Loire.

TRAVEL ROUTE 9: ***Paris–*Tours–***Castles on the Loire

See map on pages 142–143.

The castles on this tour are often described in superlatives: the most delightful (Chenonceau), the prettiest (Ussé), the most perfect (Azay-le-Rideau), the one with the most beautiful gardens (Villandry), the most beautiful setting (Amboise). Thus there is a certain consistency in beginning with another superlative: the most Gothic cathedral—at Chartres. The art historian Emile Mâle called it "the visible expression of medieval thought," adding that "nothing important has been left out."

From Paris, take Autoroute A 10 west across the rich farmlands of the Beauce plain. Continue west on this highway when it becomes Autoroute A 11 (rather than following A 10 as it turns south).

About 80 km., (48 miles) from Paris is Chartres (see page 129), where you can pick up Travel Route 8 (to Orléans) and Travel Route 7 (to Rennes). Travel Route 9 continues south on Highway N 10 to **Châteaudun** (population 17,000), which is situated on a plateau above the Loire River. The town you see today dates from the 18th century when it was largely rebuilt after a fire. Its towering *château* has a 15th-century Gothic wing on the west and a 16th-century Renaissance wing on the north, and their contrasting staircases provide a good comparison of the two different styles. The earliest part of the castle is the 12th-century watchtower. The walkway around the top of the fortress, originally used by sentries, provides fine views over the countryside. The late-Gothic (Flam-boyant) *Sainte-Chapelle* deserves a visit for its outstanding collection of expressive statues. South of the castle you can see interesting old houses. Beyond them, abutting the old ramparts of the town, stands the large *church of La Madeleine,* which has a fine Romanesque portal.

From Châteaudun, continue south on Route N 10 to the charming town of **Vendôme** (population 18,000). A ruined château in an attractive garden affords an excellent view over the countryside. The *Église de La Trinité* shows off a range of Gothic styles from the 12th to the 15th centuries. Note especially the beautiful Flamboyant *façade* and the splendid freestanding 12th-century *bell tower.* But it's the beauty of the town itself that will linger in your memory. At Vendôme the Loir River divides into many channels, and the town is situated on islands joined by a multitude of pretty bridges—an ideal place for strolling.

Vendôme is only 32 km. (20

miles) from *Blois* (see page 140), an interesting city in its own right, and a connection with Travel Route 8, if you wish to make an excursion to the châteaux of **Chambord* (see page 142), **Cheverny* (see page 142), and **Chaumont* (see page 141). For this alternative, follow Route D 957 to the southeast.

From Vendôme, Travel Route 9 proceeds southwest on Route N 10. It goes through the town of *Château-Renault,* with its tanneries and 12th-century watchtower, and passes the huge *Grange de Moslay,* formerly a tithe barn but now used for music festivals.

*Tours (population 260,000; 218 km.; 131 miles from Paris), is a major industrial city and the capital of Touraine. Its central location makes Tours a good base for trips to the lovely countryside, which is famous for fine food and wine and for magnificent châteaux. Tours itself dates from Gallo-Roman times. Saint Martin, who is remembered for sharing his cloak with a freezing beggar, became a vigorous missionary and was made bishop of Tours in about 370. Deeply venerated throughout Europe after his death, he eventually became the national saint of France. Pilgrims flocked to his tomb at Tours. Another bishop, the sixth-century Saint Gregory, won fame as the first great French historian. In the eighth century the English scholar Alcuin, adviser to the Emperor Charlemagne, made the nearby abbey of Marmoutier (see below) a center of learning

and one of the richest abbeys in Europe during his tenure as abbot there. Tours became wealthy and renowned in the 15th and 16th centuries for its silk and gold brocade fabrics.

The Rue Nationale runs south from the *Pont Wilson,* which crosses the Loire, to the *Place Jean-Jaurès,* the center of the city. Midway between the two is the Rue de la Scellerie, which leads east to the *cathedral of Saint-Gatien.* (Saint-Gatien is credited with introducing Christianity to the region in the third century.) The building is a compendium of Gothic styles, from the early 13th-century choir to the elaborate Flamboyant west façade. The two towers are topped by Renaissance domes. The stained-glass windows, which date from the 13th to the 15th centuries, are magnificent. On the north side of the cathedral is the beautiful cloister *La Psallette.* To the south is the former archbishop's palace, dating from the 17th and 18th centuries. It now houses the *Musée des Beaux-Arts,* comprising 35 rooms with many paintings, including two important works by Andrea Mantegna, sculpture, and fine furniture.

West of the Rue Nationale, beyond the *Hôtel Gouin,* is the *Place Plumereau,* the center of the old town. This picturesque area is worth exploring for its old houses and courtyards, as well as its antiques shops, cafés, and restaurants.

To visit the castles east of Tours,

leave the city on the north side of the Loire via Route N 152, heading east. After about 4 km. (2.5 miles), you will come to the remains of the once powerful *abbey of Marmoutier*, founded in 372 by Saint Martin of Tours and fortified in the 13th century. Only the *Portail de la Crosse* and some underground cells, hewn from rock between the fourth and sixth centuries, are left. A convent has been built on the site. About 6 km. (4 miles) farther east is **Vouvray,** famous for its white wine. Visits to the wine cellars are permitted. In honor of the novelist Honoré de Balzac, who was born in Tours, a statue of one of his characters, Gaudissart, has been erected in the town. About 15 km. (9 miles) to the southeast, you have a great view of the beautiful château on the far side of the Loire at ****Amboise** (population 11,500). A town and a bridge have existed at this point since ancient times. It was thus a strategic location, and the promontory, with its commanding view of the countryside, made it a logical site for a fortress. The **château still dominates the town, although it ceased being a fortress in the 15th century, when it was completely reconstructed as an elegant home for the king. Many French monarchs used it, but François I, who was the patron of the château's most famous resident, Leonardo da Vinci, is particularly associated with it. When the king entertained Emperor Charles V in 1539, torches set a wall covering on fire and the emperor nearly

suffocated from the smoke. In 1560, a Huguenot conspiracy to capture François II failed. The conspirators were killed and their bodies hung from a balcony off the *Salles d'Etats.* After that episode, the château fell into decline and was abandoned as a royal residence. During the reign of Louis XIV, the château was used as a prison. In 1818 nearly three-quarters of it was demolished. Nonetheless, what remains is imposing and elegant. The ***Chapelle le Saint-Hubert* is a jewel of Gothic architecture, both inside and out. The lintel of the portal is carved with very fine **reliefs* of Saint Christopher with the Christ Child; Saint Anthony; and the vision of Saint Hubert, the patron saint of hunters, kneeling before a deer. The **Logis du Roi (king's residence) is a fine late-Gothic building with an elaborate façade and two vaulted halls. Flanking the terrace are massive towers—the *Tour des Minimes* and the **Tour Hurtault.* In the entryway of each tower is a gently spiraling ramp which allowed horses and carriages to be brought inside. A short walk east along the Rue Victor-Hugo leads to the **Clos-Lucé,* a 15th-century manor that François I gave to Leonardo da Vinci, who, even in failing health, worked there every day until he died in 1519.

From here Route D 31 passes the **Pagode de Chanteloup,* built from 1775 to 1778 in a mélange of Chinese and Louis XIV styles, and continues through the *forest* of *Amboise,* hunting grounds of the French kings, before reaching *La Croix-en-Touraine.* Turn east and drive approximately 6 km. (4 miles) to the village of ****Chenonceaux,** where a wonderful Renaissance castle is located. The ****château of Chenonceau,** for unknown reasons, is spelled differently from the village. An avenue of magnificent plane trees leads to a drawbridge and lovely *formal gardens*—the Italian garden of Diane de Poitiers on the left and the French garden of Catherine de Médicis on the right. The pointed split in the placement and character of the gardens reflects the difference in their relationship to the king. The château itself was intimately connected with them and also with a third woman, Cathérine Briconnet, who built it. Her husband, the royal treasurer Thomas Bohier, bought the property in 1513, and because he was

Chenonceau Castle

often away, he put her in charge of the construction. After his death, the property was given to the king to satisfy the debt incurred in building it. Henri II presented it to his mistress, Diane de Poitiers, in 1547. When Henri died in 1559, his jealous wife, Catherine de Médicis, forced Diane to exchange the lovely Chenonceau for the dour Chaumont (see page 141).

Chenonceau seems to float regally, like a swan, on the River Cher. It is serene, feminine, and, most of all, romantic. The interior is splendid as well—rich in elegant furniture, ornate ceilings, and huge fireplaces. The François I room is the most elaborate. Catherine de Médicis's small library offers a charming view over the Cher; and the **Long Gallery* she added to the bridge Diane de Poitiers had built over the river is spectacular. The labyrinthine kitchens, deep in the foundations of the château, are unusual. Outside, in the stables built by Catherine de Médicis, a wax museum has been installed to show what life was like in the château.

From Chenonceaux, you can connect with Travel Route 8 by going through *Montrichard* (28 km.; 17 miles) to *Chaumont* (18 km.; 11 miles).

Travel Route 9 continues west to Route D 31 and then south to one of the most interesting small towns in France: ****Loches** (population 6,500), situated on the banks of the Indre River, has a large, picturesque, and well-preserved Medieval quarter with twisting alleys that climb to a great *château*. The massive 13th-century **Porte Royale* leads to the *Cité Médiévale,* surrounded by a wall 2 km. (1 mile) long. To the left is the 12th-century **church of Saint-Ours.* Its four conical spires are unique; the middle two are hollow and form the roof of the nave. To the north is the entrance to the **château* itself. There are two contrasting wings: one is severely Medieval in style, the other in the more ornate style of Louis XII. The château contains the tomb of Charles VII's mistress, Agnès Sorel, who died at the age of 28, allegedly poisoned by the king's son, the future Louis XI. An elegant tomb sculpture shows the beautiful Agnès guarded by two angels. The lambs at her feet may represent a pun on her Christian name, which sounds very much like the Latin *agnus* (lamb). The château also contains the *oratory* built by Charles VIII for his queen, Anne of Brittany. Its elaborate decoration includes a multitude of ermine tails, for the ermine was her heraldic insignia.

At the south end of the citadel, the part most difficult to defend, stands a massive 11th-century **fortress*—a central Romanesque keep, flanked by *round towers that contain some of the most frightening dungeons imaginable. Ludovico Sforza, the duke of Milan, was imprisoned there for eight years and died in 1508 as he was about to be released. Cardinal Jean Balue, the bishop of Evreux,

was kept for 11 years in a small cage suspended from the ceiling. You can walk around the impressive fortifications on a path outside the citadel, where the moat used to be.

To return to *Tours,* take Route N 143 northwest.

To visit the castles west of Tours, cross to the right bank of the Loire and take Route 152 west for 10 km. (6 miles) to *Luynes,* a village of quaint wooden buildings and a number of homes carved into the soft cliffs. There is a 15th-century **château,* which is surprisingly graceful despite the stern impression created by its massive round towers. Another 13 km. (8 miles) down Route N 152 lies ****Langeais** (population 4,000). The **chateau* here hasn't changed since it was built in the 15th century. As you approach it across the drawbridge, it seems severe and forbidding. There are three thick **towers* with conical roofs and a **sentry walk* all around the ramparts. The château was built between 1465 and 1469 to protect the border of Touraine against the Bretons. The need for defense was eliminated in 1491 when Charles VIII married Anne of Brittany—in this very castle. Contrasting with the stern façade, the interior of the château is elegant and filled with fine contemporary antiques. Across a beautiful **garden* is a tenth-century watchtower, reputed to be the oldest in France.

Continues west on Route N 152

and cross to ***Saumur** (population 36,000), a town that is famous for its white wines and for its riding academy, which was established in 1763. The cadets became symbols of courage and patriotism in 1940, when they mounted a futile defense against overwhelming German forces.

Strategically located between the Loire and Thouet rivers, Saumur was protected by a fortress as early as the tenth century. The present **château* dates from the 14th century. It has the sturdy towers and massive walls of a knight's castle yet is graceful enough also to suggest a Renaissance palace. The northwest side has been demolished. The château contains two museums: the **Musée des Arts Décoratifs,* with a collection that includes tapestries, enamels, statues, and ceramics, and the **Musée du Cheval,* which is devoted to the history of horses and riding. The churches of *Saint-Pierre,* near the Loire, and **Nôtre-Dame-de-Nantilly,* south of the château, were both built in the 12th century with later additions. Both are noted for their exceptional ****tapestries.** Nôtre-Dame-de-Nantilly also has a fine 12th-century wooden statue of the Madonna in a chapel on the right of the apse.

From Saumur, drive southeast on Route D 947 along the left bank of the Loire for 11 km. (6.6 miles); then turn south for 5 km. (3 miles) to ***Fontevrault** (also spelled *Fontevraud;* population 2,000). This small town won considerable fame for its important *abbey* which was influential in the history of both France and England. Founded in 1099, it soon grew to five communities—monks, nuns, lepers, other sick people, and aristocratic women wishing to withdraw from society. Madame de Montespan, a mistress of Louis XIV, retired here. Her sister, Gabrielle, was abbess during the high point of the abbey's history. There were 39 abbesses, all from the nobility, including the granddaughter of William the Conqueror and members of the House of Bourbon. The powerful abbess exercised total control—not only of the convent and its nuns but also of the monastery and its monks. The Plantagenets were generous in making gifts to the abbey, and many of them chose to be buried there.

After 700 years, the abbey's proud existence came to an abrupt

Fontevrault: Cookhouse

end with the French Revolution, when some of the buildings were destroyed. Later, Napoleon turned it into a prison, which it remained until 1963.

Even in its reduced and restored state, the abbey gives a remarkable picture of life in a Medieval monastery. The abbey church is an austere, impressive Romanesque structure, roofed by a series of domes. Henry II of England, his wife, Eleanor of Aquitaine, their son Richard the Lion-Hearted, and a daughter-in-law, Isabelle of Angoulême, were buried here; their *tomb effigies* can be seen to the right of the nave. There is a large 16th-century *cloister*. To the east stands the *chapter house,* with 16th-century wall paintings, and to the south is the spacious refectory. Next to the refectory is the 12th-century *Tour d'Evrault,* an unusual octagonal building that served as the kitchen. The odd-looking small towers and what appears to be a central spire are all chimneys for its fireplaces.

Return north to Route 947, then proceed southeast to Route D 751 for 16 km. (10 miles). As you travel along the left bank of the scenic Vienne River, you will see a Medieval fortress towering dramatically in the distance. It is the famous ****château de Chinon,** strongly associated with historical figures—Henry II of England, Richard the Lion-Hearted, Joan of Arc, the writer François Rabelais, and even Cardinal Richelieu, who used the château as a quarry to build another residence and thus

bears some of the blame for its present ruin. Even though empty and only partly restored, the chateau still makes a powerful impression, as do the splendid views from its ramparts. Perched high on a crag, the château overlooks the Vienne River, the old town, and the vineyards for which Chinon is also famous. The château is really composed of three structures: *Fort Saint-Georges,* built by Henry II in the 12th century; the *Château du Milieu,* containing the partly restored royal residence where Charles VII hid among his followers to see if Joan of Arc could identify him (enter through the slender clock tower, which now houses a small museum devoted to Joan of Arc); and the 13th-century *Château de Coudray,* the most westerly structure, with its cylindrical keep and *Tour du Moulin.*

Below the fortress, a narrow road marked "To the Echo" leads to a platform facing the castle walls, which, on a good day when there aren't too many people around to ruin the acoustics, will return a decisive "No!" to any question that ends in the word *Chinon.*

The Medieval town at the base of the cliff has been well restored. Follow the Rue Voltaire, which used to be the main thoroughfare, to the picturesque crossroads called the *Grand Carroi.* A fine museum of local history now occupies the *Maison des États-Généraux.* On this site Richard the Lion-Hearted is said to have died in 1199 from a crossbow wound received at Châlus. Rabelais spent his early years at 15 Rue de la Lamproie.

Take Route D 749 north almost to the Loire; turn right at the atomic power plant at *Avoine,* and continue for 11 km. (6.6 miles) on Route D 7 to the romantic ***Château de Ussé.** This is the turreted, white stone fantasy believed to have inspired the castle of Sleeping Beauty in Charles Perrault's fairy tale. The château rises from flowered terraces on the bank of the Indre River and stands out dramatically against the dark green hills of the forest of Chinon. Construction began in the 15th century, but most of it was done in the 16th and 17th centuries—creating a successful blend of Gothic and Renaissance styles. The 18th-century **Chambre du Roi,* a room the owners kept ready for an impromptu visit from the king, is particularly beautiful. A charming **chapel,* built between 1520 and 1538 in the park, has fine **Renaissance furnishings,* including a ceramic bas-relief by Della Robbia.

When you leave Ussé, go west on Route D 7 and then southwest on Route D 17 along the left bank of the Indre for 14 km. (8 miles) to ****Azay-le-Rideau** (population 2,800). The village is picturesque, and the *church of Saint-Symphorien* has a fine Romanesque façade. But the *pièce de résistance* is the 16th-century **château.* This masterpiece is a perfect example of how Renaissance alterations turned castles

Azay-le-Rideau

into palaces—for instance, the fortifications have been changed to decorative turrets; and although the shape is Gothic, there is Italian influence in the new symmetry. Like Chenonceau (see page 147), this elegant structure was built by a woman: Philippa Lesbahy, wife of the financier Gilles Berthelot. She supervised the construction from 1518 to 1529 and managed to create a perfect work of art. At about the time it was finished, however, her husband fell from favor with the king, who confiscated the château. It is now a **Renaissance museum* with an excellent collection of furnishings and wall hangings. The grand staircase is a particularly fine feature.

From Azay-le-Rideau, drive downstream along the right bank of the Indre, then turn north and finally northeast on Route D 7 a total of 15 km. (9 miles) to the ****Château de Villandry,** an elegant structure built in the 16th century by Jean Le Breton, a financier and minister of François I. It was remodeled in the 18th century and restored in the 20th—all the while remaining in private ownership. Villandry has a moat, a great central courtyard overlooking the Cher Valley and the Loire, and a large, square 14th-century watchtower that belonged to an earlier castle. The château displays fine furniture, 18th-century paneling, a *collection of Spanish paintings,* and a Moorish ceiling; above all, however, Villandry is famous for its spectacular **gardens.* The 16th-century gardens in formal French style were torn up in the 19th century when naturalistic English gardens became the rage; then in the early part of this century, the original geometric gardens were carefully restored from old plans and drawings. They are magnificent: three huge terraces consisting of a water garden at the highest level, a decorative garden planted and clipped in intricate symbolic patterns, and a colorful kitchen garden laid out in precise designs. Long cool avenues of trees punctuate the vast swirls of flowers and boxwood, and there is a fragrant herb garden.

From Villandry, return to Tours by driving 17 km. (10 miles) west along the Cher.

There is still one more château to see—the remarkable castle that was home to the equally remarkable statesman Talleyrand, a former bishop who became Napoleon's foreign minister and was later a revolutionary. Travel southwest from Tours on Route D 76, then turn south on Route D 956 to **Valençay** (population 3,170), which is 77 km. (48 miles) from Tours. The *château* was built in 1540 by a French financier, Jacques d'Estampes, who was influenced by the château at Chambord. A Renaissance edifice, Valençay nonetheless shows hints of the Classical style. The south wing was added in the 17th century and the New Tower in the 18th. Talleyrand bought the château in 1805, furnished it sumptuously, and lived there until his death in 1838. In addition to its lavish furniture and decorations, the château has an interesting automobile museum and a park with peacocks, flamingos, llamas, and other creatures.

TRAVEL ROUTE 10: *Tours–La Rochelle–*Royan (307 km.; 184 miles)

See map on page 154.

This route takes you west from Tours through the Poitou region with its fertile and varied landscape and Poitiers, rich in Romanesque architecture. The route continues to the Atlantic Coast harbor of *La Rochelle* and travels along the Côte de Beauté to the seaside resort of *Royan.*

The first part of this Travel Route goes to La Rochelle by way of Poitiers (follow the route marked "A" on the map). From Tours, Route N 10 crosses both the Cher and the Indre rivers then passes through *Montbazon,* with its enormous 12th century *watchtower, before continuing to **Poitiers** (population 85,000). Situated on a rocky plateau surrounded by the Clain and Boivre rivers, the city was an early center of Christianity and the old capital of Poitou, where Charles Martel, grandfather of Charlemagne, halted the invasion of the Arabs from Spain in 732. At the center of town, surrounded by an open-air market, is *Nôtre-Dame-la-Grande.* It is one of the most beautiful Romanesque churches in France, with a richly ornamented west façade flanked by two bell towers and, within, notable capitals in the choir. To the south is *Saint-Hilaire-le-Grand,* named for Poitiers' first bishop, which has a unique feature— seven naves; to the east is the **Baptistère Saint-Jean,* built in the fourth century for baptism by immersion and perhaps the oldest Christian monument in France. The large *Cathédrale Saint-Pierre,* has a somewhat clumsy façade, but an imposing interior, with stained glass from the early 13th century—the features of King Henry II of England and his queen, Eleanor of Aquitaine, who often resided in Poitiers, are discernible in the Crucifixion window in the apse; the carved choir stalls, also from the 13th century,

are the oldest in France. The *church of Sainte-Radegonde, founded in 560 by the patron saint of Poitiers, contains her tomb. A few minutes' walk away is a partly subterranean chapel of the seventh or eighth century, the *Hypogée Martyrium,* believed to have been a Christian cemetery enclosed within the pagan necropolis.

A secular structure of particular interest in the center of town is the *Palais de Justice* in which parts of the old ducal palace remain, notably the *Grande Salle,* with its magnificent Gothic window, three fireplaces, carved-wood ceiling and the donjon. Charles VII was proclaimed king here in 1442, and seven years later in this same room the Bishop of Poitiers interrogated Joan of Arc on the voices and visions that inspired her to battle.

One of Poitiers' more amusing claims to fame is that here, in 1579, a famous flea was discovered on the breast of Catherine des Roches; "La puce de Mme des Roches" became the subject of a celebrated collection of verses. Michel Foucault, the renowned structuralist philosopher, was born here in 1926.

About 7 km. (4 miles) south of Poitiers, Route N 11 branches away to the right of N 10, which leads to Bordeaux through Angoulême. Follow Route N 11 for 17 km. (11 miles) to the ancient hilltop town of *Lusignan,* home of the legendary fairy Melusine, allegedly the ancestor of the lords of Lusignan who ruled Jerusalem and Cyprus at the time of the Cru-

sades. The castle Melusine is said
to have built magically overnight
can no longer be seen, but there is
a pleasant promenade on the site.

Saint-Maixent-l'École, 26 km.
(16 miles) farther west, has an
attractive late-Gothic abbey, parts
of which date to the 11th and 13th
centuries. Several churches in the
area were desecrated or destroyed
by Huguenots in the 16th century,
and this is one that was damaged.
Continue 23 km. (14 miles) further to **Niort** (population 65,000).
Built on a sloping riverbank, this
city was the birthplace of Fran-
çoise d'Aubigne, Marquise de
Maintenon, lover and later the
secret wife of Louis XIV. Of interest is the triangular, Renaissance-
style *city hall,* a **donjon** consisting of two giant 12th- to 13th-
century towers, and an elegant
bell tower 76 meters (235 feet)
high. The old *Hôtel de Ville,* a
Renaissance mansion dating from
1535, houses the *Musée du Pilori,*
whose most interesting treasure is
a complete collection of coins
from the Carolingian mint at
Melle. The museum-minded can
also visit the *Musée des Beaux-
Arts,* which exhibits ivories, tapestries, enamels, and a series of
panels painted in the 14th century.

Farther west is *Coulon,* where
you can take boat trips on the
Marais Poitevin, peaceful, low-
lying fen country with hundreds of
canals and tree-lined streams.
Livestock as well as all crops are
moved by boat. Route N 11 bends
sharply to the west at Mauze, and
after 40 km. (25 miles) reaches **La**

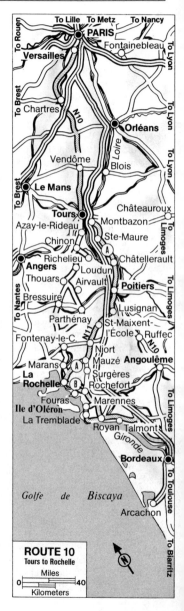

Rochelle (population 80,000; 239 km.; 148 miles from Tours), one of France's greatest maritime towns from the 14th to the 18th centuries. Ships would arrive here bearing spices, raw sugar, cocoa, and coffee, while others departed bearing emigrants to settle in Canada. The town was one of the first to trade with America. A Huguenot stronghold during the religious war, La Rochelle survived a half-year siege in 1573 by importing supplies from the English. When Cardinal Richelieu began a second siege in 1627, he built a dike across the bay, thus cutting the city off from supplies and starving it into submission; when he entered the city after 15 months, only 5,000 out of 28,000 inhabitants were still alive. La Rochelle's importance decreased greatly when the Edict of Nantes was revoked in 1685, and a century later (1763), when Canada was ceded to England. Although it has once again become a lively fishing and pleasure port, today it is not deep enough for large ships; consequently, overseas traffic arrives at the port of La Palice on the Ile de Ré, just off the coast, reaching the mainland from there by ferry.

La Rochelle is a delightful town to explore, with many well-preserved buildings and arcaded streets. Sights worth seeing include the *Old Harbor,* with its fishing boats and picturesque towers—the 14th-century *Tour Saint-Nicolas,* a mighty five-cornered donjon; opposite it, and once helping to support a chain suspended between them when the harbor was closed at night and in times of war, the *Tour de la Chaine;* and the cylindrical **Tour de la Lanterne (1445–1468), with its octagonal spire, once a lighthouse, commanding a panoramic view of the city, the harbor, the Île de Ré and, at low tide, the remains of Richelieu's dam.

From the *Old Harbor* you enter La Rochelle through the 13th-century *Porte de la Grosse-Horloge.* To the right is the opulent Renaissance *town hall,* founded in 1289 but dating mainly from 1595 to 1606, with an attractive *courtyard façade; a delicate wall with crenelated parapet protects the front entrance. Northeast of the town hall is the Rue des Merciers, with its old *arcade houses.*

The *Musée du Nouveau Monde,* located at 10 Rue Fleuriau, was opened in 1981 and holds important exhibitions relating primarily to French maritime commerce with the New World. A collection of local art and archaeology, including Gallo-Roman remains, is on display in the *Musée d'Orbigny-Bernon,* behind the cathedral. The lovely *Parc Charruyer,* with its own stream and majestic swans, runs alongside the beach. The early-morning fish auction is a noisy and exhilirating way to wake up.

Continue the trip to Royan along the coast (follow the route marked "B" on the map). Depart La Rochelle on Route N 137 heading southeast through the seaside resort of *Chatelaillon-Plage*.

Fouras (population 4,500), a small seaside resort, features a 15th century *donjon* surrounded by a triple ring of 17th-century walls. The beach extends on both sides of the *Pointe de la Fumée*. From this tongue of land, it is only 3 km. (2 miles) to *Île d'Aix*, where, in July 1815, Napoleon spent his last three days on French soil before boarding the British ship *Bellerophon*, which would take him to Saint Helena and exile. These events are the theme of exhibits in the *museum* in the *Maison de l'Empereur*.

From Fouras, continue to **Rochefort** (population 30,000), a port 15 km. (9 miles) above the mouth of the Charente River that was established in the 17th century. In the 18th century the city experienced a renewed development thanks to trade with the American colonies. Of interest are the *birthplace* of marine officer and novelist Pierre Loti (1850–1923); the *Marine Museum*, with many models of sailing ships and steamers; and the *Corderie Royale*, a rope-making center, restored in 1981.

From Rochefort you can drive directly to Royan (40 km.; 25 miles) on D 733, but the route through *Marennes* and the peninsula of *Arvert* (29 km.; 18 miles, longer) is more interesting. Leave Rochefort to the south over the *Pont du Martrou*, a bridge across the broad Charente. This route runs through *Soubise* and *Moeze*,

where the church has a fine openwork spire and a 16th century cross, to the former seaport of *Brouage*, now 3 km. (2 miles) from the ocean. Its 17th century **ramparts**, embellished with coats-of-arms and cardinals' miters, indicate that this was Richelieu's base of operations in 1628 against La Rochelle. The people of Quebec, honoring their founder, Samuel de Champlain (1567–1635), a native of Brouage, restored the town's 16th- and 17th-century church. Louis XIV, suffering from an excess of romantic ardor, once made a special detour to the town so that he could pass the night in a room that his beloved Marie Mancini had merely occupied. Marie, niece of Mazarin, was off-limits until the king's marriage with Spain (in the person of Maria-Theresa) was consummated.

About 7 km. (4 miles) farther is **Marennes** (population 4,400). This village on the mouth of the Seudre is famous for its oysters. An attractive 15th century *bell tower* dominates Marennes.

From here you can take an interesting side trip to the **Île d'Oléron** (population of 15,000), France's second-largest island after Corsica and an ideal place for those seeking luminous light, lovely sunsets, sand and sea air, and the tasty oysters, shrimps, and local wines. To get there, drive beyond *Bourcefranc* (which has an oyster museum) over the *Pont d'Oléron*; to the right is the picturesque *Fort du Chapus*, built under

Louis XIV. The flat island, bordered by high dunes and blessed with many beaches, has three small towns: On the east coast is *Le Château d'Oléron*, its 17th-century citadel washed by the sea; in the center of the island is *Saint-Pierre-d'Oleron*, with its 13th century *Lanterne des Morts*; and at the southeast cape is *Saint-Trojan-les-Bains*, a pretty seaside resort surrounded by pine forests.

To continue to Royan from Marennes, take the toll bridge over the Seudre. At *La Tremblade*, on the opposite bank, turn right on Route D 25, which leads to the seaside resort of *Ronce-les-Bains* and around the north cape of the Arvert Peninsula, passing through Coubre Forest along the coast for 25 km. (16 miles), with a view of the rootless, often stormy sea. From the seaside resort of *Saint-Palais-sur-Mer*, the Côte de Beauté extends to the broad mouth of the Gironde River, at whose center lies ***Royan** (population 21,000; 307 km.; 184 miles from Tours), cradled by the **Grande Conche*, one of the largest seaside resorts of the French Atlantic coast. Almost completely destroyed by bombs during World War II, it has since been reconstructed. At the north end of the beach is the impressive *Front de Mer*, enclosing stores and dwellings; behind it towers the bold steel-and-concrete **church of Nôtre-Dame*. Near the lively harbor is the circular *Casino* building, and to the west, the *Palais des Congrès*.

TRAVEL ROUTE 11: ***Paris–*Bordeaux–*Biarritz (749 km.; 464 miles)

See map on page 159.

Travel Route 11 offers a great amount of flexibility as you head southwest from Paris. You have the opportunity of switching to other travel routes several times before reaching the beautiful resort of Biarritz on the Atlantic coast. On Travel Route 11, you'll pass through Bordeaux and drive along the scenic Routes des Lacs de la Côte d'Argent into Basque country.

Route N 10 runs directly from Paris to Biarritz. The trip from Paris through Rambouilet and Chartres (96 km.; 60 miles) is described in Travel Route 7. The next leg of the itinerary, from Chartres to Tours (39 km.; 24 miles), through Châteaudun and Vendôme, is described in Travel Route 9 (Loire castles around Tours). Travel Route 21 also connects with Route N 10 in Tours. The trip to Poitiers (103 km.; 64 miles) is described in Travel Route 10 (Trip to Poitou). From Poitiers, Route N 10 goes through

Ruffec to ***Angoulême** (population 50,000), located on a high plateau over the Charente and Anguienne rivers. The upper town was once reserved for the nobility, while the citizenry lived in the lower town. Of particular interest in the *ville haute* (upper city) is the 12th-century Romanesque *cathedral of Saint-Pierre,* whose façade sculptures, among the most beautiful of the period, include scenes from the Last Judgment and the Ascension. Unfortunately, the cathedral has been mutilated over the centuries, especially by its insensitive "restorers."

From Angoulême you can take a 42 km. (26 mile) side trip to **Cognac.** Westbound Route N 141 passes through a lovely countryside that eventually reaches the wine region of Grande Champagne, from whose wines the famous cognac is made and where you can visit the cellars of such world-famous brands as Martell, Hennessy, and Otard. Otard occupies the former Valois castle where François I was born in 1494.

From Angoulême Travel Route 11 passes through the towns of *Barbezieux* and *Saint-André-de-Cubzac,* crossing the Dordogne on a **viaduct* constructed in 1882 by Gustave Eiffel, builder of the famous tower; it continues through the large grape-growing region of *Entre-Deux-Mers* between the Dordogne and Garonne rivers, which meet 25 km. (16 miles) north of Bordeaux and flow into the Gironde. A detailed description of the city of **Bordeaux* begins on page 69. (From Bordeaux you can work backwards using Travel Route 22 which goes from Belfort through Lyon and ends in Bordeaux.)

You can take either of two roads from Bordeaux to Bayonne: Route N 10 is direct but monotonous, passing 175 km. (108 miles) through long forest stretches of once swampy and sparsely inhabited land where herdsmen were forced to walk about on high stilts. Today the area, reclaimed by drainage and forestation, is prosperous, its economy based on cattle raising and lumber. The more interesting road is the inland **Route des Lacs de la Côte d'Argent* (Route of the Silver Coast Lakes). Although 60 km. (37 miles) longer than N 10, it offers many rewarding sights. From Bordeaux drive west on Route N 250 for 60 km. (37 miles) to the resort of ***Arcachon** (population 20,000), located at the southern edge of the *Bassin d'Arcachon,* a basin connected to the sea through a strait 3 km. (2 miles) wide. The city which is famous for its oyster beds, is divided into the *Ville d'Été* (summertime resort) along 5 km. (3 miles) beach, and the *Ville d'Hiver,* (winter resort), protected by dunes.

From Arcachon, follow the coast road 7 km. (4 miles) to the chic seaside resort of *Pyla-sur-Mer,* at the foot of the highest dune in Europe.

From *Biscarosse-Plage,* the road runs inland to the **Petit Étang de Biscarosse,* one of the

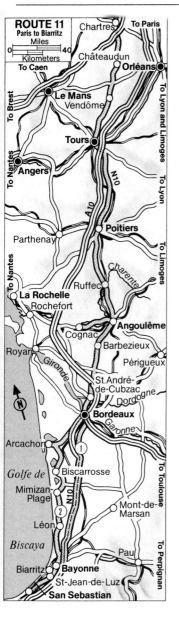

country's prettiest ponds: 9 km, (6 miles) farther is *Parentis-en-Born,* with its oil derricks; the road continues through the beach of *Mimizan,* 6 km. (3.5 miles) to the west, and leads to *Léon,* where you can take a boat trip on the *Courant d'Huchet. Continuing 31 km. (19 miles) farther south, you reach the beautiful area around *Hosségor on the *Golfe de Gascogne.* Nearby is ultrachic *Biarritz (see below), visible to the southwest from the *Plage de l'Océan.* About 7 km. (4 miles) farther the road meets Route N 10.

Follow N 10 for 13 km. (8 miles) to **Bayonne** (population 47,000), capital of the French Basque country and the southwesternmost city of France. All roads lead to this important industrial harbor that once controlled the passes of the western Pyrenees. Here, too, you are on the border of the *Pays Basques,* the country of the original inhabitants of both slopes of the west Pyrenees. A tall, good-looking people of unknown origin, the Basques in France number about a quarter of a million and speak a language (Euskara) quite distinct from any other in Europe. Of the original native costume, only the beret and rope-soled shoes remain. Bayonne is also known for its juicy hams; for a local liqueur called Izarra; and for chocolate and marzipan, both of which were introduced by the Jews after their expulsion from Spain in the late 15th century.

The town's *citadel* (1674–1679) was designed by the architect Vauban. To reach the main square, the *Place de la Liberté*, cross the bridge over the Adour and continue over the Nive on the *Pont Mayou*. The picturesque tree-lined **Rue du Port-Neuf* leads from here to the **Cathédrale Sainte-Marie* (13th–16th century) and the adjacent 14th-century cloisters. On the other side of the Nive is the ***Musée Basque,* known for its ethnographic collections detailing Basque culture and folklore. The **Musée Bonnat,* featuring the art collection of the painter Léon Bonnat, is also worth seeing.

In Bayonne, you can continue Travel Route 11 or pick up Travel Route 23.

The rocky *Côte Basque* on the Gulf of Biscaye extends for 40 km. (25 miles) from Bayonne to *Hendaye.* The direct road takes you past the mouth of the Adour and along the coast through *La Baule* (see page Travel Route 21) and *Royan* (see Travel Route 10) to **Biarritz* (population 28,000), the largest seaside resort on the French Atlantic coast, known for its bracing climate, rocky coves, and sandy beaches. Countess Montijo and her daughter Eugénie spent summer holidays here. Eugénie eventually married Napoleon III, who accompanied her to Biarritz in 1854 and built the *Villa Eugénie* (now a hotel), transforming the unassuming little fishing village virtually overnight into a famous rendezvous for "High Society." The **Grande Plage* extends northeast to the lighthouse on *Pointe Saint-Martin.* From the *Fisherman's Harbor* a tunnel leads to the chaste and solitary *Rocher de la Vierge,* or Virgin's Rock, alone in the middle of the sea. The **Musée de la Mer,* with its aquarium, sits on the Atalaya plateau that separates the fishing port from Vieux-Port beach.

To the west is the rocky inlet of the *Vieux-Port* and the aptly named **La Perspective,* where a brisk walk is rewarded by a glorious view of the Basque coast and the distant mountains of Spain; the second beach, *Plage des Basque,* connects with it.

The coast road leads to ***Saint-Jean-de-Luz** (population 10,000), where Louis XIV was married to the Spanish Infanta Maria-Theresa in 1660, though he still yearned for the forbidden niece of Mazarin. Today the town is a modish seaside resort and important fishing harbor, especially for tuna. The 13th-century *church of Saint-Baptiste* is worth seeing, particularly for its high altar.

The great French composer Maurice Ravel (1875–1937) was born in neighboring *Ciboure.* In the hinterland, a cogwheel railroad leads up the 900-meter- (2,952-feet-) high **La Rhûne,* the best observation point of the Basque country. To get from Saint-Jean-de-Luz to Hendaye you can choose between two roads: Route N 10 reaches Hendaye in 11 km. (7 miles); on the other side of the Bidassoa River is the Spanish border station of Irún, and from there it is 18 km. (11 miles) to San Sebastián in the Basque country of neighboring Spain. Alternatively, the picturesque *Route de la Corniche Basque* goes along the rocky coast for 16 km. (10 miles), to the

fashionable resort of *Hendaye-Plage* and the village of *Hendaye.* In the boundary river is the *Île des Faisons,* an island where meetings between kings and exchanges of prisoners once took place.

TRAVEL ROUTE 12: Paris–*Limoges–*Toulouse (684 km.; 425 miles)

See maps on pages 162 and 163.

This scenic route passes through the countryside of Sologne, Berry, Limousin, and the Dordogne Valley with its caves and interesting old cities. Beyond Toulouse is the Spanish border, and 176 km. (109 miles) farther is Barcelona.

The first part of the route, 115 km. (71 miles) from Paris to Orléans, is described in Travel Route 8 (trip to the ***Loire castles around Orléans). The second part—79 km. (49 miles) from Orléans to Vierzon—follows Route N 20 through the Sologne plain, a former swamp with many small lakes and ponds. You go through Lamotte-Beuvron and the forest of the same name that is a famous hunting ground. The road continues to *Salbris,* a research center for radio astronomy, then southeast to *Nançay,* and on to *Vierzon* (population 34,000), an industrial city on the north bank of the Cher.

From Vierzon to Argenton-sur-Creuse—87 km. (54 miles)—Route N 20 goes through the Berry countryside to the village of *Déols.* There is a tenth-century Romanesque *bell tower* here, the remnant of an important abbey founded in 917. In the crypt of the

parish church (12th–16th century) is the fifth-century sarcophagus of Saint Ludre.

Route N 20 passes through *Châteauroux* (population 51,000), which is 251 km. (156 miles) from Paris. Continue on N 20 through the lovely *Bouzanne Valley,* to the town of *Argenton-sur-Creuse* (population 6,900). From the high bridge here you can see the old houses with wooden porches that line the Creuse River. The road then passes through the undulating plain of Berry and finally reaches the first spurs of the Massif Central. The route from Argenton-sur-Creuse to Limoges is 93 km. (58 miles). But you can make a pleasant side trip through La Souterraine. On Route N 20, go south for 38 km. (24 miles) until you reach N 145, then drive east for 9 km. (6 miles) to **La Souterraine** (population 5,850). Built on the site of a

Roman villa, the town is dominated by a 12th-century *church.
One bay of the church supports a
13th-century tower, the other bay
has Gothic vaulting. In the crypt is
the foundation of a Gallo-Roman
altar.

Return to N 20 and go south. The
route becomes more winding and
scenic, especially along the
Ambazac mountains. When you
get into the Vienne Valley, you
come to the capital city of the old
province of Limousin, **Limoges**
(population 147,000). Since
1768, when extremely pure kaolin
was discovered nearby, this city
has been famous for the manufacture of porcelain. The city's best-
known porcelain painter was its
native son Pierre-Auguste Renoir
(1841–1919). Long before porcelain was important—indeed,
from as far back as the 12th century—Limoges was known for its
fine enamel work. In recent years
the city's importance was
increased by a decidedly 20th-
century discovery in the area:
uranium.

The *Musée National Adrien-
Dubouché* at the Place du Champ
de Foire houses a fabulous collection of porcelain from Limousin,
from other areas in France, and
from Europe and Asia. The
Musée Municipal in the Bishop's
Palace has a collection of Limoges
enamels, as well as paintings,
including several by Renoir, and
an archaeological section with a
second-century fresco discovered
in the 1960s.

ROUTE 12
Orléans to Limoges
Miles
0   20
Kilometers

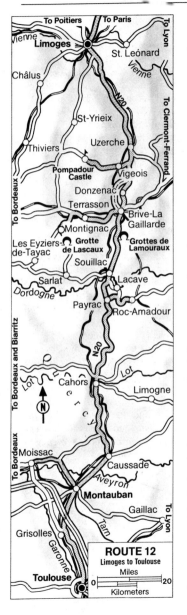

ROUTE 12
Limoges to Toulouse
Miles
0   20
Kilometers

Two old bridges span the Vienne, the 12th-century *Pont Martial* and the 13th-century **Pont Saint-Étienne.* When you cross the latter you go through the beautiful **terrace gardens* of the bishop's residence and come to the Gothic **Cathédrale Saint-Étienne,* built in the 13th, 16th, and 19th centuries. Note especially the Portal Saint-Jean at the northern transept, the fine rood screen dating from 1535, and in the three bishops' tombs in the chancel that date from the 14th and 16th centuries.

From Limoges to Brive (93 km.; 58 miles) the road winds through a beautiful landscape as it passes from the Loire River region to that of the Dordogne. In the valley of the Vézère there is a great view of ***Uzerche** (population 3,200). This town of many towers lies on a steep hill that is almost completely surrounded by the river. Because of its virtually impregnable site, the town was able to resist every siege through the ages, whereupon it proudly adopted for its town motto the words "non poluta." Even the Romanesque *church of Saint-Pierre* (12th–13th century) with its wonderful 12th-century *bell tower was fortified. A tower from this fortification still flanks the church entry today. There is a beautiful view from the terrace, the **Esplanade de la Lunade.*

About 4 km. (2.5 miles) south of Uzerche, turn west and head for the village of *Vigeois* at the entrance to a ravine called the

Gorges de la Vézère (which can be crossed only by railroad, however). From the village, take Route D 7 for 16 km. (10 miles) to *Pompadour Castle.* This is the estate that Louis XV gave to his mistress Antoinette Poisson when he conferred on her the title Marquise de Pompadour in 1745. The majestic 15th-century building has been a stud farm for thoroughbred horses since 1761.

After you return to Route N 20, go south through picturesque *Donzenac* to **Brive-la-Gaillarde** (population 52,000). The town's 12th-century Romanesque *church of Saint-Martin* is worth a visit. Unfortunately, it has undergone major renovations over the centuries. The nave was rebuilt in 1310 and the tower was added in 1896. The *Musée Ernest-Rupin,* in an elegant 16th-century house, has an interesting collection of Medieval sculpture and painting. The *Hôtel de Labenche* is in a fine 16th-century building with a lovely arcaded courtyard.

Travel Route 22 (Belfort–Bordeaux) can be picked up in Brive and takes you to the nearby (38 km.; 24 miles) **Grotte de Lascaux* with its cave paintings (see page 239). Route N 20 goes through grotto country between Brive and Cahors, a distance of 106 km. (66 miles). From Brive, follow the course of the Vézère westward, to Montignac and the *Grottes-Chapelles de Saint-Antoine,* a pilgrimage site where Anthony of Padua is said to have retreated for meditation. Its caves

have been made into chapels. Continue 4 km. (2.5 miles) farther to a path that leads to the *Grottes de Lamouraux,* which were used as refuge in the Middle Ages. At *Cressenac* you come to an especially scenic stretch of about 17 km. (10 miles) until you reach **Souillac** (population 4,350). The town, located on the Dordogne, has a 12th-century Romanesque *church.* Only about 12.5 km. (8 miles) southeast of the town are the *Grottes de Lacave,* a series of large caves with fine stalactite formations. These caves were inhabited in prehistoric times.

From *Payrac* a very curvy side road (D 673) leads east 20 km. (13 miles) to the Medieval pilgrimage site of **Rocamadour,** a picturesque village in the narrow gorge of the Alzou at the foot of a rock wall. The village consists of a single street lined with houses and four fortified gates. If you climb up the 216 steps of the *Grand Escalier,* you reach a rocky terrace. Here are the *basilica of Saint-Sauveur* and the *church of Saint-Amadour,* and nearby, a 14th-century *castle* that now serves as a priestly residence.

You can continue on D 673 to *Gouffre de Padirac,* the most famous chasm in France. It cuts 75 meters (246 feet) deep and 31 meters (102 feet) wide in the slope of a limestone plateau. An elevator takes you to an underground river that is smooth and quiet.

Route N 20 continues south from Payrac through very scenic countryside to Langeudoc. About 3 km. (2 miles) south of *Saint-Pierre-Lafeuille* a panoramic side road branches off from Route N 20. This road has a magnificent view of the Lot Valley and a spectacular view of the city of ***Cahors** (population 22,000). Located in a river bend and protected to the north by ancient ramparts, this town was settled first by the Romans, who called it Divona Cadurcorum. It became one of the most important commercial cities of France in the 13th century, with trade routes that reached as far as Scandinavia and the Levant. The town was wealthy enough to be a source of loans for kings and popes. Pope John XXII (1244–1334) was a native of the city.

Today one of the city's main attractions is the **Cathédrale Saint-Étienne* (12th–13th century) featuring an unusual nave roof with two domes. On the north portal is a famous 12th-century Romanesque ******ty*mpanum* sculpture of the Resurrection. The fortresslike 14th-century **Pont Valentré* spans the Lot River.

From Cahors to Toulouse, a distance of 111 km. (69 miles), Route N 20 passes through the fertile Quercy region and descends through the broad valley of the Lère to **Montauban** (population 50,000). The city's three most important sights, all near each other, are the **Place Nationale,* the 14th-century **Pont Vieux,* and the ***Musée Ingres.* This museum has more than 4,000 works by the great painter Jean-Auguste-Dominique Ingres (1780–1867), a native son of Montaubon. Ingres's work represents the height of the French Classical style. The museum's ground floor also has works by the Montauban sculptor Emile Antoine Bourdelle (1861–1929).

A detour on Route D 958 leads west for 31 km. (19 miles) to **Moissac.* This town on the Garonne is famous for its *abbey church* with a sculpted portal and for its monastery, founded in 506, that has a wonderful 11th-century ***cloister.* The museum is also worth seeing.

Toulouse is only 40 km. (25 miles) from Montauban on Route N 20.

*Toulouse

See map on page 167.

Toulouse (population 383,000) is located on a large plain that separates the Massif Central from the

Cahors: Fortress Bridge

Pyrenees and the Mediterranean from the Atlantic. It is the fourth-largest city in France and is known for its chemical and aerospace industries.

The city, a stronghold of the Celtic-Ligurian people, was captured by the Romans in 106 B.C. They called it Tolosa and made it the capital of the province of Gallia Narbonensis. From 419 to 506 it was the capital of the Visigoth kingdom. Under the counts of Toulouse from the 9th to the 13th centuries it had one of the most cultured and magnificent courts in Europe. From 1209 to 1229 Pope Innocent III used the city as a base from which to destroy the Albigensian sect, which he had declared heretical (the town of Albi is a short distance to the northwest). Pope Gregory IX founded the city's university in 1229 as a bulwark of orthodoxy. Europe's first literary society was created in Toulouse in the 14th century with the aim of preserving the language of the South, the "langue d'oc." After World War I, Toulouse became a center for commercial air traffic. The first airmail line to Morocco originated here in 1919; connections to Dakar followed in 1925; and service to South America was established in 1930. Among the line's pilots was the writer Antoine de Saint-Exupéry.

Today the city's center of attraction is the **Place du Capitole** (1) Here is the *Hôtel de Ville* in whose early-17th-century central court the Duc de Montmorency was exe-cuted for taking up arms against Louis XIII and the all-powerful Cardinal Richelieu.

The Rue du Taur goes north from the square to the ****Basi-lique Saint-Sernin** (2), the largest and most important Romanesque church in France and the one with the most relics. Saint Sernin, the patron saint of Languedoc, was the first bishop of Toulouse. He was martyred in A.D. 250, being dragged to his death by a bull ("taurus" in Latin, hence the Rue du Taur). The vast brick church consists of a **nave* with four side aisles, and a **transept* with two side aisles. The structure was started in 1080 and completed during the 13th century. The **tower,* 65 meters (213 feet) high, rises in six stories above the crossing; nine chapels are arranged around the apse. Especially noteworthy is the **Porte Miègeville,* with its magnificent sculptures.

The interior was designed to receive enormous crowds of pilgrims and for major ceremonies with large processions. The choir has several important features including seven **marble reliefs* in the gallery, the **choir railing,* and the late-Renaissance **choir stalls.* Opposite the main portal of Saint-Sernin is the ***Musée Saint-Raymond** (3), located in the former Collège Saint-Raymond, with a fine collection of artifacts from Early Christian times to the Renaissance.

To the west of the Place du Capitole is the ****Église des Jac-obins** (4), a two-nave Dominican

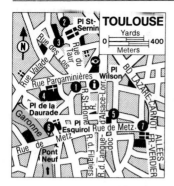

church built between 1230 and 1385, a masterpiece of southern Gothic architecture.

South of the Place du Capitole, in the old Augustine monastery, is the **Musée des Augustins** (5), which has a rich collection of Early Christian and Medieval sculptures. Between this museum and the Garonne is the Renaissance **Hôtel d'Assézat** (6), dating from 1557. This house was built for a rich woad merchant (woad is a blue dye that was used until the discovery of indigo). To the east is the *Cathédrale Saint-Étienne* (7), a large structure noted for its stylistic incongruities. It was begun in the 11th century but not completed until 600 years later; as a result, northern French Gothic clashes with southern French Gothic and the axis of the nave stands at a slant to the axis of the choir.

In Toulouse you can pick up either Travel Route 23 (Geneva–Bayonne) or Travel Route 24 (Menton–Toulouse).

It is 180 km (112 miles) from Toulouse to the Spanish border at Bourg-Madame on Route N 20; from there just 176 km. (109 miles) to Barcelona. Going south, the road winds first through the Garonne Valley and then through the valley of the Ariège, which narrows as it climbs into the Pyrenees. At an elevation of 380 meters (1,246 feet) you come to *Foix* (population 10,000). The town is dominated by a three-towered *castle* built on a giant rock, with a 15th-century detached *round tower* looming 42 meters (138 feet) high. From Foix you can take a side trip 5 km. (3 miles) northeast to the underground river of *Labouiche.*

Route N 20 continues snaking its way through the limestone walls of the Ariège Valley, passing caverns and grottoes along the way. The road also runs past the ruins of Verdun castle and then comes to *Ax-les-Thermes* (population 2,000), famous for its thermal baths, known even to the Romans. The 60 springs range in temperature from 18° C (78° F) to 78° C (173° F). In the *Place du Breilh* is a hot-water pool called the *Bassin des Ladres* (basin of the lepers) built by Saint Louis in the 13th century for pilgrims who had been cured of leprosy in the Holy Land. Today it is used as a public bathhouse.

The countryside becomes wilder as Route N 20 climbs more and more steeply, reaching *l'Hospitalet-Près-l'Andorre,* a mountain resort, at a height of 1,435 meters

(4,710 feet). The road corkscrews its way up to the fork that leads to *Andorra (see Travel Route 25), continuing through the Col de Puymorens at an elevation of 1,915 meters (6,281 feet). The pass is the watershed between the rivers Garonne and Ebro. The road then descends to Ur; the border station of Bourg-Madame is 4 km. (2.5 miles) farther. Route N 152 to Barcelona begins at the Spanish border town of Puigcerda. Here you can also pick up Route C 1313, which leads to Zaragoza through Lerida, a distance of 184 km. (114 miles).

TRAVEL ROUTE 13: ***Paris–*Bourges–**Clermont-Ferrand–**Carcassonne (770/870 km.; 447/539 miles)

See maps on pages 169 and 171.

The road from Paris to the south passes through the scenic attractions of Orléanais, Berry, Bourbonnais, Auvergne, and Languedoc, through the Massif Central to the foothills of the Pyrenees.

The first part of the route, from Paris to Bourges via Nemours, is 226 km. (140 miles). You can go to *Nemours* on Route N 6 if you wish to stop at the castle of **Fontainebleu* (see page 52) or you can take the fast and direct Autoroute du Soleil (A 6). From the old town of Nemours in the valley of the Loing, Route N 7 runs along the Loing River and a canal for 33 km. (20 miles) to **Montargis** (population 18,000). Although the town has a nice old church, the *Église de la Madeleine,* it is more famous for its praline factory. This is where pralines were invented in the 17th century, when the cook of the duke of Plessis-Praslin created a confection made of burned almonds, which he called "praslines."

You can pick up Travel Route 21 (Nancy–Nantes) in Montargis. Route N 7 continues south through wild landscape with abundant fishing.

You can make a side trip at *Nogent* to *Châtillon-Coligny,* the birthplace and burial site of Admiral Gaspard de Coligny, the Huguenot leader who was murdered during the Saint Bartholomew's Day Massacre.

Leave Route N 7 at *Les Bézards* and take Route D 940 for 14 km. (9 miles) to **Gien** (population 16,000), a town on the Loire known for its stoneware and for its *church of Sainte-Jeanne d'Arc,* which was reconstructed in 1954. There is also a castle that houses a *museum* of hunting and falconry.

From Gien you can make a side

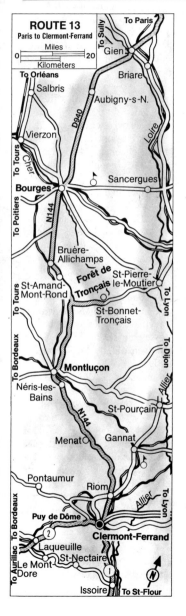

ROUTE 13
Paris to Clermont-Ferrand

trip of 23 km. (14 miles) to the Medieval Loire castle *Sully (see page Travel Route 8).

Route D 940 crosses the Loire on the Vieux-Pont and then continues in long straight stretches for 74 km. (46 miles) through the eastern Sologne, a swampy area drained in the 19th century. Visible in the distance are the towers of the cathedral of ***Bourges** (population 83,000). It was originally a Celtic settlement, then it became a Roman garrison town. The city reached its greatest prominence during the Middle Ages when it was the capital of the Duchy of Berry. During the Hundred Years' War (1337–1453) it formed the core of the territory still left to the French king; for that reason the English mockingly spoke of Charles VII as the "king of Bourges."

The major attraction in Bourges is the ****Cathédrale Saint-Étienne,* one of the most magnificent Gothic churches in France. It is noted for a remarkably consistent style. Unlike many churches of its period, it was built in less than a century—only 60 years, starting in 1200. The nave with double side aisles is 118 meters (387 feet) long and 37 meters (121 feet) high. The five **portals of the west façade are framed by two towers. The left one was reconstructed after its collapse in 1506. Above the sculpted central portal depicting the Last Judgment is a beautiful *rose window.* Magnificent stained-glass windows from the 12th through the 15th centuries are an important feature of the interior, especially the choir.

Another attractive building of the French Gothic style is the **Hôtel Jacques-Coeur,* which Charles VII's banker had built for himself between 1443 and 1451 for a princely sum of 100,000 gold ducats. Very beautiful Romanesque and Gothic *sculptures* were placed in the balconies around the cour d'honneur, where negotiations were conducted. Another sight worth visiting is the nearby *Musée du Berry,* which has a collection of Romanesque finds and folk art from the Duchy of Berry. The museum is housed in the Renaissance *Hôtel Cujas,* built in 1515.

From Bourges to Montluçon Route N 144 runs south in a straight line for 93 km. (58 miles) through **Bruère-Allichamps.** Here you can make a short detour via *Noirlac,* with the well-preserved buildings of its old Cistercian abbey that dates from the 12th to the 15th century, or you can go east for 6 km. (4 miles) by way of the magnificent *Château de Meillant,* a late-Gothic early-Renaissance castle. Then drive through the woods to **Saint-Amand-Montrond** (population 15,000), where the Paris plain changes into the foothills of the Massif Central. Here you pass from Berry into Bourbonnais.

Route N 144 follows the right bank of the Cher. You can make another short side trip (9 km.; 6 miles) to the *Château Ainay-le-Vieil* to see the castle's nine-tower

14th-century fortification. A short distance south on Route N 144 lies the **Fôret de Tronçais,* a magnificent ancient oak forest with small lakes.

Route N 144 continues south to the industrial city of **Montluçon** (population 60,000) with a well-preserved old town at its core.

Only 7.5 km. (5 miles) from Montluçon on N 144 is **Néris-les-Bains** (population 3,400), a spa favored by the Romans. The original bathing pools in the *Parc des Eaux-Chaudes* are still used today. The old city is located above the spa quarter. Dozens of other curative spas lie to the southeast, between Vichy and Le Mont-Dore.

Route N 144 runs through the hilly countryside of the Collines de Combrailles to *Menat,* with its attractive Romanesque *church; it crosses the serene Sioule Valley and then climbs to 640 meters (2,099 feet). Ahead are the volcanic mountains of Le Mont-Dore, visible as you enter the Auvergne countryside. In the valley of the Limagne, the road passes through **Riom** (population 18,000), where many Medieval and Renaissance buildings still stand. The *church of Sainte-Chapelle* (1382–1388) has magnificent 15th-century windows in the choir. Some fine old palaces are located on the main street, the Rue de l'Hôtel de Ville.

From here it is only 15 km. (9 miles) to **Clermont-Ferrand** (population 158,000), capital of Auvergne and an important indus-

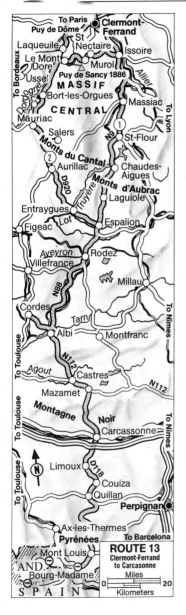

ROUTE 13
Clermont-Ferrand
to Carcassonne

Miles
0 _____ 20
Kilometers

trial city. At its center is the broad *Place de Jaude.* To the northwest, in the old town, are the two main sights of the city, standing near each other: the Gothic *Cathédrale de Nôtre-Dame* and the Romanesque *church of Nôtre-Dame-du-Port* (see below). Not far from the north end of the Place de Jaude and leading to the cathedral is the **Rue des Gras,* lined with beautifully kept houses dating from the 16th to the 18th centuries (Numbers 14, 22, and 34). Running parallel is the equally interesting Rue des Chaussetiers, location of the house in which the great French philosopher Blaise Pascal (1623–1662) was born. A plate in the wall identifies the house.

The **Cathédrale de Nôtre-Dame,* built in the 13th and 14th centuries from the region's dark volcanic rock, has an impressive west façade and magnificent 13th-century windows. **Nôtre-Dame-du-Port,* a typical example of

Notre-Dame-du-Port: Portal

Romanesque architecture in the Auvergne, is a century older and has an exceptionally beautiful choir bordered by four chapels. The building is also renowned for its sculpted capitals. Between the two churches is the *Place de la Poterne,* with its splendid *Fontaine d'Amboise.*

You can pick up Travel Route 22 (Belfort–Bordeaux) in Clermont-Ferrand.

From Clermont-Ferrand you can take a 15 km.- (9 mile-) side trip west by way of the elegant *Royat* spa, which has the interesting fortified Romanesque *church of Saint-Léger,* to **Puy de Dôme.* This long extinct volcano, at 1,465 meters (4,805 feet), towers over the 60 other volcanoes of the Chaine des Dômes. You can get a wonderful **view from the plateau at the top of the volcano. In Roman times there was a large temple here dedicated to Mercury.

You can choose between two attractive roads for the trip from Clermont-Ferrand to Rodez. The eastern route on N 9 passes through Saint-Flour (229 km.; 142 miles from Clermont-Ferrand to Rodez). The western route is 52 km. (31 miles) longer and goes through Aurillac.

Rodez via Saint-Flour

(*Follow the route marked "1" on the map on page 171.*)

Take Route N 9 southeast from Clermont-Ferrand through Coudes. The road goes through a lovely river landscape for 11 km. (7 miles) to **Issoire** (population 16,000), where the main attraction is the 12th-century **church of Saint-Paul.* This famous church, an example of Auvergnat Romanesque architecture, is larger than Nôtre-Dame-du-Port in Clermont-Ferrand. From here you can make a drive into the heart of the Massif Central.

From Issoire, you can make a 51-km. (32-mile) side trip to Le Mont-Dore by way of Saint-Nectaire. Take route D 996 through the valley of the Couze, which narrows into a gorge and continues into a geologically fascinating basalt landscape to the spa of *Saint-Nectaire.* About 2 km. (1¼ miles) beyond is the village of *Saint-Nectaire.* It also has an Auvergnat Romanesque church and outstanding carved capitals.

In *Murol,* 5 km. (3 miles) farther, there is a half-collapsed castle with a watchtower from which you can survey the volcanic landscape. As you travel along the Couze, you pass the *Lac de Chambon* and then, climbing higher, cross the *Col de la Croix-Morand* at 1,399 meters (4,589 feet). Beyond the pass the road descends, offering a charming view of the summer spa and winter-sports center *Le Mont-Dore.* From here you can take the funicular up to *Puy de Sancy* at 1,886 meters (6,186 feet). On a clear day you can see an extensive panorama of central France.

Route N 9 follows the broad Allier Valley from Issoire, passing through the Alagnon gorges to *Massiac,* where the road climbs to a high plateau and the town of **Saint-Flour** (population 9,100), situated on this basalt bluff above the confluence of two streams. From Saint-Flour the trip continues over the La Planèze plateau, crosses the Remontalou gorge, and reaches a health spa frequented by the Romans, **Chaudes-Aigues** (population 1,400). The 32 hot springs here not only serve the spa but also supply hot water and heat to the town. The road goes along the western border of the Aubrac, a farming region famous for its *cheese;* the village of *Laguiole* serves as a cattle and cheese market for the district. Continue for 32 km. (20 miles) by way of *Espalion* in the valley of the Lot to **Rodez** (population 28,000), the former capital of Rouergue, where a magnificent *bell tower* stands beside the *Cathédrale de Nôtre-Dame.*

To Rodez via Aurillac

(Follow the route marked "2" on the map on page 171.)

From Clermont-Ferrand Route N 89 goes west by way of *La Baraque* and *La Font de l'Arbre* near **Puy-de-Dôme** (described earlier). The route then follows D 922 through the *Col de la Moréno* at an elevation of 1,065 meters (3,493 feet) and the volcanic region of the Monts Dore, and on to *Laqueuille* and then to *Brive* (see Travel Route 22). The road crosses the Dordogne, ascends a plateau, and

after 30 km. (17 miles) rejoins the Dordogne at **Borte-les-Orgues** (population 5,300), which owes its name to the tall *basalt columns* that resemble nothing so much as huge organ pipes. There is a hydroelectric power station at the foot of the giant concrete *dam.* Beyond Bort, the road passes by the ruins of the *Château de Charlus* and through the scenic valley of the Sumène to **Mauriac** (population 4,600). The town boasts one of the most distinctive churches of Haute-Auvergne, the basilica of the 12th-century *Nôtre-Dame-des-Miracles,* built with the black lava of the region. From Mauriac, the road curves, rising and dipping, to the western edge of the Monts du Cantal, the remnants of a single mighty volcano that has been eroded by glaciers and streams. Today this area consists of pasture land and is a major producer of the cheeses known as Cantal and Bleu d'Auvergne.

When you reach Les Quatre-Routes, a crossroads 16 km. (10 miles) south of Mauriac, you can make a pleasant side trip of 7 km. (4 miles) to **Salers** (population 951), a town that has a completely preserved Medieval *Grand Place.*

The route along the Cantal ends at **Aurillac** (population 35,000), the ancient capital of Auvergne, where the *abbey of Saint-Geraud* is located. One of its monks was the scholar Gerbert, who became Sylvester II (999–1003), the first pope of French nationality.

The picturesque ridge road, the

Route des Crêtes, leads from here to Cantal in the northeast.

From Aurillac continue south on Route D 920 through a plateau of forests and pastures for 49 km. (30 miles) to **Entraygues** (population 1,500), where the Truyère and the Lot rivers meet. A 13th-century Gothic **bridge* crosses the Truyère. The **Rue Basse* appears unchanged since the Middle Ages. An excellent wine is made in this town. After 27 km. (17 miles) through the gorges of the Lot, the D 920 reaches *Espalion,* where the western and the eastern sections of the route meet. From there you can continue to Rodez as described earlier.

From Rodez Route N 88 proceeds to Albi over the Rouergue plateau and into the valley of the Viaur, where the railroad viaduct called the **Pont de Tanus* crosses the river. South of the industrial city of *Carmaux,* the road reaches the broad valley of the Tarn and crosses the *Pont du 22 Août* into **Albi* (population 50,000). The city is dominated by its immense *cathedral* and by the *Palais de la Berbie,* which houses the **Musée Toulouse-Lautrec.* This museum contains many works by the painter Henri de Toulouse-Lautrec (1864–1901), who was born in Albi. Both the cathedral and the palais are fortresses built in the period immediately after the defeat of the Albigensians by Pope Innocent III. Also called Cathari (the pure ones), the Albigensians

Albi

were an ascetic sect that the Church labeled heretic. The "Albigensian Crusade" of the early 13th century resulted in the murder of most of the sect's followers and the reimposition of official orthodoxy. The **Cathédrale Sainte-Cécile* was built from 1282 to 1390—after orthodoxy had won the day. It is a uniquely beautiful Gothic structure in all of southern France. The protective walls are 41 meters (134 feet) high, with windows that are also high up, and a tall 15th-century tower. A richly adorned vestibule, the so-called ***baldachin* was added to the south portal in 1535. In the interior, the magnificent ***rood screen,* circa 1500, is especially noteworthy, as are the ***choir stalls* sculpted with prophets and angels. At Albi you can pick up Travel Route 23 (Geneva–Bayonne).

From Albi you can take a side

trip of 25 km. (15 miles) to **Cordes** (population 1,200), a small town located on a hill northwest of Albi. Founded in the 13th century, it has retained its Medieval appearance to a degree that is only rarely encountered in southern France. Long stretches of the town wall remain and some houses from the 14th century still stand on the main street. The last leg of Travel Route 13 goes from Albi to Carcassonne (107 km.; 66 miles). From Albi travel south on Route N 112 through the fertile plain of Assou for 42 km. (26 miles) to the industrial city of **Castres** (population 46,000), where the socialist Jean Jaurès (1859–1915) was born. The former bishop's palace now houses the *Musée Goya*, with many important works by the Spanish painter (1746–1828).

The route continues southeast through the textile-manufacturing city of *Mazamet* (population 20,000), and beyond, to Route N 118 which passes through the Montagne Noire and then into the valley of the Dure to the walled city of ****Carcassone** (population 45,000). One of Europe's most impressive Medieval sites, the elevated fortress, **La Cité, is visible from afar. The inner wall ring—1,287 meters (4,221 feet)—was partly built by Romans and Visigoths in the sixth century; the outer wall ring measures 1,672 meters (5,484 feet) long. The walk along the **rampart walls belongs among the choicest of travel experiences. The imposing fortress was constructed around 1250 under Louis IX (Saint Louis) and added to by Philip the Bold around 1280. It has 52 towers. The *Porte Narbonnaise*, flanked by the *Tour du Trésau* is a fortress in itself, as is the *Château Comtal*, a 12th-century count's castle that abuts the inner ring wall. Rising above the tangle of narrow streets in the cité is the *Basilique de Saint-Nazaire*, which has a Romanesque nave and a Gothic choir.

TRAVEL ROUTE 14: ***Paris–*Vichy–*Perpignan (919 km.; 570 miles)

See maps on pages 176, 178, and 180.

This especially attractive route to southern France avoids the heavily travelled main roads. It passes through interesting cities such as Nevers, famous for its faïence, and the pilgrimage city of Le Puy; well-known spas such as Vichy; and beautiful natural sights such as the Gorges du Tarn. The route ends just south of Perpignan at the Spanish border.

From Paris to Nevers (237 km.; 147 miles), take the Autoroute de Soleil (A 6) to Nemours and then switch to N 7, which goes south through Montargis (see Travel Route 13). About 150 km. (93 miles) from Paris, you come to **Briare** (population 5,600), situated on the Loire. The town's main attraction is the *Pont Canal* that was designed by Gustave Eiffel and built in 1890. A bridge connects the Canal de Briare with the Loire-side canal.

Follow Route N 7 south along the right bank of the Loire through the Pouilly wine district and through *La Charité*, where there was a Benedictine abbey. Its *church of Sainte-Croix* is still impressive, even in ruins. After you pass through the spa *Pougues-les-Eaux*, you reach **Nevers** (population 49,000), famous since the 16th century for the manufacture of faïence. Among the city's attractions are the mighty Romanesque *church of Saint-Étienne* (1063–1097) southeast of the Porte de Paris; the *Place Ducale* with the *Palais Ducal*, built during the 15th and 16th centuries; and the magnificent *Cathédrale Saint-Cyr et Sainte-Juliette*, a mostly Gothic structure built from the 12th to the 16th centuries. Behind the church are the *Musée Blandin* with a good faïence collection and the elegant *Porte du Croux*, a 14th-century gate tower.

After you leave Nevers, Route N 7 crosses an 18th-century *bridge* from which you get a

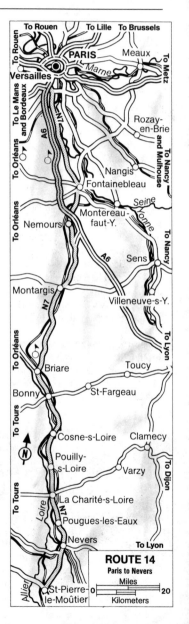

ROUTE 14
Paris to Nevers
Miles
0   20
Kilometers

lovely view of the city. The road then continues south through the foothills of the Massif Central and the town of *Saint-Pierre-le-Moûtier,* then runs along the Allier River to **Moulins** (population 27,000), the ancient capital of Bourbonnais, once the Duchy of Bourbon. The city's *cathedral* was completed in the 19th century, but it has a Flamboyant Gothic **choir* in the sacristy (1468–1507) with handsome windows from that period. There is also a famous **triptych* by the Master of Moulins, an anonymous late 15th-century artist who is now presumed to be the Flemish painter Jean Hey. Local faïence ware and the precious 12th-century **Bible of Souvigny* are displayed in the *Pavillon d'Anne de Beaujeu,* a fine Renaissance building.

Continue south on Route N 7 for 30 km. (19 miles). Just beyond Varennes-sur-Allier, at a fork in the road, turn right onto Route N 209 and go for another 27 km. (17 miles) to ***Vichy** (population 32,000), the largest and most elegant health spa in France and source of the mineral water of the same name. The city was the seat of the collaborationist French government under Marshal Pétain during World War II. Vichy was chosen at the time in part because it had many large hotels that could be requisitioned for government offices and official housing.

The focal point of spa life here is the **Parc des Sources,* with its Grand Casino, theater, and pavilion of effervescent springs. The

*Grand Établissement Thermal, the largest spa building in Europe, is located at the edge of the Parcs d'Allier, which was built by Napoleon III along the Allier. Since 1963 the river has been dammed here to create the **Lac d'Allier.*

From Vichy to Le Puy, 166 km. (103 miles), you pass through a magnificent countryside along Route D 906. After 36 km. (22 miles) you arrive at **Thiers** (population 19,000), a picturesque town above the Durolle gorge that has been famous since the time of the Crusades for its production of steel blades. Along the streets of the old city you can see half-timbered houses dating from the 15th century. Of particular interest is the *Maison du Pirou.* The **Terrasse du Rempart* offers a view of the Monts Dore and Monts Dômes.

You may pick up Travel Route 22 (Belfort–Bordeaux) here.

Route D 906 goes through the Dore Valley and the **Gorges de la Dore.* After 55 km. (34 miles) you come to **Ambert** (population 8,000), known for its handmade paper as early as the 14th century. Today only one of its 300 mills is still in operation. In the **Moulin Richard-de-Bas,* in nearby Val de Laga, you can watch paper being manufactured with centuries-old equipment.

Continue for another 13 km. (8 miles) to get to **Arlanc** (population 2,500), which has a **lace museum.* Needlework is still a cottage industry for women of this area.

The road curves and climbs through a spectacular countryside for 17 km. (11 miles) up a granite plateau of the Auvergne to **La Chaise-Dieu** (population 1,200). Among the remains of a Benedictine monastery that stood here from the middle of the 11th century to the French Revolution you can see an attractive Gothic *cloister* and the famous abbey *church of Saint-Robert,* which contains the tomb of Pope Clement VI and has magnificent 14th-century *choir stalls* carved of oak. The walls of the church are adorned with costly **tapestries* from Brussels and Arras dating from the early 16th century. On the left wall of the choir is a large three-part fresco depicting the *Dance of Death.*

Route D 906 continues on the plateau through pastures and forests. At *Bellevue-la-Montagne* the road makes a broad arc of 11 km. (7 miles) around the extinct *Peyramont volcano* to Saint-Paulien. In the distance you can see the remains of the Polignac fortress on the basalt plateau. A temple to Apollo stood here in ancient times. Atop a rocky outcrop rising from the plain in the foreground is a church, and on the peak is a colossal statue of the Virgin. Uniquely situated amid these volcanic hills is the town of **Le Puy** (population 32,000). It has been an important pilgrimage site since the Middle Ages when Louis IX (Saint Louis) brought back a

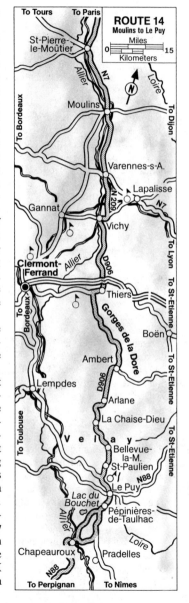

ROUTE 14
Moulins to Le Puy

statue called the *Vierge Noire* (Black Virgin) from his first Crusade. The statue stands atop a high altar in the **Cathédrale Nôtre-Dame-du-Puy*, a Romanesque church with eight domes and a west façade made of polychrome volcanic rock. The church is reached by way of a broad, steep stairway that actually passes beneath it. You can get an excellent view of the town from the foot of the enormous statue of *Nôtre Dame de France,* located at *Roche Corneille* (Corneille rock). The statue was cast in 1860 from cannons captured in Sebastopol. To the north are attractive *cloisters* with 12th-century Romanesque railings. Here also is the 11th-century *Chapelle Saint-Michel d'Aiguilhe;* to reach it you must climb a spiral staircase hewn in the rock.

Leave Le Puy on Route N 88 to go to Mende, 92 km. (57 miles) away. The road climbs to the Plan-

Le Puy

èze du Velay, a basalt plateau before you come to Pépinière du Taulhac, where you have a beautiful view over the landscape and the Loire. Stay on Route N 88 toward *Chapeauroux,* where the railroad crosses the valley of the Allier on a 28-arch viaduct. Continue through the valley of the Chapeauroux River to *Châteauneuf-de-Randon* (population 550), the large cattle market of this region. From here, Travel Route 23 (Geneva-Bayonne) joins this Travel Route as far as **Mende** (population 12,500). The town lies beneath the precipices of the Causse de Mende. Its main attraction is the *Cathédrale Nôtre-Dame,* begun in 1369 by Pope Urban V, a native of the region. The church was completed in the 15th century. In 1579 the Huguenots blew up its pillars and destroyed the bell, which had been called "La Non Pareille"; weighing 20 tons, it was the largest in Christendom at that time. Nôtre-Dame was reconstructed from 1599 to 1620 in the style of the old cathedral. The *Pont Nôtre-Dame,* a narrow bridge over the Lot, dates from the 14th century.

From Mende take Route N 106 to Route D 907b. This stretch from Mende to Millau—101 km. (63 miles)—leads through the **Gorges du Tarn,** a deeply cut canyon between the lime plateaus of Sauveterre and Méjan. Route D 907b takes you along the scenic valley of the Lot and south through the desertlike Causse de Sauveterre, a limestone plateau.

Beyond *Sainte-Enimie* you pass along high rock walls in the valley of the Tarn. The highlights of this route are the *Château de la Caze,* a 15th-century castle converted into a hotel; *La Malène,* a village at the entrance to the gorge; *Les Détroits,* between whose vertical rock walls the Tarn flows, and where the road runs through many tunnels; *Le Pas de Souci,* where the Tarn almost disappears beneath the ruins of a gigantic rock slide; and *Les Vignes,* a wine-producing area with terraced vineyards.

For a beautiful view of the gorge, take the panoramic road 13 km. (8 miles) up to *Point Sublime,* a rock 860 meters (2,281 feet) high. The valley of the Tarn gradually broadens and leads through *Le Rozier* on D 907 to **Millau** (population 25,000). The town has been famous for the manufacture of leather goods since the Middle Ages.

Route N 9 goes from Millau to Béziers (123 km.; 76 miles) and passes from Auvergne into Languedoc. On the way, you can either drive directly to La Cavalerie (20 km.; 12 miles) or, if you are a cheese-lover, detour on a side road (28 km.; 17 miles) through ***Roquefort-sur-Soulzon** (population 1,500). The town is famous for its blue-veined Roquefort cheese that ripens in massive multistoried vaults carved out of rock. You can visit the cheese factory here. Return to Route 9 and go east to *La Cavalerie,* which owes its name to a

Cellar in Roquefort

commandery of the Knights of Saint John of Jerusalem.

Southeast, the road passes through the broad hilly Causse du Larzac, a large limestone plateau. At *La Pezade* you can make a detour 4 km. (2.5 miles) northeast through ****La Courvertoirade,** a picturesque walled village where little has changed in 400 years. By way of *Le Caylar,* a rock notched at its foot, Route N 9 goes to the **Pas de l'Escalotte,* once crossable only on ladders. During the pretty downward trip into the valley of the Lergue, the landscape changes suddenly and becomes Mediterranean, with vineyards, and olive and mulberry trees. You then come to the former bishop's see of **Lodève** (population 8,000), which supplied wool from the area's sheep for the uniforms of the French armies from the reign of Louis XIII to that of Louis XVI. You can reach the fortified *Cathédrale Saint-Fulcran,* built in the

13th century, by crossing the Gothic *Pont Montifort.*

Route N 9 passes through a landscape of red sandstone, through *Clermont-l'Herault,* and into the valley of the Herault to **Pézenas** (population 7,500), where many old mansions of the nobility still stand. The most attractive of these are the 15th-century **Hôtel de Lacoste;* the 17th-century **Hôtel d'Alfonce;* and the 18th-century *Hôtel de Malibran.* The remains of a 14th-century *Jewish ghetto* are also here.

You can make an excursion of 21 km. (13 miles) to the rock village of **Saint-Guilhem-le-Désert,* to see its church cloisters. You can also pick up Travel Route 24 (Menton–Toulouse) in Pézenas.

Route N 9 continues for 2 km. (1.5 miles) to **Béziers** (population 90,000), a shipping center for the wines of Languedoc. Its main street, which is also the city's axis, is the Allées Paul-Riquet, named after the native son who from 1660 to 1680 created the Canal des Deux-Mers connecting the Mediterranean and the Atlantic. The last part of Travel Route 14 goes from Béziers to Perpignan for 89 km. (55 miles). About 2 km. (1 mile) southwest of Béziers, Route N 9 crosses the **Écluses de Fonséranes* lock and leads to the important city of **Narbonne** (population 45,000). The ancient Roman colony of Narbo Martius developed into an important seaport and became the provincial capital of the province of Gallo

Narbonensis. During the fifth century, the city was occupied by Visigoths. Arabs from Spain invaded and ruled the city from 719 to 759. Its harbor silted up in the 14th century; Narbonne now lies 4 km. (2.5 miles) from the Étang de Bages et de Sigean, the only sea inlet leading to the Mediterranean.

Near the Canal de la Robine (which crosses the city and extends 20 km. 12 miles, south to the sea) is the *Palais des Archevêques* (13th–14th century), fortified with three towers and housing the town hall and three museums. These include the *Musée Régional de l'Histoire de l'Homme,* with an interesting collection of prehistoric and ancient objects. Beyond the palace is the *Cathédrale Saint-Just;* its giant Gothic choir, at a height of 40 meters (131 feet), is among the tallest in northern France.

Route N 9 now runs south along the sea beaches. At *Étang de Leucate,* 36 km. (22 miles) from Narbonne, is the *Station Leucate-Barcarès,* a large vacation resort on the sand strips separating the lagoon from the sea. Each of its two harbors can accommodate 1,500 boats. Continue on to ***Perpignan** (population 120,000), the capital of Roussillon, which was a possession of the kingdom of Aragón from the end of the 12th century to the middle of the 17th century. During the Middle Ages the city was famous for its luminous red dyes, made from the madder plants that thrive on the Roussillon plain.

The *Palais des Rois de Majorque* (13th–14th century) in the citadel remains from the days when Perpignan was the capital of the independent kingdom of Majorca, 1278 to 1344. The other places worth seeing are all close together: *Le Castillet,* an attractive fortress gate made of brick dating from 1370; the *Loge de Mer* (1397), seat of the Medieval municipal commodity exchange; and the *Cathédrale Saint-Jean,* built in the 14th and 15th centuries in the southern French Gothic style. Noteworthy here are the famous winged altar pieces, especially the retable of the Virgin (1500) in the right apsidiole and, in the Chapelle du Christ, the 14th-century Dévot Christ, a carved crucifix that came to Perpignan from Germany.

In addition to autoroute A 9, you can take either of two roads from here to Spain. Continue on Route N 9, which leads directly south. It intersects Travel Route 25 at Bains du Boulou and reaches Le Perthus at the Spanish border after 31 km. (19 miles). Barcelona lies 162 km. (100 miles) beyond this point. The other road, N 114, runs southeast through Roussillon toward the sea, and to *Elne* (population 5,700), located only 5 km. (3 miles) from the sea. It has beautiful **cloisters dating from the 12th to the 14th century. In *Argèles* the plain ends and the rocky Côte Vermeille begins.

As it begins to curve, dip, and climb, Route N 114 becomes the *Corniche de la Côte Vermeille* for

30 km. (19 miles) along the coast to the picturesque old harbor town of ****Collioure,** a favorite haunt of the Fauvist painters André Derain, Georges Braque, and Henri Matisse. The road passes beneath the *Fort Saint-Elme,* built by Charles V in 1550, to **Port Vendres** (population 6,000), a town that maintains a lively commerce with Algiers and Oran; and **Banyuls** (population 5,000), France's southernmost seaside resort and a favorite winter spa. From a scenic lookout you can see the Spanish coast.

Route N 114 ends at the French border in **Cerbère.** *Port Bou* is on the Spanish side of the border.

TRAVEL ROUTE 15: ***Paris–*Lyon–***Avignon–Marseille (779 km.; 483 miles)

See map on page 185.

Travel Route 15 takes you south from Paris through the Burgundy wine region to the Mediterranean port of Marseille. Along the way gourmands will want to stop and sample some of the excellent regional specialties and taste the superb wines.

Two major roads lead south from Paris, interesecting each other several times: the Autoroute du Soleil (A 6 and A 7; follow the route marked "1" on the map) and Route N 6 (later N 7; follow the route marked "2" on the map), which is described below.

From Paris, take N 6 south, past *Villeneuve-Saint-Georges* and *Melun,* through the sprawling *Fontainebleau forest* filled with ancient oaks, beech, hornbeam, birch, and Scots pine trees, to the city of *Fontainebleau* and directly past ***Fontainbleau Castle* (see page 53). At *Carrefour de l'Obélisque* bear left, to the east, and follow the course of the Yonne River for 116 km. (72 miles) to **Sens** (population 27,500) with the earliest Gothic *cathedral (see page 9) in France and one of the oldest in Europe. In Sens, you can pick up Travel Route 21 (Nancy–Nantes).

The second leg of the itinerary from Sens to Saulieu—148 km. (92 miles)—goes through Burgundy. Beyond Sens, N 6 follows the Yonne River through *Joigny,* probably founded by the Romans and with half-timbered houses and two Medieval churches, to **Auxerre,** in the center of a grape-growing region that produces the white Chablis, among other wines.

The old town of Auxerre (population 42,000), founded by the Gauls and taken over by the Romans, has two architecturally notable churches. The Flamboyant Gothic *Cathédrale*

Saint-Étienne was begun in the 13th century but not completed until some 300 years later. Some of its features were reproduced in Canterbury cathedral in England. The front, with its sculptured portals, is remarkable, and some of its famous stained glass is still the original from the 13th century. *Saint-Germain abbey church,* founded by its namesake (whose statue is located on the gable of the south transept), was a learning center to which students flocked more than a thousand years ago. The oldest parts date to the ninth century, including the interesting crypt which contains Carolingian frescoes depicting the life of Saint Stephen that date to 858, the earliest in France.

Gourmands should be on the lookout for regional specialties in the shops of Auxerre—garlic sausage baked in brioche, sour-dough bread baked in wood-fired ovens, and for those with a sweet tooth, chocolate snails filled with almond praline and chocolate truffles with rum-soaked grapes.

Continue south on Route N 6 for 20 km. (12 miles), then leave the Yonne Valley and head through the woods and vineyards for the *Cure Valley* and *Vermenton,* with its twin-towered church dating from the 12th and 13th century. The road forks after 18 km. (11 miles). Follow Route N 6 west for 10 km. (6 miles) to *Avallon* where you can take Route D 951 east for a 13 km. (8 miles) detour to **Vézelay** (population 650), situated on a hill, with a commanding view of the countryside. In the Middle Ages religious pilgrims travelled here to see relics reputedly belonging to Mary Magdalen in the **Basilique de la Madeleine.* One of the largest and most beautiful Romanesque churches in France, the basilica was built in the 11th and 12th centuries. Its famous central tympanum was carved by an unknown 12th-century sculptor. The 120-meter- (394-foot-) long main aisle and the capitals are Romanesque, while the choir is early-Gothic. In 1280, when Mary Magdalen's relics were discovered to be elsewhere, the church's prosperity and popularity waned, never to recover. The omnipresent architect Viollet-le-Duc reconstructed the church in 1840–1861. In 1146 Bernard of Clairvaux called for the second crusade from Vezelay.

Route D 957 east rejoins N 6 at **Avallon** (population 11,000), which is perched on a spur 100 meters (328 feet) above the Cousin River and surrounded by ancient ramparts. Several old houses have been preserved in the inner city; on the main street you can see the *Hôtel de Condé* with its Renaissance tower and 17th-century gateway, the 17th-century Ursuline *convent,* and a *clock tower* dating from the mid-15th century. The *church of Saint-Lazare* is an example of the Burgundian-Romanesque style. There are lovely views from the *Promenade de la Petite Porte,* where you can also explore the ramparts and towers.

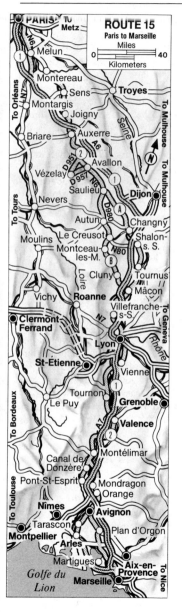

Route N 6 continues through farm country for 39 km. (24 miles) to the hilly summer resort of **Saulieu** (population 4,000), another Early-Christian pilgrimage town that later became renowned for its secular gastronomic delights. From here, there are two equally interesting routes to *Mâcon:* one through *Chalon-sur-Saône* (144 km.; 89 miles) and the other through *Le Creusot* and *Cluny.*

To Mâcon via Chalon-sur-Saône

Follow the route marked "A" on the map.

Route N 6 cuts across the Morvan plateau for 28 km. (17 miles) to *Arnay-le-Duc,* where a famous battle took place in 1570 when Protestants defeated Catholics although outnumbered two to one. Above *La Rochepot,* 27 km. (17 miles) farther on, is the picturesque 15th-century **Château de la Rochepot.* Continue on N 6 through the vineyards around *Puligny* (to the west) and *Chassagne-Montrachet,* to **Chalon-sur-Saône** (population 58,000), an important inland harbor at the confluence of the Central Canal and the Saône River and a busy commercial center for Burgundy wine. The *Musée Denon* contains important collections of archaeology and art, including a Merovingian sarcophagus, Gallo-Roman bronze figurines, and a first-century sculpture of a gladiator and a lion. A residence of the

Burgundian kings in the sixth century, the town retains its characteristic old center. Camera buffs should not miss the *Musée Niepce,* devoted to the work of Joseph Nicéphore Niepce (1755–1833), an early pioneer of photography.

Continue south on Route N 6 for 29 km. (18 miles) along the valley of the Saone, to **Tournus** (population 8,000), an old riverside town whose narrow cobblestone streets are filled with inviting antiques shops. Most of the houses and towers of the inner city were built in the Middle Ages and the Renaissance, and all buildings of historic interest are well marked. The well-preserved **abbey of Saint-Philibert* (10th–11th centuries), a unique Romanesque building in Burgundy, is actually three separate churches superimposed one on top of another. Its massive external bulk hides a surprisingly spacious, light-filled interior free of ornamentation, so that the architectural details can be seen with refreshing clarity.

Route N 6 continues along the Saône River, past the Monts du Mâconnais vineyards to **Mâcon** (population 46,000), center of the wine trade.

To Mâcon via Le Creusot and Cluny

Follow the route marked "B" on the map.

Take D 980 from Saulieu for 17 km. (11 miles), to the valley of the Ternin River and **Autun** (population 25,000), dominated by its spectacular 12th-century cathedral. Called "the other Rome" in the days of the Roman Empire, the city's good location on the large Lyon–Boulogne road was fully exploited by the military and commerce minded Romans. Of the two remaining Roman gates, the *Porte d'Arroux* is the more elegant; like the *Porte Saint-André,* it has two main arches flanked by smaller openings. Unfortunately, little remains of the 15,000-seat amphitheater, which was once the largest in Gaul.

The ***Cathédrale Saint-Lazare* is Autun's glory. It was built in 1120 on the highest point in town to house the relics of Saint Lazarus. The tympanum of the central portal, depicting the **Last Judgment,* is a triumph of Romanesque sculpture; Gislebertus, who did some of the stone carvings, is one of the rare artists of the period to sign his work. Oddly enough, these precious carvings exist today only because Voltaire scoffed at the style of the sculpture; to allay his criticism, it was plastered over between 1766 and 1834, and thus it escaped destruction by the revolutionary iconoclasts. The superb stone spire of the central tower was added by Cardinal Rolin, bishop of Autun, in the 15th century after the collapse of the Romanesque tower. The interior, with its especially fine nave capitals, projects a feeling of classic simplicity.

Small but well-arranged, the *Musée Rolin* in the *Hôtel Rolin* has magnificent works of Roman,

Gallo-Roman, and Medieval art, including an unusual *Temptation of Eve* attributed to Gislebertus. There is a view of the old circular prison from the interior courtyard.

Take N 80 for 26 km. (16 miles), where it passes 4 km. (2.5 miles) from **Le Creusot** (population 32,000), an important center of heavy industry. In 1838 the first locomotive in France was made here. The *Château de la Verrerie*, the former glassworks for Marie Antoinette, is located here.

From Le Creusot, pick up Route D 980 south to the industrial city of *Blanzy,* site of the *Musée de la Mine.* Nearby *Montceau-les-Mines* (population 26,950) is a coal-mining city with a monument (1930) by Bourdelle to those killed in action in the First World War.

Continue on D 980 southeast to *Mont-Saint-Vincent,* a division between the Atlantic ocean and the Mediterranean sea that provides a superb view. The road proceeds to **Cluny** (population 4,800), set in a lovely rolling countryside. The town contains a number of Medieval and Renaissance buildings, but only fragments remain of the great *Benedictine abbey* founded by William the Pious, Duke of Aquitaine, in 910 and expanded in the 11th century. An impression of Cluny's former power lingers among the ruins of the abbey church which was built from 1088 to 1130 and was the largest in Christendom until the construction of St. Peter's in Rome (1452–

1626). The *south crossbar of the transept* and the consecration-water tower above it still stand.

The monastery had some 300 satellite abbeys salted throughout western Europe and more than 10,000 monks observed its strict rules. In its heyday, Cluny was mightier than the papacy, which it counseled with influential advisers, and its school was so famous that it was called the "Light of the World." Before it was demolished in the 1790s to make way for a thoroughbred horse farm, the church must have been a veritable mountain range of apsidiole cupolas, nave ridges, and tower peaks. Just ten **capitals** remain from the 12th century, and they are in the grain-storage unit (13th century).

South of Cluny, Route D 980 passes through the hilly country of the Mâconnais and ends at Route N 79. From a small pass, *Col du Bois-Clair,* you can get a great view over the Saône Valley and the Bresse plain, all the way to the remote Jura mountains. Route N 79 then goes on to Mâcon.

Travel Route 15 follows Route N 6 from Mâcon to Lyon for 68 km. (42 miles). Apart from some overpasses or underpasses, N 6 and autoroute A 6 run along the west bank of the Saône River, past the vineyards of the Mâconnais. The wines produced north and south of *La Croisée-Belleville* carry the famous Beaujolais label.

South of the industrial city of *Villefranche-sur-Saône,* the former capital of Beaujolais, routes N

6 and A 6 leave the Saône River and rejoin it at ***Lyon** (see page 64). In Lyon you may pick up Travel Route 22 (Belfort–Bordeaux).

You can continue the next leg of Travel Route 15 from Lyon to Montélimar, a distance of 145 km. (90 miles), on Autoroute A 7 and Route N 7 which run south, along the west bank of the Rhone River (there isn't much to see).

The broad valley basin is bordered on the east by the foothills of the Alps and to the west by the Cevennes, the foothills of the Massif Central. You'll see many mulberry trees; these trees, along with the silkworms that thrive on them, were introduced in the 15th century to boost the silk industry in Lyon.

Proceed on N 7 for 28 km. (17 miles) to ****Vienne** (population 29,500). Situated in the center of a fruit-growing area, the town is famous for its restaurants, as well as its long-established textile and leather works. A charming Roman *temple of Augustus and Livia* (25 B.C.), stands as a fine example of architectural and spiritual adaptability. It became a church in the Middle Ages, then served as a "Temple of Reason" during the French Revolution. There are also the remains of a large *amphitheater,* built into the side of Mont Pipet. **Saint-Pierre,* rebuilt with Roman material in the ninth and tenth centuries on fourth- to sixth-century foundations, ranks among the oldest churches in France, and now houses a good **lapidary collection.* The Romanesque portals and lower story of *Saint-Maurice,* the former cathedral, are worth examining.

Proceed on Route N 7 for 55 km. (34 miles) south, through the famous vineyards of L'Hermitage, named for a hermit's cell on the hillside to the east of **Tain-L'Hermitage** (population 5,600). A Roman "taurobolium" dating from A.D. 184 that shows the ritual slaying of a bull stands in the main square. Across the Rhône is **Tournon** (population 9,700), with a pleasant riverside promenade and a much-restored 16th-century castle. The poet Stéphane Mallarmé taught English (1863–1866) at the Lycée, housed in the Renaissance buildings of the college. The two towns of Tain-L'Hermitage and Tournon were linked in 1826 by the first suspension bridge ever built.

Route N 7 intersects the Isere River 10 km. (6 miles) to the south. A monument on the bridge marks the 45th-degree latitude.

Continue for 5 km. (3 miles) to **Valence** (population 68,200), an architecturally undistinguished town perched 120 meters (397 feet) above the Rhône and facing a line of cliffs. Valence was once the capital of the Duchy of Valentinois created by Louis XII for Cesare Borgia, the son of Pope Alexander VI. The title is now held by Prince Rainier III of Monaco. Pope Pius VI, who died while a prisoner in Valence in 1799, was buried in the Romanesque *Cathédrale Saint-*

Apollinaire. (His body was moved to Rome in 1802.) Napoleon arrived in 1785 to study at the artillery school; he remained a year, and returned again in 1791. The writer Rabelais was the most famous pupil of the university. There is a series of remarkable 18th-century red chalk drawings by Hubert Robert in the *museum,* housed in the former Bishop's Palace, where the writer Madame de Sévigné was often a guest.

If you wish, you can pick up Travel Route 23 (Geneva–Bayonne) in Valence.

As you continue on Route N 7, you'll notice the landscape becomes increasingly Mediterranean south of Valence. The Provence region begins at *Loriol-sur-Drôme.* To the left is the picturesque village of **Marmande* and to the right is the *Baix Dam,* one of 22 built on the Rhone to generate electric power, provide passage for large ships, and irrigate the soil of the river basin. Continue for 13 km. (8 miles) on N 7 to **Montélimar** (population 30,200). This Provençal city has been renowned for its almond-and-honey nougat since the 16th century. Many 16th- and 17th-century houses remain in the old center with its narrow lanes that run south from a Medieval gate. The much-battered 14th-century *Adhemar Castle,* to the east, is worth a visit.

The next section of Travel Route 15 covers the 81 km. (50 miles) from Montélimar to Avignon. Take N 7 south for 7 km. (4 miles)

to the *Usine H. Poincaré,* the third-largest Rhône power plant, which is fed by a long canal that carries water from the Rochemaure Dam.

About 4 km. (2.5 miles) southwest of the power station, the Rhône narrows. The narrowest point, the "water rock," is just 300 meters (984 feet) wide, and strikes fear into the hearts of river boat pilots. The Rhône is diverted here into a canal 28 km. (17 miles) long, with the *Usine A. Blondel* power plant alongside it and the *Atomic Power Center* nearby. South of Mondragon, the canal empties into the Rhône.

At *Bollène,* to the south, N 7 and A 7 intersect Route D 94. This junction, aptly called *"La Croisière,"* is where travellers to Nîmes cross the Rhône on Route N 86 to *Pont Saint-Esprit,* an old fortified town, and proceed, via *Pont du Gard* to Nîmes (see Travel Route 16). An alternate route is autoroute A 9 between Nîmes and Narbonne.

The famous **Pont Saint-Esprit,* dedicated to the Holy Ghost and spanning a swift and shallow stretch of the Rhône, gives the town its name; 19 of its 25 original arches are from the bridge built between 1265 and 1309 by the Frères Pontifes (Pontifical Brethren). The 15th-century *Maison du Roi* in the town contains an old fresco of the bridge.

From the west side of Pont Saint-Esprit, you can make a 24-km. (15-mile) detour to **Aven d'Orgnac.* Take Route D 901 northeast through the forested foothills of the Cévennes to one of the most magnificent stalactite and stalagmite caverns in France. Its gigantic "halls" are noted for the color of their formations; an earthquake in the Tertiary period is responsible for some of the fantastic shapes. If you have time, the limestone **Gorges des Ardeches,* 47 km. (29 miles) farther along, features a natural bridge and the *Grotte d'Ebbo,* where drawings from the Aurignacian period were discovered in 1946.

From Pont Saint-Esprit, continue on N 7 to **Orange** (population 27,500), called Arausio by the Romans, an important and populous center by the time of Augustus. Charlemagne created the counts of Orange, but the counts of Nassau-Dillenburg took possession of it in 1530 with a dubious inheritance claim. Their descendants, the Nassau-Orange family, rulers of the Netherlands, decided to turn Orange into a mighty fortress, and used the ancient Roman structures as a quarry. Thus almost nothing remains of the Roman capitol, temples, baths, or the so-called Gymnasium, which was probably a circus. Excavations on the site are quite recent. The fortress was demolished by Louis IV in 1673, and Orange finally came into the possession of France in 1713.

Two justly famous Roman structures, however, are surprisingly complete. The **Arc de Triomphe,* to the north, was built

Orange: Triumphal Arch

after Caesar's victory over the Gauls in 49 B.C. Although weathered and lacking its quadriga, all its ornamental relief commemorating the founding of Arausio as a colony for veterans is intact. The 10,000-seat **Théâtre Antique* is the best preserved in all Europe. Its entire façade, 103 meters (338 feet) long and 38 meters (125 feet) high, and the colossal statue of Augustus, which has been restored and placed in a central niche, are still standing. There are two rows of supports for the posts that held up the awning (velarium) that protected the audience from the elements. The trench into which the curtain was lowered can be seen in the front of the stage. Summer festival productions of music and opera are still performed at the theater. Today's audiences sit on the same stone seats as their Roman predecessors.

If you wish, you can take a 9-km. (6-mile) detour south of Orange to *Châteauneuf-du-Pape,* a site known to all wine drinkers. Take Route 976 south to Route D 17. Only one high tower remains of the 14th century castle of the popes, which was destroyed in the religious wars. However, the famous vineyards still thrive, and there is a charming view of the valley of the Rhône and of ***Avignon** (population 91,500), the city of popes and antipopes. The mighty fortress here is among the most noteworthy sights in France. In 1305, Pope Clement V, the former Bishop of Bordeaux, moved the Holy See to Avignon to escape a Rome torn by corruption and sedition. This "Babylonian captivity" of the church lasted until 1377, during which time six more French popes reigned. The famous ***Palais des Papes,* or city fortress, considered by some to be the greatest Medieval structure in Europe, was built in this period. By 1378, the papacy officially returned to Rome, a move that was contested by several cardinals. Remaining in Avignon, they elected an antipope and thereby precipitated the Great Schism, which lasted until 1449. Avignon was administered by papal legatees until 1791, when it became part of France.

The older part of the fortress, the *Palais Vieux,* was built under Benedict XII (1334–1342), and its architecture reflects his Cistercian austerity; the more ornate "new palace," on the other hand, built by Clement VI, is an expression of that worldly love of art and extravagance that led Puritans to

Avignon: Palais des Papes

denounce Avignon as a vice-ridden pit. The outer walls of the fortress have heavy towers and few windows, and appear overbearing and starkly military. Inside, the palace, which served as a barracks from 1808 to 1906, is a labyrinth of empty halls, suites of rooms, passageways, and chapels. Noteworthy sights include the *Stag Room,* with its frescoes; the two-naved *Great Audience Hall,* which served as a courtroom, and the **Chapelle Clémentine,* which was the papal chapel. The palace is used as part of Avignon's famous drama festival, held in July.

The town is still surrounded by well-preserved Medieval ramparts. Next to the palace is the Romanesque *Cathédrale Nôtre-Dame-des-Dôms* (12th century), unfortunately disfigured over the years by insensitive alterations. Toward the Rhône, stands the *Rocher-des-Dôms* (Dome rock);

its garden, provides a view of the famous bridge of songdom, the *Pont d'Avignon,* actually called *Pont Saint-Bénézet.* Half of the bridge dates to 1669 and the rest was built between 1177 and 1188 by the Frères Pontifes. The *Musée du Petit Palais* has an outstanding collection of early Italian paintings beautifully displayed in the restored 14th-century palace, once the residence of archbishops. Two immense superimposed halls in the recently restored 14th-century *Livrée Ceccano* contain remarkable heraldic decoration.

The busy Avignon of today, centered in the *Place de l'Horloge,* is surprisingly sophisticated and chic; some of its old texture, therefore, has inevitably been eroded by the relentless renovation and commercialization that threatens to turn it into one giant historical boutique.

The last leg of Travel Route 15 runs from Avignon to *Marseille* (95 km.; 59 miles) either directly via Route N 7 or on a slightly longer route through Arles.

Take Route N 7 for 11 km. (7 miles), where it runs parallel to the Autoroute du Soleil, which circles Avignon. Route N 7 crosses the Durance River on the 14-arch *Pont de Bonpas* (1953). At the *Plan d'Orgon* intersection, go south to the ruined city of **Les Baux-de-Provence** (see Travel Route 16), a side trip of 22 km. (14 miles). Continue on N 7 for 23 km. (14 miles) to **Salon-de-Provence** (population 35,000), a busy market town. The tomb of the famous astrologer Nostradamus (1503–1566), whose book of predictions fascinated the superstitious Catherine de Médicis, is in the attractive Provence-Gothic *church of Saint-Laurent* (14th–15th century); in the center of the city is the *Château de l'Emperi* (13th–15th centuries), seat of the Archbishop of Arles. Inside there is a museum documenting 200 years of French military history.

From Salon take N 113 south to *Vitrolles,* on the eastern border of the Étang de Berre. A climb to the top of the "rock" (75 steps) provides a broad view over a landscape which is becoming increasingly industrialized. Continue on Route N 7 to **Marseille** (see page 58).

If you opt to reach Marseille through Arles, go south from Avignon on N 570, through **Tarascon** with its imposing seven-tower *Château du Roi René,* a magnificent fortress (12th–15th century), with high walls and round towers, on the bank of the Rhône. It contains several fine vaulted rooms. The town is named for the Tarasque, a child-devouring dragon that terrorized the ancient populace until Saint Martha defeated it with the Sign of the Cross. *Sainte-Martha,* named for the dragon-slayer, is a lovely Gothic church; a fifth century sarcophagus in the crypt is reputedly her tomb. The writer Alphonse Daudet (1840–1897) immortalized the town with his story about the braggart *Tartarin de Tarascon.*

Continue for 40 km. (25 miles) to *Arles (see Travel Route 16), a city that is typical of Provence. The detour continues eastward, via routes N 113 and D 568, through the impressive stony wilderness of *Plaine de la Crau, where long lines of cypresses have been planted to help break the seasonal blasts of the mistral, to the *Golfe de Fos* on the Mediterranean. *Martigues,* 11 km. (7 miles) farther down the coast, has devel-

oped from a fishing village beloved by many painters into a fishing and industrial port. One or two picturesque corners still remain, however, particularly on the Île Brescon between the banks of the canal.

The road leads into autoroute A 55, which runs along the heavily industrialized *Étang de Berre,* a large salt-water lagoon surrounded by limestone hills, over Estaque peninsula, to **Marseille** (see page 58).

TRAVEL ROUTE 16: Circular Tour through Provence (186 km.; 115 miles, or 295 km.; 183 miles including detours and side trips)

See color map.

This route crosses the heartland of Provence. The region, called Provincia by the Romans because it was the first part of Gaul they conquered, is bounded by Avignon and Pont du Gard in the north, Aigues-Mortes and La Grande-Motte in the west, the Camargue in the south, and Les Baux in the east. The clarity and purity of the landscape here is equalled by its fascinating overlay of history, encompassing majestic Roman remains and superb Romanesque and Gothic reminders of the Middle Ages, amid busy modern towns. The splendid sights of Provence are all relatively close to each other. The route is flexible: You can cover parts of it, or shorten it by dispensing with detours.

Route N 100 goes west from ***Avignon (see Travel Route 15), over the Rhône Bridge, and past the *Tour de Philippe le Bel. This tower, 32 meters (105 feet) high, was built by Philippe le Bel (Philippe the Fair) in 1307 to secure the *Pont d'Avignon. The view from the top makes a climb worthwhile. Continue on N 100 to **Villeneuve-lès-Avignon** (pop-

ulation 9,500), a delightful town often overlooked by visitors, where the mighty *Fort Saint-André (14th century) protected the border of France, which at the time ended at the Rhône. The lovely gardens provide a splendid panoramic view; a tenth-century oratory crowns the highest point. *La Chartreuse du Val de Bénédiction, the massive Carthusian monastery founded in 1356 by Pope Innocent VI, who is buried here, was once of great importance. The *museum,* located in a 17th-century hospice near the Tour de Philippe le Bel, contains Quarton's 1453 masterpiece, *The Coronation of the Virgin.* Cardinals from the papal court often chose the town as their summer residence.

Just 25 km. (16 miles) farther west on N 100 is a masterwork of ancient engineering, the lofty ***Pont du Gard.*** This aqueduct, built in 19 B.C. by Agrippa, son-in-law of Augustus, is one of the best-preserved Roman structures in France. Three series of hewn stone block arches, one atop another, span the deep valley of the Gard River. In ancient times, the 41-km.-(25-mile-) long aqueduct carried spring water from Uzès to Nîmes. You can cross the Pont du Gard on the first arch stage, which has been expanded to form a bridge, or in the water channel, which lies beneath the covering plates and does not provide a view; however, neither of these walks is recommended for those prone to dizziness.

From Pont du Gard, Route N 86, (which runs south from Pont Saint-Esprit, see Travel Route 15) goes 20 km. (12 miles) directly to *Nîmes.* Or, you can detour an additional 18 km. (11 miles) through *Uzès.*

Take Route D 981 northwest for 13 km. (8 miles) to **Uzès** (population 7,800). In this ancient town, a unique 12th-century Romanesque bell tower, the **Tour Fenestrelle,* is the sole relic of a cathedral demolished by a 16th-century bishop who embraced Protestantism; it is the only round bell tower in France. The Medieval feudal castle of the dukes of Uzès, the **Duché* (12th, 14th, 16th centuries), is also worth a visit. From Uzès, take the scenic Route D 979 south 25 km. (16 miles) to Nîmes.

**Nîmes (population 129,900) is celebrated for its outstanding Roman remains, its bullfighting tradition, and as the place of origin for the most ubiquitous fabric of modern times—denim. Founded first by the Gauls on the site of a holy spring, Nemausus, as the Romans called it, a prospered as a center of commerce for the empire. The town has an unusually large Protestant population, the Huguenots having thrived here as a result of the protection afforded them by Henri IV's Edict of Nantes. The word nicotine is derived from the name of a native son, Jean Nicot, who introduced tobacco into France in 1560. The writer Alphonse Daudet was born in Nîmes in 1840.

Most visitors come to view the remarkable Roman ruins, chief among them ***Les Arènes,* built in the first century A.D. While slightly smaller than the theater in Arles, it is much better preserved, still possessing most of the attic, or upper story. In Roman times, the theater was unquestionably magnificent. A system of movable awnings (velaria), traces of which remain in the partly preserved cor-

Nîmes: Amphitheater

bels, crowned the giant oval and protected its thrill-seeking occupants from sun and rain. The 21,000 guests, strictly separated by class, entered through the richly adorned main entrance if they were particularly important, or through one of 123 other assigned entrances if they were not. The outer shell of the theater shows off the remarkable ability of Roman master builders to add life to colossal structures through the interplay of light and shadow. The arena attracts modern day thrill seekers who come to the bullfights held here in the summer.

Follow the Boulevard Victor Hugo to the splendid ****Maison Carrée,** a marvelously preserved temple that once dominated the Roman Forum but now, unfortunately, stands alongside a superhighway. Built almost 2,000 years ago, it illustrates how architects in the age of Augustus refined Greek designs. The gracefully narrow temple is 15 meters (49 feet) high, with 30 columns ending in magnificent Corinthian capitals. The stone masonry work is magnificent. Thomas Jefferson, one of the many architects who have admired this structure over the centuries, had renderings of it sent to Virginia in 1787 as a model for the state capitol. Many fine objects are on display inside, including a perfectly preserved mosaic floor and the city's most famous sculpture, the *Venus de Nîmes.*

To the east of the Maison Carrée is the *Vieux Nîmes* or old city, centered around the cathedral. Several town houses, some with beautifully embellished façades, remain; the oldest dates from the 12th century. A series of 15 Roman mosaic panels depicting scenes of a Roman wedding are the showpiece of the *Musée des Beaux-Arts,* while other worthwhile Roman sculptures can be seen in the *Musée Archéologique.*

The *Jardin de la Fontaine,* where many buildings stood in Roman times near the Nemausus spring, is an 18th-century formal garden adorned with sculptures and a huge, shimmering reflecting pool. Some ancient structures remain. Two semicircular terraces lead down to the Nemausus spring. A park of pines and cedars extends up the slope of Mont Cavalier to the *Tour Magne,* with a hefty climb of 140 steps and a spectacular view at the top.

From Nîmes, Route N 113 goes directly to Arles (31 km.; 19 miles). However, the circular tour continues southwest, via Aigues-Mortes and the Camargue.

Proceed on Autoroute A 9, or on Route N 113, for 20 km. (12 miles) to Route D 979 south, then continue for 15 km. (9 miles) to ****Aigues-Mortes** (population 4,500), the most perfectly preserved walled town in France. This Medieval "city of the dead waters" (Aquae mortuae) was developed on swampland in the 13th century by Louis IX the Saint, who needed a port on the Mediterranean. Rather than becoming the fabulous port he envisioned, however, it became a fortified collection point for soldiers on the seventh Crusade. In 1248, 38 ships anchored beneath its walls to pick up an army of crusaders. (The harbor has long since silted up.) The Medieval sea *fortress,* enclosed by walls 8–10 meters (26–33 feet) high, has remained relatively undisturbed and is the town's principal site of interest. Fourteen towers flank the gate. The donjon, called *Tour de Constance,* is a fortress in itself: Its walls are 6 meters (20 feet) thick, and it served as a jail for hundreds of years. The inflexible Protestant Marie Durand spent 37 years of her life imprisoned there. *Nôtre Dame-des-Sablons,* a 17th-century church, is also worth a visit.

*Le Grau-du-Roi, a pretty little fishing harbor and seaside resort, is 8 km. (5 miles) to the south, on Route D 979. The road passes over a dam between lagoons and the Rhône Canal. *La Grande-Motte,* 7 km. (4 miles) to

the northwest, is a vacation center with distinctive *pyramid houses.* Its harbor has 1,000 boat slips; an additional 2,400 anchoring places are in the harbors of *Port Camargue* (southeast of La Grande-Motte and south of Le Grau-du-Roi) and *Carnon* (west of La Grande-Motte). There are very few hotels in La Grande-Motte, which consists mainly of private homes.

The route from Aigues-Mortes continues east on Route D 58, and south on D 570, through the alluvial plain between the two arms of the Rhône River, which empties into the Mediterranean here. This region is the *Camargue,* an extensive area of marshland and lagoons famed for its nature preserves and abundance of wildlife. Wild duck, rose flamingoes, egrets and ibises are plentiful. Great herds of sheep browse on reclaimed pastureland; the black fighting bulls used for the bullfights in Nîmes and Arles, as well as the small white horses said to have been introduced by the Saracens, are raised in the area by herdsmen known as "guardians." Salt production and rice cultivation, introduced in the 16th century, are the other principal pursuits of the 10,000 inhabitants of this exotic delta.

*Saintes-Maries-de-la-Mer (population 2,500) has a famous fortified and battlemented *church,* built on the site of a pagan temple, with a well inside. The church is a pilgrimage site for many gypsies, who revere the Holy Sarah and gather in late May before the dispersal of the tribes, electing a new "queen" here every few years. According to legend, Sarah accompanied the three Marias—Maria Jacobea, the sister of the Mother of God, Maria Salome, the mother of the Apostles James and John, and Maria Magdalena, the Penitent—when they landed here in A.D. 45, the first Christians to do so.

The reputed relics of Maria Jacobea and Maria Salome, conveniently discovered by King René in 1448, are in a chapel in the upper church. Those of Sarah are in the crypt. The relics of Maria Magdalena were brought to Vézelay. South of the church is the *Musée Baroncelli,* which will interest those wishing to know more about the unique flora and fauna of the Camargue. There is a tourist center at Saintes-Maries-de-la-Mer.

Take Route D 570 north toward Arles. At Albaron, a worthwhile detour leads to the ancient town of *Saint-Gilles* (13 km.; 8 miles). A 12th-century Romanesque church, part of the abbey founded in the eighth century by the Holy Agidius (Saint Gilles), has a remarkable, richly adorned **façade* that is an important work from this period.

From here, Route N 572 leads east to **Arles** (population 50,800). Vincent Van Gogh, who lived and painted here from 1888 to 1890, and Georges Bizet, who composed the *L'Arlésienne Suite,*

both thought that Arles captured the essence of Provence. Founded by maritime trading Phoenicians and Greeks, it was inevitable that this strategic site at the mouth of the Rhône should come under the eventual domination of Rome. The Romans, who left their indelible imprint here, made Arles the capital of Provence, and later capital of the "three Gauls" (France, Spain, and Britain). Christianity made its mark here as early as the first century, and the town became increasingly important as an ecclesiastical center for the early church. It was here that Saint Augustine was consecrated first bishop of Canterbury. In the 9th to 11th century it was the seat of the Burgundian kingdom of Arles. In later years, Aix became the region's political capital and Marseille its economic capital. In World War II, Arles came under heavy bombardment by the Allies.

Arles boasts an ancient 25,000-seat **amphitheatre,* the largest structure of its kind north of the Alps. Founded in the second century and used later as a fortress in the Middle Ages, it is similar to the one in Nîmes but not as well preserved. The attica, or uppermost story, is missing; 60 arches make up the two remaining stories. Provençal-style bullfighting now takes place here every summer. The Roman *theater* nearby, once used as a quarry, retains two impressive columns—called Deux Veuves (Two Widows)—which serve as a Classical backdrop for the festival plays and spectacles that are held here in July.

Painted by Van Gogh, and one of the few remaining recognizable sites of his emotionally tortured and artistically triumphant time in Arles, *Les Alyscamps,* on the city's southeast border, is a remarkable avenue of marble tombs that once formed the approach to Arles by the Aurelian Way. Miracles performed around the tomb of Saint Trophimus made the site famous; coffins of deceased citizens desiring burial at this sacred place were floated down the Rhône bearing not only the corpse but the money necessary for burial expenses. In the former *church of Sainte-Anne* (17th century), the *Musee Lapidaire Païen,* has important Roman sarcophagi, statues, and mosaics, and the *Musee Lapidaire Chrétien* has Early Christian sarcophagi, many of exceptional workmanship. The church also provides access to Roman underground galleries, the 2,000-year-old *Cryptoporticoe,* built originally to store grain. An interesting museum devoted to local life and customs, the *Museum Arlaton,* was founded by Fréderic Mistral (1830–1914), the famous Provençal poet.

Saint-Trophime, the former cathedral, is considered by many to be the finest Romanesque church in Provence. Frederick Barbarossa was crowned emperor here in 1178. Its magnificent **portal* is alive with 12th-century sculpture; the cloister, which

Saint-Trophime: Portal

consists of two 12th-century Romanesque and 14th-century Gothic column galleries, is outstanding.

Tarascon is 17 km. (11 miles) directly north of Arles on N 570. An alternative is the attractive detour through *Les Baux* (28 km.; 17 miles).

The route takes you northeast from Arles for 18 km. (11 miles) on Route D 570. It passes the remains of the *Benedictine Montmajour Abbey* (10th–12th century), with its *crypt of the church of Nôtre-Dame,* **cloister,* *tower,* and *Chapelle Sainte-Croix,* the ruins of an aqueduct, and the *Moulin de Daudet* windmill, which inspired the storyteller Alphonse Daudet, before reaching **Les Baux-de-Provence** (population 500). The dramatic ruins of this Medieval town are somewhat marred by the local souvenir industry. The town is perched on a precipitous rocky peak in the glaring white Alpilles mountains, the southernmost point of the Maritime Alps.

The road leads up the promontory, through ruins of houses and towers, some hewn out of the rock and with Romanesque, Gothic, and Renaissance details, to the ruins of a donjon (12th century), and then on to a high peak with a panoramic view. The sight is spectacular in the fall when the mistral is blowing down the Rhône Valley.

Les Baux was the seat of powerful feudal lords in the 11th century who claimed descent from Balthazar, one of the three Magi, and held important lands throughout Provence. In the 13th century it was the site of the famous "Court of Love," competitions of the minnesingers, or troubadours. Later, it became a bulwark of Protestantism, and remained so until Cardinal Richelieu razed the fortress and the walls. Since then, the city has declined, and its population, which was 6,000 in its heyday, has fallen steadily. Bauxite, the ore used in aluminum, was discovered here in 1822, and takes its name from the town.

To the northwest of Les Baux lies *Tarascon. The last leg of the circular tour goes from Tarascon to Avignon, 23 km. (14 miles) via N 570 (see Travel Route 15), and back to the starting point.

TRAVEL ROUTE 17: Geneva–Grenoble–Nice (464/496 km.; 226/308 miles)

See color map.

This route traverses the French Alps, though the Alpes-du-Nord and Alpes-du-Sud regions, and south to the Côte d'Azur. The starting point is Geneva, Switzerland. En route, you'll visit such sites as Annecy with its beautiful lake, Chambéry, and breathtaking gorges and alpine passes.

The first leg goes from Geneva to Chambéry, a distance of 90 km. (56 miles). Leave Geneva via the Arve Bridge and cross the border in 8 km. (18 miles) to ***Ponts de la Caille,** where a deep ravine is spanned by the Charles-Albert suspension bridge (1838) and the New Bridge (1928).

Just past the ravine, there is a magnificent view of *Lac d'Annecy.*

Continue south on Route N 201 for 13 km. (8 miles) to ***Annecy** (population 50,000). This delightfully situated city perched above the north end of the lake, is dominated by a *castle (12th–14th century) studded with towers and now housing the *Musée du Château,* with a good collection of items relating to archeology, geology and natural history. At its base is the attractive 15th-century *Palais de l'Isle* on a small island that boasts a theater, casino, and beach for swimming. The old quarter of the city has arcaded lanes and is crisscrossed by canals and quais brimming with flowers. The 15th-century *church of Saint-Maurice* has good Flamboyant windows in its apse. Two saints, François de Sales (1576–1622) and Jeanne de Chantal (1572–1641), founders of the Order of Salesians—came from Annecy. Pilgrims pay their respects to both at the 20th-century *Basilique de la Visitation,* with its commanding view. A more worldly resident was Jean Jacques Rousseau, who was a chorister in the 16th-century cathedral and, at the age of 16, formed an alliance with Madame de Warens, 12 years his senior.

**Lac Annecy, which is surrounded by mountain meadows and vineyards, can be circled by boat or car. The most beautiful part of the circuit leads through the 100-year-old plane-tree **Avenue d'Albigny,* and south on Route D 909A for 13 km. (8 miles) to ***Talloires.* The former ***abbey* and a magnificent 18th-century mansion, Auberge du Pere Bise, in Talloires have both become luxury hotels with excellent dining. On the way, Route D 909 passes through *Veyrier,* where a cable car climbs 1,281 meters (4,234 feet) up Mont Veyrier, providing a breathtaking panoramic view. The chic ski resort *La Clusaz* is 32 km. (20 miles) to the east.

From Annecy the route continues south for 33 km. (20 miles) on Route N 201, over a plateau and to the famous spa, ***Aix-les-Bains** (population 24,000). The city boasts the Roman triumphal arch of Campanus (third and fourth centuries). Opposite are the *Thermes Nationaux* (national public baths), built between 1857 and 1934, which include the remains of Roman baths and grottos.

To the north of the baths is the **Musée du Docteur Faure,* which has an outstanding collection of Impressionist paintings. Aix-les-Bains also has a casino and theater, and a botanical garden.

**Lac du Bourget, 3 km. (2 miles) west of the city, the largest lake entirely in France, has facilities for water sports.

The **Abbaye Royale de Hautecombe,* built in the 16th and 19th centuries, is located on the lake's west bank; 300 statues and 43 tombs of members of the House of Savoy are on display in its richly adorned church.

Chambéry (population 54,900) is 14 km. (9 miles) south on Route D 991. This ancient capital of the Duchy of Savoy is considered the cradle of the Italian royal house: The Medieval counts of Savoy moved to the upper Italian Piedmont in 1418, became kings of Sardinia in 1720, and kings of Italy in 1861.

Chambéry's picturesque **château* of the dukes of Savoy, whose center dates to the 13th century, contains the beautiful Gothic **Sainte-Chapelle,* with its *trompe l'oeil* ceiling and lancet windows richly glowing with fine stained glass. The poet Lamartine was married here in 1820. The striking *Fontaine des Éléphants*, with four life-size sculpted elephants, was built in 1838 in memory of General de Boigne, who left to the city much of the wealth he acquired in the service of Rajah Scindia in India. Close at hand is the 15th–16th century Gothic *cathedral*, with a 15th-century wooden virgin and a 10th-century Byzantine diptych. The *Musée Savoisien*, rich in history, Medieval paintings (the so-called Savoie Primitives), and a folk-art collection, stands opposite. Several old mansions, including one where Rousseau lived with Madame de Warens in 1735, are located south of the cathedral; the warren of passages behind these houses once provided access to the ramparts, and several are linked by underground passages. A surprisingly good collection of Italian paintings, including works by Titian, Uccello, Guercino, and Giordano, is housed in the *Musée des Beaux-Arts*.

The second section of Travel Route 17 leads from Chambéry south to *Grenoble*, a distance of 64 km. (40 miles). Route N 6 goes through the small spa *Challes-les-Eaux* and the broad valley of the Isère River. Route N 90 continues south along the west bank to Grenoble. Although slower, Route D 523 provides a more scenic drive as it curves up through the Chartreuse Massif.

The road climbs out of Chambéry to the 867-meter (2,844-foot) *Pas de la Fosse Tunnel*, then on to the *Col du Granier* (Granier Pass), which provides a view all the way to Mont Blanc. It continues through the Entremont gorges to *Saint-Pierre d'Entremont,* which has another great view of the Alps, and up to *Cucheron Pass.* From there, Route D 523 descends to Saint-Pierre-de-Chartreuse, starting point for a side trip to the monastery of *La Grande-Chartreuse* (5 km.; 3 miles).

Follow Route D 512 to the chief monastery of the Carthusians, which was founded in 1085 by Saint Bruno. The present structure, with its sharply sloping slate roofs, designed to prevent the accumulation of snow, has been rebuilt many times over the centuries and now mostly dates from the 17th century. You can approach the monastery on foot but sightseers are not allowed within its precincts, where 35 monks still live according to the Carthusian precepts of solitude, prayer, study, and work. The adjacent distillery where the monks' famous Chartreuse liqueur is made can be visited; a museum next to it offers exhibits on life behind the monastery's walls.

Take Route D 512 south to the *Col de Porte* (Gate Pass). A climb up the Charmont-Som of 4 km. (2.5 miles) provides a breathtaking view. The road descends to **Grenoble** (population 159,500), the original capital of the Dauphiné region, which became part of France in 1394. This once-poor city, magnificently situated in the Isère Valley with the Grande-Chartreuse Massif rising to the north, the Vercors to the southwest, and the Belldonne range to the east, developed into a large modern city when the Winter Olympics were held here in 1968. Henri Beyle, better known as the writer Stendhal (1783–1842) was born here, as was the artist Henri Fantin-Latour (1836–1904). The city was an important center for the Resistance movement in World War II. Some 30,000 students are enrolled at the University of Grenoble, founded in the 14th century.

To get a good overall view of the city and surrounding countryside, you may want to begin your visit with a ride on the cable car (*télépherique*) which leaves from the Quai Stephane-Jay and rises 427 meters (1,400 feet) to *La Bastille,* a former fortress. The *Musée des Beaux-Arts* on the Place de Verdun is one of the richest provincial museums in France. Its strong collection of old masters includes four works by the Spaniard Zurbarán; an outstanding *gallery of modern and contemporary art,* where works by Monet, Sisley, Renoir, Chagall, Klee, Miró, Modigliani, Le Corbusier, Picasso, Gris, and Braque are on view, was added in 1919. Other sights worth seeing include the new *town hall* and the architecturally daring *Palais des Sports* and the *Stade de Glace,* a 12,000-seat ice-skating arena, both built for the 1968 Winter Olympics and located in the Parc Paul-Mistral. The *church of St.-André* has a fine Gothic interior, and superb woodwork characterizes the *Palais de Justice.*

Devotees of *The Red and the Black* and *The Charterhouse of Parma* may wish to visit *Musée Stendhal,* which contains mementoes of the great French writer.

Many well-equipped winter sports centers developed around Grenoble because of the Winter Olympics; two are Chamrousse and Alpe d'Huez.

There are two ways to make the journey from Grenoble to Sisteron: south for 143 km. (87 miles) on N 75, the route of the Préalpes, which until 1930 was called the Winter Road; or, south on N 85, the *Route Napoleon,* (151 km.; 94 miles), which runs closer to the mountains and has more of an Alpine character. Nowadays, powerful snowplows make both roads passable most of the year.

To Sisteron via the Prealps

(Follow the route marked "A" on the map.)

Leave Grenoble on Route N 75 south. At *Le Pont-de-Claix,* N 75 crosses the Drac River where a modern bridge as well as one dating from 1611 stand. Continue past *Monestier-de-Clermont* to *Mont-Aiguille*—2,097 meters (6,878 feet) high—which resembles a giant domino placed on edge. The road climbs steadily to the *Col de la Croix-Haute.* Beyond the pass, the landscape begins to look more Provençal. An attractive view of the closely spaced Medieval houses of *Serres* can be seen along the way.

To Sisteron via the Route Napoleon

(Follow the route marked "B" on the map.)

While eagles soar overhead, imperial eagles appear on milestones to mark the route Napoleon took in 1815, when he left his exile on the island of Elba on his way to a fateful meeting at Laffrey. The village of Laffrey is south of Grenoble on Route N 85. East of the village is the meadow where a battalion was stationed to block Napoleon's march to Grenoble. Leaving his few faithful friends behind, Napoleon advanced alone. The soldiers, many of them veterans of his former campaigns, were ordered to shoot. Throwing open his jacket to reveal the star of the Legion of Honor, Napoleon challenged the troops to fire. Instead, they chose to join him. That evening Napoleon marched into Grenoble. An equestrian statue commemorates this historic scene.

Route N 85 continues through *La Mure* to *Corps,* south into the valley of the Drac River, and crosses the Bayard Pass. In *Gap* (population 25,500) you'll begin to feel the warmer climate of the Mediterranean; summers here can get very hot. For a side trip to *Serre-Ponçon,* the largest artificial lake in Europe, take Route D 994 just east of Gap for 28 km. (17 miles) to *Savines,* a village situated on the lake's edge.

*Sisteron (population 8,000) is farther south on Route N 85. An ancient town located in the valley of the Durance River, it is the first town in Provence. The lovely 12th-century *Nôtre-Dame-du-Roc,* formerly the cathedral, is a good example of Provençal Romanesque. Behind the apse there are steps that lead down to a Medieval warren of narrow lanes. Perched on a limestone rock the *citadel* projects above the town.

The next leg of the itinerary runs from Sisteron either to Cannes or to Nice—174–191 km. (108–118 miles)—depending on the route you choose. Both begin in the Durance Valley to *Château-Arnoux* (Route N 96 continues south to Aix-en-Provence and Marseille). Travel Route 17 continues east into the valley of the Bléone River, where *Malijai Castle* stands. Then it follows the river valley to *Digne* (population 16,400), the Roman "Diana," known for its lavender, dried fruits, honey and pentacrinites (a fossil found in the indigenous shale). It continues south into the valley of the Asse, and to the fork at Barrême, where Route N 202 goes east to Nice, and Route N 85 heads southeast to Cannes.

To Cannes

(Follow the route marked "A" on the map.)

Route N 85 winds south amid beautiful scenery, through the rocky cliffs around Colde Leques to *Castellane* (population 1,300), dramatically situated on the Verdon River and dominated by remaining sections of its 14th-century fortifications and *chapel of Nôtre-Dame du Roc*.

From Castellane Route D 952 loops west through the **Corniche Sublime** for 123 km. (76 miles) to the magnificent **Gorges du Verdon**, among the most beautiful natural sites in Europe.

Route D 71, a panoramic road with many dramatic lookouts, is a technical masterpiece. The *Artuby Bridge* is an outstanding structure bridging a ravine by a single arch. Rejoin N 85 via Route D 90. At the *Pas de la Faye*, you'll get your first views of the Mediterranean and the coast mountains of Estérel and Maures. N 85 then snakes down to **Grasse** (population 38,400), which is surrounded by orange groves and fields of flowers. An important product of the city is rose oil, a basic ingredient in manufacturing perfume. Several perfumeries here offer fragrance tours.

The city, on the sheltered southern slope of the Roquevignon, has retained its picturesque 18th-century character, and is a popular winter spa. Pauline Borghese made Grasse fashionable as a health resort, and the town was later frequented by Queen Victoria, the Belgian writer Maurice Maeterlinck, the American painter Mary Cassatt, and the English writer H. G. Wells.

From the *Cours Honoré-Cresp* building you can admire the landscape around Grasse down to the sea between Golfe du Juan and Estérel. The intriguing narrow

Grasse: Cathedral

lanes of the old town and the 18th-century arcaded *Place aux Aires* with its flower market are close at hand and worth exploring. In the nearby *Musée Fragonard* are mementoes of Jean-Honoré Fragonard (1732–1806), the Rococo painter born in Grasse; the *Museum of Provençal Art and History,* housed in a late 18th-century mansion, contains collections of furniture, glass, ceramics, and paintings. Continue on N 85 for 17 km. (11 miles) to *Cannes* (see page 215).

To Nice

(Follow the route marked "B" on the map.)

Route N 202 goes east from Barrême. At *Saint-André-les-Alpes,* it passes several lakes fed from the dam at Verdon. Then it climbs through the *Clue de Vergons* gorge to *Col de Toutes Aures* and descends through the Rouaine ravine and its colored limestone walls, to the small, well-preserved fortress city of *Entrevaux* in the Var Valley. Its 16th-century church has a notable altar screen and 17th-century doors.

Some 6 km. (4 miles) before you enter Entrevaux, Route D 902 cuts northeast for 14 km. (9 miles) to the ****Gorges de Daluis**, a 6-km. (4-mile) ravine of slate ranging in color from chocolate brown to pink.

Route N 202 continues into the valley of the Var, a region growing ever more beautiful. It passes through the village of *Puget-Théniers*, with its old houses, ruined château and church containing a 16th-century painted altarpiece, to *Pont du Cians*, where it is joined by southerly roads from the ****gorges of Daluis and Cians**. Route N 202 continues to *Pont de la Mescla*, where the Var River bends south. At this point, a secondary road runs up the Tinee Valley to the winter resorts of *Valberg* (86 km.; 53 miles from Nice on route 2205).

Travelling south through the romantic Vesubie gorge, you'll pass through the *Col de Turini*. The area is known for its winter sports facilities and as a grueling stretch (more than 100 curves) of the famous motor rally, the Grand Prix de Monaco, routed through this pass from Luceram. Several roads connect through the Turini area, which makes it easy to do a circular tour of the area. Continue south to the sanctuary of **Madonne d'Utelle*, with a magnificent view from the Maritime Alps to the sea.

South of Pont de la Mescla, the Var Valley narrows into the Chaudan Défilé, finally broadening beyond Saint-Martin-du-Var on N 202.

Shortly before the Var empties into Anges Bay, you can see the fishing village of *Saint-Laurent-du-Var* on the opposite bank. It was restored in Provençal style after its destruction in World War II and has a bathing beach at the outlet of the Var. From here, it is only 12 km. (7 miles) to Nice.

TRAVEL ROUTE 18: ****Routes des Grandes-Alpes– Nice (680 km.; 423 miles)**

See color map.

There are two starting points for this Travel Route: Evian-les Bains, on Lac Léman (Lake Geneva), and Chamonix, at the base of Mont Blanc. These routes will join in Le Fayet and continue to Bourg-Saint-Maurice, where the Route des Grandes-Alpes begins. The route winds along mountain roads and can be tiring and requires about two or three days to travel comfortably. The drive should not be attempted until early summer because of the danger of slick or snow-blocked roads in the colder months.

Evian-les-Bains to Le Fayet

Evian-les-Bains (population 6,000) is an elegant old spa on the south shore of Lac Léman, known for its healthful waters and pleasant climate. It has pretty lakeside gardens and opulent hotels, and was a spot favored by the writer Marcel Proust. The *Quai Baron-de-Blonay* is a famous esplanade in front of the casino; there are also halls here for taking the waters. From Evian take Route N 5 west along the shore of the lake for 9 km. (5.6 miles) to **Thonon-les-Bains** (population 28,000). This former capital of the Chablais region is situated on a terrace above the south bank of the lake. It has a *church* built in 1429 above a Romanesque crypt. Pick up Route D 902 south, as it follows the Dranse River upstream and through several narrow passes. Of special interest is the *Defilé des Tinés,* where a tunnel burrows under an enormous pile of stones and rocky debris from a landslide. The road climbs past the fashionable ski resort of *Morzine* (population 2,900) to *Les Gets.* This winter resort is said to have been founded by a colony of Jews exiled from Florence in the 14th century. From here, the road steeply descends, via *Taninges,* into the valley of the Arve River, which it reaches at *Cluses.* The town (population 16,000) is notable for its national watchmaking school established in 1848.

From Cluses, take N 205 south to **Sallanches** (population 11,000). This town, situated at the base of Mont Blanc, was reborn after a disastrous fire in 1840. Today it has a small airfield offering short sightseeing flights.

Take Route D 13, a serpentine road leading to the climatic health resort of ***Assy.** The town boasts a remarkable church—***Nôtre-Dame de Toute Grâce*—which some of the most famous artists of the 20th century took part in building: The architect Novarina designed it; Fernand Léger created the luminous mosaics on the façade; Lurcat did the splendid tapestry in the apse; Marc Chagall decorated the baptismal chapel; Henri Matisse and Pierre Bonnard created the side altars; Georges Rouault created the dark, glowing windows; and the controversial faceless copper crucifix is by Germaine Richier. Route D 13 continues to **Lac Vert,* situated in a forested bowl.

From Sallanches, take D 202, a mountainous road that continues southeast to the twin summer-winter health resorts of *Le Fayet–Saint-Gervais-les-Bains* (population 4,900). From Le Fayet you can take the tramway that goes up to *Le Nid d'Aigle* (Eagle's Nest) on the lower slopes of Mont Blanc and get a bird's-eye view of the scenery.

From Chamonix to Le Fayet

**Chamonix (10,000 population), one of the major attractions in the Alps, is a narrow town tucked between the Mont Blanc range and the Aiguilles-Rouges.

At the end of the 11th century an important Benedictine priory was founded here. The town's later history is closely tied to the conquest of Mont Blanc, the highest mountain in France at 4,807 meters (15,771 feet). After the mountain was first scaled, in 1786, the town developed into a world famous health and winter sports resort. Early 19th-century visitors included the poets Shelley, Byron, and Wordsworth. Today the place offers a vast array of hotels to hundreds of thousands of mountaineers and sightseers each year.

Chamonix, which includes the neighboring villages of *Argentière* and *Les Bossons* in its orbit, lies in the high *valley of the Arve River. Several glaciers of the Mont Blanc range extend into the city: Particularly impressive are the *Mer de Glace* and the *Glacier de Bossons* flowing down from *Mont Maudit.* From Chamonix, winding roads lead to the north end of the long *Mont Blanc Tunnel,* which passes under the Mont Blanc range to the Italian village of Courmayeur in the upper Aosta Valley.

Chamonix, the self-styled "Capital of Winter Sports," is in fact a giant switching station with suspension railways, chair lifts, ski tows, and two cog railways threading up through the surrounding mountains. The spectacular **funicular* ride to the ***Aiguille du Midi* ascends in two stages. The second half will at times have you dangling more than 488 meters (1,600 feet) above the earth. From there, a gondola crosses the *Vallée Blanche,* the great Mont Blanc glacier, to *Pointe Helbronner,* at an elevation of 3,452 meters (11,323 feet). From this high alpine border station between France and Italy, another funicular descends to *Courmayeur.*

From Chamonix, Route N 212 travels 20 km. (12.5 miles) through the winter resort of *Les Houches* and up the Arve River to

Mont Blanc range above Chamonix

Le Fayet–Saint-Gervais-les Bains.

Mont Blanc is visible during the entire part of the route between Le Fayet and Bourg-Saint-Maurice, a distance of 99 km. (52 miles). Route N 212 heads southwest through *Megève,* one of the largest and most elegant winter sports centers in the French Alps. From its seat on a sun-washed upland plateau, you can see *Mont Joly* and *Mont D'Arbois* as well as Mont Blanc. Much of the town dates from the 1920s, but there are also lovely 13th-century Savoyard buildings, a 17th-century church, and the round tower of an old Benedictine priory. N 212 continues through the deeply cut ravines of the *Gorges d'Arly* to *Ugine,* an industrial city with large electrochemical plants.

Albertville (population 19,000), named after founder Charles Albert of Sardinia, is the western gate to the Tarentaise, as the 90-km.- (56-mile-) long valley of the upper Isère River is called. From here, Route N 90 leads southeast and up the valley for 27 km. (16.7 miles) to **Moûtiers** (population 5,000). The old capital of this region, takes its name from a monastery founded here in the fifth century. Although the town's 15th-century cathedral is unremarkable, it includes some delightful objects, such as 12th-century ivories and enamels. The high-voltage lines crisscrossing the village carry power from surrounding hydroelectric plants to the Rhône Valley. Several other valleys fan out to the south. Heading southeast from Moûtiers on Route N 90, you can reach two well-known winter resorts on smaller roads. The first, *Méribel-les-Allues,* about 18 km. (11 miles) from Moûtiers, is the starting point for exploring the Massif du Fruit. The second, *Courcheval,* offers one of the most extensive skiing areas in France; with close to 90 ski trails totaling some 417 km. (250 miles), it has earned the sobriquet "The Star." Courcheval lies 24 km. (15 miles) from Moûtiers.

Route N 90 continues up the Isère Valley to the market town of **Bourg-Saint-Maurice** (population 6,700), where it rejoins Route D 902. Here, in this broad and beautiful spot full of orchards, the proper Grand Alps Route begins. Proceed southward and upward on Route D 902 for 49 km. (30.5 miles) to the ***Col de l'Isèran,** elevation 2,769 meters (9,082 feet). This is the second highest of the great Alpine passes. Some 23 km. (14 miles) before the top of the pass, D 902 passes the **Barrage de Tignes,* which, at 160 meters (525 feet), is the second-highest dam in Europe. On the southwest side of this elegant structure is the dramatically situated winter resort of *Le Lac de Tignes,* with mountains rising all around. Route D 902 continues on to the famous winter sports resort of **Val d'Isère* (population 2,000), immediately recognizable by its tall steeple. On this regular stop of the World Cup Ski Tour Jean-Claude Killy first gained fame. In summer, skiing is allowed on the Grand Pissaillas glacier, and you can even see bicyclists braving the area's high, winding roads. The top of the pass is just 16 km. (10 miles) farther, and the drive is surprisingly easy in spite of the massive wall of mountains towering eerily overhead. (Just keep in mind that the road is typically blocked by snow from mid-October to mid-June.)

From the Col de l'Isèran, with its enchanting *mountain church*, there is a magnificent view of the glaciers, snow fields, and surrounding peaks.

Route D 902 descends 33 km. (20 miles) to **Mont-Cenis-Lanslebourg** (population 1,000), a small winter resort at the foot of the historic Col du Mont Cenis. (Those acquainted with this pass and environs have included Charlemagne, Napoleon, and possibly even Hannibal.) From here, take N 6 southwest down the Arc River valley, through the so-called Maurienne region. This is the site of a 24-meter (79-foot) wind tunnel that is used to test aircraft. Continue to the unremarkable industrial city and ski resort of Modane—which has endured floodings, bombings, and burnings in this century—and then on for another 17 km. (10.5 miles) to Saint-Michel-de-Maurienne, another small industrial town. From here D 902 winds south for 34 km. (21 miles) through the Col du Télégraphe, past the winter sports resort of Valloire, to the **Col du Galibier.** The climb to this pass is

the longest and toughest of the great circular bicycle race, the *Tour de France.* The road goes under the summit of Galibier, one of the most beautiful passes in the Alps, through a century-old tunnel.

From the north end of the tunnel you get a rear view of Mont Blanc, and from the south end you have a view over the powerful Meije Massif, with its three main peaks. Route D 902 descends slightly to the Col du Lautaret between the Guissane and Romanche valleys. From here, Route N 91 descends southeast for the next 35 km. (22 miles) to Briançon. Here, in the southern Alps, the terrain begins to change: The slopes exposed to the sun are bald; the dark green color of the spruce gives way to the pale green of the larch; and houses display the architectural style of the Midi, the south of France.

Briançon (population 12,000) has the look of a southern city, but at 1,326 meters (4,349 feet) it is also the highest city in Europe. It is fortified by two rings of walls, and has steep, narrow streets of 18th-century houses. The *Grande Rue*, with its staircases and the "gergouille," or brook, gurgling down its center, is particularly picturesque.

From Briançon, Route D 902 climbs southwest for 21 km. (13 miles) to the Col d'Izoard, which, at 2,360 meters (7,740 feet), offers a splendid view, especially to the northwest. Just south of the pass is the **Casse-Déserte,** where rock needles jut out from steep, yellow-and-red scree slopes, creating a wild and lonely-looking landscape. Route D 902 then descends to the *Château-Queyras,* a fortress rebuilt in the 17th century by Vauban (it still has its Medieval keep). Next you come to the *gorges* of the Guil River, before reaching the town of *Guillestre* (population 2,000) where English prisoners were kept during the Napoleonic wars.

Here, D 902 resumes its climb to the *Col de Vars,* elevation 2,111 meters (6,924 feet). It passes through *Sainte-Marie-de-Vars,* which has developed from an unknown mountain village to a well-known winter sports resort. Just before the pass, a gigantic modern ski hotel has been built practically on top of the old mountain hut, "Refuge Napoleon."

Route D 902 descends for 30 km. (19 miles) through larch woods to **Barcelonnette** (population 3,400), both a summer and winter resort with a Provençal look to it. Founded in 1231, the town was involved in numerous frontier struggles. Barcelonnette maintains a curious connection with Mexico, where many of its residents emigrated in the 19th century. Route D 902 continues through the *Gorges du Bachelard* to the *Col de la Cayolle* at 2,326 meters (7,629 feet). South of the pass is the source of the Var River; follow it for 33 km. (20.5 miles) to the village of *Guillaumes,* which has a church dating to 1699 and the ruins of a 15th-century castle.

South of Guillaumes, the Var Valley narrows to the **Gorges de Daluis,** which is 6 km. (3.7 miles) long and has multicolored schist walls. You can continue south, toward Nice, or return to Guillaumes and take Route D 28 east on an interesting side trip. Cross the *Col de Valberg,* site of a new winter sports resort. Descend to *Beuil,* an ancient village turned into another winter resort. There, D 28 turns south into the *Gorges du Cians* and runs right along the bottom of the ravine next to the rushing water. The walls of the ravine come so close together that in some places you can hardly see the sky.

At *Pont du Cians* (see Travel Route 17), D 28 enters the Var Valley and merges with the Routes des Préalpes to *Nice* (a description of the city can be found in Travel Route 19).

TRAVEL ROUTE 19: **The Côte d'Azur–Toulon–**Cannes–Nice–*Monaco–Menton (311 km.; 193 miles)

See maps on pages 212 and 215.

The Côte d'Azur, also known as the French Riviera, is the stretch of Mediterranean coast extending from Cassis (just east of Marseille), through Nice and Menton to the Italian border—a distance of some 300 km. (185 miles). The French, however, limit their definition of the Côte d'Azur to the area from Hyères to Menton, excluding the stretch between Marseille and Toulon. The beauty of this region, its wonderful climate in both summer and winter, and its relaxed and casual life style have made the Côte d'Azur one of the world's best known and most desirable vacation spots. While this region, blessed with great natural beauty, has been associated with the chic and pampered set, it has also been an artists' haven. Some of the most important modern artists have lived here at one time or another. Renoir, Picasso, Matisse, Léger, Braque, Cocteau, among many others, have left some of their work in local museums, churches, town halls, and even—in one case—a restaurant.

Three mountain ranges protect the Côte d'Azur from the icy north wind known as the mistral, which rushes down the Rhône Valley to punish other parts of Provence for days at a time in the winter. The Monts des Maures shelter the coast from the west, the Estérel mountains protect the center, and the Maritime Alps, which rise so steeply from the sea that they leave only a narrow strip of coast, stand guard in the east.

The major approaches to the Côte d'Azur are from Aix-en-Provence (see Travel Route 24); from Lyon via Avignon to Marseille (see Travel Route 15); and from Grenoble to Cannes and Nice by the Route des Préalpes or the Route Napoléon (see Travel Route 17).

From Marseille, take Route D 559 eastbound. The road follows the rugged fjordlike inlets known as "the Calanques" for 90 km. (56 miles) to Toulon. Points of interest along the way include the small port of *Cassis,* famous for its white wine; *La Ciotat,* with its great shipyards; the sandy beaches of *La Ciotat-Plage* and *Les Lecques;* the bathing resort of *Bandol,* with an esplanade lined with palm, eucalyptus, and mimosa trees; and *Sanary,* with its palm-shaded quay and fishing harbor. Soon after, you arrive at **Toulon** (population 190,000), France's biggest military port and the base of its Mediterranean fleet. The source of the city's naval signifi-

cance is its excellent harbor, which is divided into the inner *Petite Rade* and the outer *Grande Rade,* both guarded by forts since the time of Napoleon. The Romans called Toulon Telo Martius; it was a center for the manufacture of purple cloth—a rare and extremely luxurious commodity in ancient times. By the end of the 16th century Toulon had become a naval base for the French king and was known and dreaded as the destination of those who were sentenced to become galley slaves, including unyielding Protestants. It was here that Napoleon began his swift ascent to eminence by defeating an English garrison that had been invited by its royalist residents to occupy the town. He was immediately promoted from captain to brigadier general. Toulon played an important, if essentially passive, part in World War II, when 60 ships of the French fleet were scuttled by a French admiral so that they would not fall into

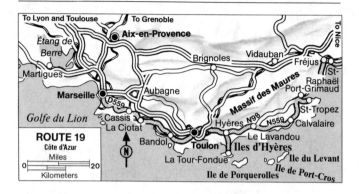

enemy hands. Allied bombers destroyed the old port. While the city was under attack by the Free French under General de Lattre de Tassigny, the occupying Germans blew up its citadel, dockyards, and harbor installations before surrendering. With the loss of France's North African naval bases, Toulon has taken on an even greater military significance for the country.

From Toulon follow Route N 98 east to ***Hyères** (population 45,000). This picturesque old city's very mild climate has made it popular as a winter resort since the 18th century—even before the English "discovered" Nice. Queen Victoria sometimes stayed here on her visits to the Riviera. The old town is now three miles from the sea, although in the Middle Ages it was a favorite port for pilgrims departing for the Holy Land.

Take D 97 south toward the sea to *Hyères-Plage,* or to the small port of *La Tour-Fondue* on the narrow peninsula of Giens; from either spot, ferries cross over to the **Île de Porquerolles,* the largest of the ***Îles d'Hyères,** 8 km. (5 miles) long and 2 km. (1.2 miles) wide. It has lovely sandy beaches on its north shore, vineyards and pinewoods in its interior, and a southern shoreline of rocky cliffs that rise as high as 150 meters (500 feet).

The neighboring island of **Île de Port-Cros* has lush subtropical vegetation. It is now a nature preserve, including the surrounding seabed, with its rare seaweeds and rockfish.

The third island in the group is the long, rocky **Île du Levant,* where one of the first nudist colonies, the Héliopolis, was established in 1931. The east end of the island belongs to the Navy and is out of bounds to tourists.

From Hyères, Route N 98 turns inland, passes the salt marshes of Hyères, then runs east for 22 km. (13.6 miles) to the fishing village and seaside resort of **Le Lavandou** (population 3,800). Route N

559, the *Corniche des Maures, begins here. On this coastal road you can enjoy the panoramic view of seaside towns along the way, among them *Cavalière, a resort with a beautiful beach, and *Le Rayol, which was built in 1925 on terraces that drop down to the sea. In Cavalière Route N 559 veers north, bypassing Cap Camarat and heading straight toward the *Golfe de Saint-Tropez and the resort **Saint Tropez** (population 6,200), an old Provençal city. Saint-Tropez is the only town on the Côte d'Azur to face north, exposing it to the mistral. Packed with tourists in the summer, it is almost deserted in the winter. The town was the most fashionable resort on the Riviera in the 1970s. You can get a particularly beautiful view of the village and the harbor, where yachts are moored next to fishing boats, from the Môle Jean Réveille and from the 16th–17th-century Citadelle. The town's famous beaches—Plage

Saint-Tropez: Harbor

des Salins, Plage de Tahiti, and Plage de Pampelonne—each with a view of Cap Camarat, are just south of the town.

Saint-Tropez is noted for art, as well as glamour and sun. The **Musée de l'Annonciade, built in 1955 in the former chapel of the Annunciation, has an outstanding collection of modern art, with works by French painters and foreign painters who lived in France. Included are works by Paul Signac (1863–1935), who "discovered" Saint-Tropez around 1890 and introduced it to his friends Pierre Bonnard and Henri Matisse, whose works are also represented.

Port Grimaud in the western corner of the gulf is a modern vacation village built in the style of a Provençal lagoon city, with its houses built on artificial spits of land so that each has its own mooring.

Route N 98 continues along a lovely stretch of the coast to the Golfe de Fréjus, passing the eastern part of the Massif des Maures. The two major seaside resorts on this part of the road are *Sainte-Maxime and Saint-Aygulf, before you come to the turnoff to the historic town of Fréjus.

Fréjus (population 31,000), now 1.5 km. (almost a mile) inland, was an important Roman port called Forum Julii. Julius Caesar founded the town to rival Marseille, which favored his enemy Pompey. He established it on the ancient road between Italy and Spain, the Via Aurelia. The ancient city, roughly twice as large

Fréjus: Cloister

as it is now, had an amphitheatre with 9,000 seats—the first of its kind in ancient Gaul—as well as a theater. It had an aqueduct, and a huge harbor connected to the sea by a channel. The port and the channel have since become silted up. This town was a bishop's seat until 1957, when the see was moved to Toulon.

Overlooking the town center is a 13th-century *cathedral,* a good example of early Provençal Gothic. On the doors of the principal entrance are richly carved Renaissance figures dating from 1530. A famous octagonal **baptismal chapel* dates from the fifth century and is one of the oldest sacred structures in France. Next to the cathedral is a 12th–13th-century **cloister,* adjoining the *Musée d'Archéologie,* which houses Greek and Roman finds from excavations here.

In December of 1959 Fréjus was the scene of a catastrophe.

The Malpasset Dam, 10 km. (6 miles) to the north, burst and caused a flood that claimed more than 400 victims.

Continuing southeast on N 98, only a few miles from Fréjus, is **Saint-Raphaël** (population 22,000). Napoleon landed here after his Egyptian campaign, and just 15 years later he left from here to go into his first exile on the island of Elba.

In the center of this old fishing village, with its narrow streets and lovely sand beach, there is an interesting 12th-century **Templar church.* It was once used as a refuge in times of danger, and its belfry served as a watchtower during the Middle Ages when the town, like the others on this coast, was preyed on by pirates. The Knights Templar were charged with defending the coast until the order was dissolved in 1308.

Saint-Raphaël marks the beginning of a magnificent stretch of the coast road known as the **Corniche de l'Estérel,* or the *Corniche d'Or.* It runs for 33 km. (20 miles) high above the sea, past red porphyry rocks under the deep green of umbrella pines, and along the brilliant blue of the inlets.

The Corniche passes the small bathing resort of *Boulouris,* the *Cap du Dramont* with its blue porphyry rocks, and the small resort of *Agay.* The aviator and writer Antoine de Saint-Exupéry, author of *The Little Prince,* who was lost in action in World War II, was last sighted flying over this spot on July 31, 1944. A memorial tablet

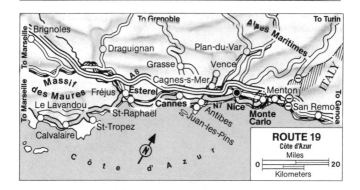

has been put up here. Route N 98 continues past *Anthéor; *Cap Roux,* with its red porphyry rocks, one of the most beautiful spots on the Corniche; the hillside town of *Le Trayas; Miramar,* which has a great view from the Col de L'Esquillon, the pass overlooking the Golfe de Napoule and Cannes; *Théoule-sur-Mer* on the slopes of the Estérel range; and *La Napoule,* with its fine beaches and a 14th-century castle, which was restored by the American sculptor Henry Clews and has been converted into a museum.

**Cannes (population 72,000) is the second largest city (after Nice) on the Côte d'Azur. (Cannes is the end point of the Route Napoleon described under Travel Route 17.) It began its rise to prominence in 1834, when an English lord named Brougham was kept out of his beloved Nice because of an outbreak of cholera. So he remained in Cannes, at that time a small fishing port. He liked the town so much that he built a

villa and stayed there for the next 34 winters. His friends, the cream of the English aristocracy, followed him and made Cannes one of the most fashionable resorts on the coast.

In the 19th century the Riviera had only a winter "season." Its summer climate was considered to be too hot and unhealthy—it would appear that the people who said this had never been there in the summer. But by the late 1920s tourists were coming to Cannes in the summer, and were finding it delightful. After World War II Cannes, with its sandy beaches, became a summer resort in earnest. The city's attractions also include its two yacht harbors, which have helped it become the premiere port on the Mediterranean for pleasure craft.

The **Croisette,* a famous palm-fringed boulevard lined with hotels, art galleries, and exclusive shops, runs along the beach, which has a casino at either end. In the west, near the port, is the

Casino Municipal, the winter casino; at the other end, near the Cap de la Croisette, is the *Palm Beach Casino.*

In the middle of the Croisette is the *Palais des Festivals.* Built in 1949, it is the site of the world-famous *International Film Festival,* held every spring.

Just off the coast are the *Îles de Lérins,* which can be reached by regular ferry service from the old port in Cannes. *Île Sainte-Marguerite* has a fort dating from the 17th century; *Île Saint-Honorat* has a *fortified monastery* dating from the fifth century. Founded in 410 by Saint Honoratus, it was a center of Christian culture in the Dark Ages. Saint Patrick probably studied here. At one time this community may have had as many as 3,700 residents, but pirate raids and occupation by the Spanish caused its decline. It was abandoned in 1788, but repopulated in the late 19th century.

From Cannes, a road leads to the *Tour Observatoire de Super-Cannes,* on top of a hill. The tower lives up to its name because it provides an unforgettable view in all directions. From here it is another 4 km. (2.5 miles) to the old Provençal pottery town of *Vallauris,* which became world famous when Pablo Picasso set up a ceramics workshop there in 1950. A statue he sculpted called *Man with a Sheep* stands in the town's main square. In the *priory of Lérins,* founded in 1227 and rebuilt in the 16th century, is a chapel in which Picasso's mural

War and Peace covers three walls. Not one of the artist's most memorable works, the painting on plywood, which was done in the 1950s takes up an area of 125 square meters (1,345 square feet).

From Cannes, take Route N 7 east to *Golfe-Juan.* It was at this sheltered roadstead that on March 1, 1815, Napoleon, having just escaped from Elba, landed with 800 men to begin the march that would lead to Waterloo and his final exile on Saint Helena.

Just east of the Golfe-Juan is the seaside resort of *Juan-les-Pins,* on the fashionable west side of Antibes. From here you can take a pleasant excursion around *Cap d'Antibes* (11 km.; 7 miles).

The coast road around the cape is one of the most beautiful roads on the Côte d'Azur. It takes you to the luxury *Hôtel du Cap* with its famous restaurant, the *Eden Roc* (which F. Scott Fitzgerald called the Hotel des Étrangers in *Tender is the Night*); the magnificent gardens of the *Villa Thuret* (where in the late 19th century eucalyptus seeds, brought from Australia, were first introduced in Europe); and the *Chapelle de la Garoupe,* which offers a splendid view of Nice and the often snow-covered peaks of the Maritime Alps.

North of Cap d'Antibes, on the edge of the broad sweep of the *Baie des Anges,* is the old city of **Antibes** (population 60,000). It was founded in 350 B.C. by the Greeks, who named it Antipolis,

Biot: Musée Fernand Léger

"city on the opposite side," because it is situated across the bay from Nice. The 16th-century **Château Grimaldi** with its 14th-century tower is worth seeing. It is now a museum housing one of the most important Picasso collections in the world, including 25 paintings, 44 drawings, 76 ceramic pieces, and some tapestries. Picasso worked on many of these right here, in 1946. The terrace of the museum provides a fine view.

From Antibes, the railroad, Autoroute A 8, and Route N 7 all follow the coastline east around the Baie des Anges.

Lovers of modern art should take Route N 7 north from *La Braque* for 3 km. (2 miles) to **Biot,** a picturesquely placed town and the site of the *Musée Fernand Léger,* which opened in 1960.

Continue east on Route N 7 for 5 km. (3 miles) to Route D 2, which

runs north to **Cagnes-sur-Mer** (population 32,000). This is a picturesque old town dominated by the *Château Grimaldi.* Built as a fortress in the 14th century, it was converted to a luxurious château in 1620 and today houses a *museum* dedicated to the olive and to olive trees. Temporary exhibits show the work of artists who have lived here, among them Marc Chagall. The *Musée Renoir* is also worth a visit. Although it contains little of the artist's work, it has some of his personal effects, including furniture, his easel, palette, and brushes, and even his coat and cravat. In 1907 Renoir bought part of an ancient olive grove and built a simple house there, where he spent every winter until his death in 1919. His studio has been preserved just as he left it.

Continue for 4 km. (2.5 miles) to **Saint-Paul-de-Vence**—often referred to simply as Saint Paul (population 1,600). This picturesque little town is situated on a hill and is surrounded by the remains of its 16th-century walls. Several great modern artists passed through here while they were still unknown, trading their work for hospitality at the restaurant *Auberge de la Colombe d'Or,* which now has a collection that includes works by Matisse, Braque, Utrillo, Bonnard, Dufy, Derain, and Vlaminck. Another important destination for art lovers is the *Foundation Maeght,* an art center that was created by Parisian dealers Marguerite and

Aimé Maeght, and the architect José Luis Sert in 1964. Some great artists worked with them: Braque contributed the stained-glass windows in the chapel and designed the fountains with Miró; Chagall and Miró both contributed mosaics; Giacometti and Calder contributed their work for the sculpture gardens. The complex of buildings is situated among lovely pine woods and includes a room devoted to Picasso, and a room devoted to Giacometti.

Just 4 km. (2.5 miles) farther north is the town of ***Vence** (population 13,400), which is best known for its famous **Chapelle du Rosaire in the Dominican monastery that was designed by Henri Matisse between 1947 and 1950. The chapel has two walls of geometrically patterned windows in yellow, blue, and green. Matisse felt that these were among his finest works. The other two walls are of white faïence, with black line drawings of faceless figures. The figures are mere outlines, leaving it to the viewer's imagination to fill them in. The effect is astonishingly beautiful.

Continue on Route N 7 via Cros de Cagnes over the Var River to **Nice,** the chief city on the Côte d'Azur and, with a population of 340,000, the fifth-largest city in France. (Nice is the end point for the Route des Préalpes—see Travel Route 17—and the Route des Grandes-Alpes—Travel Route 18.) Nice was originally settled by Phoenician traders in the fourth century B.C. The

Greeks founded a city here in 350 B.C. and called it Nikaia. When the Romans took over Gaul they renamed it Nicaea. The city was important enough to become a bishop's see in the fourth century A.D. Like much of the rest of this coast, Nice was prey to pirates, and it also suffered under the rivalry of the counts of Provence and Savoy. The city government placed itself in the hands of Savoy in 1388, was captured twice by France in the early 18th century, and eventually returned to the House of Savoy (then kings of Sardinia) in 1748, when it became known as Nizza. In an 1860 plebiscite the city voted for union with France. Nice has been a winter resort since the 18th century. Now a multinational throng joins the French in summer as well as in winter. As a seaside resort, Nice has one drawback for summer visitors: Its beaches are rocky, not sandy. The city makes up for this deficiency with activities not found elsewhere on the Côte d'Azur. It is famous for its festivals, especially the 14-day-long *carnival which climaxes on Shrove Tuesday with a parade of elaborate floats around the Place Masséna, up to the Avenue Jean Médecin, and back again.

The center of the city is the Place Masséna, named after the French general André Masséna (1758–1817), who was born here. Bordering the square on the southwest is the Jardin Albert I, a park with a 5,000-seat open–air theater. To the east is the picturesque

Old City, with its **flower market* (on the Rue François de Paule, across from the *Opera House*). South of the square the superb **Promenade des Anglais* stretches 6.5 km. (4 miles) along the Baie des Anges.

The northern suburb of *Cimiez* has some Roman ruins including a small Gaulish amphitheatre and three fine Gaulish baths that were excavated in 1965. There are three important museums in Cimiez. Two of them are in the *Villa des Arènes:* the archeological museum, which exhibits objects from Corinth and Attica as well as Etruscan and Roman works; and the **Musée Matisse,* with some of the artist's work. On the Boulevard de Cimiez is the *Musée Marc Chagall* which houses his *Biblical Message*—17 large paintings inspired by the books of Genesis, Exodus, and the Song of Songs.

You have a choice of four roads going east from Nice. The fastest route to Menton and the Italian border is Autoroute A 8. It is an expensive toll road but is easier on the nerves than the older roads. There are also three corniche roads from Nice to Menton. The **Grande Corniche,* offering magnificent views, runs above the settled areas and is the fastest of the three. It is described in Travel Route 24. The **Moyenne Corniche,* closer to the coast, also has spectacular views; it was built in 1937 to relieve the traffic that was already plaguing the lower and upper corniche routes. The **Corniche du Littoral* (described

below), also known as the *Corniche Inférieure,* passes through all the towns along the coast, providing the most intimate look at this stretch of the Côte d'Azur.

Leave Nice via Boulevard Carnot at the end of the port. Follow the corniche for 6 km. (3.7 miles) around Mont-Boron to **Villefranche-sur-Mer** (population 7,500). This town rises in terraces above one of the loveliest **bays* on the Mediterranean, the largest protected roadstead between Golfe-Juan and Genoa. Its Old City still has an 18th-century look. The 16th-century *citadel* towers over the town. On the quay of the fishing port is the **Chapelle Saint-Pierre,* decorated with frescoes by Cocteau.

A picturesque road circles the lovely Cap Ferrat, which has long been a playground of the rich and famous. Just past the peninsula's narrow neck is the *Musée de l'Île de France* with a *very good art collection and pleasant gardens. Continue to the **Villa des Cèdres,* once owned by King Léopold II of Belgium and now the site of a splendid botanical garden; the nearby zoo, *Vivarium du Cap Ferrat,* has a school for chimpanzees. On the southern tip of the cape is a lighthouse that provides a unique view extending eastward to Bordighera and westward to the Estérel mountains. At the cape's eastern point, the *Pointe de Saint-Hospice,* there is a 17th-century *watchtower* and a bronze statue of the Madonna. The chief town on the cape is *Saint-Jean-Cap-Fer-*

rat. Rejoin the Corniche du Littoral at *Beaulieu-sur-Mer* (population 5,000). Situated in a sheltered spot, this town boasts lush subtropical vegetation. It has several exclusive hotels. Continue around **Cap Roux,* where you can see the houses of ****Èze** (population 1,800). This village is perched like an eagle's aerie atop a 380 meter- (1,246 foot-) high cliff and retains the look of a Medieval town. Among its picturesque sites are the 14th-century **Chapelle des Penitents Blancs* and the ***Jardin Exotique,* where visitors can wander through exotic shrubs and cacti to the ruins of a high fortress.

Cap d'Ail, a health resort on the slopes of the Tête de Chien, is between Èze and the second-smallest independent state in Europe, the principality of Monaco.

**Monaco (population 25,000, of which 4,500 are Monégasques), a constitutional state ruled by the Grimaldi family, has been independent since 1338. The architect of present-day Monte Carlo, the casino and the modern city that grew up around it, was Prince Charles III. In 1861 he seceded the small cities of Menton and Roquebrune to Napoleon III for four million gold francs and with the proceeds he created Monaco's tourist industry. The current prince, Rainier III, was married to American movie actress Grace Kelly, who died tragically in an auto accident in 1982.

The tiny country—about half

Monte Carlo

the size of New York's Central Park—consists of the old city, *Monaco-Ville,* built on a cliff above the port; *La Condamine,* the port; the modern city of *Monte Carlo;* and *Fontvieille,* an industrial zone. Worth seeing in the old city are the **Prince's Palace* (14th–17th century) with its handsome Court of Honor and daily changing-of-the-guard ceremony at 11:55 A.M.; the *Oceanographic Museum,* founded in 1906 by Prince Albert I, with one of the largest aquariums in Europe; and the **Exotic Gardens* on the southwest border.

In Monte Carlo you must of course see the famous **gambling casino* in its dramatic setting, with its elegant terraces overlooking the sea; it was designed in 1878 by Charles Garnier, the architect of the Paris Opéra. In addition to the gambling rooms, the casino contains a theater, which was the home of the Ballets Russes de Monte Carlo. In town there is a *museum of dolls and mechanical puppets and sculptures in the rose garden.* The Monte Carlo Sporting Club is based here. The luxurious beach resort of **Monte Carlo Plage* is actually on French soil.

The *Monte Carlo Grand Prix* auto race is run every year on the principality's steep curving streets. Some three million tourists visit Monaco annually.

From Monte Carlo, the coast road passes the elegant villas of *Cap Martin* and continues to the easternmost town on the Côte d'Azur, ***Menton** (population 25,000). The town, hemmed in by mountains, is a health resort because of its mild climate. In the 19th century it was one of the most popular and exclusive towns on the Riviera, but it became unfashionable and was in fact considered dowdy. Now it is regaining its popularity. The beautiful **Promenade Georges V* leads to the breakwater of the port, which provides a marvelous view of the Old City and the mountains. On the promenade the **Musée Jean Cocteau,* housed in a 17th-century fort, has works by this versatile artist. In 1957 Cocteau designed the **Salle des Mariages* of Menton's Mairie (town hall) and decorated it with motifs from the Orpheus saga.

TRAVEL ROUTE 20: Corsica

See color map.

The Mediterranean landscape that has been domesticated and occasionally despoiled on the Riviera is still untouched and wild on the island of Corsica, 170 km. (106 miles) off the coast of France. The fourth largest island in the Mediterranean, after Sicily, Sardinia, and Cyprus, it is essentially a single block of mountains. The highest of its mountains, Monte Cinto, rises to 2,707 meters (8,800 feet). There are eight mountains that fall within 200 meters (650 feet) of it and 51 peaks on the island that are higher than 2,000 meters (6,500 feet).

Extensive forests of pine, beech, oak, and especially sweet chestnut cover much of the island. The rest is blanketed with the scrubby undergrowth that gave its name to resistance to tyranny: "maquis." The maquis blooms from mid-April through mid-June, when there is still snow on the peaks. Spring, when the scent of the blossoms saturates the island, is the best time to visit Corsica. Napoleon, a native of Corsica, once said, "With my eyes closed I would know Corsica by its smell." The 220,000 inhabitants of the island, a third of whom live in Ajaccio and Bastia, make their living from forestry and agriculture.

Corsica's history is intertwined with the history of Italy. The island was colonized by Rome between 260 and 162 B.C. Following the Empire's decline, Corsica fell into anarchy, but it was taken by the Byzantine Empire in 552. Later it was ruled by the Pope and then by a series of Italian rulers. Following a rebellion led by Pascale Paoli against the Genoese rulers, the island was sold to France in 1768 (the French defeated Paoli the following year). Napoleon Bonaparte was born in Ajaccio the same year. In 1975 Corsica was divided into two departments: Corse-du-Sud and Haute-Corse.

Corsica is most easily reached from Leghorn, Italy, but there are also boats from Nice and Marseilles, as well as flights from the French mainland. The island has two cities, the political capital Ajaccio on the west coast and the economic capital Bastia on the northeast coast. The other large towns are Corte in the north central portion of the island and Porto Vecchio on the southeast coast.

Corsica has wonderful bays for swimming. Its jagged coastline, particularly in the north and northwest makes it ideal for underwater sports. The mountainous interior is a paradise for climbers, fishermen, and hunters.

Ajaccio (population 52,000) was founded in 1492 by the Genoese, the same year that another native of Genoa discovered what came to be known as America. The city is full of reminders that it is the birthplace of Napoleon. The main street is the Cours Napoleon. On the Rue Bonaparte is the *house where he was born, on August 15, 1769. An *equestrian statue* in the main square depicts Napoleon as a Roman emperor, surrounded by his four brothers. At the Place Giraud a staircase leads to a statue of Napoleon erected in 1938. Among Ajaccio's other Napoleon memorabilia: The *cathedral* houses the basin in which he was baptized, the *Hôtel de Ville* has a Napoleon museum, and in the *Chapelle Impériale* in the Palais Fesch is the grave of Napoleon's parents.

About 12 km. (7.5 miles) west of the city is the *Punta de la Parata*. On this point of land is the *Tour de la Parata,* one of some 90 Genoese watchtowers that ringed the coast of Corsica to guard against attacks by North African pirates, a peril up to the 18th century. There is a wonderful view over the Gulf of Ajaccio and the *Îles Sanguinaires.*

The main highway in Corsica, Route N 193, runs northeast from Ajaccio to Bastia (153 km.; 95 miles). Leaving Ajaccio on the

Corsica: Genoese Tower

Cours Napoleon, the road climbs gradually up the valley of the Gravona River. As the valley narrows, the road climbs more steeply. The summer health resort of Bocognano (elevation 640 meters; 2,100 feet) is situated in a chestnut forest. The road continues its climb to the *Col de Vizzavona,* then runs through the **Vizzavona forest,* whose beech and Laricio pine trees are noted for their beauty, to the health resort of *Vizzavona.* This is the starting point for a five hour climb to *Monte d'Oro* (2,391 meters; 7,842 feet) which offers magnificent **views.

Route N 193 descends into the valley of the Vecchio River to the town of **Corte** (population 6,000). The ancient capital of Corsica, situated high in the center of the island, the town is in the Tavignano River valley. It is surrounded by mountains and dominated by a *citadel* that clings to a high rocky cliff. There is a museum in town and several statues commemorating the 18th-century struggle for independence.

You can take a pleasant side trip eastward 11 km. (6.8 miles) from Corte through the starkly beautiful ravine called *Gorges de la Réstonica* to the *Pont de Tragone.* From there you can climb to *Lake Melo* (1,996 meters; 6,547 feet) or to *Monte Rotondo* (2,625 meters; 8,610 feet high).

Route N 193 continues over the *Col de San Quilico* into the *valley of the Golo River.* Cross on the Leccia Bridge and continue to *Casamozza.* The road passes through the plain of Biguglia. Just past Casamozza, a road branches south for 5.5 km. (3.4 miles) to *La Canonica,* the loveliest Romanesque church on the island.

Bastia (population 50,000), founded by the Genoese in 1380, is the economic center of Corsica. It has a picturesque *Vieux Port* and a *citadel* built by the Genoese overlords. This fortress or *bastiglia* is the source of the city's name. The center of the port city is the Place Saint-Nicholas, which is near the Nouveau Port with its rows of palm and banana trees. Due east from Bastia is the Italian island of Elba, the site of Napoleon's first exile.

You can take a 123 km. (76 miles) roundtrip excursion from Bastia to **Cap Corse.** The cape itself is an extension of Corsica's main mountain chain, projecting northward into the sea. At *Monte Stello* the cape reaches an elevation of 1,305 meters (4,280 feet). Take Route D 80 north from Bastia along the east coast of the cape. The varied scenery includes rushing streams, valleys planted with grape vines, olive and fruit trees, and small rocky inlets with good fishing. Route D 80 veers west at *Macinaggio* and crosses the *Col de la Serra.* The pass has a **lookout point* with views of the west coast, Cap Corse itself, and the islands of Elba and Capraia. On the rugged western coast of the cape D 80 becomes a **corniche,* or cliff route, high above the sea. This truly beautiful road follows the coast south to the *Col de San Ber-

nardino. Beyond this pass the road joins Route D 81.

Route D 81 from Bastia via Calvi to Ajaccio—a distance of 256 km. (159 miles)—goes west over the *Col de Teghime* to *Saint-Florent,* which is situated on a spit of land extending into the lovely *Golfe de Saint-Florent.* Route D 81 then continues southwest through the wild and lonely *Désert des Agriates* to the *Col de Lavezzo* and another fine view. The road then drops to the sea, where it is joined by Route N 197 and follows the coast to **Île Rousse** (population 2,500). This popular beach and winter health resort has a casino, discotheque, and movie theater. Continue on N 197 along the coast and through the fertile Balagne region to **Calvi** (population 3,600). This was the capital of Corsica during the 500-year leadership of Genoa, and its *citadel* in the upper city dates from that period. The harbor is Corsica's closest one to mainland France and there is also an airport nearby. The town's sandy beaches have made it one of Corsica's main seaside resorts.

From Calvi take D 81 south along the solitary coast to the *Golfe de Galeria.* Then turn inland and cross the *Col de Palmarella,* and farther on, the *Col de la Croix.* Here you have a magnificent view over the *Golfe de Girolata* and the red cliffs of the *Golfe de Porto,* one of the most beautiful spots in Corsica. Route D 81 descends in many switchbacks to **Porto,** the most beautifully situated of the seaside resorts on the northwest coast.

Follow D 84 and the Porto River into the rugged ***Spelunca gorges,** with their towering columns of colored rock. You can return to Porto via Ota, a typically Corsican village, or continue to Evisa, a delightful summer retreat set amid a chestnut forest. The *Col de Vergio* is 33 km. (20.5 miles) farther down the road. This is the highest highway pass in Corsica.

Southwest of Porto, D 81 runs high above the sea in the midst of the jagged chaos of red rock called *Calanche* or ***Les Calanques*— one of the most beautiful sights in Corsica. This stretch ends at the charming little town of *Piana,* above the Golfe de Porto.

Route D 81 turns inland here to the *Col de Lava* and offers a dramatic look back over the Calanche, especially at twilight. The road then curves back toward the sea, cuts through the plain of the Lomberlaccio River to **Cargèse,* a settlement established by Greeks when they fled from the Turks in 1676. Route D 81 follows the Golfe de Sagone and crosses the inland foothills to Ajaccio.

You can take the 139-km. (86-mile) trip from Ajaccio to Bonifacio on Route N 196 which heads southeast into the interior. The road climbs to the *Col-Saint-Georges* (elevation 747 meters; 2,450 feet), crosses the wide valley of the Taravo River, then leads via *Petreto* to *Olmeto,* which lies among the olive groves above the Golfe de Valinco. The neighboring village of **Propriano** (population 2,800) was once simply a small lobster fishing port, but with its sandy beaches it has rapidly developed into a vacation center. Continue in a southeasterly direction through the Sartenais region with its typically Corsican landscape to **Sartène** (population 6,000), a town hewn out of dark granite. Medieval in appearance, it is the scene every year of an unusual Good Friday procession, the "Catenacciu," during which a chained "Christ" wanders the streets at night.

From here Route N 196 heads southeast through maquis covered hills and marshy coastal flats to **Bonifacio** (population 2,600). The old town is on a narrow rib of rock that thrusts outward into the sea. Protected by its stout walls

The northern tip of the island of Sardinia is only 11.5 km., (7 miles) from Bonifacio.

From Bonifacio, it is possible to return to Ajaccio via Porto Vecchio (population 6,000) on the east coast.

and a *citadel,* the town could withstand long sieges—provided there was rain, for there are no wells or springs in the giant rock upon which Bonifacio sits. Even the buttresses of the churches serve as water channels to the town's cisterns.

From the citadel, in which Napoleon served briefly as a young artillery officer, a 192-step stairway leads down to the sea. It is called the *Escalier du Roi d'Aragon,* because King Alphonse I had it cut into the rock during a siege in 1420. Since then the stairway has been a useful back way of supplying the citadel from the sea.

TRAVEL ROUTE 21: Nancy–Reims–Loire River–Nantes–La Baule (741 km.; 460 miles)

See maps on pages 228, 229, and 231.

Beginning in Nancy, this route cuts a grand swath westward across France, from the forests of the Lorraine through the vineyards of Champagne, then along the lovely Loire River Valley with its magnificent châteaux, and finally to the resort of La Baule on the Atlantic coast. If you don't mind adding an extra 300 km. (180 miles) to your trip, you can take an extended side trip to Reims and the Champagne wine-growing region. This route also intersects a number of other Travel Routes along the way.

The first part of the route goes 187 km. (116 miles) from Nancy (see Travel Route 1) to Troyes. Follow Route A 31 west for 23 km. (14 miles) on a long straightaway through a forested region to the old bishop's see of **Toul** (population 20,000), a fortified city on the left bank of the Moselle. Together with Verdun and Metz to the north, Toul was one of three bishoprics that maintained their independence during the Middle Ages. It suffered great damage during World War II, but still boasts two splendid works of Gothic art: the Flamboyant *façade* of the *Cathédrale Saint-Étienne* (built from the 13th to the 16th century), and the 13th-century Flamboyant *cloister* of the *church of Saint-Gengoult*. To the north, the restored 18th-century bishop's palace now serves as the city hall.

Cathédrale Nôtre-Dame, Reims

Side trip to *Reims

From Toul, you may make a lengthy foray into Champagne by following Route N 4 almost 90 km. (55 miles) west to Vitry-le-François, and from there proceeding north on N 44 for another 60 km. (35 miles) to ***Reims** (population 200,000), surrounded by vineyards and the center of Champagne country. An important city in Roman Gaul, it was the site of the baptism of the Merovingian King Clovis I by Saint Rémy in A.D. 496. This event marked the conversion of France to Christianity, and gave immense prestige to the town. Henceforth, nearly all the kings and queens of France were annointed and crowned at Reims. The most famous coronation was that of King Charles VII in 1429 in the presence of Joan of Arc; an *equestrian statue* of her (created in 1896 by Dubois) stands in the

square next to the ***Cathédrale Nôtre-Dame*. Built from 1211–1311, Nôtre-Dame is one of the truly great high Gothic cathedrals of France, breathtakingly tall with a multitude of pinnacles. Heavily damaged in World War I, its restoration was completed just before the outbreak of World War II. The **west façade,* lavishly decorated, is among the finest works of the Gothic period; above the *three portals* is the *rose window;* and above that the *Gallery of Kings,* over which rises the 83-meter- (52-feet-) high towers. The **statuary* of the middle portal and the "laughing angel," fondly known as "Le Sourire de Reims" (The Smile of Reims), to the left of the door of the left portal, are especially noteworthy. There are 120 statues in the 38-meter- (125-foot-) high interior. The cathedral treasury contains the coronation jewelry.

The *Musée St-Denis* is next to the cathedral. Among its holdings are cycles of wall hangings; a 16th-century Flemish tapestry depicting ten scenes from the life of Saint Rémy; Lucas Cranach's exquisitely lifelike *portrait drawings* of German princes; and the unusual **toile paintes*, painted strips of linen hung on the walls for coronation festivities. The museum also contains an excellent collection of early-to-mid-19th-century French paintings.

The *Porte de Mars* in the north part of the old city is a Roman triumphal arch embellished with reliefs of Romulus and Remus and the months of the year. It dates from the second century A.D., and served as a gate of the city during the Middle Ages. The Romanesque-Early-Gothic *abbey church of Saint-Remi*, with the grave of Saint Remingus (5th century), is in the south part of the old city. The *Caves à Champagne*, dug out of the soft chalky soil and belonging to the famous *Pommery* champagne-producers, are 18 km. (11 miles) to the east of Reims.

You may wish to take an excursion into the Champagne wine-growing region. This trip on Route N 51 to Route D 26 takes you through the region and the small city of Épernay. From Reims, the first leg is 11 km. (7 miles) to *Mont-Chenot*, on the edge of the wooded range of hills known as the *Montagne de Reims*. You will pass through the winegrowing villages of *Mailly Champagne* and *Verzenay,* with their famous champagne vineyards. Just beyond in Verzy, you will bear southwest on D 26, then continue on routes D 9 and D 34 until you drive through a forest to *Louvois,* the location of the château of the Marquis de Louvois, the famous war minister of Louis XIV. Continue southwest on D 9 through *Ay,* which produces excellent champagne, where you will pick up D 1, which will take you to **Épernay,** south on Route N 51. In Épernay, the sights of interest are the *Champagne Museum* in the Avenue de Champagne, and the extensive cellars (50 km.; 31 miles, of them) belonging to the firms *Möet et Chandon* and *Mercier.*

Heading southwest from Toul, follow Route D 960 along the southern edge of the *Côtes de Meuse.* Cross the Meuse River at **Vaucouleurs** (population 3,000), with its ruined *castle of Baudricourt.* It was here that Joan of Arc asked Governor Robert de Baudricourt for an escort to King Charles VII. When her request was granted in February of 1429, she set out from the nearby Porte de France with six men-at-arms. In 1929, on the 500th anniversary of the event, the castle's chapel was rebuilt over a late-13th-century crypt. Vaucoulers is also noted as the birthplace of Madame du Barry (1743–1793), mistress of Louis XV. About 17 km. (10 miles) farther, at the small town of Houdelaincourt, you will cross Travel Route 1.

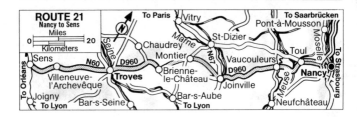

Gradually, as you leave Lorraine and enter southern Champagne, the landscape loses its austere character. At *Joinville* (population 5,100), cross the Marne, turn north on Route N 67, and travel through a wooded area to *Rachecourt*. Head west on Route E 2, a smaller road, to the ironworks town of *Wassy-sur-Blaise* (population 3,400), site of the "Wassy Massacre." Here, on March 1, 1562, a Catholic governor, annoyed by the sounds of a Protestant congregation at worship, became embroiled in an argument and was struck by a stone. Sixty Protestants were immediately killed in retaliation, and the "Wars of Religion" had begun. Follow Route D 4 west for 14 km. (8.7 miles) to where it meets Route D 384, at *Montier-en-Der* (population 2,100). The town takes its name from a monastery founded here in 672. The nave and aisles of its Romanesque *church and abbey* date from 992. Most of the village as well as the church were destroyed in 1940, but have since been restored.

Just south of Montier-en-Der, you leave the hill country behind, and head southwest on Route D 400 across a plain dotted with many ponds. After 21 km. (13 miles) you come to **Brienne-le-Château** (population 4,200), whose handsome **château* was built by Fontaine between 1770 and 1778. Napoleon Bonaparte studied at a military school here until the age of 15. Decades later, the artillery of that former school-boy did so much damage to Brienne that he eventually decided to leave the town a legacy of one million francs. A small museum contains souvenirs from his youth and mementos from his nearby battles.

Here, pick up Route D 960 and travel west about 20 km. (12.5 miles) through the "Champagne Humide" to *Piney*. The town, with its picturesque markets, signals the entry into the "Champagne Sèche," the dry part of the province. Continue on D 960 for another 20 km. to ***Troyes** (population 65,000), the Champagne region's former capital, tucked into a loop of the Seine.

Founded by the Romans to guard a crossing point of the Seine, the city achieved importance in the 10th century under the counts of Champagne who built the city into a major commercial center. The *Cathédrale Saint-Pierre-et-Saint-Paul* is famous for its colorful *windows* in the choir, dating from the 13th and 14th centuries, and in the nave, from the 15th and 16th centuries. Pope Urban IV, who was born in Troyes, built the *basilica of Saint-Urbain* in 1262–1286. It is one of the first examples of the daring Gothic architecture that extended the window area so much that the walls became little more than supporting skeletons.

Catherine of France and Henry V of England were joined in marriage in 1420 in the *church of Saint-Jean*. Their union set the seal on England's claim to the French throne. In the quarter around the church are ancient alleys and houses, including the *Ruelle des Chats* and the *Tourelle de l'Orfevre*. Troyes boasts a number of other beautiful churches.

The second leg of Travel Route 21 runs 162 km. (100 miles) from Troyes to Chateauneuf-sur-Loire. Pick up Route N 60 in Troyes and continue west-southwest along the northern edge of the *Fôret d'Othe* to *Fontvannes,* near the source of the Vanne River. Follow the river valley for about 50 km. (31 miles) as far as Sens, in the northern tip of Burgundy.

***Sens** (population 30,000) boasts one of the earliest Gothic churches in France, the *Cathédrale Saint-Étienne,* begun circa 1130. This lovely old city is best seen on foot.

From Sens, follow Route N 60 for 22 km. (14 miles). The road crosses the Yonne River, passes over the Autoroute du Soleil (Paris-Marseille), and brings you to historic **Courtenay** (population 2,600). During the 13th century, this town produced three emperors for the Latin Empire of Constantinople, established by the Crusaders after the Byzantine Empire broke up. Continue west on N 60 for 25 km. (15.6 miles) to the town of **Montargis** (population 17,600). Now an industrial town, it was the Medieval capital of the Gatinais. Crossing the tour here are Travel Route 13 and Travel Route 14.

Route N 60 goes through *Bellegarde-du-Loiret,* which boasts a Romanesque *church* with a lovely *façade* and several good paintings, as well as the massive keep of a 14th-century *castle.* Continue for another 20 km. (12.5

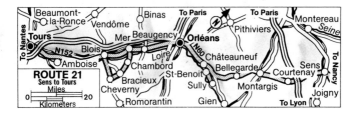

miles) through the extensive *Forêt d'Orléans.* Leave the woods at the Loire River and the pleasant town of **Châteauneuf-sur-Loire** (population 5,500). The 17th-century château, now largely in ruins, has a scenic park filled with rhododendron bushes. From here you can take a short side trip to ***Saint-Benoit** to see one of the most beautiful early-Romanesque **churches* in France, and to ***Sully,** where the mighty **fortified castle,* built by the Duc de Sully, finance minister of Henri IV, is located. These sights are fully described in Travel Route 8.

The third leg of the route goes from Châteauneuf to Tours (139 km.; 86 miles). Follow N 60 along the north bank of the Loire for 25 km. (15.5 miles) west-northwest to Orleans (described in Travel Route 8). Here, the tour also crosses Travel Route 12. Take Route N 152 for 56 km. (35 miles), usually at some distance from the banks of the Loire, to *Blois.* Along the way, there are several stops and detours worth making. In the first town of note, *Beaugency,* a picturesque bridge with 26 arches from different centuries crosses the Loire; a massive **tower* dates from the 11th century. Continue another 8 km. (5 miles) to the *Château d'Avaray,* a moated castle with beautiful gardens overlooking the Loire.

At the town of *Mer,* make a detour to two of the finest châteaux in the Loire region: ***Chambord* and ***Cheverney* (23 km.; 14 miles). Leave N 152 at Mer and go

south on Route D 112, across the Loire and through the *Fôret de Chambord,* to the 440-room Renaissance-style ****Château de Chambord,** the largest and most splendid of the Loire châteaux. (For a detailed description, see Travel Route 8.)

Passing through the great game park, go south 8 km. (5 miles) to *Bracieux* and turn west onto Route D 102. Another 9 km. (5.6 miles) brings you to the ****Château de Cheverny** (see Travel Route 8). Built in 1630, it continues to be the year-round home for the descendants of the original owners. From there, Route D 765 brings you back to N 152 and to ***Blois** (population 50,000). Its **château* was the birthplace of Louis XII, as well as the murder site of the Duc de Guise and his brother, Louis de Lorraine (Cardinal de Guise) on order of Henri III in 1588. Its importance in history, particularly art history, is due, in part, to its remarkable ***tower* and *staircase* (see Travel Route 8).

From Blois, Route N 152 closely follows the north bank of the Loire. Continue for 16 km. (10 miles) and cross the bridge to the magnificent ****Château de Chaumont.** This Gothic fortress with Renaissance detailing sits high on the south bank of the Seine. You have a choice of going back over the bridge and continuing on N 152 another 18 km. (11 miles) to ****Château d'Amboise** or of making a detour to the ****Château de Chenonceaux** To take the detour, go 18 km. (11 miles) south of Chaumont on D 111 through the *Bois de Sudais* to Montrichard on the Cher River and turn right onto Route N 76/E 13, which follows the Cher to the stately Château de Chenonceaux on the river bank (for a full description, see Travel Route 9).

About 5 km. (3 miles) down the river, at *La Croix-en-Touraine,* turn north on Route D 31 and travel through the *Forêt d'Amboise,* with its high **Pagode de Chanteloup* (1775–1778), inspired by the pagoda in Kew Gardens in London. At the *town* and ****Château d'Amboise** (see Travel Route 9), cross the Loire and pick up Route N 152. Follow the road west for 16 km. (10 miles) to **Vouvray** (population 3,000), where one of the best-known white wines of Touraine is made. Keep an eye out for road signs advertising tours and tastings.

The route continues to **Tours** (population 250,000), the lively capital of the province of Touraine. With its abundant lodging facilities and fine food, Tours is the end point of Travel Route 9, which includes visits to the nearby Loire châteaux in two loops. (From Tours, you can also connect

with Travel Routes 10 and 11.)

The fourth leg of the route, from Tours to Angers, is a distance of 108 km. (67 miles). You have a choice of continuing on Route N 152 directly to *Langeais* via *Luynes*—with its stately **castle flanked by four large round towers—or of detouring to two magnificent châteaux, as described below.

At the southern city limits of Tours, turn west on Route D 7 and travel 18 km. (11 miles) to the ****Château de Villandry,** noted for its unusual terraced Renaissance gardens (see Travel Route 9).

Continue west on D 7 for 3 km. (2 miles), turn south on D 57, and drive 8 km. (5 miles) to the graceful ****Château d'Azay-le Rideau,** which has stood on its island in the Indre River since 1527 (see Travel Route 9). From Azay, follow Route D 57 for 10 km. (6 miles) north to ****Langeais** (population 3,900), whose impressive 15th-century *château is located in the center of town. In 1491, Charles VIII of France was wed to Anne of Brittany under its roof, uniting the two powerful families.

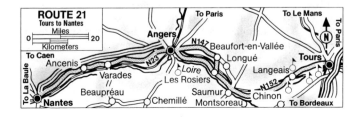

Continue to follow N 152 along the right bank of the Loire. On the forested left bank you will pass by the round towers of the *Château of Ussé* (see Travel Route 9).

A brief detour north on D 749 for 4 km. (2.5 miles) will take you to the town of *Bourgueil,* renowned for its red wine. Following Route N 152 farther downstream to where the Vienne empties into the Loire, you cross a long steel bridge to the quaint little town of *Montsoreau,* famous for its white wine.

After a short distance on N 152, you reach ***Samur** (population 36,000), on the left bank of the Loire. Its *castle* sits on a high perch, surrounded by white wine country (see Travel Route 9). From Samur, there are two ways to reach Angers. One route stays on D 952 (the extension on N 152) for 45 km. (28 miles) through *Les Rosiers,* site of a Renaissance church and steeple. A slightly longer route will bring you to Angers via Longué and Beaufort-en-Vallée, as described below.

Follow N 147 north to **Beaufort-en-Vallée** (population 3,500) in the Anjou Valley, a town dominated by the ruins of a fortress from the 14th–15th century and a church with a lovely Renaissance **bell tower.* From here the route turns west. At *Mazé,* 24 km. (15 miles) east of Angers, you can make a side trip to visit the 18th-century **Château de Montgeoffroy,* beautifully preserved from Louis XVI's day. Every piece of furniture is still

intact, and the château is decorated with fine paintings and tapestries.

*Angers (population 143,000), largely on the east bank of the Maine River, is the old capital of the mighty dukes of Anjou. Its powerful feudal ***fortress,* strengthened with 17 towers, houses the famous 14th-century ***tapestry series of the Apocalypse.* Seventy of the original 90 scenes are displayed in a specially built hall. At the heart of town is the *Place du Ralliement,* with its 19th-century theater.

The final leg of the route takes you 90 km. (54 miles) from Angers on Route A 11 or the more scenic N 23 to ***Nantes** (population 438,000).

Lying 47 km. (29 miles) from the mouth of the Loire, Nantes is a major industrial town and the sixth-largest port of France, located near the great vineyards of Muscadet and Gros Plant. Known in Gallo-Roman days as Namnetes, it competed with Rennes for the status of capital of Brittany. It was here that, in 1598, Henry IV signed the famous Edict of Nantes, which safeguarded the rights of French Protestants for almost a century. From the 16th to the 18th century, the town's wealth was based on trading black slaves from the coast of Guinea to the Antilles in exchange for raw sugar, which was then refined in Nantes (Voltaire himself had a large share in this business).

Among the important sites is the Gothic *cathedral of Saint-*

Pierre-et-Saint-Paul; its **central nave is 37.5 meters (123 feet) high; the white tufa stones used to construct it were floated down the Loire from Saumur. The south transept contains the ***tomb of Duke François II,* a masterpiece of Renaissance art made by Michel Colombe between 1502 and 1507. Holding a sword is the gracious but severe figure of Justice, whose face is that of Duchess Anne de Bretagne, wife of two French kings, François VIII and François XII. In the northern transept the **Cénotaphe de Lamoricière,* erected in 1879, commemorates a Nantes-born general who helped conquer North Africa.

Another attraction is the deeply moated castle, the *Palais Ducal.* Begun in the 13th century and rebuilt by François II in 1466, its west façade is distinguished by three massive towers. Within the spacious interior court is a well surmounted by a cast-iron ducal crown; behind the well, a staircase with four delicately ornamented loggias leads to the **Tour de la Couronne d'Or.*

Next to the Palais Ducal is the late Gothic *Grand Logis,* which houses an arts and crafts museum; the *Grand Gouvernement* building nearby houses a remarkable *museum of ethnic Breton art.

From Nantes, take Route N 165 33 km. (20 miles) to the junction near *Savenay;* there, turn left and drive 28 km. (17 miles) to **Saint-Nazaire** (population 70,000).

This thriving port and ship-building center at the mouth of the Loire was nearly destroyed during World War II. Its most ancient relic is a trilithon on the Rue du Polmen. Also of interest is the **Basse sous-marine,* a huge bunker next to the *Forme Ecluse canal that was used as a German U-boat base during the Second World War.

From Saint-Nazaire, it is an 11 km. (7 mile) drive to *Pornichet* and ****La Baule** (population 16,000), after Biarritz and Royan, the largest and most elegant beach resort on the French Atlantic coast. The semi-circular beach extends along a dike with a promenade. La Baule has all imaginable facilities for sports and entertainment, including a casino, a golf course and a pine wood, the Bois d'Amour. From La Baule the scenic Grand Côte highway takes you through *Le Pouliguen,* a small resort at the end of the beach and through *Batz-sur-Mer,* whose tall bell tower provides a panoramic view. The scenic highway encircles *Pointe du Croisic* and leads to the small sardine-fishing port of *Le Croisic,* its hill of balast offering a view of the oyster and mussel farms and many salt works of the **Marais Salants.* Only 3 km. (about 2 miles) farther is the little town of *Guérande,* with fully preserved 15th century city walls that include ten towers and four gates. It is 6 km. (about 4 miles) back to La Baule.

TRAVEL ROUTE 22: *Belfort–*Lyon–*Bordeaux (849 km.; 528 miles)

See maps on pages 235, 236, and 239.

This itinerary follows the western edge of the Jura mountains from Belfort southwest to Lyon, then crosses the northern section of the Massif Central, France's central highlands, to the volcanic Monts Dore in the Auvergne, before it continues through the Périgord region to Bordeaux.

*Belfort is a fortified city that once guarded the *Burgundian Gate* between the Vosges and the Jura mountains. The grim-looking *Lion de Belfort, built of red sandstone in 1878 by Frédéric-Auguste Bartoldi (designer of New York's Statue of Liberty), broods over the city from a platform that offers a great view of Belfort and the mountains.

The first leg of the route covers the 148 km. (92 miles) from Belfort to Poligny. Take Route N 83 southwest out of Belfort, through *Héricourt* and *l'Isle-sur-le-Doubs.* From here, N 83 follows the valley of the Doubs River to *Besançon (population 140,000). Now an important producer of watches and rayon, Besançon, positioned on a spit of land in the Doubs River, was a strategic military post for most of its history. The Romans turned it into a military stronghold called Vesontio; in the Middle Ages it was part of the "Franche-Comté," or Free Country of Burgundy; in 1674, it became part of France.

The principal thoroughfare is the 2,000-year-old Grande Rue, which runs from the *Pont de Bat-*

tant, the oldest bridge over the Doubs, to the cathedral at the foot of the city's citadel. Most of the city's main sights are on this street or close to it, including the *Palais Granvelle,* a Renaissance palace (1534–1547) with a *historical museum* containing Bruges tapestries and collections of coins and metals. The house at Number 40 is the birthplace of the great novelist Victor Hugo (1802–1885). Farther down the street is the *Square Archéologique Castan,* with the remains of a Roman theater, and the well-preserved *Porte Noire, a Roman arch covered with allegorical and military sculptures from the Antonine period. The façade of the *Cathédrale Saint-Jean* is mostly from the 18th century, but its nave is 13th-century Gothic, and the vaulting rests on 12th-century Romanesque arches. A famous painting by Fra Bartolomeo, called *Virgin and Child with Saints* (1518) is on a wall of the north aisle, and an astronomical clock built between 1857–1860 is located above the north portal.

Continue on Route N 83 for 38 km. (24 miles), past the western

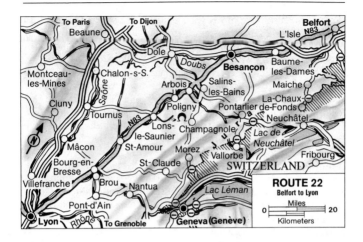

edge of the Jura mountains to the intersection of Route D 472 at *Mouchard,* where you can follow D 472 east for a 9 km. (5.6 miles) side trip to **Salins-les-Bains.** The town was built along the narrow, picturesque valley of the Furieuse River. An important producer of salt as far back as Roman times, it is now a saltwater springs resort. A curious wooden equestrian *statue of St. Maurice* may be seen in the church of that name; there are also 15th-century *towers* and the 18th-century *Hôtel de Ville.*

Return to Route N 83, and continue to **Arbois,** an attractive town famous for its wine. Arbois was the childhood home of the scientist Louis Pasteur (1822–1889), who is commemorated in a small *Pasteur Museum,* and a wine slope called *Vigne de Pasteur.* From here, you can make a short 5-km.

(3-mile) side trip southeast to the ***Reculées des Planches.** Reculée is the name for the type of blind valley formation found on the western edge of the Jura plateau. Cutting their way through the hills, these picturesque valleys end in cirques with sheer rock faces (often containing caves). Here you can see the two sources of the Cuisance, which well up 1 km. (half a mile) to the south in the **Grotte des Planches,* a natural amphitheater in the form of a horseshoe called the **Cirque du Fer à Cheval.*

Return to N 83, and continue to the town of *Poligny,* also famous for its wines.

The next leg of the itinerary runs 150 km. (93 miles) from Poligny to Lyon along the last foothills of the Jura mountains.

Lons-le-Saunier, located on the Valliere River among vineyards, is the birthplace of Rouget de Lisle (1760–1836), who composed the *Marseillaise*, the French national anthem. West of the Rue du Commerce, a charming arcaded street, is a *museum* with several notable paintings and a local archaeological collection. From Lons-le-Saunier, N 78, then D 47 lead east, for a final side trip into the Juras, to the **Cirque de Baume** (12 km.; 7.5 miles). This branching blind valley with its lofty rock walls leads to the most picturesque of all the cirques, and a magnificent lookout point, the *Belvédère des Roches de Baume.* A steep path leads to the *Grotte de Baume* with caverns up to 80 meters (262 feet) high.

N 83 leaves the Jura mountains and cuts through the fertile flatlands of the Bresse region to the busy market town of **Bourg-en-Bresse** (population 50,000). There is little to see in the town, but take N 75 to Brou, one of its suburbs, to see the remarkable **Eglise de Brou,** a late-Gothic church and cloister. It was built as the burial church of Philibert II (also called *le Beau,* or "the Handsome," a duke of Savoy) by his young widow, Margaret of Austria, who became Regent of the Netherlands in 1509, and his mother-in-law, Marguerite de Bourbon. Flemish artists were sent to work on the church, which was constructed between 1506 and 1532. Margaret, who died in 1530, never got to see it, but she is buried there with Philibert and his mother. Look for her motto on the marble stoop and throughout the church: "Fortune, infortune fort une" ("In fortune or misfortune one woman is strong"). In the choir, behind a splendid *choir screen,* are three richly decorated **tombs,** surpassed only by the tombs of the dukes of Burgundy in Dijon. The richly carved oak stalls in the choir, attributed to a local artist, are almost unsurpassed in France for their beauty.

Route N 83 continues across a lake-studded plain to *Rillieux,*

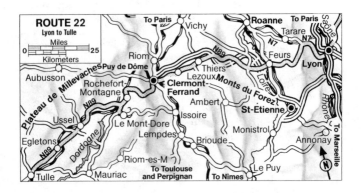

where it descends into the valley of the Rhône River, and provides an extensive view of the Alps. Continue for 10 km. (6 miles) to **Lyon,* which is described on pages 64–68.

The next leg of Travel Route 22 runs 178 km. (111 miles) from Lyon to Clermont-Ferrand, across the Massif Central of France. Heading west from Lyon on Route N 7 you'll cross the Saône River, and pass through the charmingly named suburb of *Tassin-la-demi-Lune,* and, in 26 km. (16 miles), reach *L'Arbresle.* From here, Route N 89 heads south and then west into the valley of the Brévenne, passing through *Saint-Bel* and *Sainte-Foy-l'Argentière* to the *Col du Bief,* which is the watershed between the Rhône and the Loire rivers; from here, there is a beautiful view over the Forez region. From Sainte-Foy, Route D 89 descends to *Feurs,* and crosses the Loire River; the nearby mountains are called the *Monts du Forez.*

At *Saint-Étienne-le-Moulard* you can make a short 1.5 km. (1 mile) side trip to the ***Château de la Bastie-d'Urfé.** The Medieval castle at the foot of the Madeleine peaks area, was renovated in the mid-16th century in the Italian Renaissance style. There is an equestrian gallery in the courtyard, a painted chapel, and a charming **Nymphs' Grotto,* as well as a *pavillon d'amour* (gazebo) in the adjacent grounds.

Rejoin N 89, and continue to *Boën-sur-Lignon,* where the road begins a steep climb to the valley of the Lignon, and continues through the lovely **valley of the Anzon* before descending through the valley of the Durolle to **Thiers** (see Travel Route 14), where N 89 crosses the north-south Travel Route 14 from Paris to Perpignan. The Dômes mountains lie ahead. Route N 89 crosses the Dore River and transverses the plain of La Limagne to **Lezoux,** a small town that was a center of pottery-making in ancient times; a small *museum* with a fine collection of excavated Gallo-Roman ceramics, including the celebrated *Mithras vase,* commemorates its history. From here you can make an interesting 6 km. (3.4 miles) side trip to the ***Château de Ravel,** south of Lezoux. Various parts of the château date from the 13th, 17th, and 18th centuries. Its **interior,* decorated with original furnishings, is well worth seeing, and the terrace provides a marvelous **view* over the Dômes range. The château's church dates from the 13th century.

Continue on N 89 to *Pont du Château* where you will cross the Allier River. Just 14 km. (9 miles) farther is ****Clermont-Ferrand** (described in Travel Route 13). Route N 89 crosses Travel Route 13 from Paris to Carcassone here.

The next leg of Travel Route 22 runs 176 km. (109 miles) from Clermont-Ferrand to Brive through the magnificent landscape of the ****Monts-Dômes** region, with its unusual volcanic cones.

From Clermont-Ferrand, you

can take one of two routes south-west to La Font de l'Arbre and a 6 km. (4 miles) side trip to the ****Puy de Dôme:** either via *La Baraque* or via D 68 to the elegant health spa of *Royat* (9 km.; 6 miles), with its fortified Roman-esque church of Saint-Léger. A private toll road leads from D 68 to the famous summit of Puy de Dôme, an extinct volcano which, at 1,416 meters (4,665 feet) high, dominates the 60 other volcanoes in the Dômes mountain range. From the flat summit, which in Roman times was the site of a tem-ple to Mercury, there is a magnifi-cent **view in all directions.

From *La Font-de-l'Arbre,* the road climbs to the *Col de la Moréno,* which lies between two forested volcanic mountains. The beautiful descent ends at the four-way intersection called *Les Quatre-Routes.* Rejoin N 89 here and continue to *Rochefort Mon-tagne,* which lies at the foot of an extinct volcano; from there, you can make a very worthwhile 19 km. (12 miles) side trip to ***Le Mont-Dore.** Take N 89 south, and turn left on Route D 983. You'll first come to the *Col de Guery* with an outstanding view over the two lofty crags of *Roches Tuilière* and *Sanadoire;* then skirt the **Lac de Guéry* and circle down on to the winter sports center **Le Mont-Dore* at 1,055 meters (3,460 feet). As the culmination of the trip, you can take a funicular to the top of Le Mont-Dore, the domi-nant peak of the Massif Central, which, at 1,886 meters, (6,186

feet) offers an extensive view in all directions.

N 89 continues via *Laqueille,* which has fine views back to the Dômes mountains, to a plateau called the "Roof of the Lim-ousin," and the harsh and barren Plateau de Millevaches. During France's religious wars, the forest there was burned to the ground; in 1860 it was finally replanted. N 89 descends to **Ussel** (population 9,000), which has several 15th- and 16th-century houses, but is otherwise unnotable. In the *Place Voltaire* there is a tall granite eagle, which was found in a nearby Roman encampment.

Continue on N 89 to *Rosiers-d'Egletons,* just east of which is the *Château de Maumont,* birth-place of two Avignon popes: Clement VI (1342–52) and his nephew, Gregory XI (1370–1377), who was the last of the French popes. After 17 km. (11 miles) you will reach the hamlet of *La Bitarelle,* where a road bears off to the left to one of the loveliest waterfalls in central France, the **Montane.* The nearby town of **Gimel,* set in a gorge of the Mon-tane River, has a Limoges-enam-elled shrine and other treasures in its church. From *Parc Vuilier,* you can see three waterfalls: *La Grande Cascade, La Redole,* and *La Queue du Cheval.*

Continue on N 89 for 10 km. (6 miles) along the floor of the valley of the Corrèze, to **Tulle** (pop-ulation 23,000), an unattractive industrial city known for its weapons factory. There are, however, two noteworthy sights in the Medieval old city: *de l'Enclos* is the name of a lovely 14th-century bell tower, and the 15th-century *Maison du Loyac* has a richly decorated façade.

Route N 89 now runs through the pretty, winding valley of the Corrèze for 29 km. (18 miles) to the prosperous town of **Brive-la-Gaillarde** (population 55,000). Interesting sights include the Romanesque 12th-century *church of Saint-Martin;* the *Musée Ernest Rupin,* with miscellaneous collections of tapestries, paintings, and rooms devoted to local archaeology; and the Renaissance *Hôtel de Labenche,* which has an arcaded courtyard. (In Brive, this itinerary crosses the north-south Travel Route 12.)

The last section of Travel Route 22 runs for 193 km. (120 miles) from Brive to Bordeaux. A highpoint of this section is the **Grotte de Lascaux*, with its prehistoric cave paintings.

Leave Brive by N 89, which descends through the valley of the Vézère to *Terrasson-la-Villedieu,* which has a picturesque 12th-century bridge and some atmospheric riverside houses. The truffle country of Périgord begins here.

These black, potato-sized, and nearly odorless fungi are harvested in the winter months by pigs and dogs who sniff them out. In good years, the truffle harvest in the Périgord is 150 tons; by way of comparison, 10,000 tons of nuts are harvested in the same territory.

About 6 km. (3.7 miles) farther west on N 89 is *Le Lardin-Saint-Lazare,* the starting point for a 17 km. (10.5 miles) side trip to the world famous **Lascaux Caves.** Take D 704 south to *Montignac.* From there, a side road runs 2.5 km. (1.5 miles) to the entrance to the Lascaux Caves. The caves, discovered by accident in 1940, were prehistoric "halls" covered with large, brilliant paintings of bulls, stags, and horses painted some 22,000 years ago. Unfortunately, visitors must be satisfied with seeing reproductions of these unique Ice Age cave paintings; in order to protect them from deterioration, the caves were closed to the public in 1963. Continuous slide-shows are given.

The actual center of prehistoric research in this cave-riddled area is the village of *Les Eyzies-de-Tayac,* located 24 km. (15 miles) south of Montignac on D 706. On the way there you will pass

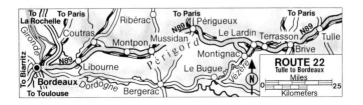

through the villages of *Le Moustier* and *Tursac,* which is the location of *La Madeleine,* the cave where the first discoveries of the late Paleolithic age, now called Magdelenian, were made. The **Musée National de Préhistoire,* in *Les Eyzies* will help to give you an idea of the importance and extent of the prehistoric finds in the area. On the return trip, bear left on D 67, which rejoins N 89 at *Thenon,* and cuts 13 km. (8 miles) off the trip.

Route N 89 runs through wooded hill country into the valley of the Manoire River before descending to **Périgueux** (population 36,000), a town famous for its truffles and *foie gras.* This capital of the Périgord region was originally two cities: Vesunna, a Roman town on the west side, and the Medieval town of Puy-Saint-Front on the east side. Its 12th-century **Cathédrale Saint-Front,* a curious structure which suffered from its 19th-century "restorations," is topped with a Romanesque bell tower, five cupolas, and 17 small bell towers. The massive interior is impressive. Also worth a visit are the *Musée Périgord,* with archaeological and Gallo-Roman collections; the remains of a Roman amphitheater on the elliptical plaza called the **Arenes Romaines;* and the *Tour de Vésone,* which was originally the cella of a temple dedicated to Vesunna, deity of the city.

Route N 89 continues west along the course of the Isle River, through *Mussidan* and *Montpon-sur-l'Isle* and then turns southwest to the city of **Libourne** (population 24,000), where the Isle flows into the Dordogne River. The town is primarily known as the commercial center for the area's numerous vineyards. On the **Grande Place,* lined with broad arcades known as *Couverts,* is the 15th-century *Hôtel de Ville,* with a small museum. From here, you can make a 7 km. (4.3 miles) side trip to ***Saint-Émilion,** a town renowned for its wine. Its major sight of interest is **Église Monolithe,* a church cut out of a rocky cliff.

From Libourne, N 89 crosses the Dordogne River and enters the winegrowing region of **Entre-Deux-Mers,* which means "Between Two Seas." Tucked into a triangular area bounded by the Dordogne and the Garonne rivers before they flow together to form the Gironde estuary, it takes its name from the tidal effects of the Atlantic, 100 km. (62 miles) away, that are felt this far inland. Continue for 31 km. (19 miles) to ****Bordeaux.** A description of this large, handsome port city begins on page 69. The seaside resort of *Arcachon* and the coast of the Landes region to the south, and the Basque coast to the Spanish border, are described in Travel Route 11.

TRAVEL ROUTE 23: Geneva–*Toulouse–Bayonne (999 km.; 621 miles)

See maps on pages 242, 245, and 246.

This itinerary traverses the alpine regions of Savoy, the mountains of the Massif Central, Albi and Toulouse, and continues through the provinces of Gascogny and Guyenne to the Basque coast on the Atlantic. It follows back roads through beautiful landscapes, including the famous Gorges du Tarn.

The first leg runs from Geneva to the attractive alpine Lac d'Annecy, to the health spa Aix-les-Bains, and continues via Chambéry, the former capital of Savoy, to Grenoble, former capital of the Dauphine and the site of the 1968 Winter Olympics. This 150 km. (93 mile) stretch is described in Travel Route 17.

The second leg runs from Grenoble to Valence, a distance of 94 km. (58 miles). You can choose between two routes, both of which lead about 100 km. (62 miles) to Valence.

The Isère Valley to Valence

(Follow the route marked "A" on the map on page 242.)

Take the Autoroute du Soleil, A 48, heading north to *Moirans,* then take Route N 92 southwest, following the west bank of the Isère River through a fertile flood-plain. You will pass through the market town of *Tullins,* known for its walnuts, *Saint-Marcellin,* with its Romanesque belfry, 13th-century castle ruins, remains of 13th–

14th-century walls, and renowned goats'-milk cheeses, to *Romans-sur-Isère,* an old leather-working town that still manufactures footwear. The Romanesque abbey **church of Saint-Bernard,* built in 1140 and restored in 1718, has an interesting portal and a polygonal 13th-century choir with three tiers of windows. Cross the Isère here to the suburb of *Bourg-de-Péage,* named for the toll (péage) that was once levied for crossing the bridge. Pick up Route N 532, and follow it for 18 km. (11 miles) to *Valence,* which is described in Travel Route 15.

The Vercors Massif to Valence

(Follow the route marked "B" on the map on page 242.)

Head west from Grenoble via the *Cours Vallier,* crossing the Drac Bridge, and pick up Route D 531 north. Near *Sassenage,* the road turns west into the mountains, climbing through the forested **Gorges d'Engins* to the health resort and winter sports center of *Villard de Lans.*

Route D 531 passes through several tunnels as it proceeds west through the *Gorges de la Bourne*, past the Bournillon cavern on the left and the Choranche cavern on the right, before reaching *Pont-en-Royans*, the old capital of the Royans. Its houses are perched on the cliffs on either side of the gorge. Continue 9 km. (5.4 miles) to the old village of *Saint-Nazaire-en-Royans*, is dominated by an

ancient aqueduct, in the valley of the Isère, where the Bourne River meets the Isère. A little farther on is the *Saint-Hilaire dam*, which was built across the Isère in 1958. Here you will join Route N 532 south along the bank of the Isère to *Bourg-de-Péage*, and continue on to *Valence*.

The next leg of the itinerary from Valence crosses the Massif Cen-

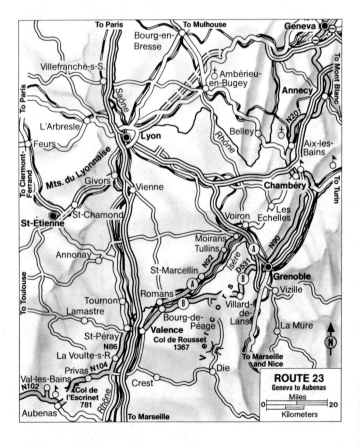

tral to Langogne, a distance of 111 km. (69 miles).

Route N 104 climbs from *Le Pouzin* to *Privas*, a town that was largely destroyed in 1629 by Louis XIII and Richelieu because of its Protestantism. There are a few old houses at the north end of town. At Privas, N 104 enters the *Cevennes*, a particularly striking section of the Massif Central, and climbs 787 meters (2,581 feet) to the *Col de l'Escrinet*, where there is a fine view. To the right, as you descend through chestnut woods, are the ruins of the *Château de Boulogne* (15th–16th century). You will enter the valley of the Ardeche River and **Aubenas** (population 13,500), located on a steep hill overlooking the Ardeche Valley. An 18th-century dome of the former Benedictine convent of Saint-Benoit is on the right. The 13th–16th century *castle* contains administrative offices. In the old town center there are one or two 17th-century houses along the Grande Rue and the restored *church of Saint-Laurent*, with a 15th-century tower. Sample one of Aubenas' famous marrons glaces. Near *Labegude*, 5 km. (3 miles) from Aubenas, a road leads to the old-fashioned health spa of **Vals-les-Bains** (population 4,500), which stretches along both sides of the narrow Volane River. The river, whose waters contain a high proportion of bicarbonate of soda, is spanned by seven bridges. The best known mineral spring here is the Source Saint-Jean.

Continue on N 102 past the ancient spa of *Neyrac-les-Bains* where, in the Middle Ages, the waters were said to cure leprosy, to *Thueyts,* situated on the Ardeche River, and the old village of *Mayres,* with its castle ruins. Here the road begins to climb into an increasingly rugged landscape, finally reaching *Col de la Chavade* (1,266 meters; 4,152 feet), the watershed of the Rhône and Loire rivers. Continue to Route N 88, and turn southwest to the once-fortified town of *Pradelles,* where there are some old houses and an arcaded market-place. Soon, you'll reach the old town of **Langogne** (population 4,800) on the Allier River. The town has a *clocktower,* five *ramparts,* an 11th–13th century Romanesque *church,* with a 15th-century Gothic façade, a Medieval gateway, and several 17th-century houses. The enormous reservoir of Naussac is to the west.

Follow Route N 88 for 21 km. (13 miles) to *Châteauneuf-de-Randon,* a cattle market and the last town captured from the English by Du Guesclin in the 14th century. Here you can pick up Travel Route 14 (Paris–Perpignan) and follow it to *Mende* and through the **Gorges du Tarn,** one of France's great scenic areas, to *Millau.*

Leave Millau on Route D 999 southwest. A smaller road branches east 3 km. (2 miles) for a side trip to *Roquefort-sur-Soulzon* (see Travel Route 14).

Rejoin D 999 and continue on for 10 km. (6 miles) to **Saint-**

Gorges du Tarn

Affrique (population 9,200), which has a 15th-century Gothic bridge and is the site of an unusual rock formation, the *Rocher de Caylus.*

Route D 999 crosses a plateau and continues through *Saint-Sernin-sur-Rance,* where there are several 15th–16th-century houses and a 15th-century church, to *Alban.* From here you can continue directly to *Albi* on D 999 or make a detour by taking the road to the north for 12 km. (7.5 miles) to the Tarn River and following its bank to ***Ambialet,** a curious village tucked into a narrow loop of the Tarn. The entrance to the peninsula is only 25 meters (82 feet) wide. An 11th-century Romanesque church, *Nôtre-Dame-de-l'Oder,* a *tower,* an old **cloister* and the *ruins* of a fortress lie on the rocky spine of the peninsula.

Follow the road along the Tarn for another 6 km. (4 miles) to *Fabas* then on to *Foncouverte,*

and finally to **Albi* (population 48,300), whose amazing fortified *church of Sainte-Cécile* and **Toulouse-Lautrec Museum* are described in Travel Route 13.

Leave Albi on Route N 88 southwest towards Toulouse, 78 km. (48 miles) away. The highway runs across a wide plain to *Gaillac,* known for its sparkling white wine. It has two churches with fortified towers, and *Rabastens,* dominated by the fortress tower of its lovely 13th–14th century **church of Nôtre-Dame-du-Bourg.* The road continues through rolling countryside to **Toulouse,* described in Travel Route 13.

There are two routes from Toulouse to Bayonne: The one through Tarbes and Pau is 294 km. (183 miles); the route through Auch and Aire is 15 km. (10 miles) shorter.

Tarbes and Pau to Bayonne

(Follow the route marked "A" on the map on page 246.)

Leave Toulouse on Route N 20, then join Route N 117 which follows the Garonne River southwest for 20 km. (12.5 miles) to *Muret.* Continue through *Saint-Martory* and across the plateau of Lannemezan to **Tarbes** (population 60,000). The original capital of the counts of Bigorre is now a lively industrial city and the center for tourism in the Pyrenees. The poet Théophile Gautier (1811–

1872) and Marshall Foch (1851–1929) were both born here.

Of special interest are the *Cathédrale Nôtre-Dame-de-la-Sède* (12th–14th century) and the *Massey Gardens.*

From Tarbes, N 117 goes directly to Pau (39 km.; 24 miles) or you can detour to the world-famous pilgrimage site of ***Lourdes** (population 19,000) following Route N 21 southwest for 20 km. (12.4 miles).

In 1858 a young peasant girl

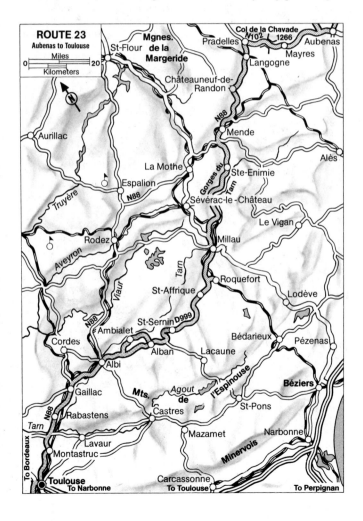

named Bernadette Soubirous had a vision of the Blessed Virgin in a grotto here and, in an act of faith, dug out the spring whose waters are said to miraculously cure the sick. Bernadette was made a saint in 1933 and Lourdes has developed into the largest pilgrimage site for Catholics—with some 2 million visitors every year.

The city, dominated by the towers of a 13th–17th century *castle* housing the *Musée Pyrénéan*, is wholly devoted to serving the needs of pilgrims and tending to the sick who come in search of their own miracles. The *Cité Religieuse* is across the Gave de Pau River. The wide *Esplanade des Precessions* is the site of eve-

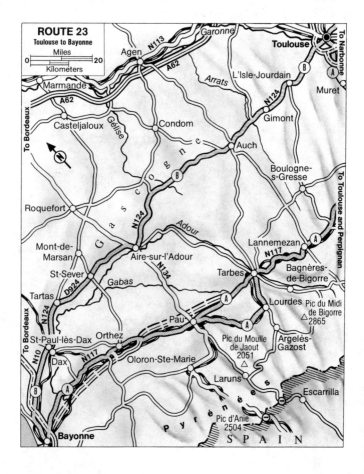

Lourdes

ning candlelight processions. Under it lies the *Basilique Souter-raine Saint-Pius X* (1958). The esplanade ends at the *Église de Rosaire* where the blessing of the sick takes place. From its plaza, ramps lead to the *Basilique du Rosaire* (1867); under the right-hand ramp are the grotto of Bernadette's visions and the bathing basins fed by the miracle-working spring. To the south is the *Chemin du Calvaire* (road of Calvary) which leads to a hill with a view.

Route D 937, following the Gave de Pau River, leads to the small pilgrimage site of *Béthar-ram* and on to **Pau** (population 135,000). The ancient capital of Béarn, Pau is dominated by the *castle* in which King Henri IV was born in 1553. According to legend, the lips of the newborn infant were brushed with a clove of garlic and moistened with a few drops of wine. Also of interest in Pau is the *Boulevard des Pyrénées*, which runs along a terrace above

the Gave de Pau and offers magnificent views of the mountains.

You can continue on Route N 117 from Pau to Bayonne (106 km; 66 miles).

Auch and Aire to Bayonne

(Follow the route marked "B" on the map on page 246.)

Leave Toulouse by the Pont-Neuf, heading west, and take Route N 124 through the gently rolling countryside on the north bank of the Save River to *L'Isle Jourdain* (population 1,300), where the tower of a former 15th-century castle became the bell tower of the 18th-century church.

Continue to *Gimont* on the Gimone River, where an enormous wooden market hall stands on the steep main street of the town. The church, dating from 1506, has an octagonal brick belfry and contains a noteworthy 16th-century triptych. Nearby are the ruins of a Cistercian abbey founded in the 12th century. Continue 25 km. (15.5 miles) to **Auch** (population 25,000), a fine old town in the heart of Gascony. The remarkable *Cathédrale de Sainte-Marie*, built from 1489–1597, and with a fine Renaissance *façade*, is famous for its early 16th-century *stained-glass windows*, which depict Biblical figures within an architectural framework, and for its truly magnificent Renaissance **choir stalls*, carved from oak and comparable to those of Amiens Cathedral. There is a seventh-century marble sarcophagus in the crypt. A slim 14th-century tower overlooks *Place Salinis,* south of the cathedral, where a monumental staircase from the 19th century leads down to the river. A collection of ceramics and local archaeological finds are housed in the *Musée,* a former Jacobin convent located near the 18th-century *Archbishop's Palace* to the north of the cathedral.

Route N 124 continues through scenic countryside, crossing several tributaries of the Garonne, before reaching the Adour River near *Aire.* The town has preserved the charming *Hôtel du Baillage,* dating from 1600, and restored the *church of Saint-Pierre,* which has a fine tower and three discernible stages of building. At *Grenade* follow the course of the Adour on Route D 924 to *Saint-Sever,* which looks out over the valley and forests of the Landes to the north. The church, founded by Benedictines in the tenth century, was rebuilt in the 12th century, and has several Romanesque features. From here, D 924 runs along the southern edge of the vast *Forêt Landaise* (see Travel Route 11), and rejoins Route N 124, passing through *Tartas,* where there are remains of a castle, to *Saint-Paul-lès-Dax.*

Dax (population 21,000), with its mild climate, is a year-round spa noted for its hot springs and mud baths. Its thermal springs were known to the Romans as Aquae Tarbellicae. Under Richard I it came under English rule, and was not incorporated into the French kingdom until 1451. The *church of Saint-Paul,* just southwest of the N 124 crossroad, has an 11th-century sculptured frieze depicting the Last Supper on its apse. From here, drive south over the Adour Bridge to the *Place Thiers,* behind which the **Fontaine Chaude,* surrounded by arcades, gushes with sulphur spring water. The uninspired Classical *Cathédrale de Nôtre-Dame,* built from 1656–1719, retains a **door* from the 13th-century English church which formerly stood on the site. Remnants of the Gallo-Roman city walls and towers may be seen in the *Parc Theodore-Denis.*

Route N 124 meets Route N 10, the main road of Travel Route 11 at *Saint-Geours-de-Maremne.* Take N 10 from here for 25 km. (15.5 miles) to *Bayonne* (see Travel Route 11).

TRAVEL ROUTE 24: *Menton–Narbonne–Toulouse (620 km.; 385 miles)

See maps on pages 250–251 and 254.

This east-west route follows main roads through lovely and historic country from the Maritime Alps near the Italian border to the Pyrenees. In places the route hugs the scenic Mediterranean coastline of the Côte d'Azur.

Begin the route in ***Menton** and ascend to the ****Grand Corniche** via *Roquebrune. This picturesque village is dominated by a handsome citadel dating from the 12th and 13th centuries. Near Le Vistaéro is one of the most magnificent lookout points on the Côte d'Azur, providing an unforgettable ****view** of Monte Carlo, the coastline, and the sea.

The Grande Corniche continues to climb to ****La Turbie**, a village situated just above Monte Carlo. The town is dominated by the splendid ruins of the **Trophée des Alpes,* a unique victory memorial that was erected in the year 5 B.C. to commemorate the Roman subjugation of the Ligurians. The ruins include the 38-sq. meter (125-sq. foot) pedestal and the row of columns above it, survivors of an attempt by the French to blow them up in 1705. The town also has an 18th-century Baroque church that contains many paintings, including a Madonna by

La Turbie: Trophée des Alpes

Louis Bréa. The panoramic Grand Corniche, which was laid out during the reign of Napoleon I, continues to climb steeply, then gradually descends through the *Col d'Èze,* providing a view of Èze (see Travel Route 19), and continues for 31 km. (19 miles) to **Nice** (see Travel Route 19). This is also the end point of the Route des Grandes-Alpes, described under Travel Route 18, and the Route des Préalpes, described under Travel Route 17.

Leave Nice on Autoroute A 8 westbound. If you continue for 59 km. (37 miles) you will bypass Cannes and come to *Fréjus* (see Travel Route 19). From here the autoroute passes through fertile plains covered with vineyards, olive groves, and fruit orchards. The soil gradually takes on a reddish cast.

Brignoles (population 11,000) is the center of bauxite mining in France, although deposits of the mineral are gradually being depleted. There is a museum that has the second-century **Gayole sarcophagus,* the earliest Christian memorial in Gaul.

Leave Brignoles on Route N 7; it forks about 13 km. (8 miles) west of town. You can drive to Arles either through Marseille (129–133 km.; 80–83 miles) or Aix-En-Provence (132 km.; 82 miles).

Marseille to Arles

(Follow the route marked "A" on the map on pages 250–251.)

Take Route D 1, which becomes N 560 after 10 km. (6 miles). Just before *Aubagne,* N 560 runs into the autoroute extension; in 22 km. (13.7 miles) you will reach **Marseille** (see page 58). From here you can take A 9, the Autoroute du Soleil, for 48 km. (30 miles) to the *Salon-en-Provence* exit. Continue on Route N 113 another 40 km. (25 miles) to ****Arles** (see Travel Route 16). For a scenic route that is off the beaten track, take Route N 568 through the Estaque Peninsula and the barren pebbled plain of La Crau, 80 km. (50 miles) to Arles.

Via Aix-en-Provence to Arles

(Follow the route marked "B" on the map below.)

From Brignoles follow Route N 7 for 6 km. (3.7 miles) to the town of *Saint-Maximin-la-Sainte-Baume,* which has a **church* that is a beau-

tiful example of the northern French Gothic style. Mary Magdalene, her brother Lazarus, her sister Martha, and several other saints are supposed to have lived in this town after they were washed ashore at Les Saintes-Maries-de-la-Mer. It is claimed that she travelled with Saint Maximin, the first bishop of Aix-en-Provence, throughout the land. She is supposed to have lived in the grotto of Saint-Maximin-la-Sainte-Baume until her death.

The ***Basilique de Sainte-Madeleine* is a splendid example of Provençal Gothic. The church was built over a long period of time; started in 1295, it was not completed until 1532. It has a fourth-century crypt that contains several Gallo-Roman sarcophagi. Adjoining the church is a former Dominican monastery.

Route N 7 follows the Arc River through its valley bordered with mountains for 44 km. (27 miles) to

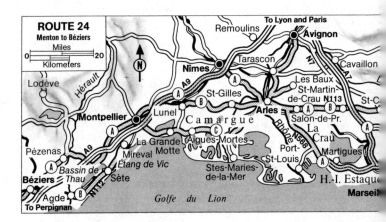

*Aix-en-Provence (population 130,000). An extremely beautiful city, Aix is also known throughout the world for its summer music festivals.

Founded by the Romans in 123 B.C., it was named Aquae Sextiae after the warm healing springs that flow here. Aix was the capital of the province of Gallia Narbonensis until the fourth century. In the tenth century it became the principal residence of the counts of Provence. In 1482, Aix, along with the rest of Provence, became part of France. Economically and politically the city has been far surpassed by neighboring Marseille, but Aix remains the cultural capital of Provence.

The main street of Aix is the **Cours Mirabeau*. Lined by handsome 18th-century houses and plane trees, the street is graced with four beautiful fountains. South of the Cours is the **Fontaine des Quatre Dauphins*, built

Aix-en-Provence: Cours Mirabeau

in 1667. Museums include the **Musée Paul Arbaud*, which houses a good ceramics collection as well as artifacts of Provence, and the **Musée Granet*, one of the most important provincial museums in France. It has unique **Celtic-Ligurian sculptures* from pre-Roman times. These are the earliest documents of Gallic art. The museum also has a rich col-

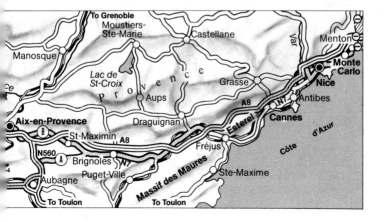

lection of 18th- and early-19th-century portraits, and it has a self-portrait of Rembrandt dating from 1665.

North of the plane-tree walk is the lovely *Place d'Albertas,* and the *Hôtel de Ville* (1658) with its famous Bibliothèque Méjanes. Nearby is the *Tour Communal,* a tower with a Medieval base and a Renaissance top that contains a 17th-century astronomical clock. Close by is the archbishop's palace, or Archevêché, which houses the *Musée des Tapisseries.* On display are 19 magnificent 17th- and 18th-century Gobelin tapestries from Beauvais. The *Cathédrale Saint-Sauveur* is a composite of the styles of many ages, from a bapistry of the fourth and fifth centuries to the capitals taken from a Roman building to a 15th-century chapel. Among the famous works in the cathedral are 15 Flemish tapestries from 1511, and the triptych of **The Burning Bush* by Nicolas Froment (1475). In the northern part of the city is the atelier of Paul Cézanne, surrounded by a somewhat neglected garden. The great painter was born and died in Aix (1839–1906).

Leave Aix on Route N 7; about 13 km. (8 miles) northwest turn left at *Saint-Cannat* onto Route N 572. Continue for 25 km. (15.5 miles) across the northern part of the stony plain of La Crau to *Saint-Martin-de-Crau.* Continue on Route N 113 for 15 km. (9.3 miles) to *Arles* (see Travel Route 16).

From Arles you can make side trips to the ruined city of *Les Baux* (see Travel Route 16), to the castle of King René in *Tarascon* and ***Avignon* (both described in Travel Route 15).

There are three routes from Arles to Montpellier, and each way has its own attractions: through Nîmes (84 km.; 52 miles), through Lunel (73 km.; 45 miles), or through the Camargue (78 km.; 48 miles).

Nîmes to Montpellier

(Follow the route marked "A" on the map on pages 250–251.)

This route is the longest in distance but the shortest in actual travel time.

Follow Route N 113 for 31 km. (19 miles) northwest to **Nîmes,** with its famous architectural monuments (see Travel Route 16). From there take the Autoroute A 9 for 53 km. (33 miles) southwest, where you can exit just south of Montpellier.

Via Lunel to Montpellier

(Follow the route marked "B" on the map on pages 250–251).

This short but not especially interesting route takes D 572 across the northern section of the Camargue via *Saint-Gilles* (see Travel Route 16) to *Lunel,* a distance of 49 km. (30 miles). From there take Route N 113 for 24 km. (15 miles) to Montpellier.

In the Camargue

Through the Camargue to Montpellier

(Follow the route marked "C" on the map on pages 250–251.)

This route is wonderfully scenic. Take Route D 570 southwest from Arles through the marshes of the Rhône delta, which is known as the Camargue (see Travel Route 16). When you have travelled 28 km. (17 miles), leave D 570 (which goes on to *Saintes-Maries-de-la-Mer*) and head west on Route D 58 for 18 km. (11 miles) to the Medieval maritime fortress of **Aigues-Mortes** (see Travel Route 16). Continue on Route D 62 past the vacation center of **La Grande-Motte** (see Travel Route 16) whose modern pyramidal buildings suggest ancient Mexican structures, over a spit of land to **Montpellier** (population 250,000). It is a flourishing commercial city best known for the wines of Languedoc

and its university. The capital of the old province of Languedoc-Roussillon, Montpellier began as a small settlement of spice traders. It was built far from the sea because of the pirates that plagued the coast throughout the Medieval period. A medical school was started here before A.D. 1000, probably by Jewish or Moslem physicians. It became part of the university that was established in the 13th century. Rabelais earned his doctorate here in the 16th century. There are now over 40,000 students at the university, of whom 7,000 are medical students.

Interesting sights include many splendid noble and merchants' *mansions;* the *Musée Fabre,* an important art museum; the *Cathédrale Saint-Pierre;* the *Promenade du Peyrou* (1689–1776) situated on the crest of a hill with two opposing terraces; an elegant six-sided water tower; an aqueduct 22 meters (72 feet) high; and the *Jardin des Plantes,* the oldest botanical garden in France (1593).

There are two routes from Montpellier to *Béziers.* You can follow Route N 113 across the interior for 49 km. (30 miles) to *Pézanas* and continue another 23 km. (14 miles) to Béziers (both towns are described in Travel Route 14; follow the route marked "A" on the map on pages 250–251). Or you can take the slightly longer but more interesting Route N 112 along the edge of the sea described below. (Follow the route marked "B".)

Sète (population 46,000) is an

important commercial and fishing port. Situated on a hill called *Mont Saint-Clair* above the town, is the *Cimetière Marin,* the sailors cemetery immortalized by poet Paul Valéry (1871–1945). He is buried here.

Route N 112 follows a spit of land 12 km. (7 miles) long between the sea and the Bassin de Thau, a lagoon that contains oyster farms, to **Agde** (population 12,000). The town is situated at the mouth of the Canal du Midi, also called the Canal des Deux Mers, because it connects the Mediterranean and the Atlantic Ocean. Of interest is the *Cathédrale Saint-Étienne,* constructed like a fortress with thick window-less walls and a high watchtower.

One of the largest vacation centers in the region is at *Cap d'Agde,* 5 km. (3 miles) to the southeast.

From Agde, Route N 112 continues for 22 km. (72 miles) to *Béziers* (see Travel Route 14).

From Béziers continue on Route N 113 (which merges with N 9 as far as Narbonne), cross over the *Écluses de Fonsérannes,* the

locks of the Canal du Midi, to Narbonne (see Travel Route 14), a distance of 27 km. (17 miles).

Between Béziers and Narbonne at the mouth of the Aude River is a resort called the *Embouchure de l'Aude.* It is a high-rise city encircled by hill villages; a bridge of shops over the Aude is a modern attempt to imitate the Ponte Vecchio in Florence.

From Narbonne N 113 turns westward, away from the sea, and into the wide lowland between the Massif Central and the Pyrenees. At **Carcassonne* you can pick up Travel Route 13.

Follow N 113 to *Toulouse,* a distance of 93 km. (58 miles). This route along the Canal du Midi offers little of interest. About 48 km. (30 miles) beyond Carcassonne is the Col de Nauroze. At an elevation of only 190 meters (623 feet), it is the watershed between the Mediterranean and the Atlantic. An obelisk commemorates the builder of the canal, Riquet de Bonrepaux, who died in 1680.

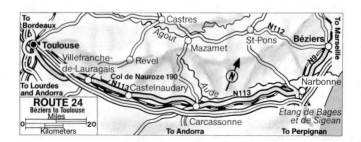

TRAVEL ROUTE 25: The Pyrenees Road from Cerbère to Hendaye (737 km.; 457 miles)

See map on pages 256–257 and 259.

The Pyrenees Road, one of the most beautiful in France, leads from the French-Spanish border town of Cerbère on the Mediterranean to the French-Spanish border town Hendaye on the Atlantic Ocean. This is not, however, one uninterrupted highway, and it has numerous curves and ascending and descending sections through the mountains. In order to fully enjoy the magnificent scenery and take recommended excursions, three to four days are needed to complete the trip.

From Cerbère, take Route N 114 along the *Côte Vermeille* (see Travel Route 14) for 30 km. (18.6 miles) to *Argelès,* where Route D 618 begins. *Saint-Genis-des-Fontaines,* whose **carved church lintel* dating from 1020 is the oldest Romanesque sculpture in France, is located on the flat plains of Roussillon.

Near *Bains du Boulou,* D 618 becomes Route N 9 for 2 km. (1 mile) from *Perpignan* to the border crossing at *Le Perthus* (see Travel Route 14). It then turns west, and continues to the old fortified town of **Céret** (population 6,000), where in mid-April France's first cherries are available. The **Pont de Céret* spans the Tech River with a wide arch; it is a remarkable example of early-14th-century bridge construction.

Along with *Collioure* (see Travel Route 14) on the coast, Céret has become a "Mecca of Cubism" to avant-gardists. From 1910 to 1920, Picasso, Braque, and other artists often came here for inspiration and to work. Paintings by several of the great modern masters are on display at the *Musée d'Art Moderne.*

Amélie-les-Bains (population 4,000), a spa with thermal springs that were used by the Romans, is 8 km. (5 miles) to the southwest. In the *Thermes Romains* (Roman baths), an ancient pavement has been preserved. A fort built by Louis XIV is visible to the west.

From here, Route D 115 leads through the valley of the Tech River, to the market town of *Arles-sur-Tech,* where the bodies of two third-century Christian martyrs were brought to the abbey **church* (11th–12th century) in the hopes that they would miraculously free the valley of dangerous beasts. The 16th-century *tower* and the 13th-century *cloister* are also noteworthy. Two major ski areas have been developed above Arles-sur-Tech. Route D 115 continues on to the picturesque winter resort and old fortress town of *Prats-de-Mollo,* which retains some of its 17th-century ramparts and a church with a Romanesque tower, to **Col d'Ares* at an elevation of

1,513 meters (4,900 feet) and the Spanish border. Travellers to Barcelona can continue via Ripoll and Vich, bypassing heavy traffic on the major highway from Le Perthus.

At *Amélie-les-Bains,* Route D 618 turns northeast, zigzagging its way to the *Col Xatard* where, on clear days, you can see the blue haze of the Mediterranean. From here, drive downhill through the canyons of the Boules River. In 5 km. (3 miles), the side road to the left leads south to *Prieuré de Serrabonne,* an Augustinian priory

built from the 11th to the 12th century. Ask to see the remarkable **choir,* with its sculptural decorations, a masterpiece of Catalanian art. Route D 618 feeds into Route N 116, which goes southwest to **Prades** (population 6,500), set amid apricot, cherry, and peach orchards. The labyrinth of old streets hides a Gothic *church* with an earlier tower. Pablo Casals (1876–1973), the famous Spanish cellist, was in exile here from 1941 to 1949; in the 1950s he organized the *Festivals de Musique* that still take place annually in

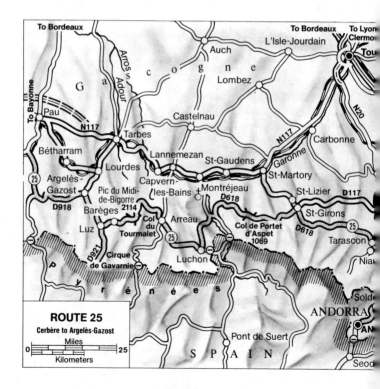

ROUTE 25
Cerbère to Argelès-Gazot

the 12th-century *abbey of Saint-Michel-de-Cuxa.*

Route N 116 climbs to *Villefranche-de-Conflent,* still surrounded by its heavy 16th-century fortifications, which has several Medieval houses. The ruins of a fort tower above the town. A 6 km. (4 mile) side trip leads from here to the spa of *Vernet-les-Bains,* beautifully situated at the foot of *Mont Canigou,* the highest peak in this area. It was particularly popular with the English from 1850 on, but has now somewhat faded. Climbers will find this a good base

for an ascent of the Canigou. A castle and an austerely beautiful 11th-century abbey, *St.-Martin-du-Canigou,* accessible only by jeep or on foot, look down on the modern town. The abbey, which fell into ruins after the Revolution, has been carefully restored and is now used for retreats. N 116 continues through the narrow canyon of the *Defilé des Graus* to the health resort of *Thuès-les-Bains,* where 42 steaming hot springs are used to help a variety of ailments. Continue to ***Mont-Louis** (population 800), the highest garrison

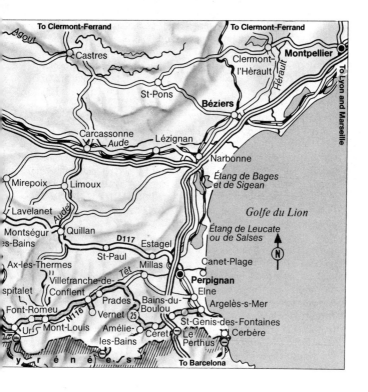

town in France at 1,600 meters (5,248 feet) and now a flourishing resort. In earlier days this little town, surrounded by walls built by Vauban in 1681 and dominated by a citadel, was an important fortress guarding the Languedoc and Rousillon plains from Spain.

At this point the Pyrenees road leaves Route N 116 and continues via Route D 618 through the Cerdagne, an upland plain of meadows and pine forests, climbing through the health resort of *Superbolquère* to the *Ermitage de Font-Romeu.* This place of pilgrimage has a richly adorned 17th-century chapel that once contained a 12th-century representation of the Virgin. From here you have a panoramic view.

Just a short way beyond is the summer resort and winter sports center regularly used by athletes for altitude training, *Font-Romeu.* It is situated 1,800 meters (5,900 feet) above sea level. With a climate so dry and sunny that the road is called "solana," the sunny road, it's no wonder that the neighboring small village of *Odeillo* has been selected as the location for an experimental project in the field of solar energy. Some of the scientists live in the small solar-heated houses nearby.

Route D 618 begins to wind downhill, crossing the aptly named *Chaos Granitique de Targassonne,* a gorge filled with a tumble of granite boulders. It joins Route N 20 near the town of *Ur,* whose church has a rich gilt interior.

The Pyrenees road winds its way up through the valley of the Carol River, crossing the *Col de Puymorens,* 1,915 meters (6,280 feet) high. Just 3 km. (2 miles) on the other side of this pass the road forks: to the south 36 km. (22 miles) is *Andorra;* the Pyrenees route continues north to *l'Hospitalet.*

Take the south road where N 20 forks past Col de Puymorens and continue to the *Pas de la Case,* where you'll see the country's radio transmission tower, and cross the border to ***Andorra.** The free state of Andorra (population 40,000) is just 453 sq. km. (172 square miles) in size and is Europe's last surviving feudal protectorate, governed jointly by the French head of state (formerly by the Count of Foix) and the Spanish bishop of Seo d'Urgel. This tiny republic's tax exempt status has led to an unfortunate situation: The ceaseless demand for duty-free goods has turned even the smallest villages on the main road into concrete shopping nightmares—casual visitors expecting traditional charm will be sorely disappointed.

Livestock breeding and a traditional Andorran way of life is still practiced in a few isolated hamlets in the side valleys off the main road. The road climbs up to the *Port d'Envalira,* where you have a view of the *Cirque dels Pessons,* a basin-shaped valley dotted with small lakes. Continue through the valley of the *Valira del Orient* and the rugged narrow pass of *Enamp* at 1,300 meters (3,608 feet) to

Andorra

Andorra la Vella (population 10,900), where the Andorran Parliament meets in a 16th-century building.

Return to the fork. Route N 20 goes back by way of *l'Hospitalet* and **Ax-les-Thermes* (see Travel Route 12), a spa of ancient origin

and birthplace of the architect François Mansart (1598–1666). The town has remains of a 13th-century hospital bathing pool. Continue downhill to *Tarascon-sur-Ariège*. Here you see two towers, one rising from an old castle, the other from the 15th-century church of Saint-Michel. You will find the church of La Daurade with a 16th-century door. The Romanesque Nôtre-Dame-de-Sabart is situated at the junction of two valleys. From here the Pyrenees route heads west, via D 618.

Just south of *Tarascon-sur-Ariège*, Route D 8 leads to the **Grotte de Niaux,* a cave with remarkably well-preserved prehistoric animal paintings.

Back on Route D 618, you'll pass the *Col de Port* continuing for 58 km. (36 miles) to *Saint-Girons.* Route D 618 goes west through

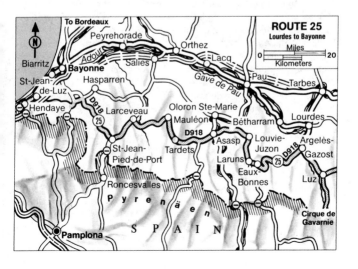

ROUTE 25
Lourdes to Bayonne

the valley of the Lez up to the *Col de Portet d'Aspet,* where you get a panoramic view, and then downhill, into the valley of the Garonne River. Cross the river via the Pont de Chaum and continue on Route N 125 south, through the charming *Vallée de Luchon* to *Bagnères-de-Luchon,* simply known as ***Luchon** (population 3,900), the most fashionable resort of the Pyrenees and close to the well-equipped winter sports area at *Superbagnères,* just 18 km. (11 miles) up a road, where the view is especially good. Used as a bathing resort by the ancient Romans, Luchon has 68 springs, including the *Lepape* spring. The springs fell into disuse and were not rediscovered until the 18th century, when new promenades were laid out. The *Musée du Pays de Luchon,* concerned with local history and culture, is worth a brief visit. The railroad station for the train to Superbagnères, the thermal springs, and the delightful *Parc des Quinconces* are all located on the *Allées d'Etigny,* the town's main street. You can see the old village around the 19th-century *Nôtre-Dame,* which has a preserved 16th-century doorway from an earlier church on the site.

The Pyrenees Road becomes even more breathtaking from this point on.

From Luchon, Route D 618 continues to *Saint-Aventin,* whose 12th-century church has capitals on its porch depicting the life of the saint; inside is a Romanesque basin for holy water and 12th-century ironwork. A side road goes off for 5 km. (3 miles) to the picturesque **Vallée d'Oueil,* with it superb lookout point, *Ciosque de Mayrègne.* Route D 618 climbs to the **Col de Peyresourde* (1,563 meters; 5,126 feet) with a good view of a glacier and the mountains of Luchon. Route D 618 descends to *Arreau,* where it meets Route D 918. (To the south, a tunnel goes to Bielsa in Spain and on to Huesca.) Continue on D 918 to the **Col d'Aspin* and its fine view. The road down the pass leads, via the marble quarry of *Carrière de Marbre de Campan,* to *Sainte-Marie-de-Campan,* where D 918 turns south through a hairpin curve and then continues uphill toward the *Col du Tourmalet,* the highest main-road pass of the Pyrenees. This is one of the toughest segments of the "Tour de France" bicycle race. Continue through the recently developed winter ski resort of *La Mongie,* where a cable car carries passengers to the *Pic du Midi de Bigorre.* Route D 918 continues to climb steeply through relatively unspoiled mountain scenery, finally reaching the ***Col du Tourmalet** at 2,114 meters (6,934 feet). A toll road goes up to the summit of the **Pic du Midi de Bigorre* at 2,865 meters (9,397 feet), which offers an unsurpassed view across the Pyrenees and the Gascogne region. The **Observatoire et Institut de Physique du Globe,* the geophysical observatory and institute founded in 1880, is located just below the peak.

Drive downhill on Route D 918

to *Barèges*, a mountaineering and ski center as well as a health resort that first became popular after a visit by Madame de Maintenon in 1677. There is a cable car to the *Pic d'Ayré*. Continue through the valley meadows to *Luz*, a charming village with the Gave de Bastan flowing through it. It has a strange church built by the knights of Saint-John of Jerusalem in the 12th and 13th century that is surrounded by fortified ramparts. *Saint-Sauveur-les-Bains*, on the west bank of the Gave de Gavarnie, is the twin town of Luz. The ruins of a château from the 14th and 15th centuries overlook the two villages to the north.

Take D 921 through the magnificent and rugged countryside of the *Gorge de Saint-Sauveur* and the stony *Chaos de Coumélie*, past the hydroelectric power plant of *Pragnères*, and into the magnificent **Cirque de Garvarnie,** situated at 1,670 meters (5,477 feet), an enormous natural amphitheater with steep vertical walls rising in terraces to a summit comprised of half a dozen snow-covered peaks. About 30 waterfalls, including the glacier-fed *Grande Cascade*, Europe's highest, plummet into this basin.

From Luz, the Pyrenees road leads via Route D 921 through the *Gorge de Luz* and down to the health resort of *Argelès-Gazost*, where it meets Route D 918. You can take a 13-km. (8-mile) side trip to *Lourdes* (see Travel Route 23).

From Argelès-Gazost, the narrow Route D 918 climbs 30 km.

(18 miles) up to the *Col d'Aubisque* (1,710 meters; 5,600 feet) with its splendid view, and then winds its way high above the *Cirque du Litor*. The beautiful drive descends via the ski resort of *Gouretta* (with a cable car to the *Pic de Ger*) and the little spa of *Eaux-Bonnes*, whose sulphurous waters helped to cure Bearnais troops wounded in 1525 in Pavia. The drive ends at *Laruns*. Here, in the scenic *Vallée d'Ossau*, where routes D 918 and D 934 run north together, continue north on D 918 to *Louvie-Juzon*, then turn west and continue through the *Bois du Bager* to *Assap*.

In Assap, Route N 132 crosses the Pyrenees Road and goes south through the Vallée d'Aspe to the *Col du Somport* and the Spanish border. Continue instead on Route D 918 to the pleasant village of *Tardets*, gateway to the Basque country of Navarre. Continue through *Mauleon-Licharre*, dominated by ruins of a 15th-century castle and with a Renaissance building in the center of town. Then go over the *Col d'Osquich* to **Saint-Jean-Pied-de-Port** (population 1,900), named thus because of its position at the foot of the pass of Roncesvalles, where Charles the Great fought off the Basques. The town is situated on the banks of the Nive River. A citadel and the fortified lower town remain from the 16th century. The narrow *Rue de la Citadelle*, lined with 16th- and 17th-century houses, climbs to the *Porte Saint-Jacques*, which is part of earlier defenses erected in the 15th century. A good view of the old houses built along the Nive may be found at the *Porte d'Espagne.*

Continue on D 918 northwest, past remote Basque villages like *Bidarray,* with a Medieval bridge; *Louhossoa,* whose great church tower carries a 17th-century external stair; *Itxassou,* an ancient place known for its cherries; and *Cambo-les-Bains,* a village for convalescents. From the village of *Espelette,* you can make a side trip of 6 km. (3.5 miles) via Route D 20 to the charming and typical Basque village of *Aïnhoa* with its 17th-century houses.

D 918 continues through *Saint-Pée-sur-Nivelle,* where you will find a ruined 16th-century château and an early-15th-century keep, to the Atlantic Ocean, which it reaches at *Saint-Jean-de-Luz* (see Travel Route 11).

The Pyrenees Road runs from *Luchon* to *Hendaye,* a distance of 343 km. (206 miles).

The village of Conques was an important stop for pilgrims journeying to the grave of Saint James in Santiago di Compostela, Spain.

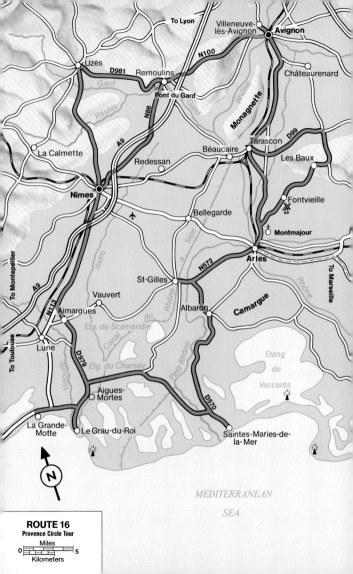

ROUTE 16
Provence Circle Tour

Miles
0   5
Kilometers

Nantua
Geneva
St-Julien
Annemasse
Bonneville
Cluses
Martigny
SWITZERLAND

N205
Chamonix
Sallanches
Flumet N212
Mégève
Courmayeur

Annecy
Lac du Bourget
N201
17
Belley
To Lyon
Rhône
Lac d'Annecy
Albertville
Bourg-St-Maurice
Aosta

Aix-les-Bains
N90

Chambery
C. du Granier
Challes les
Eaux
Moutiers
Val d'Isère
Col de l'Iseran
2769
18

ITALY

Chartreuse
N90
St-Michel-de-
Maurienne
Lanslebourg
D902

Grenoble
Vizille
Valloire
C. du Galibier
2556
C. du
Lautaret
2058
Susa
Turin (Torino)

To Valence
Vif
Laffrey
Briançon
Pinerolo
Po

Monestier-
de Clermont
La Mure
Corps
C. d'Izoard
2360
Château-
Queyras

C. de la
Croix-Haute
1176
Drac
D902
Guillestre
A
N75
B
Chorges
Col de
Vars
St-Paul

Aspres-
sur-B.
Gap
Col de Larche
1991
Cuneo

Tallard
Barcellonnette
D902
Vinadio
To Savona

Serres
C. de la
Cayolle
2326

Sisteron
Colmars
18
C. de
Valberg 1669
Beuil
Col de
Lombarde
2350

Château-
Arnoux
Digne
Guillaumes
Gorges
de Daluis
N202
Puget-Théniers

N
17
St-Andre-les-
Alpes
Entrevaux
Ventimiglia

Barrême
Castellane
B
Monte Carlo
Menton

A
N85
Nice

Grasse
N7
Antibes

ROUTES 17 AND 18
Geneva to Nice

Miles
0   20
Kilometers

Cannes
To Marseille

Three panoramic roads—the corniches of the Riviera—offer superb views along the Côte d'Azur.

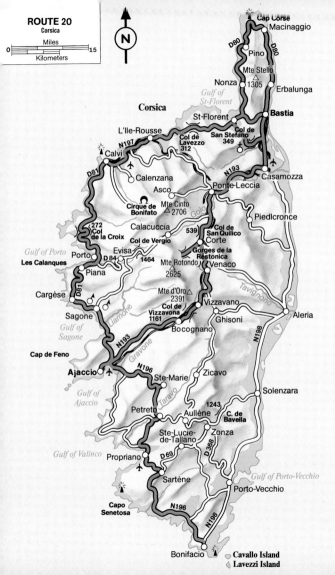

The island of Corsica is best known for the rugged beauty of its beaches, coves, and mountain peaks.

The highest sand dune in France, the Dune du Pilat, rises over 100 meters (328 feet) and extends south of Arcachon.

Reached by cable car, the summit of Le Brévent provides a majestic view of Mont Blanc, the highest peak in the Alps.

Practical Information

The following chapter is divided into two sections. The first, **General Trip Planning,** offers information you'll need for planning and researching your trip as well as tips on transportation to and around France and other items of interest. (See listing in Contents for the full range of subjects covered.)

The second section, **Town-by-Town,** is organized alphabetically by town and provides information that will be helpful on site, such as local tourist offices, hotels, and transportation.

General Trip Planning

Choosing When to Go. Travelling in France can be splendid in all seasons. At any time of the year there is an area of the country suitable for vacationing, and Paris is superb in any season.

Winter is the time to revel in the beautiful vistas of ski resorts, such as Alpe d'Huez, located in the Isère region, and Chamonix and Mégève, both situated in the Haute-Savoie region. Fall is perfect for visiting the wine-harvesting areas of Alsace, Bordeaux, Burgundy, and Champagne. Spring flowers in the provinces, making them appear like the veritable Elysian Fields, and the summer offers festivals of every kind, especially in Paris, where it is the cultural high season. In June, Paris holds its International Air Show (usually in odd-numbered years) and Strasbourg has its International Music Festival; in July, Paris hosts the Tour de France, the famous bicycle race, and Reims has the annual French Grand Prix, the equally famous auto race.

France's peak season lasts from May to September. During the off-peak season, prices in hotels can be reduced by as much as 30 percent— except in resort hotels. July and August are good months to visit France, due to the fine weather and the fact that most French people are on vacation. However, keep in mind that many restaurants and shops in the larger cities may be closed for one month during the summer season.

Average Temperature and Climate. France's climate is delightfully mild throughout the year. Most of France lies in the temperate zone, which accounts for the moderate climate and lack of extreme fluctuation in temperature. The western region (Nantes, Brest, and Rennes) receives a greater amount of precipitation than the rest of France; the eastern region (Dijon, Lyon, and Strasbourg) has cooler winters and hotter summers; the southern region (Biarritz, Toulouse, and Marseille) has warmer temperatures in both summer and winter, but there is no humidity; and the northern region (Lille, Rouen, and Reims) has colder weather in winter and comfortable temperatures in summer.

The temperature in France is measured in degrees centigrade. Below is a listing of average daily temperatures in centigrade and Fahrenheit by month in France:

Average Daily Temperatures

	January F°	January C°	February F°	February C°	March F°	March C°
Brest	43	7	43	6	47	9
Paris	39	4	40	4	46	8
Nice	48	8	48	9	51	11
Corsica	47	8	47	9	51	11

	April F°	April C°	May F°	May C°	June F°	June C°
Brest	49	10	53	12	58	15
Paris	52	11	58	15	64	18
Nice	56	13	62	17	68	20
Corsica	55	13	60	16	66	20

	July F°	July C°	August F°	August C°	September F°	September C°
Brest	61	16	61	16	59	15
Paris	67	20	67	17	62	17
Nice	73	23	73	23	69	21
Corsica	71	22	71	22	68	21

	October F°	October C°	November F°	November C°	December F°	December C°
Brest	54	12	48	9	45	7
Paris	53	12	45	8	40	5
Nice	62	17	54	12	48	9
Corsica	62	17	55	13	49	10

National Holidays. Listed below are the national holidays in France. Specific dates for some holidays vary from year to year.

New Year's Day (January 1)
Easter Monday
Labor Day (May 1)
European Armistice Day of 1945 (May 8)
Ascension (5 weeks after Easter)

Pentecôte (Whitmonday)
National Day (July 14; capture of the Bastille in 1789)
Assumption (August 15)
All Saints' Day (November 1)
Armistice Day of 1918 (November 11)
Christmas (December 25)

It is especially important to remember that virtually everything closes during holidays. If you intend to drive, make certain that your gas tank is full because gas stations will probably not be open.

Metric/U.S. Weight, Measure, Temperature Equivalents.
Throughout the text, metric weights and measures are followed by U.S. equivalents in parentheses; likewise, Fahrenheit degrees are provided for centigrade temperatures. The following table is a quick reference for U.S. and metric equivalents.

Metric Unit	U.S. Equivalent	U.S. Unit	Metric Equivalent
Length		**Length**	
1 kilometer	0.6 miles	1 mile	1.6 kilometers
1 meter	1.09 yards	1 yard	0.9 meters
1 decimeter	0.3 feet	1 foot	3.04 decimeters
1 centimeter	0.39 inches	1 inch	2.5 centimeters
Weight		**Weight**	
1 kilogram	2.2 pounds	1 pound	0.45 kilograms
1 gram	0.03 ounces	1 ounce	28.3 grams
Liquid Capacity		**Liquid Capacity**	
1 dekaliter	2.38 gallons	1 gallon	0.37 dekaliters
1 liter	1.05 quarts	1 quart	0.9 liters
1 liter	2.1 pints	1 pint	0.47 liters

(*Note: there are 5 British Imperial gallons to 6 U.S. gallons.*)

Dry Measure		**Dry Measure**	
1 liter	0.9 quarts	1 quart	1.1 liters
1 liter	1.8 pints	1 pint	0.55 liters

To convert centigrade (C°) to Fahrenheit (F°):
$C° \times 9 \div 5 + 32 = F°$.
To convert Fahrenheit to centigrade:
$F° - 32 \times 5 \div 9 = C°$.

Time Zones. Paris is on Central European Time (one hour ahead of Greenwich Mean Time and six hours ahead of Eastern Standard Time). Therefore, if it is noon in New York and Toronto, Canada, it is 6:00 P.M. in Paris; and when it is noon in London, it is 1:00 P.M. in Paris. There is a 14-

hour time difference between Sydney, Australia, and Paris. Therefore, when it is noon in Sydney, it is 2:00 A.M. the following day in Paris.

France observes Daylight Savings Time (Central European Time plus one hour) from early April until late September. Remember that the French use a 24-hour clock to differentiate between the morning and evening hours. Therefore, midnight is expressed as 2400 hours; 1:00 A.M. is 0100 hours; noon is 1200 hours; 1:00 P.M. is 1300 hours, etc.

Passport and Visa Requirements. Since 1986, French customs require all visitors entering France to carry a visa. These forms can be obtained through your travel agent or a French consulate. You can get a visa for a period of time lasting from one week to several months. All visitors to France must also carry a valid passport to gain entrance into the country.

Customs Entering France. Personal items used for professional or private purposes (i.e., jewelry, cameras, watches, radios, portable type-writers, etc.) do not have to be declared upon arrival in France. There is no limit on the amount of national currency and foreign bank notes that can be brought into the country. In the case of foreign bank notes worth 5,000 francs or more, you should fill out a special form called a "Declaration of Foreign Currency Brought into France." It can be obtained from any customs office. There is no declaration requirement on forms of payment such as traveller's checks and letters of credit.

Customs Returning Home from France. To simplify passage through customs, travellers who have nothing to declare are now commonly given a green card. Travellers with goods that have to be declared must follow the red signs.

If you travel with items from home that were manufactured abroad (i.e., cameras), carry all receipts with you so that you will not have to pay duty.

U.S. residents may bring back $400 worth of foreign goods duty free to the U.S. A 10 percent duty is levied on the retail value of the next $1,000 worth of merchandise. Beyond $1,400 worth of merchandise, the rate of duty is decided by the customs officer. Exempt merchandise includes no more than one liter of alcohol, 100 cigars, 200 cigarettes, and one bottle of perfume.

You may also ship goods duty free if you mail them to a residence other than your own. Packages must be marked "Unsolicited Gift—Value Under $50."

U.S. citizens may find it helpful to obtain "Know Before You Go," a publication provided by the U.S. Customs Service which lists all goods you are prohibited from bringing home, including products from endangered species. Contact: U.S. Customs Service, Customs Information,

Room 201, 6 World Trade Center, New York, N. Y. 10048; tel. (212) 466-5550.

Canadian residents may return with $150 worth of foreign purchases duty free if you have been out of the country for two days, or $300 if you have been out of the country for seven days. Canadians may also return with 40 ounces of alcohol, 50 cigars, 200 cigarettes, and two pounds of tobacco. You can also send packages duty free marked "Unsolicited Gift—Value Under $40."

Australians over the age of 18 may return with $400 worth of foreign articles, one liter of alcohol, and 250 grams of tobacco products.

Residents of Great Britain may return with £250 worth of foreign goods, 200 cigarettes, 50 cigars, one liter of alcohol, and 50 grams of perfume.

Embassies and Consulates in France. Help and information can be obtained from the following offices:

American Embassy
2, Avenue Gabriel
F 75008 Paris
tel. (1) 42 96 12 02

U.S. Consulates:

4, Rue Esprit-des-Lois
F 33000 Bordeaux
tel. 56 65 95 00

9, Rue Armeny
F 13006 Marseille
tel. 91 54 92 00

7, Quai Général-Sarrail
F 69006 Lyon
tel. 78 24 68 49

2, Rue St. Florentin
F 75001 Paris
tel. (1) 42 60 14 88

15, Avenue d'Alsace
F 67000 Strasbourg
tel. 88 35 31 04

Canadian Embassy
35, Avenue Montaigne
F 75008 Paris
tel. (1) 47 23 01 01

Canadian Consulates:

4, Rue Ventadour
F 75001 Paris
tel. (1) 40 73 15 83

Croix du Mail
Rue Claude-Bonnier
F 33008 Bordeaux
tel. 56 96 15 61

24, Avenue du Prado
F 13006 Marseille
tel. 91 37 19 37

10, Place du Temple-Neuf
F 67007 Strasbourg
tel. 88 32 65 96

Australian Embassy
4, Rue Jean Rey
F 75008 Paris
tel. (1) 45 74 62 60

British Embassy
109, Rue de Faubourg Saint-Honoré
F 75008 Paris
tel. (1) 42 66 91 42

British Consulates:

15, Cours de Verdun F 33081 Bordeaux tel. 56 52 28 35	24, Rue Childbert F 69388 Lyon tel. 78 37 59 67
11, Square Dutilleul F 59800 Lille tel. 20 52 87 90	24, Avenue du Prado F 13006 Marseille tel. 91 53 43 32

10, Rue du Général de Castelnau
F 67001 Strasbourg
tel. 88 36 64 91

French Embassies and Consulates.

In the U.S.:

French Embassy 444 North Michigan Ave., Suite 3140 Chicago, Ill. 60611 tel. (312) 787-5359	934 Fifth Avenue New York, N.Y. 10021 tel. (212) 606-3600

8350 Wilshire Blvd., Suite 310
Beverly Hills, Calif. 90211
tel. (213) 653-3120

French consulates are also located in Boston, Detroit, Houston, Miami, New Orleans, Puerto Rico, San Francisco, and Washington, D.C.

In Canada:

French Embassy 42, Promenade Sussex Ottawa, Ont. K1M 2C9 tel. (613) 232-1795	1201-736 Granville Street Vancouver, B.C. V6Z 1H9 tel. (604) 681-2301

1110 Avenue des Laurentides
Quebec, P.Q. G1S 3C3
tel. (514) 688-0430

French consulates are also located in Moncton, Montreal, and Toronto.

In Great Britain:
French Embassy

58 Knightsbridge   24 Rutland Gate
London SW1 7JT   London SW7
tel. (01) 235-8080   tel. (01) 581-5292

11 Randolph Crescent
Edinburgh EH3 7TT
tel. (01) 225-7954

There are currently no French consulates located in Australia.

Getting to France by Air. *From the U.S.:* The major air carriers flying from the United States to France include Aeromexico, Air France, American, Continental, Delta, Egypt Air, Pakistan International, Pan Am, and TWA.

From Great Britain: The major air carriers that fly from Great Britain to France include Air France, Jersey, Aer Lingus, Air U.K., Aurigny Air, Brit Air, British Airways, British Caledonian, British Midland Airways, Dan Air, Swissair, Touraine Air Transport, and Air Vendée.

From Canada: The major air carriers that fly nonstop from Canada to France include Air Canada, Air France, and Canadian Airlines.

From Australia: The major air carriers that fly from Australia nonstop to France are UTA and KLM. Quantas Air, British Airways, and Air France also fly to France with stopovers in Germany, Hong Kong, and London.
There is a bewildering variety of ever-changing special fares, hotel packages, fly-drive, and other deals that depend upon the travel season, the amount of time you can spend, the number of places you wish to visit, etc. You also have the option of flying the Concorde via Air France, which flies from New York to Paris in about four hours; the fare is approximately 20 percent higher than the amount you would pay for first class on a regular airline. Keep an eye on the advertisements in your newspaper's travel section, and make your travel arrangements through a reliable travel agent or tour operator to get the best fares and packages.

Getting to France by Boat. The only transatlantic passenger ship that sails from North America to France is the Cunard Lines' *Queen Elizabeth II* which sails from April to December between New York, Great Britain, and France. Although expensive, an ocean cruise is a sumptuous, relaxing way to travel. More detailed information can be obtained from travel agencies, or you can contact:

Cunard Lines
555 Fifth Avenue
New York, N.Y. 10017
tel. (212) 880-7500
Nationwide reservation: 1-800-5-Cunard

You can also travel to France cross-Channel from Great Britain. There are a number of ferries that shuttle passengers back and forth between various ports in France and Great Britain. The services include the Brittany ferries, the Condor (a hydrofoil service), Emeraude ferries, the Hoverspeed, Sally Line ferries, Sealink ferries, and Townsend Thoresen ferries.

Hotels and Other Accommodations. France offers an abundance and variety of wonderful accommodations. You can choose to spend your evenings in an opulent hotel, settle into a cozy inn, or rent a private apartment in Paris.

You can get free information about accommodations from any French Government Tourist Office before you leave home, or get it in the Office de Tourisme in towns throughout France. Every year the government issues its "Guide des Hôtels de France," which gives a complete listing of the better hotels and their price ranges. The pamphlet can be obtained from French Government Tourist Offices or from Bureaux et Service de l'Annuaire, 94 Boulevard Beaumarchais, F 75011 Paris.

In this guide, accommodations have been classified according to our four categories: Luxury (🏨🏨🏨); First Class (🏨🏨🏨); Good (🏨🏨); and Less Expensive (🏨). Both Luxury and First Class are delineated by three stars, a designation that indicates the quality of service and accommodations. The higher prices for luxury hotels are reflected in the amenities they offer.

It is always advisable to book rooms in advance, especially during the high season. The peak travel season extends from May to October, when rates are highest and hotels are the most crowded.

Note: While most hotel rooms include some type of shower facility, they do not always have bath tubs. If you prefer a tub rather than a shower, check ahead to find out if your hotel can accommodate you.

Château accueil: You can arrange for accommodations in extraordinary châteaux, which are usually occupied by private owners who let rooms for high prices. These fees are more easily overlooked when you are in the breathtaking surroundings in which these châteaux are frequently located. Reservations can be made through Visafrance, 8, Rue de la République, 78100 Saint-Germain-en-Laye; tel. 30 61 23 30. You can write to this address for information only: Madame de Bonneval,

Château de Thaumiers, Thaumioro 18210 Charenton-du-Cher; tel 48 61 81 62.

You can rent apartments and houses in Paris through Paris Accueil, 485 Madison Avenue, Suite 1310, New York, N.Y. 10022; tel. (212) 838-2444.

Paris Accueil also has listings for Bed and Breakfast establishments located in rural areas.

You can also arrange to stay in former castles, manor houses, and abbeys, all of which have been reconverted for modern use. Contact Relais et Châteaux, 10, Place de la Concorde, 75008 Paris; tel. (1) 47 42 00 20 for information.

Gîtes—Chambres d'Hôte: You can rent a room or rooms in a private house in a village and stay for up to a month. They offer clean accommodations, and the price of a room can include a hearty breakfast and other meals if you arrange it with your host. Contact: La Maison du Tourisme Vert, Fédération Nationale des Gîtes Ruraux de France, 35, Rue Gogot-de-Maury, 75009 Paris; tel. (1) 47 42 20 20.

Bed and Breakfasts: You can stay in a room on a farm or in a village for a few days under the same roof as your host. The price of a room includes breakfast, which can range from a simple Continental affair of coffee, rolls, and jam to a breakfast extravaganza, complete with farm sausages, eggs, and fresh biscuits. For complete information, contact: The French Experience, 171 Madison Avenue, Suite 1505, New York, N.Y. 10016; tel. (212) 683-2445.

Currency Regulations. French currency is based on the franc (FF), which is subdivided into 100 centimes (c). Coins of 10, 3, 2, and 1 FF, and of 50, 20, 10, and 5 centimes are in circulation. Bank notes are in denominations of 500, 200, 100, 50, 20, and 10 francs. The 10 franc notes are being gradually withdrawn from circulation in favor of the 10 franc coins.

French numbers are written as follows: Six thousand francs (6,000 FF) is written as 6.000 FF. However, a smaller number, such as six francs, fifty centimes (6.50) is written as 6,50 FF.

There are no limits on the amount of currency that can be brought into or taken out of the country. But regulations are subject to sudden change, and we recommend that you check with your bank before leaving. Your national currency may be exchanged at most banks or at the airport. Try not to exchange currency at hotels or restaurants, as they usually have less favorable rates and are accompanied by a surcharge. To obtain the best rate of exchange before leaving home, first track currency fluctuations in the newspaper, and then change your money at a bank. One helpful source of information is the International Herald Tribune, written in English and published in Paris.

Business Hours and Closings. Banks are usually open in the cities from 9:00 A.M. to 5:00 P.M., Monday through Friday, with a two-hour lunch break starting at 12:00 noon or 1:00 P.M. Similar hours apply to banks in small villages and towns, which are open from Tuesday to Saturday.

Government offices and businesses are open from 9:00 A.M. to 6:00 P.M., with a two-hour lunch break beginning at 12:00 noon or 1:00 P.M. Department stores are open Monday through Saturday, 9:30 A.M. to 6:30 P.M. One or two nights a week, they may stay open late until 9:00 or 10:00 P.M., and some stores may close Monday mornings. Smaller shops are open from 9:00 A.M. to 5:00 P.M., with the customary lunch break. Food shops are open from 7:30 A.M. until 12:30 P.M., close for about three hours, and reopen from 3:30 P.M. to 7:00 P.M.

Museums are generally closed on Mondays or Tuesdays; check the museum before embarking on a long day's journey, as hours vary greatly. Churches are generally open from 7:00 A.M. to 12:00 noon, and from 3:00 P.M. to 7:00 P.M.

Postage. Post offices are open Monday through Friday, 8:00 A.M. to 7:00 P.M., Saturdays from 8:00 A.M. to 12:00 noon, and on Sundays in smaller towns from 8:00 A.M. to 12:00 noon. The post offices and assistance stations of the Postal, Telegraph, and Telephone Administration (PTT) offer multiple services, ranging from selling stamps and aerograms to sending telegrams and placing long-distance phone calls. (You can also purchase stamps at the local tobacco shop, called a *tabac*.) The main post office in Paris is open 24 hours a day; it is located at 52, Rue du Louvre, 75001 Paris; tel. (1) 42 33 71 60.

Airmail not exceeding 5 grams whose destination is the U.S. costs 4,20 FF. For mail up to 10 grams going to the U.S., it costs 4,80 FF. Airmail to Canada not exceeding 5 grams is 2,80 FF, and up to 10 grams is 3,40 FF. Mail to Great Britain of up to 5 grams costs 2,20 FF, and up to 10 grams is also 2,20 FF. Airmail to Australia not exceeding 5 grams costs 4,50 FF, and up to 10 grams is 5,40 FF.

Telephones. There are three types of telephones available in France. Public pay phones usually take coins, and can be used for local and long-distance calls. Local calls cost one franc. To place a local call, insert coins before dialing. If your party doesn't answer, the coins will be returned when you hang up. If you wish to extend your conversation longer than five minutes, you must continue to feed coins into the machine as you speak.

When you make international calls, just put a handful of coins in the machine; they will automatically drop as you speak. Any coins not used for the duration will be returned after you hang up.

Some public phones only take tokens, called *jetons*. These can be purchased from cashiers in tabacs. To use a token, you must insert it in the telephone and, after your party answers, press the button on the front of the phone for the token to drop and connect you.

Coin telephones are currently being replaced by phones that only accept Télécartes. There are two types of Télécartes: the Bleue Claire, worth 40 unités, or units, and the Bleue Française, worth 120 unités. Each unit is equivalent to 20 minutes of conversation. Télécartes may be purchased at post offices and at railway ticket booths.

For international calls, first dial 19, wait for the dial tone, then dial the country code and the individual subscriber's number. For an operator-assisted call, you can ask for help in placing a collect call—"en PCV" (pronounced *ahn pey sey vhey*)—or for a person-to-person call—"avec preavis" (pronounced *ah veck prey ah vee*). You can also get assistance in a post office when placing international calls by specifying the type of call you wish to place. You will then be directed to a cabine, or booth, and the postal clerk will put your call through. Due to the vast increase in telephone subscription, numbers in France have now expanded to eight digits instead of seven. Paris numbers have the prefix "1," which precedes its eight-digit number.

Travelling in France. From the modern highways to the convenience of the Paris métro system, travelling in France can be a highly pleasurable affair. There is a profusion of transportation alternatives available; depending upon your objective, you can journey leisurely through the countryside by bicycle, drive on highways framed by lovely scenery, take a quick train ride, or travel from town to town by bus.

Taxis. A taxi ride from Roissy/Charles de Gaulle airport to central Paris should run about 170–210 FF, and from Orly airport it should cost about 150–190 FF.

Taxis are ordinarily very hard to hail, with the exception of the Champs-Elysées area; it is better to request that someone from your hotel hail one for you. Try to agree upon a fixed price before you enter the cab to avoid being overcharged. Fares should run approximately 2,50 FF per kilometer during the day and 5,50 FF per kilometer during the evening.

Métro System. Paris has a unique subway system, which extends throughout the city both above the ground and beneath it. You can purchase tickets for 10 rides by asking for "un carnet" (pronounced *uhn car nay*) or "une carte orange" (pronounced *oon cart or ange*), which entitles you to unlimited travel on the subway during the period of one month. You can purchase first- or second-class tickets for the métro.

Air Travel. Perhaps the easiest method of travel between major cities in France is via air. Air Inter and Touraine Air Transport offer inflight domestic travel in any direction within France. You can reach any corner of France in about an hour. Contact Air France, Air Inter's agent at 1, Avenue du Maréchal Devaux, 91550 Paray Vieille-Poste; tel. 46 75 12 12 or 45 39 25 25 for reservations.

Long-Distance Buses. Bus lines are operated by the French National Railways, called the Société Nationale des Chemins de Fer (SNCF), and by many private companies. There are long-distance bus lines, round-trip service through the major tourist areas, and excursion routes from the major cities. For information, contact: Eurolines, 52 Grosvenor Gardens, London SW1; Europabus, Service Routier Voyageurs, 9, Rue Pablo Neruda, 92532 Levalois Perret Cedex, France.

Driving in France. The French road system covers some 700,000 km. (435,000 miles), and is so well maintained that even side roads in out-of-the-way areas are in superb condition. To date, approximately 5,600 km. (3,475 miles) of autoroutes (expressways) have been built in France. Tolls are charged along the autoroutes, depending upon which category your vehicle falls into; i.e., category 1 (passenger cars) or category 2 (passenger cars with trailers).

As in most countries, major traffic jams occur at the start of holiday periods, particularly on August 1, the day on which, by tradition, half of Paris seems to leave the city and stream out to vacation spots throughout France and the Continent.

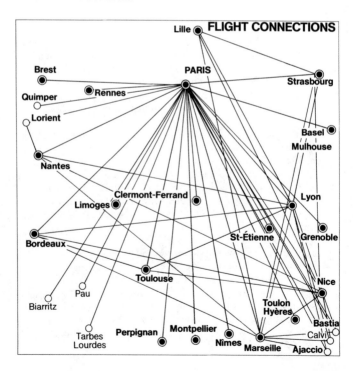

FLIGHT CONNECTIONS

Minimum Age and Documentation All drivers must be at least 18 years old, carry their own national driver's license, and, if driving their own vehicle, have national car-registration papers. A nationality symbol must be displayed on the rear of cars owned by citizens of EEC countries. If you wish, you may obtain an International Driving Permit from your local American Automobile Association (AAA) or AAA headquarters, located in the U.S. at 8111 Gatehouse Road, Falls Church, Va. 22047.

You must also have an International Insurance Certificate green card in your vehicle. It is available through your travel agent or the AAA, and is administered for periods of 8, 15, or 30 days. It is wise to take out temporary insurance through a French company in case of an accident to assure the authorities of your ability to pay potential damages. The Automobile Club de France (ACF), with branches in 50 cities, has its headquarters at 6, Place de la Concorde, 75008 Paris; tel. (1) 42 65 34 70.

Car Rentals. Car rental agencies can be found throughout the country's major cities and at the airports. Major companies such as Avis, Budget, Milleville, Citer, Europcar, Hertz, Interrent, Mattei, Serval, T. T. Car Transit, and others have local branches almost everywhere in France.

Road Warning Signs. You should familiarize yourself with the following words that appear on road signs:

Attention	Caution
Au pas	Proceed slowly
Chantier	Construction site
Danger (de mort)	Danger (of death)
Déviation	Detour
Gravier	Gravel, loose rocks
Halte	Stop
Impasse	No through road
Limitation de vitesse	Speed limit
Passage interdit	Do not enter
Passage protégé	Yield
Priorité à droite	Car to the right has right of way
Ralentir	Reduce speed
Sens unique	One way
Route barrée	Road closed
Virage dangereux	Dangerous curve
Voie unique	Single-lane traffic
Zone bleue	Parking only with special parking sticker
Zone rouge	No parking—tow-away zone

Traffic Regulations. In France, as in the United States, driving is on the right side of the road. The general rule is that the car on the right has the right of way, even in a traffic circle, unless there is a right-of-way sign to the contrary. On inclines, the car going up has the right of way. Drivers

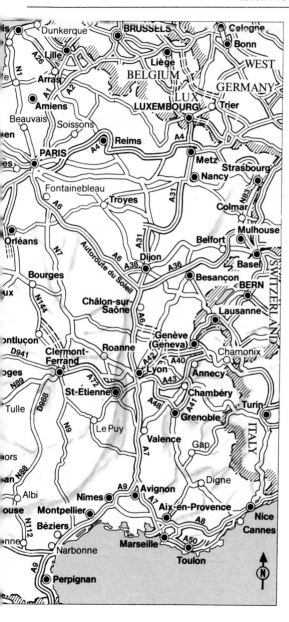

are extremely aggressive in France, so be prepared—especially in congested areas.

Passing is prohibited just before and at intersections and junctions.

Honking in congested areas is only allowed in cases of emergency. Honking is not allowed anywhere at night.

Parking lights are permissible only on well-lighted streets and roads at night.

Gasoline. Unleaded gasoline is available in France and sold by the liter.

Safety Belts. It is compulsory for the driver and the front-seat passenger to use seat belts in the car.

Parking on the roadways is prohibited outside of towns, but it is permitted on unpaved shoulders. Within towns, red-and-yellow or red-and-white stripes on the curb indicate that parking is prohibited. Blocks that have alternate-side-of-the-street parking are marked with signs. *Blue Zones* are areas in which cars displaying a round parking sticker (disques de contrôle) are permitted to park for one hour only from 9:00 A.M. to 12:30 P.M. and from 2:30 P.M. to 7:00 P.M. Parking stickers can be obtained from tourist offices and police stations. The time restrictions do not apply on Sundays and holidays.

Speed limits are 130 km. per hour on the autoroutes; 110 km. on divided highways; 90 km. on other nonurban roads; and 60 km. within towns. When the roadway is wet, the speed limit on autoroutes is 100 km.; on country roads, 80 km.

Traffic accidents. A police report is written up only when personal injury occurs. If there is only property damage, it is customary to settle the matter "à l'aimable," or by mutual agreement. Preprinted forms called "constat à l'aimable" provided with French insurance policies are to be filled out on the spot by each party.

Assistance and towing services are well organized in France. On heavily travelled roads there are emergency call boxes roughly every 4 km. (2.5 miles). The police can be summoned by dialing 17. You may also wish to check up on the condition of the roads you will be travelling that day. Information can be obtained through Centre National Information Routière (CNIR), a 24-hour-a-day service that reports on the weather and general driving conditions; its number in Paris is (1) 48 57 20 83; in Bordeaux 56 44 23 23; in Lille 20 52 22 44; in Lyon 78 54 33 33; and in Marseille 91 47 20 20.

Trains. Train travel is a delightful way to introduce yourself to France's serenely beautiful provinces. There are multiple advantages to taking a train: France's high-speed trains (TGV) are renowned as the swiftest in the world, the plethora of available routes make travel within France and to other countries convenient and affordable and, if you are driving, there are many trains that will transport your car.

The track network of the French National Railways extends for approximately 35,000 km. (21,000 miles) State-owned trains can be divided into four categories: the TGV (Train à Grande Vitesse), the EC (Euro Cité), the IC (Intercité), and the Rapide. The TGV is a train with the highest speed capacity on record, achieving a momentum of up to 280 km. (175 miles) per hour. The new Euro Cité trains have superseded the TEE system (Trans Europe Express), which had formerly been touted as the most efficient train network in Europe. Intercité trains are second-class cars that have been joined to the old TEE cars; they travel shorter distances. The Rapide is a fast train that makes limited stops. Information on schedules and brochures are available at major train stations and at travel agencies throughout France. You may also obtain information from the following French National Railways offices:

In the U.S.:

610 Fifth Avenue
Rockefeller Center
New York, N.Y. 10020
tel. (212) 582-2816

11 East Adams Street
Chicago, Ill. 60603
tel. (312) 427-8691

323 Geary Street
San Francisco, Calif. 94102
tel. (415) 982-1993

In Canada:

1500 Stanley Street, Suite 436
Montreal, Quebec H3A 1R3
tel. (514) 288-8255/6

409 Granville Street, Suite 452
Vancouver, B.C. V6C 1T2
tel. (604) 688-6707

55 University Place, Suite 600
Toronto, Ontario MSJ 2E7
tel. (416) 368-8639

In Great Britain:

179 Piccadilly
London, England W1V OBA
tel. (01) 499 21 53

There is no office currently located in Australia.

The central information office (Paris) for schedules and general inquiries is open daily from 7:00 A.M. to 10:00 P.M.; tel. (1) 45 82 50 50. The trains run on two schedules: summer, which begins in June, and winter, which begins in October. The central reservations office in Paris is open daily from 8:00 A.M. to 8:00 P.M.; tel. (1) 45 65 60 60. There is also a general information number for English-speaking tourists: (1) 45 82 08 41.

Different kinds of passes are offered for train travel; there are a variety of discounts available depending upon your individual agenda. Each

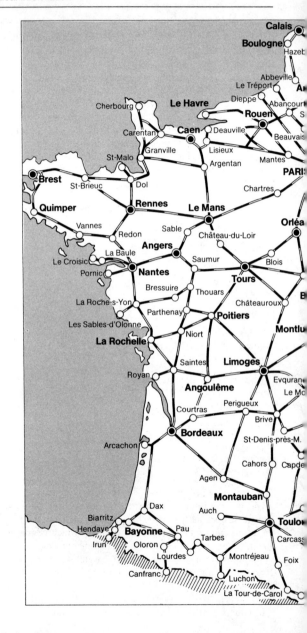

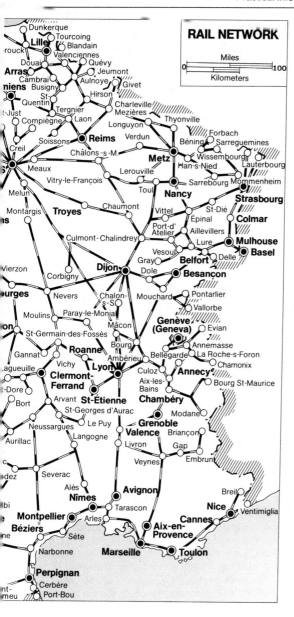

RAIL NETWORK

Miles

0 ⊢———————————⊣ 100

Kilometers

Dunkerque
Tourcoing
Lille
Blandain
rouck
Valenciennes
Douai
Quévy
Arras
Jeumont
Cambrai
Aulnoye
Givet
niens
Busigny
St-
Quentin
Hirson
t-Just
Tergnier
Charleville
Mézières
Compiègne
Laon
Longuyon
Thyonville
Soissons
Verdun
Forbach
Creil
Reims
Béning
Sarreguemines
Châlons-s-M.
Metz
Wissembourg
Meaux
Han-s-Nied
Lauterbourg
Lerouville
Sarrebourg
Mommenheim
Vitry-le-François
Toul
Nancy
Strasbourg
Melun
Chaumont
Vittel
St-Dié
Montargis
Troyes
Port-d'
Epinal
Colmar
s
Atelier
Aillevillers
Mulhouse
Culmont-Chalindrey
Lure
Basel
Vesoul
Belfort
Delle
Vierzon
Corbigny
Dijon
Gray
Besançon
Dole
urges
Nevers
Chalon-
Mouchard
Pontarlier
Moulins
s-S
Vallorbe
Paray-le-Monial
Gannat
St-Germain-des-Fossès
Mâcon
Genève
(Geneva)
Evian
on
Roanne
Bourg
Annemasse
aguelle
Vichy
Ambérieu
Bellegarde
La Roche-s-Foron
Clermont-
Lyon
Culoz
Chamonix
-Dore
Ferrand
Aix-les-
Annecy
Bort
Arvant
St-Étienne
Bains
Bourg St-Maurice
St-Georges d'Aurac
Chambéry
Neussargues
Le Puy
Modane
Aurillac
Langogne
Grenoble
Valence
Briançon
Livron
Gap
c
Severac
Veynes
Embrun
dez
Alès
Avignon
Breil
Ibi
Nîmes
Nice
e
Tarascon
Cannes
Ventimiglia
Montpellier
Arles
Béziers
Aix-en-
ne
Sète
Provence
Narbonne
Marseille
Toulon
Perpignan
Cerbère
nt-
meu
Port-Bou

pass requires that you journey during specific days and times. Most discount passes only entitle you to travel during the periode bleue (blue period), which designates off-peak travel from noon on Monday to noon on Friday, and noon on Saturday to 3:00 P.M. on Sunday. Periode blanche (white period) tickets are valid for peak hour travel, from noon on Friday to noon on Saturday, and 3:00 P.M. on Sunday to noon on Monday. The periode rouge (red period) tickets correspond to dates when traffic is anticipated to be heavy—i.e., on holidays.

All tickets may be purchased at the railroad station or at travel agencies displaying the official SNCF sign. It is advisable to buy your ticket before your train departs, as there is an additional 10 percent fine added to the regular cost if you board without it. You can guarantee your seat by making a reservation (it is required to reserve on all TGV lines and during holidays to ensure your place). When you reserve ahead, you may also specify a smoking versus a nonsmoking car, a window seat, or a private compartment. You can also reserve seats by telephone.

First-class tickets cost 50 percent more than second-class tickets. Remember to stamp your ticket manually before boarding; composteurs, or stamping machines, are located in every station. If you fail to do this, your ticket will not be valid and cannot be honored on the train. You will then have to pay the cost of a new ticket plus an additional 20 percent fine. Remember also if you make a brief stop along your journey, you must restamp your ticket before reboarding the train.

Sleeping Accommodations: Most trains have sleeping accommodations. You can choose between a couchette (sleeping berth), of which there are four in first class and six in second class; a voiture-lit, which includes washing facilities; or a cabines 8, a semi-reclining lounger in second class. The conductor can provide you with a 15-minute wake-up call before a station stop.

Trains plus Transportation: The SNCF's *Train and Auto* service reserves cars for train passengers with pickup in over 150 cities. Through the *Train and Velo* service, the SNCF offers bicycles for rent at more than 200 train stations in France upon presentation of a personal identification document and a deposit. The TAC (Trains Autos Couchettes) and the TAJ (Trains Autos Jours) are car-carrying trains that travel to limited destinations.

There are also a number of reduced-fare programs available:

Billet de Séjour. This is a 25 percent discount for travel within France for a minimum round-trip distance of 1,000 km. (620 miles) in first or second class. You must travel at least 200 km. each way. The journey must begin during a blue (off-peak) period, and must be extended to include a Sunday or a holiday. Tickets are valid for two months.

Carte Vermeil. Senior citizens (men 62 years of age and older, and women 60 years of age and older) may purchase the Carte Vermeil, entitling them to purchase tickets at a 50 percent discount of the basic fare. The Carte Vermeil pass is valid for one year, and any tickets purchased are valid for two months. This card also entitles the holder to purchase the Rail Europe card for international travel in either first or second class, with a 30–50 percent fare reduction for any time period travelled.

France Railpass. This card is good for all routes in the SNCF rail network, and is available for first or second class. It is valid for longer periods of travel; with four nonconsecutive days of travel, which must be used within a 15-day period; nine nonconsecutive days, which must be used within one month; or 16 nonconsecutive days, which must also be used within one month. The card entitles the purchaser to multiple bonuses, such as free first-class travel to the Paris airports (Orly and Roissy/Charles de Gaulle), up to two days' free car rental, and unlimited travel up to two days on the Paris bus and subway system.

France Saverpass. This pass is economical for two people travelling together; the discount price includes nine nonconsecutive days of travel to be taken within one month. Dates for this offer are limited to the period from October through March 31.

Eurail Pass: This pass allows the traveller unlimited first-class travel on rail networks through 16 European countries. Passes are valid for 15 days, 21 days, or one, two, or three months, and entitle travellers to a variety of special discounts. There is a *Eurail Youthpass* for travellers under 26 years of age, allowing unlimited second-class rail travel on passes valid for one or two months. The *Eurail Saverpass* offers unlimited first-class travel to three or more people travelling together. The pass is valid for 15 days. All passes must be used within six months.

Further reduced fares: A *Family Card* gives a 50 percent reduction for the second person or two people travelling together. This pass is valid for five years. With an R.E.F. (Rail Europe Famille), families of at least three can travel first or second class with a reduction for all but one person. This pass is also valid for trips out of France. Similarly, a *Billet de Groupe* permits you a 20 percent reduction in first or second class with a group of six people or more.

There are many combinations of family reduced fares. The *Familles Nombreuses* pass is offered to a group with at least three children, one of whom must be 18 years old. This results in an individual fare reduction of 30–75 percent for each parent and child more than 18 years old. Children under four years of age ride for free if you do not request a separate seat. A *Billet Bambin* entitles a child to his or her own seat at a fare discount of 75 percent. There is a 50 percent fare reduction for children ages 4–12, which can be extended to a 75 percent reduction for children if their parents hold a *Family Card.*

Restaurants. France is renowned throughout the world for its superb cuisine. From chic dining establishments to humble cafés, France offers a wide range of cooking that will satisfy and delight any discriminating palate.

Most social activity between the French occurs in restaurants and cafés, especially in Paris, where it is unusual to be invited to someone's house for dinner. Friends usually meet to talk over wine or drinks and a meal. Therefore, it is especially important to make dinner reservations in advance in larger cities to ensure seating.

Cafés are fantastic places to grab a bite and watch the world go by. The French take eating very seriously; it is not unusual to linger over a cup of café exprès for two hours. Cafés generally offer a selection of light sandwiches and salads, and beverages that include soft drinks, an assortment of coffees, wine, and hard liquor. Cafés are generally open from mid-morning to late in the evening, when their menus will sometimes list dinner selections.

One of the most exciting food establishments to visit is a *pâtisserie.* The French shop at pâtisseries daily for bread and especially on weekends to purchase a special tart or cake for the Sunday family dinner. Pâtisseries offer a superlative assortment of pastries—which are probably the best in the world—and baguettes, long loaves of bread that are crisp on the outside and soft on the inside. Try a pain au chocolat (bread with chocolate) or a crusty baguette with fresh farm butter. You will see why pâtisseries are considered a necessary element for the French diet!

Tipping. If the check at a restaurant or a café does not say "Service Compris" (charge for service included), a tip of 15 percent is expected. General guidelines for tipping should be as follows: Porters should receive 5 FF per bag; the chambermaid should receive 10 FF per day; cinema ushers should receive 2 FF; hairdressers should receive 10 percent of your bill; tour guides should receive 5 FF; and taxi drivers should receive 10–15 percent of the total charge.

Electricity. France runs on 220 volts in most areas, although there may be some towns or private homes where 110 voltage is still used. You should buy an adapter for your electrical appliances.

Sports. Among the many sports that are assiduously followed in France, there are spectator sports, like soccer, and there are participant sports, such as hang gliding, water skiing, parachuting, cycling, fishing, tennis, golf, sailing, and horseback riding. Listed below are some vacation alternatives to suit your preferences.

Resorts and Spas. On the Channel, the Atlantic, and the Mediterranean, there are numerous resorts and spas. Prices are modest in many of them, although such famous international watering places as Le Touquet-Paris-Plage, Trouville-Deauville, La Baule, Royan, Biarritz, Nice, Saint-Tropez, Saint-Raphael, and Cannes are much more expensive. Newer vacation resorts have been built to the west of Marseille all the way to Peripignan. Spas are also very popular in France, and are widely visited by vacationers and those who seek therapeutic assistance. Many people frequent spas for the health-giving atmosphere and water, which is believed to purify the system. There are over 90 thermal spas in the Vosges, Auvergne, and Pyrénées areas. For information, contact: Syndicat National des Établissements Thermaux de France, 10, Rue Clemont-Marot, 75008 Paris.

Ballooning. Excursions may be taken in balloons over the wine-growing hills of Burgundy from May through October. For information, contact: Centre Aérostatique de Conlommiers, 21200 Beaune; or Fédération Française d'Aérostation (F.F.A.), 29, Rue de Sèvres, 75006 Paris.

Boat Trips. A trip down the rivers or canals for one day or several days (with opportunities for side excursions; e.g., on rented bicycles) is highly recommended. An especially lovely boat trip is the one through Burgundy, passing through Auxerre (with its magnificent cathedral dating from the 13th century), Dijon, and Sens (home of one of France's oldest Gothic cathedrals). For more information, contact: Quiztour, 19, Rue d'Athenes, 75009 Paris. The lagoons of the Camargue delta, home to magnificent wildlife, can be toured in a cabin cruiser. The starting point is in Saint-Gilles/Petit Rhône. Beautiful rivers, ideal for boating and canoeing, abound throughout the south of France, too.

For information on boat trips throughout France, contact: Syndicat National des Loueurs de Bâteaux de Plaisance, Port de la Bourdonnais, 75007 Paris.

Bicycling. Well-built roads make it possible to cross the entire country by bicycle. For information on bicycle routes through the provinces, contact: La Fédération Française de Cyclotourisme, 8, Rue Jean-Marie-Jego, 75013 Paris; or Le Bicyclub de France, 8, Place de la Porte-Champerret, 75017 Paris.

The French National Railways (SNCF) rents bicycles in over 200 stations throughout France.

Golf. All-inclusive golf tours (including wine-tasting) in the Bordelais can be booked through Loisirs Accueil Gironde, 12, Cours du 30 Juillet, 33080 Bordeaux.

Equestrian Trips. The island of Corsica is crisscrossed by some 300 km. (186 miles) of bridle paths. The paths run from the edge of the sea through picturesque villages into the mountainous inland of the island. For information on horseback riding or horse-drawn caravans in France, contact: Association Nationale pour le Tourisme Équestre, 15, Rue Bruxelles, 75009 Paris.

Hiking. Some 2,500 km. (1,500 miles) of marked hiking trails cross the country. "Sentiers de Grande Randonée" (long-distance trails) are uniformly marked by two parallel bars. In addition, circular trails that are geared for excursions of one to three weeks are laid out in each region.

For information, contact: Comité National des Sentiers de Grande Randonnée, 8, Avenue Marceau, 75008 Paris.

Water Sports. Aside from the plethora of water sports available in France, you can also journey on the Philippe Cousteau Aquascope from the fishing port of Cap d'Agde for a marvelous underwater experience. For information, contact: Néonautes SARL, 36, Rue des Lavandes, Saint-Clement la Rivière, 34980 Saint-Gely du Gesc.

Shopping. France may very well be the leading nation in designer fashion; Paris offers astounding talent in the fashion industry that lures shoppers from around the globe.

Designers show two collections a year; the autumn-winter showings last from July through December, and the spring-summer collections are shown from January through May. You can obtain an invitation to these collections by requesting an invitation card through your concierge in your hotel or at the salon itself. Below is a listing of some of the better fashion houses located in Paris:

Balmain, 44, Rue François Ier, tel. (1) 47 20 35 34.
Cerruti 1881, 27, Rue Royale, tel. (1) 42 65 68 72.
Chanel, 29, Rue Cambon, tel. (1) 42 62 83 35.
Chlöe, 71, Avenue Franklin-Roosevelt, tel. (1) 43 59 15 63.
Christian Dior, 28, Avenue Montaigne, tel. (1) 47 23 54 44.
Courrèges, 40, Rue François Ier, tel. (1) 47 20 70 44.
Dorothée Bis, 33, Rue de Sèvres, tel. (1) 42 22 02 90.
Emanuel Ungaro, 2, Avenue Montaigne, tel. (1) 47 23 61 94.
Givenchy, 3, Avenue Georges-V, tel. (1) 47 23 81 36.
Grès, 1, Rue de la Paix, tel. (1) 42 61 58 15.
Guy Laroche, 29, Avenue Montaigne, tel. (1) 47 23 78 72.
Hanae Mori, 17, Avenue Montaigne, tel. (1) 47 23 52 03.
Hermès, 24, Faubourg-Saint-Honoré, tel. (1) 42 65 21 60.
Jean Patou, 7, Rue Saint-Florentin, tel. (1) 42 60 36 10.
Jean Louis Scherrer, 51, Avenue Montaigne, tel. (1) 43 59 55 39.
Kenzo, 3, Place des Victoires, tel. (1) 42 36 56 86.
Lanvin, 22, Faubourg Saint-Honoré, tel. (1) 42 65 14 40.
Nina Ricci, 39, Avenue Montaigne, tel. (1) 47 23 78 88.
Pierre Cardin, 27, Rue de Marigny, tel. (1) 42 66 92 25.
Schiaparelli, 21, Place Vendôme, tel. (1) 42 96 14 50.
Sonia Rykiel, 6, Rue de Grenelle, tel. (1) 42 22 43 22.
Yves Saint-Laurent, 5, Avenue Marceau, tel. (1) 47 23 72 71.

Department stores in Paris are open Monday through Saturday from 9:30 A.M. to 6:30 P.M., sometimes later. Many stores remain open until 9:00 or 10:00 P.M. one or two nights a week. Winter sales take place in mid-December and early January, and the summer sales take place in June and July. Major department stores are listed below:

Au Bon Marché, 38, Rue de Sèvres, 75007; tel. (1) 45 49 21 22.

Bazar de l'Hôtel de Ville, 52, Rue de Rivoli, 75001; tel. (1) 42 74 90 00.

Galeries Lafayette, 40, Boulevard Haussmann, 75009; tel. (1) 42 82 34 56.

Galeries Lafayette (Montparnasse), 22, Rue du Départ, 75015; tel. (1) 45 38 52 87.

Au Printemps, 64, Boulevard Haussmann, 75009; tel. (1) 42 82 50 00.

Au Printemps (Italie), Centre Galaxie—Place d'Italie, 75013; tel. (1) 45 81 11 50.

Au Printemps (Nation), 21-25, Cours de Vincennes, 75012; tel. (1) 43 71 12 41.

Au Printemps (République), 10, Place de la République, 75011; tel. (1) 43 55 39 09.

Au Printemps (Ternes), 30, Avenue des Ternes, 75017; tel. (1) 43 80 20 00.

Samaritaine (Pont-Neuf), 19, Rue de la Monnaie, 75001; tel. (1) 45 08 33 33.

Aux Trois Quartiers, 17, Boulevard de la Madeleine, 75001; tel. (1) 42 60 39 30.

Shopping Centers in Paris.

Palais des Congrès de Paris Boutiques, 2, Place de la Porte-Maillot, 75017; tel. (1) 46 40 22 22.

Montparnasse Shopping Center, Rue de l'Arrivée et la Rue du Départ, 75014.

Forum les Halles, 1-7, Rue Pierre-Lescôt, 75001.

Shopping is not restricted to Paris alone. There is a profusion of fine-quality goods for which France is famous, including delicate faïence, beautiful linens, exotic perfumes, and fine crystal. Below is a listing of areas in France and their specialties:

Aix-en-Provence is well known for its wonderful sweets, its Provençal cotton fabric designs, and its wines. Also renowned for wines, *Alsace* produces some of France's best. You can find hand-blown glass, rare books, and sweets in *Avignon*. *Biarritz* is devoted to designer resort fashions, and fine perfumes. Unusual antiques can be found in *Bordeaux,* along with good-quality cheese. *Cannes,* like Biarritz, displays high fashion in its shop windows. *Chartres* offers handmade pewter and pottery. *Dijon* is known for its mustard, as well as excellent honey. *Lyon,* an area made famous for its silk production, offers exquisite painted silk, as well as toys and textiles. In *Marseille* you can find interesting shoes, biblical figurines called "santons," and the ever-popular "navettes," a concoction of half bread and half cake. *Monaco* and *Monte Carlo* also have high-fashion shops, as well as fine flatware and crystal. *Nice* boasts an astonishing variety of foie gras, and its open-air markets are not to be missed. *Reims* is famous for its superb champagne, and *Rouen* offers such dainties as antique lace, jewelry, and toys for children. *St. Tropez,* like other resorts, sells high-fashion clothing, while *Strasbourg* is best known for its handicrafts, like needlework and faïence.

VAT Refund. In larger stores and shops, you may be able to apply for the VAT Refund (Value Added Tax), which will give you a discount of approximately 20 percent. You must spend about 2,400 FF if you are a resident of the EEC in order to qualify, or about 1,200 FF if you are not a resident of the EEC. Special forms must be filled out by you and the store, and the refund will be deposited directly into your bank account at home.

Clothing Sizes. Listed below are standard clothing size equivalents for the United States, Great Britain, and Europe:

		U.S.	U.K.	Europe
Chest	*Small*	34	34	87
	Medium	36	36	91
		38	38	97
	Large	40	40	102
		42	42	107
	Extra Large	44	44	112
		46	46	117
Collar		14	14	36
		14$^1/_2$	14$^1/_2$	37
		15	15	38
		15$^1/_2$	15$^1/_2$	39
		16	16	41
		16$^1/_2$	16$^1/_2$	42
		17	17	43
Waist		24	24	61
		26	26	66
		28	28	71
		30	30	76
		32	32	80
		34	34	87
		36	36	91
		38	38	97
Men's Suits		34	34	44
		35	35	46
		36	36	48
		37	37	49$^1/_2$
		38	38	51
		39	39	52$^1/_2$
		40	40	54
		41	41	55$^1/_2$
		42	42	57

	U.S.	U.K.	Europe
Men's Shoes	7	6	39$\frac{1}{2}$
	8	7	41
	9	8	42
	10	9	43
	11	10	44$\frac{1}{2}$
	12	11	46
	13	12	47
Men's Hats	6$\frac{3}{4}$	6$\frac{5}{8}$	54
	6$\frac{7}{8}$	6$\frac{3}{4}$	55
	7	6$\frac{7}{8}$	56
	7$\frac{1}{8}$	7	57
	7$\frac{1}{4}$	7$\frac{1}{8}$	58
	7$\frac{1}{2}$	7$\frac{3}{8}$	60
Women's Dresses	6	8	36
	8	10	38
	10	12	40
	12	14	42
	14	16	44
	16	18	46
	18	20	48
Women's Blouses and Sweaters	8	10	38
	10	12	40
	12	14	42
	14	16	44
	16	18	46
	18	20	48
Women's Shoes	4$\frac{1}{2}$	3	35$\frac{1}{2}$
	5	3$\frac{1}{2}$	36
	5$\frac{1}{2}$	4	36$\frac{1}{2}$
	6	4$\frac{1}{2}$	37
	6$\frac{1}{2}$	5	37$\frac{1}{2}$
	7	5$\frac{1}{2}$	38
	7$\frac{1}{2}$	6	38$\frac{1}{2}$
	8	6$\frac{1}{2}$	39
	8$\frac{1}{2}$	7	39$\frac{1}{2}$
	9	7$\frac{1}{2}$	40
Children's Clothing (*One size larger for knitwear*)	2	16	92
	3	18	98
	4	20	104
	5	22	110
	6	24	116
	6X	26	122
Children's Shoes	8	7	24
	9	8	25
	10	9	27
	11	10	28
	12	11	29

Clothing Sizes, (cont'd)

	U.S.	U.K.	Europe
	13	12	30
	1	13	32
	2	1	33
	3	2	34
	4^1/$_2$	3	36
	5^1/$_2$	4	37
	6^1/$_2$	5^1/$_2$	38^1/$_2$

General Sources of Information. Below are the addresses of the French Government Tourist Offices in the U.S., Canada, Great Britain, and Australia:

In the U.S.: 610 Fifth Avenue
New York, N.Y. 10020
tel. (212) 757-1125

645 North Michigan Ave., Suite 630
Chicago, Ill. 60611
tel. (312) 337-6300

9401 Wilshire Blvd.
Los Angeles, Calif. 90212
tel. (213) 272-2661

In Canada: 1981 McGill College, Suite 490
Montreal, Quebec H3A 2W9
tel. (514) 288-4264

1 Dundas Street West, Suite 2405, Box 8
Toronto, Ontario M5G 1Z3
tel. (416) 593-4723

In Great Britain: 178 Piccadilly
London W1V OAL
tel. (01) 493-6594

In Australia: 33 Bligh St.
Sydney N.S.W. 2000
(612) 231-5241

For tourist information in France, you can call (1) 47 20 94 94. You can also call for information for English-speaking tourists by phoning (1) 47 20 88 98. The Office du Tourisme de Paris is located at 127 Avenue des Champs-Élysées, and is open from 9:00 A.M. to 8:00 P.M. Monday through Friday.

Town-by-Town

Each town listing below includes region as well as information on local tourist offices, hotels, and transportation such as airports, train stations and bus connections. Hotels are classified according to our rating system and the one used by the French Government Tourist Office (for a full explanation, see page 270).

Abbeville (Picardie)

Information: Syndicat d'Initiative, Place de la Libération. **Transportation:** *Train:* Paris, Amiens. *Bus:* Dompierre-s.-A. Fort-Mahon, St-Pol.-s.-T., Hesdin. **Accommodations:** 🏨 France; Relais de l'Europe; Relais Vauban. 🏨 Du Chalet.

Agde (Languedoc-Roussillon)

Information: Syndicat d'Initiative, Arcades Hôtel de Ville. **Transportation:** *Train:* Bordeaux, Lyon, Nice, Toulouse. *Bus:* Béziers-Marseillan, Le Cap d'Agde, Pinet. **Accommodations:** 🏨 Sablotel; La Voile d'Or. 🏨 Saint-Clair.

Aigues-Mortes (Languedoc-Roussillon)

Information: Syndicat d'Initiative, Tour Gardette. **Transportation:** *Train:* Nîmes, Le Grau-du-Roi. **Accommodations:** 🏨 Hostellerie des Remparts; Saint-Louis. 🏨 Bourse. 🏨 Laporte; Provence.

Aix-en-Provence (Provence–Alpes-du-Sud)

Information: Office du Tourisme, Place du Général-de-Gaulle. **Transportation:** *Train:* Marseille. **Accommodations:** 🏨 La Caravelle; Grand Hôtel Negre-Coste; Le Manoir; Les Thermes Sextius. 🏨 De France; Le Moulin; Concorde; Pasteur; Moderne. 🏨 Du Casino; Paix; Paul.

Aix-les-Bains (Alpes-du-Nord)

Information: Syndicat d'Initiative, Place M.-Mollard. **Transportation:** *Air:* Paris, Geneva, Toulouse, Nice, Marseille, and others. *Train:* Geneva, Grenoble, Paris, and others. *Bus:* Geneva, Grenoble, Lyon, Côte d'Azur, Annecy. **Accommodations:** 🏨 Astoria; De la Cloche; International Rivollier; Le Manoir; Bristol. 🏨 Métropole; Du Casino; Paix; Azur. 🏨 Angleterre; Le Bon Coin; De Genève.

Ajaccio (Corsica)

Information: Syndicat d'Initiative, Hôtel de Ville, Avenue Serafini. *Air France,* 3, Boulevard Roi-Jérôme. *Air Transport:* Aéroport de Campo dell'Oro. *Compagnie G. Transatlantique:* Quai L'Herminer. **Transportation:** *Air:* Marseille, Nice, Paris, Toulon, Nîmes (in summer). *Bus:* regular service on the island. *Boat:* Genoa, Marseille, Nice, Porto Torres, Toulon, and others. **Accommodations:** 🏨🏨🏨 Castel Vecchio; Fesch; Costa. 🏨🏨 Bellavista; Du Golfe; Ideal. 🏨 Aria Marina; Bonaparte.

Albertville (Alpes-du-Nord)

Information: Syndicat d'Initiative, Place de la Gare. **Transportation:** *Train:* Bourg-St-Maurice–St. Pierre–Chambéry. *Bus:* Annecy, Arèches, Bourg-St-Maurice, Crest-Voland, Megève, Les Saisies. **Accommodations:** 🏨🏨🏨 La Berjann; Million. 🏨🏨 Le Costaroche; Terminus.

Albi (Midi-Pyrénées)

Information: Syndicat d'Initiative, 19, Place Ste-Cécile. **Transportation:** *Train:* Toulouse–Rodez. *Bus:* Montauban, Millau, St-Affrique. **Accommodations:** 🏨🏨🏨 Chiffre; Grand Hôtel du Vigan. 🏨🏨 George V; Grand Hotel d'Orléans; Relais Gascon. 🏨 Parc Rochegude; Le Lyonnais.

Alençon (Normandie)

Information: Syndicat d'Initiative, 60, Grande-Rue. **Transportation:** *Train:* Tours–Rouen. *Bus:* Paris, La Ferté–Mace, L'Aigle, Domfront, Le Mans, Nogent, Tinchebray. **Accommodations:** 🏨🏨🏨 Du Grand Cerf. 🏨🏨 De la Gare; De France. Grant St-Michel. 🏨 Normandie; De l'Industrie.

Ambert (Auvergne)

Information: Syndicat d'Initiative. **Transportation:** *Train:* Arlau–Vichy. *Bus:* Clermont-Ferrand. **Accommodations:** 🏨🏨 Le Livradois. 🏨 De la Gare; Terminus.

Amboise (Loire)

Information: Syndicat d'Initiative, Quai Général de Gaulle. **Transportation:** *Train:* Tours–Paris. **Accommodations:** 🏨🏨🏨 Chanteloup; Novotel Amboise; Bellevue. 🏨🏨 Parc; Lion d'Or.

Amélie-les-Bains (Languedoc-Roussillon)

Information: Office Municipal du Tourisme et Thermalisme, Place de la République. **Accommodations:** ⌂⌂⌂ Catalogne; Grand Hôtel des Thermes. ⌂⌂ Castel Émeraude; Martinets. ⌂ Central; Du Fin Gourmet; De France.

Amiens (Picardie)

Information: Syndicat d'Initiative, Rue Jean-Catelas. **Transportation:** *Train:* Paris–Calais, Laon, Lille, and others. **Accommodations:** ⌂⌂⌂ Carlton-Belfort; De l'Univers. ⌂⌂ Spatial; De la Paix; Le Normandie. ⌂ De l'Est; Rallye; Renaissance.

Andorra la Vella (Andorra)

Information: Syndicat d'Initiative, Place Prince Benlloch. **Accommodations:** ⌂⌂⌂ Parc Hôtel; Andorra Palace. ⌂⌂ Celler d'En Toni; Eden Roc; Mirador; Montserrat; Meritxell. ⌂ Les Arcades; Cassany; Consul; Enclar; Sant Jordi; Pyrénées-Hôtel.

Angers (Centre–Val-de-Loire)

Information: Office du Tourisme, Place de la Gare; Place Kennedy. **Transportation:** *Train:* Paris, Nantes, Tours. *Bus:* Many bus lines in the area. **Accommodations:** D'Anjou; Du Progrès. ⌂⌂ De France; De l'Univers; De la Boule d'Or. ⌂ Belle Rive; Continental; De la Mairie; Relais.

Angoulême (Poitou-Charentes)

Information: Syndicat d'Initiative, Place de l'Hôtel de Ville. **Transportation:** *Train:* Bordeaux, Dax, Hendaye, Royan, and others. *Bus:* Bordeaux, Matha, Mussidan, Perigueux. **Accommodations:** ⌂⌂⌂ Epi d'Or; Trois Piliers. ⌂⌂ Terminus; Les Valois; Du Palais; D'Orléans. ⌂ Central; Gasté; Thalie.

Annecy (Alpes-du-Nord)

Information: Syndicat d'Initiative, Place Hôtel de Ville. *Travel bureau:* Wagon-Lits, and others. **Transportation:** *Train:* Paris–St-Gervais, Nice, Grenoble. *Bus:* Duingt. Cable car to Mont Veyrier. **Accommodations:** ⌂⌂⌂ Splendid; Abbaye; Carlton. ⌂⌂ Parc; Du Parmelan; De Savoie. ⌂ Super Panorama; Du Bellvedere; Savoyard; Les Terrasses.

Antibes (Côte d'Azur)

Information: Syndicat d'Initiative, Place-du-C. de Gaulle. **Transportation:** *Train:* Cannes, Marseille, Nice, Paris. **Accommodations:** ⌂⌂⌂ Josse; Royal. ⌂⌂ Belle Epoque; Relais du Postillon. ⌂ Auberge Provençale; Méditerranée; Modern-Hôtel; Toulouse; Riviera.

Arbois (Franche-Comté)

Information: Syndicat d'Initiative, Hôtel de Ville. **Transportation:** *Train:* Besançon. *Bus:* Besançon. **Accommodations:** 🏨 Les Messageries; De Paris. 🍴 Poste.

Arcachon (Gironde)

Information: Office du Tourisme, Quinconce de la Gare. **Transportation:** *Train:* Bordeaux. *Bus:* Pilat-Plage, Cazaux-Lac. **Accommodations:** 🏨 Grand Hôtel Richelieu; Moderne; Vagues; Parc. 🏨 Gascogne; Marinette; De Menton; Nautic. 🍴 Les Caureuils; St-Christaud; La Riviera.

Argenton-sur-Creuse (Centre–Val-de-Loire)

Information: Syndicat d'Initiative, Ancien Hôtel de Scévole. **Transportation:** *Train:* Paris–Toulouse. *Bus:* Poitiers, La Chatre, Eguzon, Lignac. **Accommodations:** 🏨 Manoir de Boisvillers. 🍴 De France.

Arles (Provence–Alpes-du-Sud)

Information: Office du Tourisme, Esplanade des Lices. **Transportation:** *Train:* Marseille, Avignon, Miramas, Tarascon, Toulouse. *Bus:* Lunel, Nîmes, S.-de-Girand, Les Stes-Maries-de-la-Mer, Port-St.-Louis-du-Rhône, Salon, Marseille. **Accommodations:** 🏨 D'Arlatan; Du Forum; Mireille. 🏨 Constantin. 🍴 Gauguin; Terminus et Van Gogh; De la Poste; Lamartine.

Arromanches-les-Bains (Normandie)

Information: Syndicat d'Initiative, Place 6 Juin. **Transportation:** *Bus:* Bayeux–Courseulles. **Accommodations:** 🏨 De la Marine. 🍴 De Normandie.

Assy (Alpes-du-Nord)

Information: Syndicat d'Initiative, Maison Communale. **Transportation:** *Bus:* St-Gervais–Guebriant. **Accommodations:** 🏨 Tourisme. 🍴 Les Edelweiss; Family; Sabaudia.

Aubenas (Vallée-du-Rhône)

Information: Syndicat d'Initiative, Place Airette. **Transportation:** *Bus:* Le Puy, Alès, Montélimar, Valence, Avignon, Thueyts, Langogne, Vals le Bain. **Accommodations:** 🏨 Cévenol; Le Provence. 🍴 Le Dôme.

Auch (Midi-Pyrénées)

Information: Syndicat d'Initiative, Maison du Tourisme. **Transportation:** *Train:* Agen, Toulouse, *Bus:* Mirande, Montauban, Riscle, Tarbes, and others. **Accommodations:** 🏠🏠🏠 Le Robinson. 🏠🏠 De la Poste; Lion d'Or. 🏠 Modern' Hotel.

Audierne (Bretagne)

Information: Syndicat d'Initiative, Place de la Liberté. **Transportation:** *Bus:* Pointe du Raz–Brest, Quimper, Douarnenez. **Accommodations:** 🏠🏠🏠 Du Goyen. 🏠🏠 Le Cornouailles; De la Plage. 🏠 Dunes; Roi Gradlon.

Aurillac (Auvergne)

Information: Syndicat d'Initiative, Place du Square. **Transportation:** *Train:* Bort-les-Orgues, Capdenac, Libourne. *Bus:* Couques, Le Brezon, Ste-Geneviève-s.-Arg., Maurice. **Accommodations:** 🏠🏠🏠 La Thomasse; Map Bordeaux. 🏠🏠 De l'Univers; Du Square; Le Terminus. 🏠 Beauséjour, Du Commerce.

Autun (Bourgogne)

Information: Syndicat d'Initiative, 3, Avenue Charles de Gaulle. **Transportation:** *Train:* Chalon-sur-Saône, Paris, Vierzon. *Bus:* Chalon-sur-Saône, Château Chinon, Montceau-1.-M. **Accommodations:** 🏠🏠🏠 St-Louis; Hostellerie du Vieux Moulin. 🏠🏠 Les Arcades; Moderne et de la Tête Noire. 🏠 Commerce et Touring Hôtel; France.

Auxerre (Bourgogne)

Information: Syndicat d'Initiative, 1-2, Quai de la République. **Transportation:** *Train:* Laroche–Autun. *Bus:* Gien, St-Florentin-V., Montargis. **Accommodations:** 🏠🏠🏠 Le Maxime; Du Cygne. 🏠🏠 Normandie; De la Poste. Seignelay.

Avallon (Bourgogne)

Information: Syndicat d'Initiative, 24, Place Vauban. **Transportation:** *Train:* Paris–Autun. *Bus:* Ravières, Dijon, Vézelay. **Accommodations:** 🏠🏠🏠 (*Luxury*) Hostellerie de la Poste. 🏠🏠🏠 Moulin des Ruats. 🏠🏠 Le Manoir du Morvan; Relais Fleuri. 🏠 De Paris.

Avignon (Provence–Alpes-du-Sud)

Information: Syndicat d'Initiative, 41, Cours Jean-Jaurès. **Transportation:** *Train:* Dijon, Lyon, Marseille, Nice, Paris, Toulon, Ventimiglia and international connections. *Bus:* Europabus: Paris–Antwerp. **Accommodations:** 🏨🏨🏨 Bristol Terminus; Cité des Papes; Novotel Avignon Sud. 🏨🏨 Mistral; Auberge de France; D'Angleterre; Regina. 🏨 Bourse, 6, Rue du Portail Bouquier; Le Magnan, 63, Portail Magnanen; Henri IV, 4, Rue Galante; Innova, 100, Rue Vernet; Cezanne, 11, Rue Bancasse.

Ax-les-Thermes (Midi-Pyrénées)

Information: Syndicat d'Initiative, 2, Avenue Delcassé. **Transportation:** *Train:* Toulouse. Cable car, chair lifts and ski jump. **Accommodations:** 🏨🏨🏨 Mapotel Royal Thermal. 🏨🏨 De France; Moderne; Roy René; Terminus. 🏨 Du Parc; Carrière.

Azay-le-Rideau (Centre–Val-de-Loire)

Information: Syndicat d'Initiative, Place de la République. **Transportation:** *Train:* Tours–Chinon. **Accommodations:** 🏨🏨 De Biencourt.

Baccarat (Lorraine-Vosges-Alsace)

Transportation: *Train:* Nancy–Sélestat–Colmar. *Bus:* Badonviller. **Accommodations:** 🏨 Renaissance.

Ballon d'Alsace (Vosges)

Transportation: *Train:* nearest railroad station, St-Maurice. *Bus:* St-Maurice. **Accommodations:** 🏨 Tourtet; Saint de la Truite; La Chaumière.

Bandol (Provence–Alpes-du-Sud)

Information: Syndicat d'Initiative, Allées Vivien. **Transportation:** *Train:* Marseille, Toulon. *Bus:* Marseille, Toulon. **Accommodations:** 🏨🏨🏨 De la Baie; La Réserve. 🏨🏨 La Brunière; Les Galets; Golf. 🏨 Bel Ombra; Coin d'Azur; Florida; De la Mer.

Banyuls-sur-Mer (Pyrénées-Oriental)

Information: Syndicat d'Initiative, Hôtel de Ville. **Transportation:** *Train:* Paris–Port Bou. **Accommodations:** 🏨🏨🏨 Catalan. 🏨🏨 Les Elmes. 🏨 Bon Accueil; Le Manoir; Pergola.

Barbizon (Paris–Île-de-France)

Transportation: *Bus:* Arbonne, Melun. **Accommodations:** 🏨 Hostellerie La Clé d'Or; Auberge de la Dague. 🏨 Angelus St-Herem; Auberge des Alouettes.

Barcelonnette (Provence–Alpes-du-Sud)

Information: Syndicat d'Initiative. **Transportation:** *Bus:* Digne, Gap, Larche. Sauze (4 km.; 2.5 miles), chair lifts, Pra-Loup (8.5 km.; 5 miles), cable cars and rope tows. **Accommodations:** 🏨 Grand Hôtel; Alpes.

Barentin (Normandie)

Transportation: *Train:* Rouen, Le Havre. *Bus:* Rouen, Fécamp, Veulettes, St-Valery-en-Caux, Yvetot, Dieppe, Veules-les-Roses, Le Havre, and others. **Accommodations:** 🏨 Auberge du Grand St-Pierre.

Barfleur (Normandie)

Information: Syndicat d'Initiative, 60, Rue St-Thomas. **Transportation:** *Train:* Cherbourg–Valognes. **Accommodations:** 🏨 Du Phare. 🏨 Moderne.

Bar-le-Duc (Lorraine)

Information: Syndicat d'Initiative, Mairie. **Transportation:** *Train:* Frankfurt, Munich, Vienna, Luxembourg, Nancy, Metz, Strasbourg, and others. *Bus:* St.-Dizier, Ligny, Sommeilles, Verdun. **Accommodations:** 🏨 Grand Hôtel de Metz et du Commerce. 🏨 Bertrand; Exelmans.

Bar-sur-Aube (Champagne-Ardennes)

Information: Syndicat d'Initiative, 42, Rue d'Aube. **Transportation:** *Train:* Paris, Chaumont–Troyes. *Boat:* Chaumont–Troyes. **Accommodations:** 🏨 Commerce. 🏨 Pomme d'Or.

Bastia (Corsica)

Information: Syndicat d'Initiative, 35, Boulevard Paoli. *Air France:* 6, Émile-Sari. *Comp. G. Transatlantique:* Hôtel de la Chambre de Commerce. **Transportation:** *Air:* Marseille, Paris, in summer autotransport to Nice and Nîmes. *Bus:* Regular service on the whole island. *Boat:* Marseilles, Nice, Toulon, Livorno, Genoa, Porto Torres, Portoferreio, Piombino, Viareggio, and others. **Accommodations:** 🏨 Île-de-Beauté. 🏨 Bonaparte; Des Voyageurs; Central; Napoléon. 🏨 De l'Univers; Riviera; Laetitia.

Bayeux (Normandie)

Information: Office du Tourisme, 1, Rue Cuisiniers. **Transportation:** *Train:* Paris–Cherbourg. *Bus:* Courseulles, Grandcamp-les-Bains, Isigny. **Accommodations:** 🏨 Pacary; Le Lion d'Or. 🏨 Le Bayeux. 🏨 De la Gare.

Bayonne (Aquitaine)

Information: Syndicat d'Initiative, Place de la Liberté. **Transportation:** *Train:* Dax, Lourdes, Madrid, Paris, Toulouse, and others. *Bus:* Biarritz, Anglet, St-Jean-de-Luz, Ustaritz. **Accommodations:** 🏨 Agora. 🏨 Basses-Pyrénées; Bordeaux; Côte Basque; Loustau. 🏨 San Miguel.

Beaune (Bourgogne)

Information: Syndicat d'Initiative, Hôtel Dieu (Vis-à-Vis). **Transportation:** *Train:* Dijon, Lyon. *Bus:* Autun, Dijon, Saulieu. **Accommodations:** 🏨 Cloche; Closerie; Central. 🏨 Le Home; Bourgogne. 🏨 Château de Challanges.

Beauvais (Paris)

Information: Syndicat d'Initiative, 6, Rue Malherbe. **Transportation:** *Air:* Ashford, East Midland-Skyways. *Train:* Paris, Creil, Le Tréport. *Bus:* Le Crocq, Ansauvillers, Breteuil, Compiègne, Formerie, Gisors. **Accommodations:** 🏨 Du Palais. 🏨 Bristol Hôtel; Cygne; Croix d'Or.

Belfort (Vosges)

Information: Syndicat d'Initiative, Place Dr.-Corbis (Pavillon du Tourisme). **Transportation:** *Train:* Basel, Milan, Vienna, Zürich, Nancy, Paris, and others. **Accommodations:** 🏨 Hostellerie du Château Servin; Grand Hotel du Lion. 🏨 De France; Modern Hotel; De Paris. 🏨 Astoria; Du Chalet.

Berck-Plage (Nord–Pas-de-Calais)

Information: Syndicat d'Initiative, Esplanade Parmentier (seasonal). **Transportation:** *Bus:* Etaples, Lille, Rang-du-Fliers. **Accommodations:** 🏨 Renaissance. 🏨 Concorde; Médicis.

Bergues-Saint-Winoc (Nord–Pas-de-Calais)

Information: Syndicat d'Initiative, Beffroi, Place de la République. **Transportation:** *Train:* Dunkerque. *Bus:* Bollezede, Dunkerque, Oost-C. **Accommodations:** 🏨 Au Tonnelier.

Besançon (Franche-Comté)

Information: Syndicat d'Initiative, Place de la 1ʳᵉ Armée Française.
Transportation: *Train:* Belfort, Lyon, Paris, Strasbourg, and others.
Bus: Europabus: Luxembourg–Brussels–Ostende. **Accommodations:**
🏨🏨🏨 Mercure; Novotel-Besançon; Frantel. 🏨🏨 Foch; De Paris; Terrass
Hôtel; Du Nord; Gambetta; Franc-Comtois. 🏨 Régina; Carnot.

Beuil (Côte d'Azur)

Transportation: *Bus:* Nice, Valberg. **Accommodations:** 🏨🏨 L'Esca-
pade. 🏨 Edelweiss; Millou; Le Tremplin; Bellevue.

Béziers (Languedoc-Roussillon)

Information: Syndicat d'Initiative, 27, Rue Quatre-Septembre.
Transportation: *Train:* Bordeaux, Marseille, Lyon, and others. *Bus:*
Lacanne-1. B., Cruzy, Lodève, Marseille, Valras. **Accommodations:**
🏨🏨🏨 Europ Hôtel; Imperator; Du Midi. 🏨🏨 Splendid; Le Castelet; Ter-
minus. 🏨 Excelsior; Roussillon; De Paris.

Biarritz (Aquitaine)

Information: Syndicat d'Initiative, Square d'Ixelles. **Transporta-
tion:** *Air:* Paris, London, and Lourdes (in summer). *Train:* Bordeaux,
Madrid, Paris, and others. **Accommodations:** 🏨🏨🏨 Florida; Mirador;
Windsor; Marbella; Le Président. 🏨🏨 Atlantic; Eduard-VII; Monguillot;
Central; Port Vieux; Milady. 🏨 Bellevue; Bon Coin; Palym.

Biot (Côte d'Azur)

Information: Syndicat d'Initiative, Mairie. **Transportation:** *Train:*
Cannes, Nice. **Accommodations:** 🏨 Arcades.

Blois (Centre–Val-de-Loire)

Information: Syndicat d'Initiative, 3, Rue du Jean-Laigret. **Trans-
portation:** *Train:* Paris–Royan. **Accommodations:** 🏨🏨🏨 Novotel Blois.
🏨🏨 Du Château; Gare et Terminus; Hostellerie de la Loire. 🏨 Du Bellay;
Croix Blanche; Médicis; Saint-Nicolas.

Bonifacio (Corsica)

Information: Syndicat d'Initiative 17, Quai Comparetti. **Transportation:** *Bus:* Regular service on the island. *Boat:* Santa Teresa, La Mad-
dalena. **Accommodations:** 🏨🏨🏨 Solemare; La Caravelle. 🏨🏨 Résidence
du Centre Nautique. 🏨 Les Étrangers; Golfe; Les Voyageurs; La Pergola.

Bordeaux (Aquitaine)

Information: Syndicat d'Initiative, 12, Cours du 30-Juillet. *Air France:* 29, Rue Esprit-des-Lois. *Air Inter:* Allées de Tourny. **Transportation:** *Air:* Marseille, Nantes, Paris, Tours; in summer: Algiers, Barcelona, Clermont-Ferrand, Las Palmas, London, Lyon, Rabat, Sta. Cruz de Tenerife, Toulouse. *Train:* Paris, domestic and foreign connections. *Boat:* International port. **Accommodations:** 🏨 Le Bristol; Arcade; Balzac; La Tour-Intendance; Continental; Goya. **Accommodations:** 🏨 Cheval-Blanc; Fenelon; Bourgogne; Opéra; Du Parc; Lion d'Or.

Bort-les-Orgues (Limousin)

Information: Syndicat d'Initiative, Au barrage. **Transportation:** *Train:* Aurillac, Neussargues. *Bus:* Meymac. **Accommodations:** 🏨 Central Hôtel; Bourdoux.

Boulogne-sur-Mer (Nord–Pas-de-Calais)

Information: Office du Tourisme, Place F.-Sauvage. **Transportation:** *Train:* Paris–Calais, Arras. *Bus:* St-Omer, Douvres, Calais. **Accommodations:** 🏨 Marmin. 🏨 Alexandra; Ibis. 🏨 Arts; Mirador.

Bourg-en-Bresse (Vallée du Rhône)

Information: Syndicat d'Initiative, 1, Place P. Goujon. **Transportation:** *Train:* Geneva, Chambéry, Dijon, Lyon, Paris. *Bus:* Chalon-sur-Saône, Arinthod, Lons-le-Saunier, Lyon, Villefranche. **Accommodations:** 🏨 Le Logis de Brou; De France. 🏨 Mail; Les Negociants. 🏨 Genève; Midi; Du Parc; Sporting.

Bourges (Centre–Val-de-Loire)

Transportation: Syndicat d'Initiative, 14, Place E. Dolet. **Transportation:** *Train:* Paris, Montluçon, Vierzon. *Bus:* St-Amand, Corne, Gien, Issoudun, La Charité, Moulins, Nancy, Sancoins. **Accommodations:** 🏨 d'Angleterre. 🏨 Le Cygne; Les Tilleuls. 🏨 Agriculture; Etape; Ideal Hôtel; Normandie; Le Rocher; De Tours.

Bourg-Saint-Maurice (Alpes-du-Nord)

Information: Syndicat d'Initiative, Place de la Gare. **Transportation:** Mountain airstrip. *Train:* Geneva, Aix-les-Bains, Chambéry, and others. *Bus:* Albertville, Lac de Tignes, La Rosière. Gondolas, rope tows. **Accommodations:** 🏨 Vallée-de-l'Arc. 🏨 Au Bon Repos; Petite Auberge; Du Centre.

Brest (Bretagne)

Information: Syndicat d'Initiative, Place de la Liberté. *Air Inter:* Aéroport Guipavos. **Transportation:** *Air:* Paris. *Train:* Bordeaux, Lyon, Paris, Quimper. *Bus:* Argenton, Brignogan, Camaret-sur-Mer; Châteauneuf-du-Faou, Guisseny, Le Frêt, Le Huelgoat, Lilia, Lampaul-Plouarzel, Pointe du Raz, Quelern, Quessant, Roscoff, and others. **Accommodations:** 🏨 Les Ajoncs d'Or; Continental; Voyageurs. 🏨 France; Vauban. 🏨 De l'Avenue; Escargot; Pasteur; De la Rade; Comédiè; Saint-Louis; Siam Hôtel; Magenta.

Briançon (Provence–Alpes-du-Sud)

Information: Syndicat d'Initiative, 45, Avenue République. **Transportation:** *Train:* Marseille. *Bus:* Cesana, Clavière, Grenoble, Le Monetier, Refuge. **Accommodations:** 🏨 Vauban. 🏨 De Paris; Montbrison; Auberge le Mont Prorel. 🏨 De la Paix; De la Chaussée; Univers.

Briare (Vallée-du-Rhône)

Information: Syndicat d'Initiative, Place de l'Église. **Transportation:** *Train:* Saincaize-Gien. **Accommodations:** 🏨 Hostellerie le Canal. 🏨 Du Cerf.

Brienne-le-Château (Champagne)

Information: Syndicat d'Initiative, Hôtel de Ville. **Transportation:** *Bus:* Vitry-le-François, Troyes-St-Dizier. **Accommodations:** 🏨 De la Croix Blanche.

Brignoles (Provence–Alpes-du-Sud)

Transportation: *Bus:* Toulon, Cotignac, Carnoules, Marseille. **Accommodations:** 🏨 Château. 🏨 Fabre de Piffard; De Provence.

Brive-la-Gaillarde (Limousin)

Information: Syndicat d'Initiative, Place du XIV Juillet. **Transportation:** *Train:* Paris, Périgueux, Toulouse, and others. *Bus:* Benayes, Pompadour, St-Cere, Tulle, and others. **Accommodations:** 🏨 La Truffe Noire; Du Chapon Fin. 🏨 Le Ferry; Crémaillère; Terminus. 🏨 Plaisance; De l'Avenir; De la Gare.

Cadillac (Aquitaine)

Information: Syndicat d'Initiative, Château des Ducs d'Épernon. **Transportation:** *Bus:* Bordeaux, Langon. **Accommodations:** 🏨 Commerce.

Caen (Normandie)

Information: Syndicat d'Initiative, Place St-Pierre. **Transportation:** *Train:* Argentan, Cherbourg, Flers, Le Mans, Paris. *Bus:* Argentan, Courseulles, L'Evêque, Fougères, Honfleur, Lion-s.-M., Vers.-M. **Accommodations:** 🏨 Malherbe; Moderne. 🏨 Métropole; Royal; Bristol. 🏨 Le Fuchsia; L'Escale; Du Havre; Saint-Jean; De Bernières.

Cagnes-sur-Mer (Côte d'Azur)

Information: Syndicat d'Initiative, 26, Avenue A.-Renoir. **Transportation:** *Train:* Cannes, Marseille, Nice. *Bus:* Grasse, Nice, Vence. **Accommodations:** 🏨 Tierce Hôtel. 🏨 Motel Bagatelle; Savournin; Chantilly. 🏨 Motel La Gelinotte; Golf.

Cahors (Midi-Pyrénées)

Information: Syndicat d'Initiative, Place A.-Briand. **Transportation:** *Train:* Brive-la-Gaillarde, Capdenac, Monsempron, Toulouse–Paris. *Bus:* St-Cère, Belmontet, Labastide-Murat, Lanzerte, Marminiac. **Accommodations:** 🏨 Chartreuse; Terminus. 🏨 Melchior. 🏨 Chez Jean-Pierre.

Calais (Nord–Pas-de-Calais)

Information: Office du Tourisme, 12, Boulevard Clemenceau. **Transportation:** *Train:* Basel, Dunkerque, Lille, Paris, and others. *Bus:* Boulogne, La Panne, St-Pols-sur-Ternoise. *Boat:* Dover, and others. **Accommodations:** 🏨 Meurice. 🏨 George V; Bellevue; Du Sauvage. 🏨 Victor-Hugo; Armoric.

Calvi (Corsica)

Information: Syndicat d'Initiative, Place de la Gare. *Air Inter:* Airport. *Comp. G. Transatlantique:* Quai A.-Landry. **Transportation:** *Air:* Nice, Lyon, Paris, Marseille and Nîmes in summer with autotransport. *Bus:* Regular service on the island. *Boat:* Calvi, Marseille, Nice, and others. **Accommodations:** 🏨 La Revellata; St-Christophe; Abbaye. 🏨 Aria Marina; Balanea; Caravelle; Christophe-Colomb; Corsica; Cyrnea. 🏨 Bon Accueil; Sole e Mare; Il Tremento.

Cambrai (Nord–Pas-de-Calais)

Information: Syndicat d'Initiative, 17, Mail St-Martin. **Transportation:** *Train:* Dijon, Paris, Lille–Reims. **Accommodations:** 🏨 Beatus. 🏨 De France; Le Mouton Blanc. 🏨 Commerce.

Cannes (Côte d'Azur)

Information: Office du Tourisme, La Croisette. **Transportation:** *Train:* Lyon, Nice, and many international connections. *Bus:* Paris, Brussels, Amsterdam, Geneva, Genoa, San Remo, Lucéram–Peira Cava, Beuil-Valberg, Avignon, Vence, Allos, Tende-la-Brigne, Monaco, Grasse, Saint Raphaël, Mongins, Vallauris, Valbonne. **Accommodations:** 🏨 Acapulco, 16, Boulevard d'Alsace; De Paris, 34, Boulevard d'Alsace, 🏨 Bristol, 14, Rue Hoche; Chantilly, 34, Boulevard Alexandre III.; Cheval Blanc, 3, Rue Guy de Maupassant; Des Etrangers, 6, Place Sémard; Riviera, 35, Avenue Hoche. 🏨 Florella, 55, Boulevard de la République; Le Florian, 8, Rue du Commandant André; Des Glycines, 32, Boulevard d'Alsace; Les Iris, 77, Boulevard Carnot; Du Nord, 6, Rue Jean Jaurès; Pyrénées, 8, Rue Châteauneuf.

Cap Corse (Corsica)

Transportation: *Bus:* Regular service on the island. **Accommodations:** 🏨 30 hotels near Bastia and Cap Corse.

Cap d'Antibes (Côte d'Azur)

Information: Syndicat d'Initiative, 12, Place G.-de-Gaulle. **Transportation:** *Train:* Genoa–Milan–Vienna, San Remo, Ventimiglia, Marseille–Paris, and others. **Accommodations:** 🏨 Residence Beau Site; Castel Garoupe–Motel Axa; Gardiole; Du Levant; Miramar. 🏨 Helvetia. 🏨 Château Fleuri; Maryland; Val Fleuri.

Cap-Ferrat (Côte d'Azur)

Information: Office Municipal du Tourisme; Avenue Denis Semeria, in St-Jean-Cap-Ferrat. **Transportation:** *Train:* Nearest railroad station, Beaulieu-sur-Mer. **Accommodations:** 🏨 (*Luxury*) La Voile d'Or. 🏨 Belle Aurore; L'Oursin. 🏨 Bagatelle; Clair Logis. 🏨 De la Bastide; La Costière; Dauphin; La Fregate.

Carcassonne (Languedoc-Roussillon)

Information: Syndicat d'Initiative, Boulevard Camille-Pelletan. **Transportation:** *Train:* Bordeaux, Marseille, Toulouse, and others. *Bus:* Europabus: Toulouse–Barcelona; Foix, Mazamet, Pamiers, Tuchan. **Accommodations:** 🏨 Terminus; La Vicomté; Donjon; Logis de Trencavel. 🏨 Bristol; Central; Royal Hôtel. 🏨 De la Poste.

Carentan (Normandie)

Information: Syndicat d'Initiative, Place Valnoble. **Transportation:** *Train:* Caen, Carteret, Cherbourg–Paris. *Bus:* Carteret, Coutances, Cherbourg–St.-Lo. **Accommodations:** 🏠 Commerce et Gare; Auberge Normande.

Cassis (Provence–Alpes-du-Sud)

Transportation: *Train:* Marseille, Toulon. **Accommodations:** 🏠🏠🏠 Les Jardins des Campanilles; De la Rade; De la Plage. 🏠🏠 Le Golfe; Du Grand Jardin.

Castres (Midi-Pyrénées)

Information: Syndicat d'Initiative, Place Alsace-Lorraine. **Transportation:** *Train:* St-Pons–Toulouse. *Bus:* Brassac, Castelnandary. **Accommodations:** 🏠🏠🏠 Grand Hôtel. 🏠🏠 Cheval Blanc.

Caudebec-en-Caux (Normandie)

Information: Syndicat d'Initiative, Mairie. **Transportation:** *Bus:* Yvetot, Rouen, Le Havre. **Accommodations:** 🏠🏠🏠 De la Marine; Manoir de Rétival. 🏠🏠 De Normandie. 🏠 Cheval Blanc.

Cerbère (Languedoc-Roussillon)

Information: Syndicat d'Initiative, Mairie (in summer). **Information:** *Train:* Barcelona, Geneva, Lyon, Narbonne, Paris, Strasbourg. **Accommodations:** 🏠🏠🏠 La Dorade. 🏠 Le Belvedere du Rayon Vert.

Céret (Languedoc-Roussillon)

Information: Syndicat d'Initiative, Rue Clemenceau. **Transportation:** *Bus:* Perpignan. **Accommodations:** 🏠🏠 Arcades; Pyrénées.

Cernay (Lorraine-Vosges-Alsace)

Information: Syndicat d'Initiative, Journal d'Alsace, 12, Rue Thann. **Transportation:** *Train:* Mulhouse–Kruth. *Bus:* Sewen, Guebwiller. **Accommodations:** 🏠 Hostellerie d'Alsace; Des Trois Rois.

Chalon-sur-Saône (Bourgogne)

Information: Syndicat d'Initiative, Square Chabas. **Transportation:** *Train:* Cluny, Lyon, Mâcon, Marseille, Paris, and others. **Accommodations:** 🏠🏠🏠 Mércure; Saint-Regis. 🏠🏠 Central; De l'Europe; Aux Vendanges de Bourgogne; Saint-Jean. 🏠 Rive Gauche; La Gloriette; Kiosque; Le Régal.

Châlons-sur-Marne (Champagne)

Information: Syndicat d'Initiative, 2 bis, Boulevard Godart. **Transportation:** *Train:* Innsbruck, Munich, Vienna, Bucharest, Dijon, Lille, Paris, Strasbourg, and others. *Bus:* Château-Thierry, Ambonnay, Épernay, Troyes. **Accommodations:** 🏨 D'Angleterre. 🏨 Bristol; Du Pot d'Etain; Pasteur; Du Renard. 🏨 Central; Au Bon Accueil.

Chambéry (Alpes-du-Nord)

Information: Syndicat d'Initiative, Place Monge. **Transportation:** *Air:* Ajaccio, Grenoble, Paris. *Train:* Geneva, Grenoble, Lyon, Paris. *Bus:* Many bus lines in the area. **Accommodations:** 🏨 Novotel Chambéry; Des Princes. 🏨 Croix Blanche; Aux Pervenches; Lion d'Or. 🏨 Home Savoyard; Bon Accueil; Du Château.

Chambord (Centre–Val-de-Loire)

Transportation: *Bus:* Blois. **Accommodations:** 🏨 Saint-Michel.

Chamonix (Alpes-du-Nord)

Information: Office du Tourisme, Place de l'Église. **Transportation:** *Train:* Geneva, Vallorcine–St.-Gervais. *Bus:* Milan, Geneva, Annecy, Les Houches, Megève, Grenoble, Le Tour. Cog railways, cable cars, chair lifts. **Accommodations:** 🏨 Mapotel Alpina; Sapinière-Montana; Park-Hôtel Suisse. 🏨 Richemond; Les Gentianes; Univers. 🏨 Du Lion d'Or; Beauséjour; Des Lacs; La Varappe; Le Corzolet.

Chantilly (Picardie)

Information: Syndicat d'Initiative, Avenue M. Joffre. **Transportation:** *Train:* Amiens, Compiègne, Paris–Creil, Senlis. *Bus:* Orly-la-Ville. **Accommodations:** 🏨 D'Angleterre; Étoile.

Chartres (Normandie)

Information: Syndicat d'Initiative, Cloître Nôtre-Dame. **Transportation:** *Train:* Le Mans, Nantes, Paris, Saumur. *Bus:* Rouen, Châteaudun, Dreux, Orléans, and others. **Accommodations:** 🏨 Mapotel Grand Monarque. 🏨 Jehan de Beauce; De l'Ouest; De Paris. 🏨 Métropole.

Châteaudun (Normandie)

Information: Syndicat d'Initiative, 2, Rue Toufaire. **Transportation:** *Train:* Paris–Tours. *Bus:* Chartres, Orléans. **Accommodations:** 🏨 De Beauce; Armorial.

Châteauneuf-du-Pape (Provence–Alpes-du-Sud)

Information: Syndicat d'Initiative, Place Porteil. **Transportation:** *Train:* Nearest railroad station, Orange. **Accommodations:** 🏠🏠🏠 Hostellerie du Château des Fines Roches.

Châteauneuf-sur-Loire (Vallée-du-Rhône)

Transportation: *Bus:* Orléans. **Accommodations:** 🏠🏠 La Capitainerie.

Château-Thierry (Picardie)

Transportation: *Train:* Paris–Nancy. *Bus:* Châlons-sur-Marne, La Ferté, Marigny, Montmirail, Soissons. **Accommodations:** 🏠🏠 Île de France.

Chaudes-Aigues (Auvergne)

Transportation: *Bus:* Laguiole-St-Flour. **Accommodations:** 🏠🏠 Aux Bouillons d'Or. 🏠 Chaumière; Résidence.

Chenonceaux (Centre–Val-de-Loire)

Transportation: *Train:* Vierzon–Tours. **Accommodations:** 🏠🏠🏠 Bon Laboureur et du Château.

Cherbourg (Normandie)

Information: Office du Tourisme, 2, Quai Alexandre III. **Transportation:** *Train:* Paris, Coutances. *Bus:* Auderville, St-Lo, Valognes. *Boat:* International port. **Accommodations:** 🏠🏠🏠 Mercure. 🏠🏠 Du Louvre; De France; Renaissance; Angleterre. 🏠 Moderna; Du Centre.

Chinon (Centre–Val-de-Loire)

Information: Syndicat d'Initiative, 12, Rue Voltaire. **Transportation:** *Train:* Tours. *Bus:* Richelieu. **Accommodations:** 🏠🏠 Boule d'Or; Chris' Hôtel; De France; Diderot. 🏠 Point du Jour; Du Progrès; Lion d'Or.

Clermont-Ferrand (Auvergne)

Information: Office Municipal du Tourisme; 69, Boulevard Gergovia. *Air Inter,* 69, Boulevard Gergovia. **Transportation:** *Air:* Bordeaux, Lyon, Paris, Toulouse, Geneva, Ashford (in summer). *Train:* Lyon, Bordeaux, Nîmes, Paris, Toulouse, Nancy, Marseille. *Bus:*

Ambert, Le Puy, Vichy, Le Mont-Dore, Moulins, Aubusson. **Accommodations:** 🏨🏨🏨 Mapotel Colbert; Galliéni; Lafayette. 🏨🏨 Excelsior, Bristol; Ravel. 🏨 Fleury; Splendid Hôtel Terminus; Gare; Foch.

Cognac (Poitou-Charentes)

Information: Syndicat d'Initiative, Place François Ier. **Transportation:** *Train:* Paris–Royan. *Bus:* Bordeaux. **Accommodations:** 🏨🏨🏨 François Ier. 🏨🏨 Moderne; L'Étape. 🏨 Cheval Blanc.

Col de Valberg (Côte d'Azur)

Information: Office du Tourisme. Syndicat d'Initiative. **Transportation:** *Bus:* Nice. **Accommodations:** 🏨🏨🏨 Adrech de Lagas. 🏨🏨 Chalet Suisse; Vallée Blanche; Clé des Champs. 🏨 Blanche Neige; Flocons.

Col du Bonhomme (Lorraine-Vosges-Alsace)

Transportation: *Bus:* Mulhouse–Colmar–St-Dié. 🏨🏨 Relais Vosges-Alsace.

Collioure (Languedoc-Roussillon)

Information: Syndicat d'Initiative, Boulevard Camille-P. **Transportation:** *Train:* Cerbère-Narbonne. **Accommodations:** 🏨🏨🏨 Madeloc; La Frégate. 🏨🏨 Bon Port; Hostellerie des Templiers. 🏨 Bona-Casa; Le Majorque.

Colmar (Lorraine-Vosges-Alsace)

Information: Syndicat d'Initiative, 4, Rue d'Unterlinden. **Transportation:** *Train:* Lyon, Luxembourg, Mainz, Metzeral, Brussels–Basel–Milan. *Bus:* Epinal St-Dié, Labaroche, Orbey, Marckolsheim. **Accommodations:** 🏨🏨🏨 Terminus-Bristol; Champ de Mars; Park Hotel. 🏨🏨 Majestic; Fecht; Motel Azur. 🏨 Au Cerf; Europe; Rapp.

Compiègne (Picardie)

Information: Syndicat d'Initiative, Place Hôtel de Ville. **Transportation:** *Train:* Paris, Scandinavian-Express Copenhagen–Stockholm, Brussels–Antwerp, Amiens. **Accommodations:** 🏨🏨🏨 De Harlay. 🏨🏨 De Flandre; De France. 🏨 Lion d'Or; Solferino.

Concarneau (Bretagne)

Transportation: *Train:* Rosporden. *Bus:* Quimper-Lorient, Quimperlé. **Accommodations:** 🏨🏨🏨 Promotel du Cabellou. 🏨🏨 Grand Hôtel; Des Sables Blancs. 🏨 La Bonne Auberge; Gare; Atlantic; Halles.

Contrexeville (Vosges)

Information: Syndicat d'Initiative, Parc de l'Établ. **Transportation:** *Train:* Clermont–Metz, Nancy–Langres. **Accommodations:** 🏨 Du Parc; Cosmos. 🏨 Des Sources; De France. 🏨 Beauséjour; Bains; Dessez.

Cordes (Midi-Pyrénées)

Information: Syndicat d'Initiative, Mairie. **Transportation:** *Bus:* Vindrac-C. **Accommodations:** 🏨 Grand Écuyer. 🏨 Hostellerie du Vieux Cordes.

Corte (Corsica)

Information: Syndicat d'Initiative, Cours Paolie. *Compagnie G. Transatlantique.* Avenue Calizi. **Transportation:** *Bus:* Service throughout the island. **Accommodations:** 🏨 De la Paix; Sampiero. 🏨 Poste.

Dax (Aquitaine)

Information: Syndicat d'Initiative, Place Thiers. **Transportation:** *Train:* Bordeaux, Irún, Paris, and others. *Bus:* Leon, Mimizan, and others. **Accommodations:** 🏨 Grand Hôtel; Régina; Tarbelli. 🏨 Des Baignots; Thermes; Modern' Hôtel; De la Paix. 🏨 De la Néhé; Peyroux; Beausoleil; Auberge des Pins.

Deauville (Normandie)

Information: Office du Tourisme, Hôtel de Ville, Rue V. Hugo. *Air France:* Rue du G. Léclerc. **Transportation:** *Air:* Paris. *Train:* Lisieux. *Bus:* Caen–Le Havre. **Accommodations:** 🏨 La Bajocasse; P. L. M. Port Deauville; Royal; Du Golf; Marie-Anne 🏨 Brise-Marine; Paradis; Patio. 🏨 Aux Sports; Des Prairies.

Dieppe (Normandie)

Information: Office du Tourisme, Boulevard Général de Gaulle. **Transportation:** *Train:* Paris, Rouen. *Bus:* Le Havre, Le Tréport, Rouen, St-Valéry-en-Caux. *Boat:* England. **Accommodations:** 🏨 La Présidence; De l'Univers; Aguado. 🏨 Windsor; De la Plage. 🏨 La Falaise; De Pontoise.

Digne-les-Bains (Alpes-du-Sud)

Information: Syndicat d'Initiative, 2, Boulevard V.-Hugo. **Transportation:** *Train:* St.-Auban. *Bus:* Avignon, Barcelonnette, Geneva–Nice. **Accommodations:** 🏨 Bourgogne; Le Coin Fleuri; Central-Hotel; Thermal. 🍴 Provence; Tivoli; Julia; Du Petit-Saint-Jean.

Dijon (Bourgogne)

Information: Office du Tourisme, 34, Rue des Forges. **Transportation:** *Air:* Paris. *Train:* Bern, Luxembourg, Lyon, Milan, Metz, Nancy, Paris. **Accommodations:** 🏨 Chapeau Rouge; Morot et Geneve; Des Ducs; Jura. 🏨 Nord; Montchapet; Le Jaquemart; St.-Bernard; Thurot; Rosiers. 🍴 Bagatelle; Confort; La Lorraine.

Dinard (Bretagne)

Information: Syndicat d'Initiative, 5, Rue du Maréchal-Leclerc. **Transportation:** *Train:* Rennes. *Bus:* St-Brieuc, St-Malo, Rennes. **Accommodations:** 🏨 Le Crystal; La Reine Hortense. 🏨 Emeraude-Plage; Des Bains; Dunes; Balmoral; Du Mont-St-Michael Plage. 🍴 Sables; De la Paix; Beauséjour; Altair.

Domrémy-la-Pucelle (Vosges)

Transportation: *Bus:* Neufchâteau–Toul. **Accommodations:** 🍴 De la Basilique.

Dormans (Champagne–Ardennes)

Transportation: *Train:* Château-Thierry, Épernay. *Bus:* Château-Thierry–Châlons. **Accommodations:** 🍴 Demoncy.

Douarnenez (Bretagne)

Information: Syndicat d'Initiative, Rue D.-Mével. **Transportation:** *Train:* Quimper. *Bus:* Brest–Pointe du Raz. **Accommodations:** 🏨 France; Bretagne. 🍴 Halles.

Dreux (Centre–Val-de-Loire)

Information: Syndicat d'Initiative, 4, Rue P.-Chartraine. **Transportation:** *Train:* Bueil, Chartres, Granville, Paris. *Bus:* Evreux, Maintenon. **Accommodations:** 🏨 Au Bec Fin.

Dunkerque (Nord–Pas-de-Calais)

Information: Syndicat d'Initiative, Hôtel de Ville. **Transportation:** *Train:* Calais, Metz, Paris, Strasbourg, and others. *Bus:* Bollezeele, Calais, Hondschoote, Oost-Cappel. *Boat:* England; and others. **Accommodations:** ♜♜♜ Borel. ♜♜ Select. ♜ Terminus-Nord.

Entraygues (Midi-Pyrénées)

Information: Syndicat d'Initiative, Tour de Ville. **Transportation:** *Bus:* Rodez. **Accommodations:** ♜♜ La Truyère.

Épernay (Champagne)

Information: Syndicat d'Initiative, Place Thiers. **Transportation:** *Train:* Paris, Reims, Strasbourg, Munich–Vienna. *Bus:* Châlons-sur-Marne, Reims, Romilly, Sézanne, Troyes, and others. **Accommodations:** ♜♜♜ Des Berceaux; Champagne. ♜♜ De l'Europe. ♜ Du Chapon Fin; De la Cloche.

Épinal (Vosges)

Information: Syndicat d'Initiative, 13, Rue de la Comédie. **Transportation:** *Train:* Belfort, Chaumont, Nancy, Remiremont, Strasbourg. *Bus:* Charmes, Colmar, Jussey, Lure, Les Bains, Le Val-d'Ajol, Royan, Thann. **Accommodations:** ♜♜♜ Relais des Ducs de Lorraine. ♜♜ Bristol; Le Columbier; La Résidence. ♜ Azur Hôtel; Commerce.

Étretat (Normandie)

Information: Syndicat d'Initiative, Hôtel de Ville. **Transportation:** *Bus:* Bréauté–Beuzeville, Le Havre, Fécamp, Dieppe. **Accommodations:** ♜♜♜ Dormy-House Golf Hôtel. ♜♜ Des Falaises; Welcome. ♜ Escale; Angleterre; Normandie.

Eu (Normandie)

Information: Office du Tourisme–Syndicat d'Initiative, Place Carnot. **Transportation:** *Train:* Abbeville, Paris. *Bus:* Dieppe, Le Tréport, Neufchâtel, Rouen. **Accommodations:** ♜♜ Relais.

Évian-les-Bains (Alpes-du-Nord)

Information: Office du Tourisme, Place d'Alinges. **Transportation:** *Train:* Geneva, Paris, Lyon, Marseille. *Bus:* Europabus, Turin, Geneva, Chamonix. *Boat:* Lausanne, Geneva, Montreux. **Accommodations:** ♜♜♜ (*Luxury*) Royal Hôtel. ♜♜♜ La Verniaz et ses Chalets; Bellevue; De la Plage. ♜♜ Bon Séjour; Continental; Beau Rivage; Les Cygnes; Savoy Hôtel. ♜ Du Léman.

Evreux (Normandie)

Information: Comité Départemental de Tourisme de l'Eure, Evreux.
Transportation: *Train:* Cherbourg–Caen–Paris, l'Aigle. *Bus:* Rouen–
Evreux–Chartres. **Accommodations:** 🏨 Normandy Hôtel. 🏨 Biche;
Bellevue. 🏠 Bretagne; De Paris.

Èze-Bord-de-Mer (Côte d'Azur)

Accommodations: 🏨 (*Luxury*) Cap-Estel. 🏨 La Bananeraie. 🏠
Mimosas-Cottage.

Èze-Village (Côte d'Azur)

Accommodations: 🏨 (*Luxury*) Château de la Chèvre d'Or. 🏨 Hermitage du Col d'Eze; Golfe. 🏠 Auberge des Deux Corniches; *Motel:* Cap
Roux.

Fécamp (Normandie)

Information: Syndicat d'Initiative, Place Bellet. **Transportation:**
Train: Le Havre. *Bus:* Dieppe, Étretat, Le Havre, Rouen. **Accommodations:** 🏨 De la Poste; Angleterre. 🏠 Moderne et Gare.

Foix (Midi-Pyrénées)

Information: Office du Tourisme, Cours Gabriel Fauré. **Transporta-
tion:** *Train:* Toulouse. *Bus:* St-Girons, Toulouse. **Accommodations:** 🏨
La Barbacane; Pyrène. 🏨 Audoye-Lons; Echauguette. 🏠 Eychenne;
Lac.

Fontainebleau (Paris et Île-de-France)

Information: Syndicat d'Initiative, 38, Rue Grande. **Transportation:** *Train:* Paris–Laroche, Montargis, Nevers, Saincaize. **Accommodations:** 🏨 Napoléon; Legris et Parc. 🏨 La Carpe d'Or; Chan-
cellerie; M. Hôtel Île de France. 🏠 De Neuville; Salamande.

Font-Romeu (Languedoc-Roussillon)

Information: Office du Tourisme, Avenue E. Brousse. **Transporta-
tion:** *Train:* Villefranche-V.–La Tour-d.-C. *Bus:* Ermitage, Quillan, La
Tour-d.-C. **Accommodations:** 🏨 Soleil d'Or. 🏨 Cara Sol; Carlit
Hôtel; Ermitage. 🏠 Villa-Saint-Paul; Grillons; Castel Négro.

Fougères (Bretagne)

Transportation: *Train:* Vitre. *Bus:* Caen, St-Malo, Rennes. **Accommodations:** 🏨 Des Voyageurs. 🏠 Moderne; Du Commerce; Flaubert.

Fouras (Poitou-Charentes)

Transportation: *Bus:* Rochefort, La Rochelle–St-Palais-sur-Mer. *Boat:* Île d'Aix. **Accommodations:** ⌂⌂ Grand Hôtel des Bains. ⌂ La Roseraie.

Fréjus (Provence–Alpes-du-Sud)

Information: Syndicat d'Initiative, Place Calvini. **Transportation:** *Train:* Cannes, Marseille. *Bus:* St-Raphaël, Toulon. **Accommodations:** ⌂⌂⌂ Catalogne. ⌂⌂ Azur; Le Lion d'Or.

Gérardmer (Vosges)

Transportation: *Train:* Bruyères. *Bus:* Épinal, Bruyères, Colmar. **Accommodations:** ⌂⌂⌂ Hostellerie des Bas Rupts; Du Saut des Cuves. ⌂⌂ Des Bains; De la Jamagne. ⌂ Interlaken; Les Sapins; Sarcelles.

Gien (Centre–Val-de-Loire)

Information: Syndicat d'Initiative, Rue Anne-de-Beaujeu. **Transportation:** *Train:* Paris–Nevers. *Bus:* Several bus lines. **Accommodations:** ⌂⌂ Le Rivage. ⌂ Terminus.

Grand Ballon (Lorraine-Vosges-Alsace)

Transportation: *Train:* Moosch–Lautenbach–Guebwiller. Rope tow. **Accommodations:** ⌂ Grand Ballon.

Grasse (Côte d'Azur)

Information: Syndicat d'Initiative, Place de la Foux. **Transportation:** *Bus:* Cannes, Draguignan, Nice, St-Auban. **Accommodations:** ⌂⌂⌂ (*Luxury*) Le Régent. ⌂⌂ Bellevue. ⌂ Les Palmiers; Vauban; Paradis.

Grenoble (Alpes-du-Nord)

Information: Maison du Tourisme, 14, Rue de la République. *Air France:* 4, Place Victor-Hugo. **Transportation:** *Air:* Chambéry, Nice, Paris, Metz. *Train:* Paris, Lyon. *Bus:* Alpe-d'Huez, Chamrousse, Les Deux Alpes, Col de Porte, Alpe du Grand-Serre. **Accommodations:** ⌂⌂⌂ Grand Hôtel; Gallia; Mercure; D'Angleterre; De Savoie. ⌂⌂ Bristol; Gloria; Splendid; Stendhal; Gambetta; Trianon. ⌂ Beau Soleil; Clé d'Or; Lakanal.

Guillaumes (Côte d'Azur)

Information: Syndicat d'Initiative, Mairie. **Transportation:** *Bus:* Nice. **Accommodations:** ⌂⌂ Renaissance. ⌂ Des Alpes.

Guingamp (Bretagne)

Transportation: *Train:* Brest–Paris, Carhaix, and others. *Bus:* Morlaix, St-Quay–Portrieux. **Accommodations:** 🏨 L'Hermine. 🏨 L'Escale.

Ham (Picardie)

Transportation: *Train:* Amiens–Laon. *Bus:* St-Quentin, Noyon. **Accommodations:** 🏨 De France.

Harfleur (Normandie)

Transportation: *Train:* Paris, Rouen, Le Havre. *Bus:* Le Havre. *Boat:* Le Havre, Rouen, Dieppe. **Accommodations:** 🏨 Bellevue.

Honfleur (Normandie)

Information: Office du Tourisme, 35, Cours Fossés. **Transportation:** *Train:* Lisieux. *Bus:* Evreux, Caen. **Accommodations:** 🏨 Hostellerie Lechat. 🏨 Belvedere; De la Tour; Du Dauphin.

Houlgate (Normandie)

Information: Syndicat d'Initiative, Rue d'Axbridge. **Transportation:** *Train:* Lisieux–Dives–Cabourg. *Bus:* Caen–Honfleur–Le Havre. **Accommodations:** 🏨 Du Centre. 🏨 Le Bar Normand; De la Plage.

Hyères (Provence–Alpes-du-Sud)

Information: Office du Tourisme, Avenue de Belgique. **Transportation:** *Bus:* Toulon, St-Raphaël. *Boat:* Toulon. **Accommodations:** 🏨 Bona; Vieille Auberge St-Nicolas. 🏨 Central Hôtel; Mozart; Le Suisse. 🏨 Comme chez Soi; Calypso; Lido; De la Poste.

Île de Bréhat (Bretagne)

Transportation: *Boat:* Island connections. **Accommodations:** 🏨 Vieille Auberge. 🏨 Belle-Vue.

Île d'Oléron (Poitou-Charentes)

Information: La Brée-les-Bains: **Transportation:** *Boat:* Saintes–St-Denis-d'Oléron.

Île d'Ouessant (Bretagne)

Transportation: *Boat:* Brest. **Accommodations:** 🏨 Duchesse Anne; Du Fromeur; Roch'Armor.

Île Rousse (Corsica)

Transportation: *Bus:* Regular service throughout the island. **Accommodations:** ⌂⌂⌂ La Pietra. ⌂⌂ Splendid. ⌂ La Bergerie.

Issoire (Auvergne)

Transportation: *Train:* Paris–Nîmes. *Bus:* Clermont–St.-Flour–Le Puy. **Accommodations:** ⌂⌂ Florida. ⌂ Le Pariou; Tourisme; Terminus; Parc.

Josselin (Bretagne)

Transportation: *Bus:* Vannes, Pontivy, Redon. **Accommodations:** ⌂⌂ Du Château; Le Commerce.

Juan-les-Pins (Côte d'Azur)

Information: Syndicat d'Initiative, 11, Place de Gaulle. **Transportation:** *Train:* Nice, Cannes, Marseille. **Accommodations:** ⌂⌂⌂ Beach-ôtel; Des Mimosas; Courbet; Cyrano; Astoria. ⌂⌂ Alexandra; Colbert; Eden; Juan Beach. ⌂ Casino; De la Gare; Impérial; Pacific; Paprika.

Kaysersberg (Lorraine-Vosges-Alsace)

Information: Syndicat d'Initiative, Rue C.-de-Gaulle. **Transportation:** *Bus:* Colmar–St-Dié, Orbey. **Accommodations:** ⌂⌂⌂ Les Remparts. ⌂ Du Château; A l'Arbre Vert.

La Baule (Pays de la Loire)

Information: Office du Tourisme, 8, Place de la Victoire. **Transportation:** *Train:* Tours–Paris. *Bus:* Connections to nearby areas. **Accommodations:** ⌂⌂⌂ Alexandra; Les Alizes; Majestic; Christina; Les Pléiades; Flepen. ⌂⌂ Concorde; Welcome; Des Dunes. ⌂ Oceanic; Parc; Violetta;

Lacanau-Océan (Aquitaine)

Information: Syndicat d'Initiative, Place de l'Europe. **Transportation:** *Bus:* Bordeaux. **Accommodations:** ⌂⌂ L'Étoile d'Argent. ⌂ Grand Hôtel de la Côte d'Argent; Commerce.

Lac du Bourget (Alpes-du-Nord)

Information: Office du Tourisme, Syndicat d'Initiative, Place Général-Sevez. **Transportation:** *Bus:* Chambéry. **Accommodations:** ⌂⌂ Port. ⌂ La Cerisaie; Beaurivage; Savoy.

La Chaise-Dieu (Auvergne)

Information: Syndicat d'Initiative, Place Mairie. **Transportation:** *Train:* Vichy–Darsac. *Bus:* Le Puy. **Accommodations:** 🏨 Au Tremblant; Terminus et du Monastère; Hostellerie du Lion d'Or.

La Ciotat (Côte d'Azur)

Information: Office Municipal du Tourisme, Vieux Port. **Transportation:** *Train:* Toulon, Marseille. *Bus:* Ceyreste, Marseille, Bandol. **Accommodations:** 🏨 Miramar; King. 🏨 De la Rotonde; Plaisance; Croix de Malte–Mare Nostrum; Provence-Plage. 🏨 Beau Rivage; Gare.

Langeais (Centre–Val-de-Loire)

Information: Syndicat d'Initiative, 12, Rue Gambetta. **Transportation:** *Train:* Tours–Angers. **Accommodations:** 🏨 Hosten; La Duchesse Anne.

Langogne (Languedoc-Roussillon)

Information: Syndicat d'Initiative, 15, Boulevard des Capucins. **Transportation:** *Train:* Nîmes–Paris. *Bus:* Le Puy, Aubenas, Mende. **Accommodations:** 🏨 Voyageurs. 🏨 Gaillard.

Lannion (Bretagne)

Transportation: *Train:* Pleumeur. *Bus:* Morlaix, Paimpol, Trégastel, Île Grande, Trebeurden. **Accommodations:** 🏨 Terminus. 🏨 A l'Arrivée.

Lanslebourg (Alpes-du-Nord)

Information: Syndicat d'Initiative, Mairie. **Transportation:** *Bus:* Modane. Chair lifts; rope tows. **Accommodations:** 🏨 Alpazur. 🏨 Relais des 2 Cols. 🏨 Le Roc Noir; Marmottes.

Laon (Picardie)

Information: Syndicat d'Initiative, Place Parvis. **Transportation:** *Train:* Amiens, Chaumont, Dijon, Hirson, Liart, Lille, Paris, Reims, and others. *Bus:* Chauny, Le Cateau, Montcornet, St.-Quentin, Reims. **Accommodations:** 🏨 L'Ecrin Provençal. 🏨 Du Commerce.

La Rochelle (Poitou-Charentes)

Information: Syndicat d'Initiative, 10, Rue Fleur'Au (Tourist kiosk).
Transportation: *Train:* Paris, Bordeaux, and others. *Bus:* St-Palais-sur-
Mer. **Accommodations:** 🏨🏨🏨 De France et d'Angleterre; Champlain; Les
Brises. 🏨🏨 Tour de Nesles; Du Commerce; François 1er. 🏨 Du Béarn;
Atlantic; Centre.

La Turbie (Côte d'Azur)

Transportation: *Bus:* Monaco, Nice, Peille. **Accommodations:** 🏨
Césarée; France.

Laval (Pays de la Loire)

Information: Syndicat d'Initiative, Place 11 Novembre. **Transportation:** *Train:* Caen, Paris–Brest. *Bus:* Fougères, Gorron, Sable, and
others. **Accommodations:** 🏨🏨 Impérial; Ouest Hôtel; Grand Hôtel de
Paris; Ibis Relais d'Amour. 🏨 Le Zeff; Moderne.

Le Creusot (Bourgogne)

Information: Syndicat d'Initiative, 1, Rue Maréchal Foch. **Transportation:** *Train:* Chalon-sur-Saône, Nevers. *Bus:* Montceau–Chalon-
sur-Saône, Autun. **Accommodations:** 🏨🏨 Moderne. 🏨 Voyageurs.

Le Croisic (Pays de la Loire)

Information: Office du Tourisme, Syndicat d'Initiative, Place de la
Gare. **Transportation:** *Train:* Tours, Paris. *Bus:* La Baule, St.-Nazaire,
Nantes. **Accommodations:** 🏨🏨 Skipper; Les Nids. 🏨 Le Tréhic-
L'Estacade; Jonchères.

Le Fayet-St-Gervais (Alpes-du-Nord)

Information: Syndicat d'Initiative, Avenue de la Gare. **Transporta-
tion:** *Train:* Paris, Lyon. *Bus:* Guebriant, Megève, Annecy–Chamonix,
Glacier de Bionnassay. Cable cars. **Accommodations:** 🏨🏨 Chaumière;
Les Deux Gares.

Le-Grau-de-Roi (Languedoc-Roussillon)

Information: Office du Tourisme–L'Imperial. Syndicat d'Initiative,
Quai Colbert. **Transportation:** *Train:* Nîmes. *Bus:* Montpellier.
Accommodations: 🏨🏨 Splendid'Hôtel; De la Plage. 🏨 Saint-Louis.

Le Havre (Normandie)

Information: Office du Tourisme, Place de l'Hôtel de Ville. **Transportation:** *Air:* Paris, London. *Train:* Fécamp, Paris, Rouen. *Bus:* Fécamp, Rouen, Caen. *Boat:* International port. **Accommodations:** ⌂⌂⌂ De Bordeaux. ⌂⌂ Gambetta; Astrid; Bauza; Richelieu; Celtic. ⌂ Atlantic; Chambord; Île de France.

Le Lavandou (Provence–Alpes-du-Sud)

Information: Office du Tourisme, Syndicat d'Initiative, Quai Gabriel Péri. **Transportation:** *Bus:* Toulon, St.-Raphaël. *Boat:* Îles d'Hyères. **Accommodations:** ⌂⌂⌂ Auberge de la Calanque; L'Espadon. ⌂⌂ Beau Rivage; Petite Bohème. ⌂ California; Le Rabelais; Terminus.

Le Mans (Pays de la Loire)

Information: Syndicat d'Initiative, Place de la République. **Transportation:** *Train:* Nantes, Paris, Tours, and others. **Accommodations:** ⌂⌂⌂ Novotel Le Mans; Moderne. ⌂⌂ Central; L'Escale; De l'Étoile; De Rennes; Du Saumon; Maine-Atlantique Hôtel. ⌂ Normandie; Suède; Le Pélican.

Le Mont-Dore (Auvergne)

Information: Office du Tourisme. **Transportation:** *Train:* Laqueuille. *Bus:* Clermont-Ferrand. Cable cars; T-bar; rope tows. **Accommodations:** ⌂⌂⌂ (*Luxury*) PLM Carlina. ⌂⌂⌂ Panorama. ⌂⌂ Metropol; Les Cascades; Du Louvre; Nouvel Hôtel; Du Parc. ⌂ Continental; Royal Hotel; Terminus.

Le Pouliguen (Pays de la Loire)

Information: Office du Tourisme–Syndicat d'Initiative, Port Sterwitz. **Transportation:** *Train:* Le Croisic–Paris. *Bus:* Nantes–St.-Nazaire–Le Croisic. **Accommodations:** ⌂⌂ Orée du Bois; Neptune; Beau Rivage. ⌂ Galion.

Le Puy-en-Velay (Auvergne)

Information: Office du Tourisme, Place du Breuil. **Transportation:** *Train:* Clermont, Lyon, St-Étienne, and others. *Bus:* Annonay, Aubenas, Duniers, Vichy, Craponne, Langeac, Langogne, Monastier, St-Chély, St-Étienne. **Accommodations:** ⌂⌂⌂ (*Luxury*) Christel. ⌂⌂⌂ Régina. ⌂⌂ Bristol; Cygne; Val Vert. ⌂ Grand Cerf; De la Verveine.

Les Baux-en-Provence (Provence–Alpes-du-Sud)

Transportation: *Train:* Closest railroad station, Maussane. **Accommodations:** 🏨🏨🏨 Bautezar; La Benvengudo. 🏨🏨 Hostellerie de la Reine Jeanne.

Les Eyzies-de-Tayac (Aquitaine)

Information: Syndicat d'Initiative, Place de la Mairie. **Transportation:** *Train:* Périgueux–Agen. **Accommodations:** 🏨🏨🏨 Du Centenaire; Cro-Magnon; Les Glycines. 🏨🏨 Du Centre. 🏨 Perigord.

Le Touquet-Paris-Plage (Pas-de-Calais)

Information: Syndicat d'Initiative, Hôtel de Ville. **Transportation:** *Air:* London, Lydd (in summer), Southend (in summer). *Bus:* Étaples. **Accommodations:** 🏨🏨🏨 Côte d'Opale; La Chaumiere; Manoir Hotel et Golf Club. 🏨🏨 Artois; Nouvel Hôtel; Saint-Christophe; Windsor; De la Plage; Chalet. 🏨 Touquet; Moderne.

Le Tréport (Normandie)

Information: Office du Tourisme–Syndicat d'Initiative, Esplanade Plage. **Transportation:** *Train:* Paris Nord, Abbeville, and others. *Bus:* Dieppe, Rouen. Cable car to Calvary Terrace. **Accommodations:** 🏨🏨 De Picardie. 🏨 Rex; Petit-Trianon.

Libourne (Aquitaine)

Information: Office du Tourisme–Syndicat d'Initiative, Place Abel Surchamp. **Transportation:** *Train:* Bordeaux, Paris, and others. *Bus:* Bordeaux, Rauzan, and others. **Accommodations:** 🏨🏨🏨 Loubat. 🏨🏨 Orient. 🏨 France; Moulin Blanc.

Lille (Nord)

Information: Syndicat d'Initiative, 16, Place d'Armes. *Air France:* 810, Rue Jean-Roisin, *Air Inter:* 10, Rue Anatole-France. **Transportation:** *Air:* Barcelona (in summer), London (in summer), Palma (in summer), Paris. *Train:* Paris, Basel, Brussels, Calais, and others. *Bus:* Berck-Plage, Boulogne, Béthune, Condecourt, St.-Omer. **Accommodations:** 🏨🏨🏨 Grand Hôtel Bellevue; Mapotel-Carlton; Royal Hôtel. 🏨🏨 Monte-Carlo.

Limoges (Limousin)

Information: Syndicat d'Initiative, Boulevard Fleurus. **Transportation:** *Air:* Paris. *Train:* Brive, Bordeaux, Lyon, Munich, Paris. *Bus:* Several buslines serve the area. **Accommodations:** 🏨🏨🏨 Luk Hotel. 🏨🏨 Du Faisan; De l'Europe; Claridge. 🏨 Le Relais Lamartine.

Lisieux (Normandie)

Information: Office Municipal du Tourisme, 11, Rue Alençon. **Transportation:** *Train:* Tours–Rouen, Paris–Cherbourg, Dives–Cabourg. *Boat:* Channel Islands, England. *Bus:* Honfleur, Deauville, Livrarot. Orbec, Vimoutier. **Accommodations:** 🏨🏨🏨 Mapotel De la Plage. 🏨🏨 La Bretagne; La Coupe d'Or; Grand Hôtel de L'Epérance; De la Paix; Terrasse Hôtel. 🏨 De l'Avenue; De la Gare; De Lisieux; Le Rond-Point; Sainte-Thérèse; Saint-Michel; Les Sports.

Lodève (Languedoc-Roussillon)

Information: Syndicat d'Initiative, 17, Boulevard Liberté. **Transportation:** *Bus:* Montpellier–St-Affrique, Beziers. **Accommodations:** 🏨🏨🏨 Domaine du Canalet. 🏨🏨 De la Croix Blanche. 🏨 Du Nord.

Lourdes (Midi-Pyrénées)

Information: Syndicat d'Initiative, Place du Champ. *Air Inter:* Grand Hôtel de la Grotte. **Transportation:** *Air:* In summer, Barcelona, Biarritz, Brussels, Dublin, Nice, Paris. *Train:* Paris–Pierrefitte, Geneva-Hendaye, Toulouse, Marseille, and others. *Bus:* Arrens, Bagnères and several lines serve the outlying areas. **Accommodations:** 🏨🏨🏨 Christina; Du Gave; Ambassadeurs. 🏨🏨 Golgotha; Central; Florence; Lutétia; Beausite; Miramont; Concorde; Corona; Majestic. 🏨 De Paris; Mirella; Du Donjon; Barcelone.

Luchon (Midi-Pyénées)

Information: Syndicat d'Initiative, 18, Allée Étigny. **Transportation:** *Train:* Montrejeau-S.P. **Accommodations:** 🏨🏨🏨 Sacaron; Corneille. 🏨🏨 Des Bains; Beau-Site; Bon Accueil; Concorde; Royal-Hôtel; Hôtel d'Étigny. 🏨 Henri Sors; De la Paix; Dardenne; Deux Nations.

Lunéville (Lorraine)

Information: Syndicat d'Initiative, 22, Rue Haxo, Château de Lunéville (right wing). **Transportation:** *Train:* Sarrebourg–Nancy, St.-Dié, Bruyères. **Accommodations:** 🏨🏨 Europe; Voltaire. 🏨 Central et des Vosges; Au Cheval Gris.

Lyon (Alpes-du-Sud)

Information: Office du Tourisme de Lyon/Communauté Syndicat d'Initiative, Place Bellecour. *Travel bureaus:* Agence Française de Tourisme, 75, Rue de la République; Wagon-Lits-Cook, 105, Rue Pdt-Herriot. *Cruiselines:* Passenger Office, 6, Place des Terreaux. *Airlines: Air France:* 10, Quai Jules-Courmont. **Transportation:** *Train:* Bron, Lille, Marseille, Mulhouse, Nancy, Nantes, Nice, Paris. In summer only: Ajaccio, Algier, Bordeaux, Casablanca, Clermont-Ferrand, London, Milan, Toulon, Toulouse, Tours, Tunis, Zürich, Poitiers, Reims, Strasbourg. *Bus:* Domestic and international connections in all directions. Ambérieu, Annecy, Bourg, Cours, Dolomièn, Montbrison, Yenne. **Accommodations:** ⌂⌂⌂ Bristol; Carlton; Des Étrangers; Des Beaux-Arts. ⌂⌂ Le Montblanc; Axotel; Continental; Dubost; Bayard; De la Loire. ⌂ Bretagne; Genève; Du retour.

Mâcon (Bourgogne)

Information: Syndicat d'Initiative, Avenue de Lattre-de-Tassigny. **Transportation:** *Train:* Geneva, Paris, Ventimiglia, and others. *Bus:* Paray-le-Monial, Marcigny, Fleurville, Montceau, Pont de Vaux. **Accommodations:** ⌂⌂⌂ Novotel Macon Nord; Motel La Vieille Ferme. ⌂⌂ La Promenade; Terminus; Des Champs-Élysées. ⌂ La Savoie.

Magny-en-Vexin (Paris–Île-de-France)

Information: Syndicat d'Initiative, Mairie. **Transportation:** *Bus:* Chars, Les Mureaux. **Accommodations:** ⌂ G. H. Cerf; Cheval-Blanc.

Mantes-la-Jolie (Paris–Île-de-France)

Information: Office du Tourisme, 5, Place Jean XXIII. **Transportation:** *Train:* Caen, Cherbourg, Le Havre, Lisieux, Paris, Plaisir-Grignon, Rouen. **Accommodations:** ⌂⌂ Les Glycines. ⌂ Commerce.

Marennes (Poitou-Charentes)

Information: Syndicat d'Initiative, Place Verdun. **Transportation:** *Bus:* Saintes-St-Denis-d'Oléron, Rochefort–Le Chapus. **Accommodations:** ⌂ Du Commerce.

Marseille (Côte d'Azur)

Information: Office du Tourisme, 4–6, La Canebière. **Transportation:** *Air:* Algiers, Casablanca, Dakar, Djibouti, Geneva, London (in summer), Milan, Oran, Palma (in summer), Rabat, Rome, Tunis, Mexico. Ajaccio, Bastia, Bordeaux, and Calvi in summer, Constantine,

Lyon, Nice, Paris, Strasbourg. *Train:* Barcelona, Brussels, Geneva, Rome, and elsewhere. Bordeaux, Nice, Paris, Strasbourg, and others. *Bus:* Arles, Miramas, Carro, Martigues, Aix-en-Provence, Port-de-Bouc, Bandol, Barjols, Draguignan, Avignon, Turin. *Boat:* Ajaccio, Algiers, Oran, Tunis, Casablanca, Dakar, Pointe Noire. **Accommodations:** ☖☖☖ (*Luxury*) Frantel, Rue Neuve Saint Martin; Grand Hôtel Noailles, 64–68, La Canebière. ☖☖☖ Bristol, 18, La Canebière; Carlton Hôtel, 395 bis, Corniche Kennedy; Concorde Palm Beach, 2, Promenade de la Plage; De Genève, 3 bis, Rue Reine-Elisabeth; Grand Modern Hôtel, 5, La Canebière. ☖☖ Bellevue, 34, Quai du Port; Esterel, 124/125, Rue Paradis; Européen, 115/117, Rue Paradis; Grand Hôtel de Paris, 11–15, Rue Colbert. ☖ Azur, 24, crs F. Roosevelt; Du Caire, 12, Rue Beauvau; Edmond-Rostand, 31, Rue Dragon.

Martigues (Côte d'Azur)

Information: Syndicat d'Initiative, Musée du Vieux. **Transportation:** *Train:* Avignon, Marseille. *Bus:* Aix-en-Provence, Marseille. **Accommodations:** ☖☖☖ Eden; Saint-Roch. ☖☖ Lido; Le Venitien.

Maubeuge (Nord)

Information: Office du Tourisme Syndicat d'Initiative, Port de Bavay. **Transportation:** *Train:* Amsterdam, Berlin, Brussels, Copenhagen, Stockholm, Paris. *Bus:* Valenciennes, Avesnes, Bettiguies, Mons. **Accommodations:** ☖☖ Grand Hôtel de Paris. ☖ De Provence, De la Poste.

Mauriac (Auvergne)

Transportation: *Train:* Aurillac. *Bus:* Aurillac, Riomès-Mont. **Accommodations:** ☖☖ De l'Écu de France, Central Hôtel; Des Voyageurs la Bonne Auberge.

Mazamet (Midi-Pyrénées)

Information: Syndicat d'Initiative, Rue Georges-Tournier. **Transportation:** *Train:* St-Pons–Toulouse. *Bus:* Carcassonne. **Accommodations:** ☖☖☖ Le Grand Balcon. ☖☖ Les Comtes d'Hautpoul. ☖ Boulevard.

Meaux (Paris–Île-de-France)

Information: Syndicat d'Initiative, 2, Rue Nôtre-Dame. **Transportation:** *Train:* Paris–Château-Thierry, Reims. *Bus:* Crépy en Valois, Coulommiers, Dammartin. **Accommodations:** ☖☖☖ De la Sirène. ☖☖ Le Richemont. ☖ De la Gare.

Megève (Alpes-du-Nord)

Information: Syndicat d'Initiative, Avenue A.-Martin. **Transportation:** *Train:* Nearest train station, Sallanches. *Bus:* Albertville, Geneva, Annecy–Chamonix, Sallanches, St-Gervais. Cable cars, chair lifts, rope tows. **Accommodations:** 🏨🏨🏨 (*Luxury*) Chalet Mont d'Arbois; Mont-Blanc. 🏨🏨🏨 Grand Hôtel du Parc; Du Mont-Joly; Au Coin du Feu. 🏨🏨 Nid du Mage; La Marmotte; Week-End; Les Sapins; Le Megevan; Fleur des Alpes; Les Roseaux; Des Neiges. 🏨 Mon Ideal; Les Fougères; Sylvana; Les Primevères; La Croix de Savoie.

Mende (Languedoc-Roussillon)

Information: Syndicat d'Initiative, 16, Boulevard Soubeyran. **Transportation:** *Train:* Paris, Marseille. *Bus:* Alès, Rodez, Florac, Langogne. **Accommodations:** 🏨🏨🏨 Mapotel des Lions d'Or. 🏨🏨 De France; Pont Roupt; Grand Hôtel de Paris et de la Poste.

Menton (Côte d'Azur)

Information: Syndicat d'Initiative, Avenue Boyer. **Transportation:** *Train:* Ventimiglia, Metz. *Bus:* Europabus Nice–Brussels. **Accommodations:** 🏨🏨🏨 Beau Rivage; Chambord; Du Parc; Aiglon; Viking. 🏨🏨 Carlton; Le Globe; Londres. 🏨 Claridge; Magenta; Terminus; Benzo; Richelieu; Villa Louise.

Metz (Lorraine)

Information: Syndicat d'Initiative, Porte Serpenoise. **Transportation:** *Train:* Basel, Amsterdam, Brussels, Luxembourg, Rome, Nancy, Paris, and others. *Bus:* Many buses serve the area. **Accommodations:** 🏨🏨🏨 (*Luxury*) Royal. 🏨🏨🏨 Frantel Metz; Le Crinouc. 🏨🏨 Du Centre; Moderne; Bristol; Cecil Hôtel; Gare; Foch; Métropole. 🏨 La Pergola; De France.

Millau (Midi-Pyrénées)

Information: Syndicat d'Initiative, 1, Avenue Merle. **Transportation:** *Train:* Paris–Béziers. *Bus:* Many buses serve the area. **Accommodations:** 🏨🏨🏨 International Hôtel. 🏨🏨 Du Commerce; La Capelle. 🏨 Mon Hôtel; Royal; De la Vallée.

Mirecourt (Vosges)

Transportation: *Train:* Chaumont, Épinal, Nancy. *Bus:* Charmes. **Accommodations:** 🏨 De la Gare.

Monaco (Côte d'Azur)

Information; Direction du Tourisme et des Congrès de la Principauté de Monaco, 2a, Boulevard des Moulins, tel. (93) 50 60 88. **Transportation:** *Air:* International airport. *Train:* Lyon, Marseille, Nice, Paris, Strasbourg. *Bus:* Compagnies Rapides Côtes d'Azur. **Accommodations:** 🏨🏨🏨 (*Luxury*) Hôtel de Paris, Place du Casino; Monte-Carlo Beach, Avenue du Bord de Mer; Beach Plaza, 22, Avenue Princesse Grace. 🏨🏨🏨 Alexandra, 35, Boulevard Princesse-Charlotte; Balmoral, 12, Avenue de la Coste; Miramar, 1 bis, Avenue J.-F. Kennedy; Splendid, 4, Avenue de Roqueville; Versailles, 4–6, Avenue Prince Pierre. 🏨🏨 Le Siècle, 10, Avenue Prince Pierre; Résidence des Moulins, 27, Boulevard des Moulins; Terminus, 9, Avenue Prince Pierre. 🏨 Cosmopolite, 4, Rue de la Turbie; De la Poste, 5, Rue des Oliviers; De l'Étoile, 4, Rue des Oliviers; De France, 6, Rue de la Turbie; Helvetia, 1 bis, Rue Grimaldi.

Montargis (Centre–Val-de-Loire)

Transportation: *Train:* Paris–Nevers. *Bus:* Paris, Orléans, Auxerre, Malherbes. **Accommodations:** 🏨🏨 De la Gloire; Grand Hôtel de France, De Lyon 🏨 Bon Gîte; Le Cheval Blanc.

Montauban (Midi-Pyrénées)

Information: Syndicat d'Initiative, Rue Collège. **Transportation:** *Train:* Bordeaux, Paris, Port Bou, Toulouse, Marseille. *Bus:* Albi, Auch, and others. **Accommodations:** 🏨🏨🏨 Mapotel-Ingres. 🏨🏨 Du Midi; Bristol; Au Lion d'Or; Prince Noir. 🏨 Du Commerce; Poste; Le Sélect.

Montceau-les-Mines (Bourgogne)

Information: Syndicat d'Initiative, Place H.-de-Ville. **Transportation:** *Train:* Chagny, Clermont-Ferrand, Paris. **Accommodations:** 🏨🏨🏨 Du Commerce. 🏨🏨 De Bourgogne. 🏨 Du Lac; Epoque.

Montélimar (Vallée du Rhône)

Information: Maison du Tourisme, Allées Champs-de-Mars. **Transportation:** *Train:* Marseille–Lyon–Paris, Nice–Marseille–Dijon. *Bus:* Valreas, Valence, Lafarge, Aubenas, Valvigneres, Privas, Laon, Avignon, Nyons; Europabus Paris–Nice. **Accommodations:** 🏨🏨🏨 Relais de l'Empereur; Motel Vallée du Rhône. 🏨🏨 Sphinx; Dauphiné-Provence; Beau Soleil. 🏨 Pierre; Chez Nous; De la Croix d'Or; Genève; Saint-Gaucher.

Mont-Louis (Languedoc-Roussillon)

Information: Syndicat d'Initiative, Mairie. **Transportation:** *Train:* Perpignan. **Accommodations:** 🏨 Clos Cerdan.

Montpellier (Languedoc-Roussillon)

Information: Office du Tourisme, Syndicat d'Initiative, Place de la Comédie. **Transportation:** *Air:* Paris, Bordeaux, Lyon, Nice, London, Valencia. *Train:* Marseille, Nîmes, Geneva, Toulouse, and others. *Bus:* Ganges, Palavesles-Flots, Le Grau-du-Roi, St-Affrique, Sète. **Accommodations:** 🏨 Frantel; Royal Hôtel; George V. 🏨 De la Comédie; Le Mistral; Paris; Edouard VII; Angleterre. 🏨 Cosmos; Polygone Stade.

Mont-Saint-Michel (Normandie)

Information: Syndicat d'Initiative, Corps de Garde des Bourgeois. **Transportation:** *Bus:* Pontorson, Granville. **Accommodations:** 🏨 La Mère Poulard. 🏨 Duguesclin; K-Motel; Du Mouton Blanc. 🏨 Vieille Auberge.

Morlaix (Bretagne)

Transportation: *Train:* Carhaix, Brest–Paris, Roscoff. *Bus:* Carantec, Carhaix, Guingamp, Lannion, Quimper. **Accommodations:** 🏨 D'Europe. 🏨 Calvez.

Moulins (Auvergne)

Transportation: *Train:* Clermont-Ferrand, Montluçon, Paray-le-M., Paris. *Bus:* Bourges, Bourbon, Châteauroux, Clermont-Ferrand, Le Donjon, Montluçon. **Accommodations:** 🏨 (*Luxury*) De Paris. 🏨 Moderne. 🏨 Ibis; Le Parc; Grand Hôtel du Dauphin. 🏨 De l'Agriculture; Le Français; Danguin-Terminus.

Moutiers (Alpes-du-Nord)

Transportation: *Train:* Chambéry–Bourg-St-Maurice. *Bus:* Pralognan, Courchevel, Albertville–Bourg-St-Maurice, Meribel, St-Martin-de-B., Le Villard-du-Planay, Pralognan. **Accommodations:** 🏨 Ibis; Terminus. 🏨 Auberge des Alpes.

Mulhouse (Lorraine-Vosges-Alsace)

Information: Office du Tourisme, 9, Avenue Foch. *Air Inter:* Aéroport Saint-Louis. **Transportation:** *Air:* Lyon, Milan, Paris. *Train:* Amsterdam, Basel, Brussels, Luxembourg, Milan, Rome, Vienna, Zürich, Belfort, Paris, Strasbourg, and others. *Bus:* Altkirch, Bellemagny, Belfort, Leymen, Sewen, St-Dié, Thann. **Accommodations:** Novotel Sausheim; De la Bourse; Europe; Mercure Sausheim; Bristol. National; Strasbourg; Paris. Le Paon d'Or; Schoenberg; Taverne.

Munster (Lorraine-Vosges-Alsace)

Information: Syndicat d'Initiative, Place de la Salle des Fêtes. **Transportation:** *Train:* Colmar-Metzeral. *Bus:* Epinal-Colmar. **Accommodations:** De la Cigogne; Des Vosges. A la Schlucht.

Nancy (Lorraine)

Information: Office du Tourisme, 14, Place Stanislas. *Air Inter:* Aéroport Essey. **Transportation:** *Air:* Epinal, Lyon, Paris. *Train:* Munich, Vienna, Metz, Paris, Strasbourg. *Bus:* Conthil, Thezey, Verdun, Toul. **Accommodations:** Américain; De l'Europe. Albert Ier; Ariane; Carnot; De la Poste. Des Beaux-Arts; Lycée.

Nantes (Bretagne)

Information: Office du Tourisme, Syndicat d'Initiative, Place du Change. *Air France:* Place Neptun. *Air Inter:* 6, Place Royale. **Transportation:** *Air:* Bordeaux, Lyon, La Rochelle, Marseille, Paris, Nice. *Train:* Bordeaux, Lyon, Paris, and others. *Bus:* Cholet, Les Herbiers, Prefailles, Redon, St Brévin. **Accommodations:** Supotel; Vendée; De France; Astoria; De Bourgogne. Graslin; De Paris; Des Trois Marchands. De la Bourse; Grand Monarque; Surcouf; Longchamp; Orléans; Trianon.

Narbonne (Languadoc-Roussillon)

Information: Office du Tourisme–Syndicat d'Initiative de Narbonne et sa Région, Jardin de la Maison Vigneronne, Place Roger Salengro. **Transportation:** *Air:* Lézignan, Carcassonne, Béziers, Perpignan. *Train:* Bordeaux, Cerbère, Marseille, and others. *Bus:* La Caunette, Monthoumet, Sigean, Maillac, St-Pierre-s.-M. Neviau. **Accommodations:** Du Languedoc; La Résidence. Le Fin Gourmet; Du Midi; France; Lion d'Or. De Paris.

Nemours (Paris–Île-de-France)

Information: Syndicat d'Initiative, Office du Tourisme, 17, Rue des Tanneurs. **Transportation:** *Train:* Montargis–Moret–Paris. *Bus:* Paris. **Accommodations:** 🏨🏨🏨 Euromotel-Etap-Hôtel. 🏨🏨 De l'Écu de France; Saint-Pierre. 🏨 De l'Ecluse.

Néris-les-Bains (Auvergne)

Transportation: *Bus:* Montluçon–Vichy, Commentry. **Accommodations:** 🏨🏨 Parc des Rivalles; De la Source; Dumoulin; Splendid Hôtel. 🏨 Du Casino; Central Hôtel; Du Centre; Du Rhône et Thermes.

Neufchâteau (Lorraine-Vosges-Alsace)

Transportation: *Bus:* Bar-le-Duc, Mirecourt, Chaumont, Dijon, Nancy, Pagny, Toul. **Accommodations:** 🏨🏨 Saint-Christophe.

Nevers (Bourgogne)

Information: Syndicat d'Initiative, 3, Rue des Remparts. **Transportation:** *Train:* Besançon, Clermont-Ferrand–Paris, Vierzon. *Bus:* Clamecy, Cercy-la T., Château–Chinon, Saulieu. 🏨🏨🏨 Magdalena. 🏨🏨 Molière; Terminus; Auberge Sainte-Marie; Moderne; Clèves. 🏨 Du Morvan; Thermidor; Villa du Parc.

Nice (Côte d'Azur)

Information: Office du Tourisme, Avenue Thiers. *Air France* and *Air Inter:* 7, Avenue Gustave V. *Lufthansa:* Aéroport Côte d'Azur. **Transportation:** *Air:* Ajaccio, Bastia, Calvi, Lourdes (in summer), Lyon, Marseille, Nice, Nîmes, Olbia, Paris, Algier, Amsterdam, Athen, Barcelona, Béziers (in summer) Bordeaux, Brussels, Casablanca, Copenhagen, Dakar, Lisbon, London, Luxembourg, Milan (in summer), New York, Rome, Tunis, Zürich. *Train:* Autotrains toward the north and Paris, among other destinations. *Bus:* Lyon, Paris, Grenoble, Briançon, Marseille, Monaco-Menton, Saint-Martin–Vésubie, Grasse, Grande-Corniche–Monte-Carlo. *Boat:* Corsica. **Accommodations:** 🏨🏨🏨 (*Luxury*) Mercure, 2, Rue Halevy; Park-Hôtel, 6, Avenue de Suède. 🏨🏨🏨 Agata, 46, Boulevard Carnot; Ambassador, 8, Avenue de Suède; Carlton, 26, Boulevard Victor-Hugo; La Résidence, 18, Avenue Durante. 🏨🏨 Carnot, 8 Boulevard Carnot; Impérial Hôtel, 8, Boulevard Carabacel; De la Mer, 4, Place Masséna; Miron, 4, Rue Miron; De Mulhouse, 9, Rue Chauvain. 🏨 Monclar, 29, Boulevard Magnan; Le Gourmet Lorrain, 7, Avenue Santa-Fior; Panoramic, 107, Boulevard Bischoffsheim; Pension des Studios, 11, Avenue Dr.-Roux; Soleil d'Or, 16, Avenue des Orangers.

Nîmes (Languedoc-Roussillon)

Information: Syndicat d'Initiative, 6, Rue Auguste. **Transportation:** *Air:* Paris, Nice. *Train:* Clermont-Ferrand, Lyon, Toulouse, Marseille, and others. *Bus:* Tarascon, Sommières, St-Gilles, Arles, Avignon, Camargue. **Accommodations:** 🏨🏨🏨 (*Luxury*) Imperator. 🏨🏨🏨 Cheval Blanc et des Arènes; Grand Hôtel du Midi. 🏨🏨 Amphithéâtre; Carrière; Empire; Le Louvre; Temple. 🏨 Central; Du Dauphiné; Doré; Forum; Menausa; Modern; De Paris.

Niort (Poitou-Charentes)

Information: Syndicat d'Initiative, Place Poste. **Transportation:** *Train:* Paris, Saintes, La Rochelle, and others. *Bus:* Couture-d'Argen, Angers, Sauze–Vaussais, and others. **Accommodations:** 🏨🏨🏨 Grand Hôtel. 🏨🏨 Parc; Terminus; Paris; Central. 🏨 De l'Europe, De Bordeaux.

Nogent–le-Rotrou (Centre–Val-de-Loire)

Information: Syndicat d'Initiative, 22, Place St.-Pol. **Transportation:** *Train:* Paris–Le Mans. *Bus:* Alençon. **Accommodations:** 🏨🏨 Du Dauphin; Du Lion d'Or.

Noyon (Picardie)

Information: Office du Tourisme–Syndicat d'Initiative, Hôtel de Ville. **Transportation:** *Train:* Paris–St-Quentin. *Bus:* Ham, Compiègne. **Accommodations:** 🏨🏨 Le Grillon; St-Éloi.

Obernai (Alsace)

Transportation: *Train:* Strasbourg-Sélestat. **Accommodations:** 🏨🏨🏨 Le Grand Hôtel; Du Parc. 🏨🏨 De la Cloche; Hostellerie la Diligence.

Omaha-Beach (Normandie)

Accommodations: 🏨 Casino.

Orléans (Centre–Val-de-Loire)

Information: Syndicat d'Initiative, Place Albert-Ier. **Transportation:** *Train:* Bordeaux, Paris, Toulouse, Tours, and others. **Accommodations:** 🏨🏨🏨 Saint-Aignan; Les Cèdres; Terminus; D'Orléans. 🏨🏨 Central; Marguerite; Saint-Martin; De l'Abeille et du Commerce. 🏨 Trévise; Des Carmes; Bannier; Étoile d'Or; Touring.

Paimpol (Bretagne)

Information: Syndicat d'Initiative, Place de la République. **Transportation:** *Train:* Guingamp. *Bus:* Pontrieux, Pointe de l'Arcouest, St-Brieuc, Lannion. **Accommodations:** 🏨🏨🏨 Relais Brenner. 🏨🏨 Groëlo; De la Marne. 🏨 Berthelot.

Paris (Paris–Île-de-France)

Information: *Le Bureau d'Accueil de l'Office du Tourisme de Paris:* 127, Avenue des Champs-Élysées (open daily, 9:00 A.M.–10:00 P.M.). Information can also be obtained at the following train stations: *Bureau Gare de l'Est:* Place du 11-Novembre 1945 (open daily except Sunday, 7:00 A.M.–1:00 P.M. and 5:00 P.M.–11 P.M.). *Aérogare des Invalides:* Esplanade des Invalides (open weekdays, 9:00 A.M.–10:00 P.M., Sundays 10:30 A.M.–1:30 P.M. and 3:30 P.M.–7:30 P.M.). *Bureau Gare de Lyon:* Station ticket office open daily except Sundays, 6:30 A.M.–12:30 P.M. and 5:00 P.M.–11:00 P.M. *C.I.P. Porte Maillot:* open daily except Sunday 10:00 A.M.–8:00 P.M. *Bureau Gare du Nord:* station ticket office or 18, Rue de Dunkerque; open daily except Sundays, 8:30 A.M.–10:00 P.M.

Post offices: Post offices are open Monday–Friday, 8:00 A.M.–10:00 P.M. and Saturdays, 8:00 A.M.–12:00 noon. The following post offices are open on Sundays and holidays: 49, Rue la Boëtie; 103, Rue de Grenelle (7e); 8, Place de la Bourse (1er); Main post office, 48–52, Rue du Louvre (1er).

Money exchange: Most banks are open Monday–Friday, 9:00 A.M.–12:00 noon and 2:00 P.M.–4:00 P.M., before holidays open only until noon. Exchange offices open late every evening are located at the three airports and at the *Aérogare des Invalides,* open 5:30 A.M.–11:00 P.M.; the *Gare d'Austerlitz* (7:30 A.M.–11:30 P.M.); *Gare d'Est* (7:45 A.M.–10:00 P.M.); the *Gare de Lyon* (6:30 A.M.–11:00 P.M.); the *Gare St. Lazare* (6:00 A.M.–10:00 P.M.); the tourist office *OTP* at 127, Champs-Élysées (9:00 A.M.–12:00 midnight); and in the *Centre International CIP,* Port Maillot (7:00 A.M.–11:00 P.M.).

City tours: If you prefer to take an organized tour of the city with a group, you can contact any of the following organizations: *Cityrama-Rapid Pullman:* 4, Place des Pyramides (1er; Tel. 260-30-14) and 21, Rue de la Paix (2e; Tel. 073-60-20). *Paris-Vision:* 5, Rue d'Alger. Paris-Excursions: 1, Rue Auber (9e), *S. N. C. F.* (French National Railroad): 36, Rue de Léningrad (8e) and at the information booth: 127, Avenue des Champs-Élysées (8e; Tel. 720-12-80).

Guides: The *Bureau Officiel des Guides-Interprètes*, 83, Rue Taitbout (Tel.: 874–14–08) supplies English-speaking guides.

Transportation: *Train stations:* Gare d'Austerlitz (travels to the southwest), 55, Quai d'Austerlitz, Paris 13ᵉ arrondissement; Paris-Est (travels to the east), Place du 11 Novembre 1918, Paris 10ᵉ arrondissement; Paris-Sud-Est (travels to the southeast), Place Louis Armand, Paris 12ᵉ arrondissement; Paris-Montparnasse (travels to the west), 17, Boulevard de Vaugirard, Paris 15ᵉ arrondissement; Paris-Nord (travels to the north), 3, Rue Ambroise Paré, Paris 10ᵉ arrondissement; Paris-St.-Lazare (travels to the northwest), 13, Rue d'Amsterdam, Paris 8ᵉ arrondissement. *Bus:* Paris is served by 55 bus lines within the city and 134 suburban lines. The green bus stops, labeled as *points d'arrêt,* are marked by round yellow and red signs that indicate the line number and direction. Buses stop only on request, so waiting passengers must signal the driver to stop. *Métro:* The subway system (Métropolitain), called Le Métro for short, service begins at 5:30 A.M. from outlying terminals. The last trains at night reach their terminals at 1:15 A.M. Accordingly, there is no subway service in central Paris between about 12:45 A.M. and 6:00 A.M.

Accommodations: 🏨🏨🏨 (*Luxury*) Inter-Continental, 3, Rue Castiglione; Ritz, 15, Place Vendôme; Meurice, 228, Rue de Rivoli; Madeleine Palace, 8, Rue Cambon; Cambon, 3, Rue Cambon. 🏨🏨🏨 Brighton, 218, Rue de Rivoli; De Calais, 5, Rue des Capucines; Du Continent, 30, Rue de Mont-Tabor; G. H. de Champagne, 17, Rue Jean-Lantier; Du Loiret, 5, Rue des Bons-Enfants; Molière, 21, Rue Molière; Régence Opéra, 5-7, Rue Thérèse; Sainte-Anne Ladbroke, 10, Rue Sainte-Anne; Des Tuileries, 10, Rue Saint-Hyacinthe; Violet, 7, Rue Jean-Lantier. 🏨🏨 Des Ducs de Bourgogne, 19, Rue du Pont-Neuf; Londres-Stockholm, 13, Rue St-Roch; Montpensier, 12, Rue de Richelieu; Timhôtel le Louvre, 4, Rue Croix-des-Petits-Champs; Washington-Opéra, 50, Rue de Richelieu. 🏨🏨 De Nice, 42 bis, Rue de Rivoli; Mary-Hôtel, 32, Rue Sainte-Anne; Du Palais, 2, Quai de la Mégisserie; Résidence Vauvillers, 6, Rue Vauvillers; Richelieu-Mazarin, 51, Rue de Richelieu; De Rouen, 42, Rue Crois des Petits Champs.

Périgueux (Aquitaine)

Information: Syndicat d'Initiative du Tourisme, 1, Avenue d'Aquitaine. **Transportation:** *Train:* Bordeaux, Agen, and others. *Bus:* Riberac, Bordeaux, Angoulême. **Accommodations:** 🏨🏨🏨 Du Domino; Bristol. 🏨🏨 Regina Hôtel. 🏨 Fenelon; Lion d'Or; Le Toulouse; De l'Univers; Charentes.

Péronne (Picardie)

Information: Syndicat d'Initiative. **Transportation:** *Bus:* Montdidier–Chaulnes–Cambrai. **Accommodations:** 🏨 Hostellerie des Remparts.

Perpignan (Languedoc-Roussillon)

Transportation: *Air:* Perpignan/Riversaltes airport. *Train:* Narbonne, Port Bou, Le Tour de Carol. *Bus:* Europabus Toulouse–Barcelona; Quillan, La Preste-les-B., Le Perthus, Le Barcarès, St-Cyprien, Fourques, Thuir. **Accommodations:** 🏨 De la Loge; De France; Le Catalogne. 🏨 Des Pyrénées; Regina; Victoria; Christina; Méditerranée; Paris-Barcelone. 🏨 Le Mermoz; Le Helder; Florida; Du Midi.

Pézenas (Languedoc-Roussillon)

Transportation: *Bus:* Agde, Béziers–Lodève. **Accommodations:** 🏨 Genieys. 🏨 Grand Hôtel Molière.

Phalsbourg (Lorraine)

Transportation: *Bus:* Saverne, Strasbourg–Sarrebourg. **Accommodations:** 🏨 Ercmann-Chatrian.

Pleyben (Bretagne)

Information: Syndicat d'Initiative. **Transportation:** *Train:* Charhaix–Châteaulin. *Bus:* Quimper–Morlaix. **Accommodations:** 🏨 Auberge du Poisson Blanc.

Ploërmel (Bretagne)

Information: Syndicat d'Initiative, Place Lamennais and 16, Boulevard Foch. **Transportation:** *Train:* Rennes–La Brohiniere–Ploërmel. *Bus:* Rennes–Vannes, Questembert, Pontivy-Redon, La Trinité-Prohoët. **Accommodations:** 🏨 Du Commerce; Saint-Marc.

Plombières-les-Bains (Vosges)

Information: Syndicat d'Initiative, 16, Rue Stanislas. **Transportation:** *Train:* Paris. *Bus:* Épinal–Le Vas d'Ajol, Aillevillers, Vesoul-Remiremont. **Accommodations:** 🏨 Beauséjour; Grand Hôtel. 🏨 Des Abbesses–Relais des Capucins; G. H. des Bains; La Fontaine Stanislas. 🏨 Bolmont-Bernier; Central; Du Commerce; Maison Blanche; Riviera; Sources.

Poitiers (Poitou-Charentes)

Information: Office du Tourisme et Syndicat d'Initiative, Rue Victor Hugo. **Transportation:** *Train:* Bordeaux, Limoges, Paris, and others. *Bus:* Argenton, Charroux, Confolens, Loudun, Parthenay, St-Cauvant. **Accommodations:** 🏨🏨🏨 (*Luxury*) Mapotel de France. 🏨🏨🏨 Royal-Poitou. 🏨🏨 De l'Europe; Régina; Du Chapon Fin. 🏨 Grand Cerf; Lion d'Or.

Poligny (Franche-Comté)

Transportation: *Train:* Besançon-Lyon. *Bus:* Besançon, Dole. **Accommodations:** 🏨🏨🏨 Hostellerie des Monts de Vaux. 🏨🏨 Hotellerie Vallée Heureuse; De Paris. 🏨 Charmilles; Nouvel Hôtel.

Pontoise (Paris–Île-de-France)

Information: Syndicat d'Initiative, 6, Place Petit-Martroy. **Transportation:** *Train:* Creil, Dieppe, Gisors, Paris. *Bus:* Les Mureaux, St.-Germain. **Accommodations:** 🏨 De Pontoise.

Pont-Saint-Esprit (Languedoc-Roussillon)

Information: Office Municipal du Tourisme, Place Pasteur. **Transportation:** *Train:* Lyon–Nîmes. *Bus:* Avignon, Arles, Ardèche, Montélimar, Orange, Nîmes. **Accommodations:** 🏨🏨 Commerce. 🏨 Europe et Poste.

Port Grimaud (Côte d'Azur)

Information: Syndicat d'Initiative. **Transportation:** *Air:* Nice. *Train:* St. Raphaël. **Accommodations:** 🏨🏨🏨 Du Port.

Porto (Corsica)

Transportation: *Bus:* Regular service throughout the island. **Accommodations:** 🏨🏨🏨 Kallisté. 🏨🏨 Cyrnéa; Idéal-Hôtel; Monte Rosso. 🏨 Beauséjour; Bellavista; Le Golfe.

Porto-Vecchio (Corsica)

Transportation: *Bus:* Regular service throughout the island. *Boat:* Island traffic by boat. **Accommodations:** 🏨🏨🏨 Cala Verde. 🏨🏨 Les Roches Blanches; Chez Franca; L'Aiglon; Le Hameaux de Palombaggia. 🏨 Da Mama.

Port-Vendres (Languedoc-Roussillon)

Information: Syndicat d'Initiative. Office du Tourisme, Place de l'Obélisque. **Transportation:** *Train:* Cerbère, Perpignan. *Boat:* Balearen–Porto–Alcadia. **Accommodations:** 🏨 La Résidence; Saint-Elme; Les Tamarins. 🛏 Des Albères; Castallane.

Propriano (Corsica)

Transportation: *Boat:* Marseille, Toulon, Nice. *Bus:* Regular service throughout the island. **Accommodations:** 🏨 Arena Bianca; Roc e Mare; Du Valinco. 🏨 Claridge; Lido; Ollandini.

Quiberon (Bretagne)

Information: Office du Tourisme, 7, Rue de Verdun. **Transportation:** *Boat:* Le Palais (Belle Île). *Train:* Auray, Vannes. **Accommodations:** 🏨 Beau Rivage; Relais des Îles. 🏨 Hoche; Bellevue; Europa; Mer; Idéal. 🛏 Caravelle; De l'Océan; Mener Vro.

Quimper (Bretagne)

Information: Syndicat d'Initiative, 3, Rue du Roi-Gradlon. **Transportation:** *Air:* Paris. *Train:* Brest, Bordeaux, Douarnenez, Lyon, Paris. *Bus:* St.-Brieuc, Morlaix, Lorient, Camaret, Pointe du Raz, Beg-Mail, St-Guenole, and others. **Accommodations:** 🏨 Griffon. 🏨 La Tour d'Auvergne. Gradlon; Moderne; Le Transvaal. 🛏 Celtic; De l'Odet; Pascal Frères; Terminus.

Quimperlé (Bretagne)

Information: Syndicat d'Initiative. **Transportation:** *Train:* Quimper, Paris. *Bus:* Quimper, Le Pouldu. **Accommodations:** 🏨 Hermitage. 🛏 De l'Europe; Moderne; Tour d'Auvergne.

Rambouillet (Paris–Île-de-France)

Transportation: *Train:* Paris. *Bus:* Ablis, Dourdan, Limours, Montfort, St-Remy. **Accommodations:** 🏨 St-Charles. 🛏 Relais du Château.

Reims (Champagne)

Information: Office du Tourisme, 3, Boulevard de la Paix. **Transportation:** *Train:* Brussels, Dijon, Épernay, Lille, Luxembourg, Paris, Strasbourg, and others. *Bus:* Épernay, Rethel, St-Menehould, Soissons, Vouziers, Charleville-Mézières. **Accommodations:** 🏨 Mercure Reims Est; De la Paix. 🏨 Grand Hôtel du Nord; De l'Univers; Grand Hôtel Continental; Welcome; Cecyl. 🛏 Arcades; Jeanne d'Arc; Libergier; Monopole; D'Alsace.

Rennes (Bretagne)

Information: Syndicat d'Initiative, Place de la République. **Transportation:** *Train:* Brest, Paris, Quimper, St-Malo. *Bus:* Dinan, Dinard, Guer, Fougères, Angers, Loudeac, Mont St-Michel, Redon, Paramé, St-Malo, and others. **Accommodations:** 🏨 Frantel; Central Hôtel; Du Guesclin; Président; Anne de Bretagne. 🏨 Cheval d'Or; Garden Hôtel; Astrid; Angélina; Le Sévigné. 🏨 De Nemours; Paris; Angleterre; Beaumont.

Ribeauvillé (Alsace)

Information: Office du Tourisme–Syndicat d'Initiative, 1, Grande-Rue. **Transportation:** *Train:* Mulhouse–Sélestat, Strasbourg–Basel. *Bus:* Colmar–Ribeauvillé. **Accommodations:** 🏨 (*Luxury*) Clos St.-Vincent; Pepinière. 🏨 De la Tour; Au Cheval Blanc; Des Vosges. 🏨 Du Mouton.

Riom (Auvergne)

Transportation: *Train:* Châtel-Guyon, Clermont-Ferrand. *Bus:* Châtel-Guyon, Clermont-Ferrand, Vichy. **Accommodations:** 🏨 Mikege; Le Pacifique; Des Voyageurs. 🏨 La Caravelle; Lyon; Du Square.

Rocamadour (Midi-Pyrénées)

Transportation: *Train:* Paris–Rodez. **Accommodations:** 🏨 De l'Ascenseur; Mapotel Beau Site et Nôtre-Dame. 🏨 Sainte-Marie; Panoramic; Bellevue. 🏨 Des Voyageurs.

Rochefort-sur-Mer (Poitou–Charentes)

Transportation: *Train:* Bordeaux, Nantes, Paris. *Bus:* Fouras, Le Chapus, La Rochelle, Port-des-Barques. **Accommodations:** 🏨 Caravelle. 🏨 Colbert; Du Grand Bacha.

Rodez (Midi-Pyrénées)

Transportation: *Train:* Toulouse, and others. *Bus:* Millau, St-Affrique, Albi, and others. **Accommodations:** 🏨 Le Parc; Biney. 🏨 Moderne; Le Concorde. 🏨 De l'Avenir; Beauséjour; Soulie.

Romans-sur-Isère (Vallée-du-Rhône)

Information: Syndicat d'Initiative, Place J.-Nadi. **Transportation:** *Train:* Valence-Grenoble, Paris. *Bus:* Beaurepaire, Le Grand-Serre, Grenoble, Vercors, Tournon-Bourg-de-Péage, Valence, Vassieux. **Accommodations:** 🏨 Magdaleine; Terminus; Des Ors; Au Tahiti; Valence.

Roquebrune-Cap-Martin (Côte d'Azur)

Information: Syndicat d'Initiative, 20, Avenue Paul-Doumer. **Accommodations:** 🏨 (*Luxury*) Monte Carlo Beach Hôtel. 🏨 Regency; Alexandra; Victoria et Plage. 🏠 Westminster.

Roquefort-sur-Soulzon (Midi-Pyrénées)

Transportation: *Bus:* Tournemire–St-Affrique. **Accommodations:** 🏨 Grand-Hôtel.

Roscoff (Bretagne)

Transportation: *Train:* Morlaix. *Bus:* Brest. **Accommodations:** 🏨 Régina. 🏨 Talabardon; Bellevue. 🏠 Des Arcades; D'Angleterre; Du Centre Chez Janie.

Rosheim (Alsace)

Transportation: *Train:* Strasbourg–Sélestat. *Bus:* Ottrott. **Accommodations:** 🏠 Auberge du Cerf.

Rouen (Normandie)

Information: Office du Tourisme, 25, Place Cathédrale. **Transportation:** *Train:* Amiens, Dieppe, Le Havre, Le Mans, Paris. *Bus:* Paris, Dieppe, Le Tréport, Fécamp, Le Havre, Deauville, Caen, Lisieux, Chartres, Gournay, Neufchâtel, Aumale. **Accommodations:** 🏨 (*Luxury*) Frantel; De Dieppe. 🏨 De Bordeaux; Normandie; Solférino; Bristol; Régina; Astrid. 🏠 Des Arcades; Chapeau Rouge; Gare Rive Droite; Modern Hôtel; Napoléon; Préfecture; La Tour de Beurre.

Rozay-en-Brie (Paris–Île-de-France)

Transportation: *Train:* Bordeaux, Clermont-Ferrand, Paris. *Bus:* Coulommiers–Melun. **Accommodations:** 🏨 Régina; Métropole. 🏨 Parc Majestic; Belle-Meunière; Richelieu. 🏠 Royal; Cottage; Castel; Paix; Chalet Camille; Ste-Eugénie; Pépinière; Victoria.

Saint-Affrique (Midi-Pyrénées)

Transportation: *Air:* Montpellier, Belmont. *Bus:* Albi, Millau, Montpellier, Rodez. *Train:* Tournemine, Roquefort. *Boat:* Sète. **Accommodations:** 🏨 Moderne. 🏠 France; Du Pont Neuf.

Saint-Amand-Mont-Rond (Centre–Val-de-Loire)

Information: Syndicat d'Initiative, Place de la République. **Transportation:** *Train:* Bourges, Montluçon, Paris. *Bus:* Bourges, Moulins, Montluçon. **Accommodations:** 🏨 De la Poste. 🏨 Central Hôtel.

Saint-Denis (Paris–Île-de-France)

Information: Office du Tourisme, 2, Rue de la Légion d'Honneur. **Accommodations:** 🏨 Moderne. 🏨 Poste.

Saint-Dié (Vosges)

Information: Syndicat d'Initiative, 31, Rue Thiers. **Transportation:** *Train:* Nancy–Sélestat, Épinal, Strasbourg. *Bus:* Plaintaing, Raon–L'Étape. **Accommodations:** 🏨 Du Parc; Du Globe; Des Vosges. 🏨 Acacias; Moderne; Du Commerce; Voyageurs; Montcalm.

Saint-Dizier (Champagne)

Information: Syndicat d'Initiative, Pavillon du Jard. **Transportation:** *Train:* Reims, Dijon. *Bus:* Troyes, Doulevant-les-Ch., Commercy, Bar-le-Duc. **Accommodations:** 🏨 Gambetta. 🏨 Le Picardy; Gare et Voyageurs; Commerce.

Sainte-Maxime-sur-Mer (Côte d'Azur)

Information: Syndicat d'Initiative, Avenue de la IVe-République. **Transportation:** *Bus:* St-Raphaël, Toulon. **Accommodations:** 🏨 Beau Site; Chardon Bleu; Le Calidianus; La Croisette. 🏨 L'Ensoleillé; Motel Royal Bon Repos; Grand Hôtel; Des Palmiers. 🏨 Lou Paouvadou; Des Sports.

Saint-Émilion (Aquitaine)

Information: Syndicat d'Initiative, Place du Clocher. **Transportation:** *Train:* Libourne–Bergerac. *Bus:* Bordeaux–Libourne. **Accommodations:** 🏨 *(Luxury)* Hostellerie de Plaisance. 🏨 Auberge de la Commanderie.

Saintes-Maries-de-la-Mer (Côte d'Azur)

Information: Syndicat d'Initiative, Avenue van Gogh. **Transportation:** *Bus:* Arles. **Accommodations:** 🏨 Des Amphores. 🏨 Bellevue. 🏨 Bord de Mer.

Saint-Flour (Auvergne)

Transportation: *Train:* Paris. *Bus:* Laguiol. **Accommodations:** 🏨🏨🏨 Grand Hôtel l'Étape. 🏨🏨 Grand Hôtel L'Europe; Nouvel Hôtel La Bonne Table; Grand Hôtel des Voyageurs; Les Messageries; Saint-Jacques. 🏨 De France; Nord; Parc et Terminus.

Saint-Germain-en-Laye (Paris–Île-de-France) ·

Information: Office du Tourisme, 1 bis, Rue de la République. **Transportation:** *Train:* Métro, R.E.R. *Bus:* Versailles, Maisons-Lafitte, Pontoise, Poissy. **Accommodations:** 🏨🏨🏨 Pavillon d'Estrées. 🏨🏨 Le Cèdre. 🏨 Bel Air.

Saint-Jean-de-Luz (Aquitaine)

Information: Office du Tourisme, Place du M.-Foch. **Transportation:** *Train:* Paris–Madrid. *Bus:* Socoa, Sare, Hasparren. **Accommodations:** 🏨🏨🏨 Grand Hôtel de la Poste; Madison; Villa Bel Air; Les Goëlands. 🏨🏨 De la Plage; Le Petit Trianon; Agur; De Paris; Continental; Argentina; Atherbéa. 🏨 Jardin; Tocki Ona.

Saint-Jean-Pied-de-Port (Aquitaine)

Information: Syndicat d'Initiative, Maison Mansard. **Transportation:** *Train:* St-Étienne–St-Palais. **Accommodations:** 🏨🏨🏨 Continental. 🏨🏨 Central; Des Pyrénées. 🏨 Ramuntcho; Xoko-Goxoa; De la Paix.

Saint-Malo (Bretagne)

Information: Office du Tourisme, Esplanade St-Vincent. **Transportation:** *Train:* Rennes, Dol. *Bus:* Cancale, Dinard, Fougères, Rennes, and others. **Accommodations:** 🏨🏨🏨 Central; Des Thermes. 🏨🏨 Bristol-Union; Alba Hôtel; Grand Hôtel de Courtoisville; Hostellerie de la Grotte aux Fées; Des Voyageurs. 🏨 Arc en Ciel; Suffren; Eden; Le Croiseur; Courlis; Des Voyageurs; Annick.

Saint-Maxime-sur-Mer (Côte d'Azur)

Information: Office du Tourisme, Syndicat d'Initiative, Promenade Simon Lorrière. **Transportation:** *Train:* Saint-Raphaël. *Bus:* Marseille, Toulon. *Boat:* St-Tropez–St-Raphaël. **Accommodations:** 🏨 France.

Saint-Palais-sur-Mer (Poitou-Charentes)

Information: Syndicat d'Initiative, Avenue de la Grande Côte. **Transportation:** *Bus:* Meschers, La Rochelle. **Accommodations:** 🏨🏨🏨 Le Cordouan. 🏨🏨 Primavera; Plage. 🏨 Auberge les Falaises; Atlantic; La Grande Côte.

Saint-Paul-de-Vence (Côte d'Azur)

Transportation: *Train:* Nearest train station, Vence. **Accommodations:** 🏨🏨🏨 La Colombe d'Or. 🏨🏨 Les Remparts.

Saint-Quentin (Picardie)

Information: Syndicat d'Initiative. **Transportation:** *Train:* Quévy, Aulnoye, and others. *Bus:* Cambrai, Guise, Hendicourt, Villers, and others. **Accommodations:** 🏨🏨🏨 Grand Hôtel. 🏨🏨 France-Angleterre; Carillon; De la Paix et Albert 1er. 🏨 Terminus.

Saint-Raphaël (Côte d'Azur)

Information: Syndicat d'Initiative, Square Gallieni. **Transportation:** *Train:* Toulon–Marseille–Nice. *Bus:* Europabus Paris–Nice; Toulon, Fayence. **Accommodations:** 🏨🏨🏨 Etap Cap Boulouris; San Pedro; Continental; Beauséjour. 🏨🏨 Europe et Gare; France; Parc Santa Lucia; Vieux Port; Des Pyramides; Select Hôtel; Jean-Bart; La Bonne Auberge; La Colombette; Amandiers.

Saint-Tropez (Côte d'Azur)

Information: Office du Tourisme, Quai J.-Jaurès. **Transportation:** *Bus:* St-Raphaël, Toulon. **Accommodations:** 🏨🏨🏨 Ermitage; Résidence des Lices; Yaca. 🏨🏨 De la Méditerranée; Coste; Lou Cagnard. 🏨 La Frégate; Les Lauriers; Romana.

Sallanches (Alpes-du-Nord)

Transportation:*Train:* St-Gervais–Lyon–Paris. *Bus:* Geneva–Megève, Annecy–Chamonix, Cordon, Guebrian. **Accommodations:** 🏨🏨🏨 Les Sorbiers; La Cremaillière. 🏨🏨 Saint-Jacques; Ibis; Beau-Séjour; Du Mont-Blanc. 🏨 Arts et Metiers; La Régence.

Salon-de-Provence (Provence–Alpes-du-Sud)

Information: Office du Tourisme, 56, Cours Gimon. **Transportation:** *Train:* Avignon, Marseille. *Bus:* Arles, Marseille, Avignon. **Accommodations:** 🏨🏨 Grand Hôtel d'Angleterre; Le Roi René; Vendôme. 🏨 Le Paris; Terminus.

Sartène (Corsica)

Transportation: *Bus:* Bus service throughout the island. **Accommodations:** 🏨 Les Roches. 🏨 Fior di Riba.

Saulieu (Bourgogne)

Information: Syndicat d'Initiative, 38, Rue Marché. **Transportation:** *Train:* La Roche–Autun. *Bus:* Europabus: Paris–Lyon, Dijon, Beaune, Nevers, Semur. **Accommodations:** 🏨 De la Côte d'Or. 🏨 De Bourgogne; De la Poste. 🏨 Aux Quatre Vents; Au Petit Marguery.

Saumur (Pays de la Loire)

Information: Syndicat d'Initiative, 27, Rue Beaurepaire. **Transportation:** *Train:* Paris, Tours, Angers, and others. *Bus:* Cholet, Fontevrault, Loudun. **Accommodations:** 🏨 Budan. 🏨 Du Roi René; Hôtel de Londres; Terminus. 🏨 Croix Verte; Cristal; De Bretagne; Central; Volney.

Saverne (Alsace)

Information: Syndicat d'Initiative, Grand-Rue. **Transportation:** *Train:* Munich, Vienna, Rome, Basel, Brussels, Paris, Sarrebourg, Strasbourg. *Bus:* Drulingen, Molsheim, Sarrebourg, Sarre Union, and others. **Accommodations:** 🏨 Geiswiller RN 4; Le Bœuf Noir; Chez Jean; Fischer. 🏨 National; De la Marve.

Sélestat (Alsace)

Information: Syndicat d'Initiative, Place de la République. **Transportation:** *Train:* Basel, Mulhouse, Metz, Nancy, Strasbourg, and others. *Bus:* Ville, Sundhouse, Markkolsheim, Haut-Koenigsb., and others. **Accommodations:** 🏨 Vaillant. 🏨 L'Ill.

Senlis (Picardie)

Information: Syndicat d'Initiative, Place Gare. **Transportation:** *Train:* Chantilly. *Bus:* Creil, Crepy. **Accommodations:** 🏨 Point du Jour. 🏨 Du Nord.

Sens (Bourgogne)

Information: Syndicat d'Initiative, Place Jaurès. **Transportation:** *Train:* Paris–Marseille, La Roche-M. *Bus:* Montargis, Troyes. **Accommodations:** 🏨 De Paris et de la Poste. 🏨 Résidence René Binet; De la Croix Blanche. 🏨 Le Bourgogne; Des Deux Ponts.

Sète (Languedoc-Roussillon)

Information: Office du Tourisme, Syndicat d'Initiative, 22, Quai d'Alger. **Transportation:** *Train:* Marseille, Narbonne, Nîmes, Toulouse. *Boat:* Tanger, Oran. *Bus:* Montpellier. **Accommodations:** 🏨🏨🏨 Grand Hôtel; Mapotel Impérial. 🏨🏨 Les Algues; Laconga; Régina Hôtel; Du Bosphore; Brise-Lames; Les Tritons. 🏨 Le Floride; Le Venise.

Soissons (Picardie)

Information: Office du Tourisme, Syndicat d'Initiative, Avenue Général-Leclerc. **Transportation:** *Train:* Paris–Hirson. *Bus:* Many bus lines serve the area. **Accommodations:** 🏨🏨🏨 Picardie. 🏨🏨 Le Lion Rouge; Le Rallye. 🏨 De la Marine.

Souillac (Midi-Pyrénées)

Information: Syndicat d'Initiative, Office du Tourisme, Boulevard L. J. Malvy. **Transportation:** *Train:* Paris–Toulouse. *Bus:* Sarlat. **Accommodations:** 🏨🏨 Des Ambassadeurs; La Roseraie; Le Quercy. 🏨 Auberge de la Cascade; Auberge du Puits; Du Périgord.

Strasbourg (Lorraine-Vosges-Alsace)

Information: Office du Tourisme, Pont de l'Europe and Place de la Gare. *Air France:* 11, Rue du Vieux-Marché-aux-Vins. *Air Inter:* 14, Rue des Orphelins, and 4, Rue des Francs-Bourgeois. **Transportation:** *Air:* Milan, London, Paris, Lille, Lyon, Marseille. *Train:* Innsbruck, Rome, Calais, Brussels, Basel, Munich, Frankfurt, Barcelona, Geneva, Paris, and others. *Bus:* Ottrott, Truchtersheim, Westhoffen, Marckolsheim, Bitche, Sarrebourg, St-Odile. **Accommodations:** 🏨🏨🏨 (*Luxury*) Le Grand Hôtel, 12, Place de la Gare; Novotel Strasbourg Centre Halles, Quai Kléber. Bristol, 4, Place de la Gare; De la Dauphiné, 30, Rue de la 1ʳᵉ Armée; Monopole Metropole, 16, Rue Kuhn. 🏨🏨 Astoria, 70, Rue Rosheim; De Bruxelles, 13, Rue Kuhn; Eden, 16 Rue Obernai; Hostellerie Louis XIII, 133 Route de Colmar 🏨 De la Couronne, 26, fg. de Saverne; Gare, 15, Petite-Rue de la Course; Reech, 26, Rue Rosheim.

Sully-sur-Loire (Centre–Val-de-Loire)

Information: Syndicat d'Initiative, Place de Gaulle. **Transportation:** *Bus:* Orléans. **Accommodations:** 🏨🏨 Hostelliere du Grand Sully; De la Poste.

Tarascon (Provence–Alpes-du-Sud)

Information: Syndicat d'Initiative, Avenue de la République. **Transportation:** *Train:* Avignon, Marseille. *Bus:* Cavaillon. **Accommodations:** 🏨 Terminus; Le Provençal.

Thann (Alsace)

Information: Office du Tourisme, 6 Place Joffre. **Transportation:** *Train:* Mulhouse–Kruth. *Bus:* Épinal, Mulhouse. **Accommodations:** 🏨 Parc; Kléber. 🏨 Moschenross; A l'Ours Blanc.

Thiers (Auvergne)

Transportation: *Train:* Clermont-Ferrand, St-Étienne. **Accommodations:** 🏨 Fimotel. 🏨 De l'Aigle d'Or; Nouvel Hôtel; Du Nord.

Thonon-les-Bains (Alpes-du-Nord)

Information: Syndicat d'Initiative, Place H.-de-Ville. **Transportation:** *Train:* Evian-les-Bains–Lyon. *Bus:* Evian, Geneva, Annecy, St-Gingolph, Morzine, Châtel Lullin, Bellevaux. *Boat:* Lausanne, Geneva–Saint-Gingolph. **Accommodations:** 🏨 Savoie et Léman. 🏨 Duché de Savoie; Clos Savoyard. 🏨 Le Chalet; Léman; Victoria; De Lausanne; Du Stade; Thonon et Terminus.

Toulon (Côte d'Azur)

Information: Office du Tourisme, 8, Avenue Colbert. *Air France:* Chambre de Commerce, Aéroport de Toulon. **Transportation:** *Air:* Ajaccio, Lyon, Paris in summer. *Train:* Paris, Lyon, Marseille, Nice, Cannes, and others. *Bus:* St-Raphaël and nearby. *Boat:* Corsica. **Accommodations:** 🏨 (*Luxury*) Grand Hôtel; La Corniche; Frantel La Tour Blanche. 🏨 Amirauté; Moderne; Maritima; Nouvel Hôtel. 🏨 Rex Hôtel; Molière; Lutetia; Prémar; Du Sud.

Toulouse (Midi-Pyrénées)

Information: Syndicat d'Initiative, Donjon du Capitole. *Air France:* 2, Boulevard de Strasbourg. *Air Inter:* 15, Boulevard Bon-Repos. **Transportation:** *Air:* Algiers, Barcelona, Geneva, Marseille, Oran, Palma (in summer), Bordeaux, Lyon, Nice, Paris, Rabat, Tours. *Train:* Domestic and international train service. *Bus:* Europabus Barcelona. Many buses serve the area. **Accommodations:** 🏨 (*Luxury*) Concorde, 16, Boulevard Bonrepos; Frantel Wilson, 7, Rue Labéda. 🏨 La Caravelle, 62, Rue Raymond-IV; De Diane, 3, Route Saint-Simon; Grand Hôtel de l'Opéra, 1, Place du Capitole. 🏨 D'Europe; 10, Boulevard Bonrepos;

De France, 5, Rue d'Austerlitz; Métropole, 18, Rue d'Austerlitz; Touristic Hôtel, 23, Place Victor Hugo. 🛏 La Bascule, 14, Avenue Maurice Hauriou; Florence, 21, Boulevard de Strasbourg; Glycines, 295, Avenue Grande-Bretagne.

Tourcoing (Nord–Pas de Calais)

Transportation: *Train:* Paris, Antwerp, Dijon. **Accommodations:** 🛏🛏 Ibis. 🛏 Grand Hôtel Verdy.

Tournus (Bourgogne)

Information: Syndicat d'Initiative, Place Carnot. **Transportation:** *Train:* Paris–Dijon–Lyon–Marseille. *Bus:* Bourg, Châlons, Mâcon. **Accommodations:** 🛏🛏🛏 Mapotel Le Sauvage. 🛏🛏 Aux Terrasses; De la Paix. 🛏 Bellevue; Nouvel Hôtel; Saône.

Tours (Centre–Val-de-Loire)

Information: Office du Tourisme, Place de la Gare. **Transportation:** *Air:* Bordeaux, Bourges, Toulouse (in summer), Clermont-Ferrand, Lyon. *Bus:* Bordeaux, Paris, and others. **Accommodations:** 🛏🛏🛏 De l'Univers; Royal; Bordeaux. 🛏🛏 Des Châteaux de la Loire; Colbert; Mondial; De Rosny. 🛏 Grammont; Voltaire; Idéal; Saint-Eloi.

Tréguier (Bretagne)

Information: Syndicat d'Initiative, Mairie. **Transportation:** *Bus:* St-Brieuc-Port Blanc, Paimpol, Larmor. **Accommodations:** 🛏 Estuaire.

Trouville (Normandie)

Information: Office du Tourisme, Place M.-Foch. **Transportation:** *Train:* Paris–Deauville. **Accommodations:** 🛏🛏🛏 Bellevue; Flaubert; Le St. James. 🛏🛏 Reynita; Les Sablettes; Chatham; Carmen; Central. 🛏 La Coquille; De la Paix; Le Florian.

Troyes (Champagne)

Information: Syndicat d'Initiative, 16, Boulevard Carnot. **Transportation:** *Train:* Basel, Milan, Paris, Vienna, Belfort, Chaumont-Châlons-sur-Marne, and others. *Bus:* Tonnere, Plancy, Vitry-le-Fr., St-Dizier, Épernay, Sens, Chatillon, Chaumont, Sens. **Accommodations:** 🛏🛏🛏 Grand Hôtel; Poste; Royal. 🛏🛏 Thiers; Le Champenois; Splendid.

Tulle (Limousin)

Information: Syndicat d'Initiative, Place Baluze. **Transportation:** *Train:* Argentat, Uzerche, Vichy–Bordeaux. *Bus:* Limoges, Neuvic–D'Ussel, Bugeat, St.-Privat, Brive. **Accommodations:** 🏨 Le Limouzi. 🏨 Toque Blanche. 🏨 Saint-Martin; Bon Accueil.

Ussel (Limousin)

Information: Syndicat d'Initiative, Place Voltaire. **Transportation:** *Train:* Limoges, Clermont-Ferrand, Brive, and others. *Bus:* Neuvic-d'Ussel, Bort–Meymac. **Accommodations:** 🏨 Les Gravades. 🏨 Des Messageries; Teillard.

Uzerche (Limousin)

Information: Syndicat d'Initiative, Rue Porte-Bécharie. **Transportation:** *Train:* Tulle–Argentat, Paris–Toulouse. *Bus:* Brive, Tulle–Limoges. **Accommodations:** 🏨 Hostellerie Chavant; D' Ambroise.

Valençay (Centre–Val-de-Loire)

Information: Syndicat d'Initiative, Rue Nationale. **Transportation:** *Train:* Salbris–Ecuelle. *Bus:* Châteauroux, Chabris, Blois. **Accommodations:** 🏨 (*Luxury*) D'Espagne. 🏨 Le Lion d'Or.

Valence (Vallée-du-Rhône)

Information: Maison du Tourisme, Place Gén.-Leclerc. **Transportation:** *Air:* Chabeuil airport, 7 km. (4.5 miles) southwest. *Train:* Paris. **Accommodations:** 🏨 Novotel Valence Sud. 🏨 Continental; Du Grand St-Jacques; Des Voyageurs. 🏨 Splendid.

Valenciennes (Nord–Pas-de-Calais)

Information: Syndicat d'Initiative, Rue Askièvre. **Transportation:** *Train:* Paris, Nancy, Calais, Lille, Maubeuge, Basel, and others. *Bus:* Bry, Caudry, Le Quesnoy, Maubeuge, Mons, Rombies. **Accommodations:** 🏨 Novotel Valenciennes; Grand-Hôtel. 🏨 Bristol; Modern-Hôtel; Nôtre-Dame. 🏨 Franco Belge.

Vals-les-Bains (Vallée-du-Rhône)

Information: Syndicat d'Initiative, 12, Avenue Farincourt. **Transportation:** *Bus:* Aubenas, Valence, Lalerade, Arles, Avignon, Laviolle, La Souche. **Accommodations:** 🏨 Grand Hôtel des Bains; Du Vivarais. 🏨 Europe; De Lyon; Touring-Hôtel. 🏨 Poste; Du Stade.

Vaucouleurs (Lorraine-Vosges-Alsace)

Information: Syndicat d'Initiative. **Transportation:** *Bus:* Nancy, Neufchâteau. **Accommodations:** 🏠 Jeanne d'Arc; Le Relais de la Poste.

Vence (Côte d'Azur)

Information: Office du Tourisme, 1, Place Gd.-Jardin. **Transportation:** *Bus:* Grasse, Nice. **Accommodations:** 🏨 Le Floreal; Miramar. 🏨 Florida; Le Provence; Régina; Auberge des Seigneurs. 🏠 Closerie des Genêts; Coq Hardi.

Vendôme (Centre–Val-de-Loire)

Information: Office du Tourisme, Syndicat d'Initiative, Hôtel de Bellay. **Transportation:** *Train:* Paris–Tours. *Bus:* Blois–Pont-de-Braye, Tours. **Accommodations:** 🏨 St-Georges. 🏠 Château.

Versailles (Paris–Île-de-France)

Information: Syndicat d'Initiative, 7, Rue Réservoirs. **Transportation:** *Train:* Paris. *Bus:* Arpajon, Menlan, St-Germain, St-Remy. **Accommodations:** 🏨 Royal. 🏨 Eden Hôtel. 🏠 Du Palais.

Vézelay (Bourgogne)

Transportation: *Train:* Sermizelles-Vézelay. *Bus:* Bazoches–Sermizelles–Vézelay, Avallon. **Accommodations:** 🏨 Poste et Lion d'Or. 🏠 Relais du Morvan; Du Cheval Blanc.

Vichy (Auvergne)

Information: Office du Tourisme et de Thermalisme, 19, Rue Parc. **Transportation:** *Train:* Clermont-Ferrand–Metz, Bordeaux, Paris, Dorsac. *Bus:* Montluçon, St-Just-en-Ch., Clermont-Ferrand, Chantelle. **Accommodations:** 🏨 *(Luxury)* Aletti Thermal Palace, 3, Place J. Aletti; Pavillon Sévigné, 52, Boulevard Kennedy. 🏨 Albert-1er, Avenue Paul-Doumer; D'Amérique, 1, Rue Petit; Carlton, 28, Rue du St Wilson; Du Louvre, 15, Rue de l'Intendance; Magenta, 23, Avenue Walter-Stucki. 🏨 Balmoral et de Menton, 4, Rue Galliéni; Des Charmilles, 70 Boulevard Kennedy; Colbert, 23, Rue Maréchal-Foch; Du Grand Condé, 12, Rue Desbrest. 🏠 Alsace-Lorraine, 24, Place Charles de Gaulle; Antilles, 16, Rue Desbrest; Beau Site, 9, Avenue Aristide Briand.

Vienne (Alpes-du-Nord)

Information: Syndicat d'Initiative, 3, Cours Brillier. **Transportation:** *Train:* Strasbourg–Avignon–Nice. **Accommodations:** 🏨🏨🏨 Central; Grand Hôtel du Nord. 🏨🏨 De la Poste. 🏨 De l'Union; De Provence; Musée.

Villefranche-sur-Mer (Côte d'Azur)

Information: Syndicat d'Initiative, Square F.-Binon. **Transportation:** *Train:* Nice, Ventimiglia. *Bus:* Bus service along the coast. **Accommodations:** 🏨🏨🏨 Le Versailles; Welcome; Saint-Estève; Le Vauban. 🏨🏨 La Flore; Le Provençal; De la Darse. 🏨 Bellevue; Pension Patricia.

Villeneuve-les-Avignon (Languedoc-Roussillon)

Information: Office du Tourisme, Syndicat d'Initiative, 1, Place Charles David. **Transportation:** *Train:* Lyon–Nîmes. *Bus:* Avignon. **Accommodations:** 🏨🏨🏨 Hostellerie du Vieux Moulin. 🏨🏨 L'Atelier; Cèdres; Coya; Auberge du Canard. 🏨 Beau Séjour; Chêne Verte.

Villers-Cotterêts (Picardie)

Transportation: *Train:* Paris–Laon. *Bus:* Compiegne, Soissons. **Accommodations:** 🏨🏨🏨 Le Régent. 🏨 Commerce.

Vitré (Bretagne)

Transportation: *Train:* Paris–Rennes–Vitré, Lavel–Vitré–Paris. *Bus:* Fougères, Châteaubriant. **Accommodations:** 🏨🏨 Le Petit Billot. 🏨 Du Chêne Vert.

Vitry-le-François (Champagne)

Information: Office du Tourisme, Syndicat d'Initiative, Place Giraud. **Transportation:** *Train:* Paris, Strasbourg, Chaumont. *Bus:* Troyes, Brienne-Le Château, Châlons-sur-Marne. **Accommodations:** 🏨🏨 De la Poste; De la Cloche. 🏨 De l'Étoile; De Nancy; Bon Séjour.

Vittel (Lorraine-Vosges-Alsace)

Information: Syndicat d'Initiative, Palais des Congrès. **Transportation:** *Train:* Nancy–Langers. **Accommodations:** 🏨🏨🏨 Angleterre; Rue de Charmey. 🏨🏨 Bellevue, 503, Avenue de Châtillon; De la Providence, Avenue de Châtillon. 🏨 Le Relais des Sources, Avenue Georges Clemenceau.

Vouvray (Centre–Val-de-Loire)

Information: Syndicat d'Initiative. **Transportation:** *Train:* Tours–Blois. *Bus:* Tours–Vendôme. **Accommodations:** 🏨 Auberge du Grand Vatel.

Vouziers (Champagne)

Information: Bureau du Tourisme, Syndicat d'Initiative. **Transportation:** *Train:* Rethel-Paris. *Bus:* Charleville–Rethel, Reims. **Accommodations:** 🏨 A la Ville de Rennes. 🏨 Deux Ponts; Relais des Ardennes.

Yvetot (Normandie)

Transportation: *Train:* Paris, Rouen, Le Havre. *Bus:* Rouen, Fécamp, Veulettes-sur-Mer. **Accommodations:** 🏨 Du Havre.

Index

(If more than one page number appears next to the name of a site, the number in boldface indicates the page where the detailed description appears in the text.)